Two Grammatical Models
of Modern English

GERMANIC LINGUISTICS

Routledge publish the Germanic Linguistics series under the editorship of Ekkehard König (Free University of Berlin) and Johan van der Auwera (Belgian National Science Fund and University of Antwerp).

After a period during which linguistic theorizing was closely associated with the study of a single Germanic language, viz. English, the importance of comparative evidence for linguistic theory is now widely recognized. The Germanic languages are among the best described in the world and exhibit a considerable degree of variation. Yet, with the exception of English, their properties and structural variance have yet to be fully exploited for linguistic theory. The purpose of the present series is to promote more intense interaction of general linguistics with the field of Germanic linguistics as a whole. We welcome any study, whether synchronic or diachronic, on one or several of the Germanic languages, which is theoretically informed and fulfils high scholarly standards. Comparative studies, as well as detailed descriptive studies of certain areas of grammar, semantics and pragmatics, are a major focus of the series.

Two Grammatical Models of Modern English

The old and the new from A to Z

Frits Stuurman

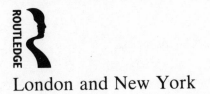

London and New York

First published in 1990
by Routledge

Paperback edition first published in 1993
by Routledge
11 New Fetter Lane, London EC4P 4EE

Simultaneously published in the USA and Canada
by Routledge
29 West 35th Street, New York, NY 10001

© 1990, 1993 Frits Stuurman

Typeset by J&L Composition Ltd, Filey, North Yorkshire
Printed in Great Britain by T. J. Press, Cornwall

British Library Cataloguing in Publication Data
Stuurman, Frits
   Two grammatical models of modern English: the old
   and the new from A to Z. – (Germanic linguistics
   series)
   1. English language. Grammar. Theories
   I. Title
   425

Library of Congress Cataloging in Publication Data
Also available

   ISBN 0–415–09344–9

For my father-in-law
C. B. van Bergen

Contents

Contents

Contents

Preface

I have been working on this book off and on since the autumn of 1985; also incorporating even earlier materials. In the course of so many years so many people have assisted me in one way or another that on the one hand I am afraid I may not remember them all (and some of the most helpful commentary has been anonymous); on the other hand some may not even recognize that what they once saw or heard is now part of this book. Nevertheless, I would like to mention the following names and extend my gratitude to them, and to anyone I may have forgotten: Prof. D. J. Allerton, Johan van der Auwera, Bert Bourgonje, Anne Dijkstra, Martin Everaert, Jelle Kaldeway, Konrad Koerner, Gerhard Leitner, Rob van Oirsouw, James Pankhurst, Jonathan Price, Adrian J. Stenton, Marijke Stuurman-van Bergen, Herman Wekker. Anonymous will also have to remain the students who have been subjected to embryonic versions of my material; and whose reactions have been among the most soberingly useful that I have had.

I dedicate this book to my father-in-law, Cees van Bergen. His professional career of over forty years, with ups and downs, has been an example to me; his achievements will remain a source of inspiration.

Finally I would like to apologize to Marijke, Kobus, and Neeltje; I am pretty certain that what they only get out of it all is learning that there is one thing worse than having to live with a grammar fanatic; viz. with an alphabetically obsessed one.

Abbreviations

C	Curme
CGoEL	Quirk *et al. A Comprehensive Grammar of the English Language*
CM&LF	Celce-Murcia and Larsen-Freeman *The Grammar Book*
CulWil	Culicover and Wilkins *Locality in Linguistic Theory*
GCE	Quirk *et al. A Grammar of Contemporary English*
GLME	Poutsma *A Grammar of Late Modern English*
Handbook	Kruisinga *A Handbook of Present-Day English* (1931–1932)
J	Jespersen
K	Kruisinga
L&P	Lakoff and Peters 'Phrasal conjunction and symmetric predicates'
LGB	Chomsky *Lectures on Government and Binding*
MEG	Jespersen *A Modern English Grammar on Historical Principles*
NEG	Sweet *A New English Grammar*
OED	*Oxford English Dictionary*
P	Poutsma
Q72	Quirk *et al. A Grammar of Contemporary English*
Q85	Quirk *et al. A Comprehensive Grammar of the English Language*
S	Sweet
SS&P	Stockwell *et al. The Major Syntactic Structures of English*
Survey	Survey of English Usage
A	adjective
A	adverbial
Adj	Adjectival

Abbreviations

AP	Adjective Phrase
AUX	auxiliary
c	clause
copu+Q	Q after a copula
DET	determiner
EST	extended standard theory
e	empty
I	infinitive
I*	I takes object, represented elsewhere
if-Q	embedded question characterized by introductory *if*
L	a particular language
m	mutual relation
MOD	modifier
N	noun
N-bar	nominal word-group
Neg	negative
nice	negation, inversion, code, emphasis
NP	Noun Phrase
O	object
p	*to*
P	predicative
PRO	pronoun
Q	quasi-question
Q-float	Tq-move
S	subject
S=init	*that*-S initially
S=subj	*that*-S initially, specifically in the position of subject
SJC	subjunctive
SSC	Specified Subject Constraint
t	item like *though* around which transposition can take place
T	transformation
T	transposed phrase
that-S	embedded statement introduced by *that*
Tq-move	Tquantifier-movement
v	lesser verb
V	verb
V-bar	verbal word-group
VP	Verb Phrase
whether-Q	embedded question characterized by introductory *whether*
X-bar	word-group with X as Head

XP	phrase with X as Head
x-to-x	extraposition *to* extremities
?	questionable example
*	unacceptable example
≠	does not equal
==%==>	speakers vary as to whether or not they apply the rule

Introduction

A–Z, the brief label by which this book will refer to itself, collects together, and from a consistent perspective comments on, various accounts of particular points of Modern English grammar. 'Modern' here covers the twentieth century; the grammatical descriptions date from the same period (with an excursus to Sweet 1891–1898; see section 2.1). The descriptions of Modern English grammar looked at are taken to represent two approaches: roughly, an 'older' approach (1891– . . .) and a 'newer' approach (1957– . . .). Although these approaches may coincide to the extent that both deal with Modern English and its grammar, the essential aim of *A–Z* is to present them as entirely separate in fundamental respects: inductive vs. deductive, and consequently comprehensive vs. exclusive; which we will capture by the polar opposites *open* and *narrow* as technical terms. Accordingly, we will talk about the juxtaposition of OG = (older) *open* grammar and NG = (newer) *narrow* grammar.

The OG of *A–Z* is variously known: traditional, traditional-descriptive, scholarly traditional, the Great Tradition, etc.; and similarly NG has been advertised under various labels: generative, transformational, formal, Chomskyan. . . . The terms OG and NG are in the first instance merely conveniently short labels which allow one to circumvent the problems that the variety of more familiar labels entails. For instance, an OG account – say in Quirk *et al.* (1985) – may actually be newer than an NG account – say in Chomsky (1957). In fact, under juxtaposition, it is one of the purposes of *A–Z* to present OG and NG as equally relevant and equally going concerns today – in particular, equally and independently going towards their aims of accounting for Modern English grammar, though pursuing these aims in diametrically opposed directions.

However, it is not in fact altogether uncontroversial that the various OG accounts of Modern English grammar represent a

1

single, coherent approach; and to some extent the same applies to NG. The fundamental significance of the terms OG and NG is thus rather to embody abbreviatorily one of the claims of *A–Z*: that the coherence of OG as fundamentally *open* grammar emerges by means of juxtaposing it to NG as fundamentally *narrow*. NG should be more easily recognized by itself: it constitutes what, since the 'Chomskyan revolution' of 1957, has somehow – sometimes even along apparently disparate lines – presented itself as Chomskyan generative grammar; but for NG, too, the ultimate characteristic is consistent *narrow*ness.

The purpose of *A–Z* then is to juxtapose to one another contributions made by OG and by NG to the description of Modern English grammar. *A–Z* is thus directed at anyone to whom such juxtaposition may be more or less uncongenial. Such may be linguists who have already come to be working in one approach, and worry about its relation to the other. Under juxtaposition, we promote proper acquaintance with different approaches; and especially appreciation of the differences between approaches, as the indispensable foundation for their independent contributions to the study of Modern English grammar. The trained specialist committed to working within one approach or another may be inclined to look at other approaches as if they were just other, and often implicitly or explicitly inferior, ways of achieving similar goals; and whose results had better be transferable to one's own approach. For them, also, *A–Z* maintains that various approaches to Modern English grammar have their separate aims; that their contributions should be respected – and only be respected – accordingly; and that thus at no point can apparent similarities and/or transferability be used as an evaluation measure: under juxtaposition, OG and NG are antithetic, such that there cannot be sufficient common ground between them to serve as a basis for relative rankings.

But in so far as the aim of *A–Z* is thus ultimately to promote a mentality – grammatological tolerance, and understanding of the need for pluriformity in Modern English grammar – *A–Z* especially addresses those who are not yet firmly committed either way, and whose mentalities may still be most pliable. Many university students are likely to be made acquainted with Modern English grammar through being introduced to both OG and NG: and they naturally tend first to see these as unnecessarily different ways of doing much the same thing. *A–Z* therefore presupposes courses in Modern English grammar along the lines of introductory OG and NG: working through *A–Z* should inform such students, or at least reinforce for them, how fundamentally different one approach to a given point of Modern English grammar actually is from the other; and how their contributions are valid precisely provided those from one approach be kept carefully distinct from those of any other approach.

It might well be argued that OG and NG, in their separate ways, are just two out of many – if perhaps among the more productive – current approaches to Modern English grammar. But regardless of whether they are, there are still a number of closely related arguments for using OG and NG for the purposes of *A–Z*: to emphasize the independence, and independent achievements, of separate approaches. Let us look at three such arguments.

1 Firstly, it has been argued (Newmeyer 1986) that the 'Chomskyan revolution' manifests itself in that generative grammar, NG, has been established as the inevitable reference point in linguistics. Even if only a (small) minority of grammarians are committed to NG, the majority will still feel obliged to note explicitly, and to attempt to motivate, deviance from NG. In this context, after the Chomskyan revolution, any presentation of OG, even if it were intended as an entirely independent exercise, must necessarily concern itself with outlining the position of OG *vis-à-vis* NG. The juxtaposition of OG to NG in *A–Z* makes a virtue out of this necessity.

2 Secondly, a recurrent phenomenon in the history of NG is a claim that (some version of) NG has the merit of a special relationship with (some version of) OG; or vice versa. Specifically, from the perspective of NG – by 1 above the dominant perspective since the Chomskyan revolution – the major representative of OG is Otto Jespersen (1860–1943): as essentially 'Otto's grammar', OG in fact appears quite regularly in NG, 'Noam's (= Chomsky's) grammar', as if there was no juxtaposition. Looking at OG and NG in juxtaposition, *A–Z* can take a critical stance towards putative OG↔NG relationships; and especially towards Jespersen's OG↔NG in particular. As *A–Z* develops a proper perspective on both OG and NG, a grammarian like Hendrik Poutsma (1856–1937) emerges as at least as typical a representative of OG

3 Thirdly, although there are many different approaches, among these *A–Z* looks at OG and at NG as extreme cases: diametrically juxtaposed poles among approaches to the description of Modern English grammar. OG stands for *open* grammar, in full contrast to NG for *narrow* grammar. The juxtaposition = polar

contrast between *open* and *narrow* informs the entirety of *A–Z*. Once the reader has thoroughly assimilated the ways in which such entirely disparate approaches to Modern English grammar are each possible – and indeed valuable – under juxtaposition, it is assumed that s/he will be able to carry this tolerance over to one or more of the approaches more or less intermediate between *open* and *narrow*.

In line with the above orientations, the material in *A–Z* which represents OG and NG is of three main sorts. Part I collects statements about OG and NG, both by practitioners and outsiders, to establish the juxtaposition of *open* and *narrow* approaches as a frame of reference. Part II surveys statements about OG in NG, to show how juxtaposition can contribute towards a more proper perspective on their relationships. For Parts I and II, 'from A to Z' in this book's title is an alphabetical metaphor, as OG and NG are at opposite ends among approaches to grammar under juxtaposition. In Part III, 'from A to Z' (also) refers directly to the alphabet itself. Part III selects, for each letter of the alphabet, statements about Modern English grammar in OG and in NG, to show their actually juxtaposed practices; alphabetically arranged, Part III is the real core of *A–Z*'s juxtaposition of OG and NG. Note that *A–Z* thus does not claim to present anything that is genuinely novel or original. Rather, what is new is the systematic collection of the various materials from sometimes obscure and/or impenetrable sources; and more importantly, the perspective imposed on the material: the juxtaposition of OG and NG.

Part I surveys large OG and NG grammars of Modern English; in the case of NG, this is supplemented by an explanation of the relative scarcity – and also relatively early dates – of such large grammars; and the material which – especially more recently – 'makes up for' this scarcity: the vast NG 'literature'. In these presentations, the emphasis is on establishing in general terms the coherence of OG as an *open* approach to Modern English grammar, juxtaposed to NG as a *narrow* approach.

Part II takes up NG attitudes to OG, especially as these tend to go counter to *A–Z*'s juxtaposition, towards perceived benefits of conjunction. Arguments are indicated which allow *A–Z* to dissent from these views and to maintain beneficial juxtaposition.

Finally, Part III contains the core of *A–Z*: an alphabetical series of points of Modern English grammar, for each of which both OG and NG accounts are represented. The detailed practical case-studies in Part III give substance to the general points outlined in Parts I and II. In half the number of cases, full discussion in 'majuscule' sections shows how individual differences among OG or among NG accounts dwindle into insignificance as compared to the juxtaposition between OG on the one hand and NG on the other. Moreover, *A–Z* allows its readers ample opportunity to draw conclusions by themselves. Majuscule sections contain 'discussion and extensions', encouraging the readers to extend the observations and conclusions already given. In addition, for the remaining points of Modern English grammar covered by *A–Z*, in 'miniscule' sections, there are outlines of OG and NG accounts so as to help the reader to recognize more independently the juxtaposed contributions made by OG and by NG. From there on, readers are expected to be able, and prepared, to juxtapose OG and NG, and other approaches to Modern English grammar, entirely by themselves.

Part I
OG and NG

1

Two approaches to Modern English grammar

Many men, many minds. Grammarians of English, also, may account for various points of Modern English grammar in more or less individual ways. Still, it is usually possible to group grammarians together in that their accounts are in some fundamental sense more similar to one another than to those of other grammarians. *A–Z* is about two such approaches shared by grammarians: an earlier approach, let us say 'older' grammar or OG; and a more recent approach, 'newer' grammar or NG. The purpose of this first chapter is to identify in preliminary fashion the dimension on which OG and NG are fundamentally 'juxtaposed'. Many of the points to be made here can be extended and/or modulated; where appropriate, and space allows, this is indeed catered for elsewhere in *A–Z*. But in the first instance, we concentrate on points germane to juxtaposition of OG and NG.

Although there have been significant developments within NG, it should still be relatively easy to recognize; and NG is in fact fairly well-established as one common approach. The publication by Noam Chomsky of *Syntactic Structures* in 1957 sparked off the 'Chomskyan revolution' in linguistics; many grammarians have since adopted Chomsky's approach as it developed (e.g. Chomsky 1965, 1970, 1981, etc.), variously known as 'transformational', 'generative', 'lexicalist', 'government-binding', ...; or indeed simply 'Chomskyan'. The central position of Chomsky in NG, today as much as in 1957, may be recognized by reading NG as 'Noam's grammar'. It is less obvious, and it may accordingly be more controversial, that the grammarians that *A–Z* collects under OG really have a single approach in common. *A–Z* contends that OG *can* be seen as a genuinely common approach to Modern English grammar, by juxtaposing OG to NG.

Below we juxtapose quotations as an initial basis for the juxtaposition of OG and NG in the rest of *A–Z*:

A: Above all one ought to abstain from wresting the available evidence . . . into harmony with some pre-conceived theory

Z: the requirement that the grammar be constructed in accordance with . . . the associated linguistic theory

the *pertinent* facts . . . a notion that is linked to theory

Consideration of *A* (quoted from Poutsma 1928:viii) and *Z* (from Chomsky 1964:52, 1979:107 respectively) will reveal two contrasts. Firstly, 'from A to Z' there is essentially the juxtaposition between *induction* and *deduction* as one dictionary defines these scientific methods. *A* is 'using *known facts* ['available evidence'] to produce general laws', i.e. inductive; *Z* is 'determining *from general principles* ['in accordance with the theory'] in relation to a particular ['pertinent'] fact', i.e. deductive. Accordingly, *A* and *Z* disagree about what range of facts to cover: *A*'s 'available evidence' assumes a *comprehensive* collection of facts about Modern English grammar; *Z*'s 'pertinent facts' presupposes a *selection*, motivated by the theory. Along these two parameters, the fundamentally juxtaposed significations of OG and NG are '*open* grammar' and '*narrow* grammar' respectively. *Open* grammar is inductive: without 'pre-conceived theory', it can only attempt to cover comprehensively the 'available evidence'. *Narrow* grammar is deductive; limited by an 'associated linguistic theory', it needs to cover only selectively the 'pertinent facts'.

Once again, the suitability of characterizing NG as *narrow* is relatively evident. The point about the Chomskyan programme has always been for linguistic theory to *narrow*ly characterize language, by excluding everything that is *not* language. In other words, in NG linguistic theory should provide sets of *constraints*: for something to be language, it must according to the theory be like this, not like that, etc. NG thus wants grammatical accounts to be limited, or constrained, or *narrow*ed by linguistic theory, a representation of what enables human beings, and only human beings (another limitation), to learn and to use language. Correspondingly, Chomsky explicitly rejects the *open* aim of comprehensiveness: "Comprehensiveness . . . does not seem to me a serious or significant goal . . . Gross coverage of data can be achieved in many ways" (1964:53). 'Many ways' leaves things *open*, not *narrow*, and thus for Chomsky comprehensiveness is of no interest; only a *narrow* account of only the pertinent facts may be constructed in accordance with the preconceived theory, and thus reveal something about the deep nature of grammar.

On the other hand, 'many ways' leaves room for considerable

apparent variability in pursuing comprehensiveness, accounting for some difficulty in recognizing OG as a common approach.

Therefore, one point about NG's antagonism to comprehensiveness is that it will serve to juxtapose NG to OG, if it can be shown that for all its variability OG *does* have fundamentally in common comprehensiveness as a serious and significant goal. *A–Z* asserts that this demonstration can be given for the grammars of Modern English by Sweet, Poutsma, Kruisinga, Curme, Jespersen, and Quirk *et al.*, which accordingly represent OG.

Unfortunately, OG is not always as explicitly *open* as is Poutsma in the quotation for *A* above. Therefore, Part III of *A–Z* is intended as a series of demonstrations that in practice – specific accounts of individual points of Modern English grammar – at least, OG and NG *are* juxtaposed as *open* and *narrow*. In addition, and by way of an introduction to OG in Part III, in Chapter 2 we will probe for *open* comprehensiveness as a goal by taking a more global look at OG. Such an exercise is more straightforward for the *narrow*ness of NG in Chapter 3: in accounts of Modern English grammar, commitment to the Chomskyan approach will typically appear from explicit adoption of a *narrow* programme (in turn, in NG *narrow*ness may well be programmatic rather than practically effective; *A–Z* takes issue with the affinity between OG and NG that may accordingly be perceived in Part II).

In the meanings adopted here, the use of the abbreviations OG and NG, and of the terms *open* and *narrow* that it is their fundamental function to embody, is probably unique to *A–Z* (and related material by the author). Of course, the terms 'old(er) grammar' and 'new(er) grammar', which OG and NG also abbreviate, have been used elsewhere; but even then, apparently not in the specific senses intended here. For instance, Cattell (1969:1–13) contrasts 'Grammar old and new', i.e. 'traditional' and 'transformational-generative' grammar respectively. But for Cattell old, 'traditional', grammar is not *A–Z*'s OG but an approach that dates back to the eighteenth century; and which was prescriptive, based on Latin and logic, and restricted to written language – all this is not the case for OG. In fact, Cattell's 'old grammar' does not juxtapose to *A–Z*'s NG either: "the gulf is ... not as great as may at first appear. Chomsky himself has pointed out that his form of grammar is closer to ... [old] grammar than many others are" (1969:30). For Chomsky and OG, see Part II of *A–Z*. But here, old and new grammar in Cattell's senses would *both* be juxtaposed to OG.

Similarly, Robinson (1975) labels Chomskyans the 'new grammarians', to bring out that "Chomsky has reinstated grammar, in the old school sense of the word" (1975:15). Both 'old school grammar' and the 'new grammarians' are equally *narrow*, i.e. "very restricted" (1975:35); both therefore also juxtapose to an approach which is *open* to "accounting for the whole of language" (1975:169). What exactly the latter *open* approach would be represented by, Robinson does not make explicit; but cf. "Reading Jespersen, looking up some point or other, I am always surprised and fascinated by the ... diversity of English" (1975: 173): probably, Robinson takes *A–Z*'s OG – at least OG in Jespersen – to be the approach that does set its sights at comprehending the 'whole of language'.

Finally, note that juxtaposition of OG and NG in *A–Z* does not imply a comparative evaluation, of one approach as superior to the other. On the contrary, *A–Z* assumes that, precisely because of their being juxtaposed, there is no genuine possibility of comparing OG and NG, let alone of ranking them. Comparison presupposes something in common as a basis for comparing; juxtaposition of OG and NG in *A–Z* denies that they have anything sufficiently fundamental in common to serve as a valid basis for comparison. *A–Z* pleads that several approaches to Modern English grammar be seen to exist productively alongside one another. OG vs. NG is just one – if a particularly strong – case in point: *A–Z* lacks the space to repeat the exercise for the many other approaches that are available. OG and NG have juxtaposed goals, *open* vs. *narrow*; there should thus be general tolerance of pluriformity in grammar by a variant of the old aphorism: many men, many minds – and many grammars, many goals.

2

OG. Older grammar, open grammar

An *open* approach to Modern English grammar, which under induction aims at comprehensive coverage, would lead to extensive representations of the 'available evidence'. If OG is indeed *open* grammar, then one should therefore look for OG among the larger grammars of Modern English. If one restricts oneself to such grammars *in* English, this means that *A–Z* (cf. McKay 1984:93) will attempt to identify as OG the really huge grammars of Modern English by Poutsma (five volumes), Kruisinga (three volumes), Curme (two volumes), Jespersen (seven volumes), and Quirk *et al.* (1972: 1000 pages; 1985: 1600 pages). In the various subsections of this chapter, for each grammar in order of date of completion, more substantial motivation than just mere size will be given that it belongs to OG. Preferably, a grammar should advertise itself as *open* by directly stating the aim to be comprehensiveness, and/or the methodology induction. However, it will appear that there are no such really explicit statements in the grammars of Modern English by non-natives: Poutsma (Dutch), Kruisinga (Dutch), Jespersen (Danish).

Trying to trace, and to account for, the relations between non-nativeness and *open* grammar would require extending our programme beyond the primary concerns of *A–Z*; but (non-)nativeness will remain a recurrent subsidiary issue in *A–Z* (cf. Bourgonje and Dijkstra 1982). Here it may be tentatively noted that non-native grammarians will be more readily comprehensive than native ones. "[T]he foreign student ... has to rely mainly on ... observation ... The native student has another source of information at his disposal, viz. introspection" (Zandvoort 1961:23; cf. section C for complementation). Thus, non-native grammarians will raise observations to a scholarly level in pursuing all the available evidence; and hence they may tend to remain silent about their 'self-evident' aim of comprehensiveness. By contrast, the native grammarian who alongside introspection 'unnaturally'

13

aims for comprehensive coverage by observation will want to have this noted, by stating such an aim explicitly.

Whatever the effects of (non-)nativeness may be, *A–Z* has essentially three reasons for counting Poutsma, Kruisinga, and Jespersen as OG in the sense of *open* grammar, even if they make no direct statements to that effect. Firstly, Poutsma (1928:vii), Kruisinga (1931:xviv), and Jespersen (1927:vi) do all acknowledge a debt to Sweet. And Sweet is identified as a pioneer of OG in section 2.1, where in fact his grammar (two volumes) turns out to be explicitly *open*. Poutsma, Kruisinga, and Jespersen are thus at least under *open* influence from Sweet. Secondly, Poutsma, Kruisinga, and Jespersen are argued to give *open* accounts of Modern English grammar in Part III. And thirdly, in the relevant subsections below, more or less indirect evidence is presented that Poutsma, Kruisinga, and Jespersen did indeed aim to be comprehensive.

2.1 Henry Sweet (1845–1912) *A New English Grammar* (1891, 1898)

Henry Sweet is especially well known as an early British phonetician: G. B. Shaw's character Henry Higgins, who teaches Eliza Doolittle how to sound like a lady in *Pygmalion*, is generally said to be based on Sweet (for discussion, see Collins 1988:132–8). But Sweet was a versatile man: he has also made seminal contributions to the study of Old English. And the two volumes of his *New English Grammar* (*NEG*) published in 1891 and 1898 also extensively trace historical developments from Old to Modern English. But we will here concentrate on Sweet's *NEG* accounts of Modern English grammar.

The debts acknowledged by Poutsma, Kruisinga, and Jespersen to Sweet have already been recorded; there is a similar acknowledgement in Quirk *et al.* (1985:38). *NEG* has duly been seen to belong to OG like these later grammars, on the basis of comprehensiveness: "One of the reasons for the continuing appeal and importance of men like Jespersen and Sweet ... is ... the completeness of their coverage" (Levin 1960/1964:49; for 2.5, note the testimony to Jespersen's comprehensiveness as well). Most significantly, however, Sweet himself seems to have recognized the need (for him, as a native?) to state explicitly that his *NEG* is the as yet modest beginning of a then novel, *open* approach: "by comparison with other grammars ... my syntax is fairly complete" (1898:v). Although in Part III of *A–Z*, *NEG* will regularly be seen to fall somewhat behind later OG in actual comprehensiveness, *NEG* does clearly appear to have pioneered

OG, as *open* grammar (whether in the 1890s *NEG* was indeed 'complete by comparison with other grammars' is an interesting issue, which would however require to be researched much beyond the limits of *A–Z*). At the least, with Sweet, OG starts about 60 years earlier than NG (*Syntactic Structures*, Chomsky 1957); although OG may be as recent as 1985 (Quirk *et al.*), in age it is therefore still older than NG, newer grammar.

[Biography: Sebeok 1966a:512–32; Sweet 1964:iii–iv]

2.2 Hendrik Poutsma (1856–1937) *A Grammar of Late Modern English* (1904–1929)

The Dutchman Hendrik Poutsma was by profession a teacher of English in secondary schools in Holland. His teaching duties apparently left him time to produce between 1904 and 1926 not only five volumes of his *Grammar of Late Modern English* (*GLME*), but in 1928 and 1929 also second, enlarged editions of the first two volumes (to mention only his larger grammatical works). The sheer size of *GLME* already suggests comprehensive coverage. But Poutsma, a non-native grammarian of English, does not seem to have got round to stating directly that he aims at comprehensiveness. Still, in Chapter 1, Poutsma has already been cited for *A*, as he expresses somewhat circumstantially the general OG approach: "Above all, one ought to abstain from wresting the available evidence ... into harmony with some pre-conceived theory" (1928:viii). Under the inductive approach here intimated, the 'available evidence' will in fact be *all* the evidence, i.e. comprehensive coverage and *open* grammar.

And indeed, the comprehensiveness of Poutsma's *GLME* has since been recognized as its fundamental merit: "exhaustive description ... as in Poutsma's [*GLME*]" (Hill 1958:v); "a more copious grammatical thesaurus of the English language than appeared before or after it" (translated from Dutch, Zandvoort 1964:7); etc. In spite of the subsequent appearance of Quirk *et al.* (1972, 1985) many sections in Part III of *A–Z* suggest that Poutsma's *GLME* is still the most comprehensive among OG grammars of English (but see Aarts 1975:95, 1986:376, cited in section 2.6).

[Biography: Zandvoort 1937; Stuurman 1988]

2.3 Etsko Kruisinga (1875–1944) *A Handbook of Present-Day English* (1909–1911 (first edition), 1931–1932 (fifth edition))

Etsko Kruisinga, another Dutchman, is a somewhat controversial figure, in more than one sense. Kruisinga seems to have been uncannily prone to antagonizing and quarrelling with people. More pertinently to *A–Z*'s purposes, the proper interpretation of Kruisinga's work on Modern English grammar is rather difficult. One reason for the latter problem is that Kruisinga's major grammar went through five editions between 1911 and 1932, each of which differs more or less radically from the previous one. As such it would be gross over-simplification to state that the fifth edition of *A Handbook of Present-Day English* (1931–1932) (*Handbook*) is *only* aimed at comprehensiveness. Kruisinga practically denies this by saying that "the new edition does not supply much new material" (1931:viii); i.e. the fifth edition was not intended to be more comprehensive than the fourth. The fact is that Kruisinga in *Handbook did* have a preconceived theory, viz. that in grammatical accounts only form should be considered. Note that 'only form' is a *narrow* concept (in fact quite similar to 'structuralist' theory; see Part II). On the other hand, *Handbook* occasionally betrays Kruisinga's *open* reliance on induction, e.g.: "the impossibility . . . to presuppose [deductively] . . . the body of knowledge that the study of the subject may be hoped to reveal to us [inductively]" (1932b:178).

Moreover, it seems possible to see *Handbook* as *open* by inheritance. Thus, in the first edition, Kruisinga *did* directly commit himself to induction: "the study of English grammar is chiefly a matter of observation" (1911:341). Accordingly, the third edition *is* purely aimed at a greater measure of comprehensiveness: "Although the book has remained substantially unchanged, its size has increased considerably" (1922:v). And indeed, on occasion of the fourth edition, comprehensiveness has duly been recognized as a fundamental merit of non-native Kruisinga: "It has been left to a foreigner, writing for foreign students, to produce the most comprehensive account in English of the phenomena of our present-day language" (Grattan 1926: 243). In view of all this, the reports in Part III of *A–Z* about Kruisinga's *Handbook* may be seen as as many confirmations of the claim that *Handbook* is, whatever else, ultimately especially *open* grammar.

[Biography: Van Essen 1983]

2.4 George Oliver Curme (1860–1948) *A Grammar of the English Language* (1931, 1935)

The American G. O. Curme was a Professor of German at Northwestern University, Illinois. In 1922 he published a grammar of German which is "still unsurpassed as a comprehensive reference

grammar of ... German" (McKay 1984:148): for German OG, too, it seems that there may be some correlation between (Curme's) non-nativeness and comprehensiveness (for Dutch see Stuurman 1986). Conversely, because of his profound familiarity with German, Curme may be counted as a kind of pseudo-non-native when he subsequently turned to the grammar of Modern English. Moreover, Curme acknowledges his indebtedness to "the large works of the foreign students of our language, the grammars of Jespersen, Poutsma, Kruisinga" (1931:v); he himself thus correlates comprehensive ('large') and non-native ('foreign'). At any rate, Curme explicitly subscribes to the *open*ness of OG when he states the aims of his grammar of Modern English: "to describe fully" (1935:v), or initially at least "to present ... a rather full outline" (1931:v).
[Biography: Hatfield *et al.* 1930:5–7]

2.5 Otto Jespersen (1860–1943) *A Modern English Grammar on Historical Principles* (1909–1949)

Among students of language the Dane (Hans) Otto (Jens) Jespersen is one of the best-known scholars. It has quite appropriately been said that one of the few who could have earned a Nobel prize for language studies, if there was one, would have been Jespersen. Rather significantly for the purposes of *A–Z*, Jespersen's Nobel-worthy merit is then said to be size, suggesting *open* grammar: "Jespersen's *Modern English Grammar*, and a very few other monumental tomes ... are genuine landmarks of achievement" (Pullum 1985:266). Still, in the juxtaposition of OG and NG, *A–Z*'s allocation of Jespersen to OG is somewhat contentious: NG has regularly claimed Jespersen as a precursor of NG to some extent or another. In *A–Z* the discussion of such claims belongs to Part II, where NG views of OG are surveyed.

Anticipating the conclusion of Part II that Jespersen belongs to OG rather than to NG, we may here recall that Jespersen (1927:vi) acknowledges his debt to Sweet, *open* according to 2.1 (but Sweet, and Jespersen, are both made out to be proto-NG in Ohlander 1980; see II.4 for discussion); and that Jespersen is a non-native grammarian of Modern English, and hence perhaps 'naturally' *open* (it is at least important not to Americanize Jespersen by spelling his name as Jesper*so*n, a mistake frequently made; cf. Tervoort 1981:265; Pullum 1983:437). More fundamentally, Jespersen associates himself with those who have an "aversion ... to the idea of a grammar arrived at by ... deductive reasoning" (1924:48) (while deduction is essential to NG). It may also be

noted that Jespersen's *Modern English Grammar* (*MEG*) has regularly been interpreted as comprehensive (cf. Robinson 1975:173 cited in Chapter 1; and Levin 1960/1964:49 cited in section 2.1): "Jespersen's ... seven-volume grammar ... manages to touch on just about every imaginable topic of English grammar" (Langendoen 1970:ix; cf. also section O); "Jespersen ... undoubtedly one of the best of the large comprehensive grammars" (Huddleston 1976:16). Finally, the proof of Jespersen's OG pudding is again in Part III of *A–Z*: *MEG*'s consistently comprehensive accounts of points of Modern English grammar.
[Biography: Sebeok 1966b:148–73; Reynolds 1969:7–34]

2.6 Randolph Quirk (born 1920) *et al. A Grammar of Contemporary English* (1972), *A Comprehensive Grammar of the English Language* (1985)

If Jespersen might have won a Nobel prize, Randolph Quirk did earn a knighthood: he is now Sir Randolph. But in fact *A–Z*'s final OG grammars of Modern English are collective efforts: *A Grammar of Contemporary English* (*GCE*) and *A Comprehensive Grammar of the English Language* (*CGoEL*) by three Britons – besides Quirk, Sidney Greenbaum (born 1929), Geoffrey Leech (1936) – and a Swede (another non-native) – Jan Svartvik (1931). Although the others should clearly not be neglected, the customary abbreviation to Quirk *et al.* is quite appropriate (and intentional: note the deviation from alphabetical order to put Quirk first). Quirk is clearly the senior partner, not only in age but in input. In particular, Quirk is the founder of the Survey of English Usage, a vast collection of data on Modern English grammar, in University College London (see Svartvik and Quirk 1980); both *GCE* and *CGoEL* are based on this *Survey*, by induction. If this inductive basis does not already serve to establish *GCE* and *CGoEL* as OG, then the authors do not leave any doubt by explicitly espousing comprehensiveness; after first stating that "the present work ... aims at ... comprehensiveness" (1972:v), they go on to actually call their second grammar the *Comprehensive* (1985). And at least the earlier attempt at comprehensiveness of *GCE* has been found successful: Aarts (1975:98, 1986:376) subscribes to the claim that *GCE* is "the fullest and most comprehensive synchronic description of English ever written".

Note that we would now have a succession of 'most comprehensive' OG grammars: in 1926 Kruisinga's *Handbook* (section 2.3, Grattan 1926:243), in 1964 Poutsma's *GLME* (section 2.2,

Zandvoort 1964:7), and in 1975/1986 *GCE*; another indication that OG is a genuine tradition, in the sense of *open* grammar. [Biography: none yet written. Quirk "studied together with Chomsky at Yale in the early fifties ... and we have been in close touch and on first name terms ever since" (interview with Quirk, January 1984 issue of *Quill*, students' journal University of Utrecht). Bibliography of Quirk: Greenbaum *et al.* 1979:xi–xvi]

3

NG. Newer grammar, narrow grammar

A–Z has no occasion to give an account of NG in its own right; nor to outline its history. As for the former, the reader of *A–Z* may want to be acquainted with NG through recent general introductions such as Van Riemsdijk and Williams (1986) or Radford (1988), and/or with applications of NG theory to Modern English grammar as in Rigter and Beukema (1985) or Wekker and Haegeman (1985) (cf. section b). For an authoritative history of NG the reader is referred to Newmeyer (1980). Newmeyer's history does not contain much on *A–Z*'s concern: NG's relations to OG. In this sense, the information in Part II of *A–Z*, on NG's interpretations of OG and on developments that occurred therein, provides something of an appendix to Newmeyer's internal history.

In our Introduction, *A–Z* adopted the abbreviation NG to refer to work written since, and on the basis of, the Chomskyan revolution of 1957. One may well ask why one of the more familiar labels should not have been used: 'transformational grammar', 'generative grammar', some combination of these, and so on. The reason is that in the roughly thirty years since the Chomskyan revolution there has not been the uniformity that labels as specific as 'transformational' or even 'generative' would suggest (nor have NG's relations to or perceptions of OG been constant; see Part II). This chapter introduces NG work that will be juxtaposed to OG in Part III; the purpose here is to establish that NG in its various stages and guises can indeed consistently be presented in *narrow* terms; although NG's *narrow*ness may be programmatic, and less in effective evidence. Thus section 3.1 identifies the fundamentally *narrow* elements in what are by common consent (cf. Van Riemsdijk and Williams 1986) Chomsky's definitional works: *narrow*ness equally in 1957, 1965, and 1981, in spite of the intervening developments.

Broadly, one would expect that NG will juxtapose less notably with OG as long as NG is programmatically rather than effectively *narrow*. This may be seen to have been the case in one way or another throughout the history of NG: thus, in earliest NG, which could indeed appropriately be called 'transformational' (roughly 1957–1968); in 'generative semantics' (roughly 1968–1973); and in 'relational grammar' (since roughly 1973) (for the latter two see Part II). The development from relatively *open* to more effectively *narrow* NG only took place in the later work of Chomsky and his closest associates (since roughly 1968); see section II.1. It should be remembered that *A–Z*'s case for juxtaposition of OG and NG is quite naturally at its strongest with respect to more effectively *narrow*, generally later NG.

NG, whether only programmatically or also effectively *narrow*, has largely been true to Chomsky's precepts (as presented in Chapter 1) of deduction, and hence of coverage only of pertinent facts (although the range of pertinent facts may vary widely in correlation to actual *narrow*ness). It has thus never been natural for NG to produce general grammars of Modern English like those of OG. Rather, most NG accounts of points of Modern English grammar are scattered in NG 'literature' – papers, or sections of books, sometimes even unpublished, in which one point or another is pertinent as long as a particular theoretical position is adopted. In Part III, *A–Z* therefore has to sample from such NG literature in juxtaposing NG to OG. The difference between the general OG grammars of Chapter 2 and the highly specific NG literature here is in fact an important pointer that OG and NG are juxtaposed: the comprehensiveness of the *open*ly receptive OG grammars vs. the fragmentation of *narrow*ly exclusive NG literature.

From this perspective, it is incumbent on *A–Z* also – if not especially – to note NG attempts which do appear to resemble grammars, and thus OG, counter to juxtaposition. In this chapter, two notable such cases for Modern English will be looked at: Stockwell *et al.* (1973) in section 3.2; and Emonds (1976) in section 3.3. Note at once that these NG 'grammars' are relatively early NG: it is one sign of the effectuation of *narrow*ness in NG that more recently no 'general' grammars have been attempted. Correspondingly, for the points of Modern English grammar of Part III, OG accounts in the grammars of Sweet, Poutsma, Kruisinga, Curme, Jespersen, and Quirk *et al.* will be juxtaposed to NG accounts in Chomsky's various seminal works, and in Stockwell *et al.* and Emonds, if the point has ever been pertinent in any of these; otherwise, if possible, at least two representatives of the – generally later – further NG literature are selected because in each case some theoretical position or other did serve to make the point at issue seem to be a pertinent one.

3.1 Avram Noam Chomsky (born 1928)

Chomsky inaugurated NG in 1957, when the publication of *Syntactic Structures* led to the 'Chomskyan revolution' in linguistics. One of the more readily visible constants in NG has since remained Chomsky's decisively authoritative influence. Our purpose here is to show that an effect of Chomsky's influence will indeed have been consistently to foster *narrow*ness.

To begin with *Syntactic Structures*, then (cf. also Chapter 1), its Preface – the preface to NG in its entirety – instantly adopts a *narrow* programme: "The search for rigorous formulation . . . [an] attempt to avoid . . . loose formulation" (1957:5). But rather notably, this programme is as yet executed only partially: "we limit the direct description . . . to . . . basic sentences . . ., deriving all other sentences from these . . . by transformation" (1957: 106–7). In *Syntactic Structures*, *narrow* limits on the description of basic sentences are relatively well-explored; *narrow* limits on transformations are not yet really in sight however.

Next, in 1965 Chomsky proclaimed what was to become a 'standard theory' of NG in *Aspects of the Theory of Syntax*. Chomsky again "requires a precise and *narrow* delimitation of the notion 'generative grammar'" (1965:35; emphasis added). Chomsky now also espouses a deductive approach: "grammar . . . is in no sense an 'inductive generalization'" (1965:33). Moreover, the relative *open*ness of transformations is now programmatically taken up at least, (1965:133): as yet "the theory . . . permits a great deal of latitude . . . of transformations"; but the *narrow* programme should be applicable here as well, and would "suggest . . . restrictions on . . . transformations" also.

Finally, in 1981 Chomsky canonized a number of developments in NG theory in *Lectures on Government and Binding* (*LGB*). But whatever the changes in specific respects, in *LGB* too "the correct theory . . . will . . . sharply restrict the class of attainable grammars and *narrowly* constrain their form"; accordingly, "a grammar . . . will in general lack . . . an inductive basis" (1981:3–4; emphasis added). And the relatively *open* transformations of earlier NG are now effectively *narrow*ed as well: "In early work in generative grammar, it was assumed, as in traditional grammar, that there are . . . transformations . . . In subsequent work . . ., these . . . were gradually reduced . . . This development, largely in the work of the past ten years, represents a substantial break from earlier generative grammar, or from the traditional grammar on which it was in part modelled" (1981:7; cf. section v).

Chomsky's views on NG and 'traditional' grammar, and the

extent to which NG could ever be seen as 'modelled' on OG, are discussed in Part II – where *A–Z* largely dissents from Chomsky. We may accept for NG, however, Chomsky's authority for NG's consistently *narrow* programme; and for the development towards effectively *narrow* NG – notably with a reduction, up to the point of elimination, of *open* transformations.

At this point it may be appropriate to acknowledge an important possibility to challenge *A–Z*'s entire notion that NG is inherently averse to comprehensiveness. One of the early slogans of NG, which may in fact well have helped to achieve the Chomskyan revolution, was that the purpose of NG was for a grammar of a particular language L to account for 'all and only the grammatical sentences of the language'. This might be derived from Chomsky (1957:13): "the grammar of L will ... be a device that generates all of the grammatical sequences of L and none of the ungrammatical ones". In various ways this fits closely *A–Z*'s presentation of NG as *narrow*. 'Generate' is a technical term tantamount to 'proceeding deductively'; and 'none of the ungrammatical ones' is a pointer to NG's exclusiveness (for discussion of '(un-)grammatical', see section II.4). But beyond all this, '*all* of the grammatical sentences' appears to espouse comprehensiveness.

It is important to note that this point particularly arises for earlier NG; more recently, the 'all and only' slogan seems to be bandied about much less. But even at the time, the slogan may be seen to have been a misinterpretation – if not for political reasons a deliberately oversimplified misrepresentation – of Chomsky (1957). That is, it has been ignored that Chomsky at once continues, "to set the aims of grammar *significantly* it is sufficient to assume a *partial* knowledge of sentences and non-sentences ... In ... intermediate cases we shall be prepared to let the grammar itself decide" (1957:13–14; emphases added). Even in 1957, Chomsky associates 'significant' aims with 'partial' coverage, counter to comprehensiveness. In fact, in the NG sense of the term, a sentence is 'grammatical' precisely if and only if it is 'decided' by the grammar that it is a sentence; in this sense, it is a tautology to say that 'a grammar generates all and only the sentences of a language'. At least, all of this is explicitly *partial*, and thus a far cry from the comprehensiveness espoused in OG, full coverage of evidence assumed to be available independently from the grammar.

[Biography: Lyons 1977:174–5; Newmeyer 1980:33–5]

3.2 Robert P. Stockwell (born 1925) *et al.* **The Major Syntactic Structures of English (1973)**

Like the largely native, British Quirk grammars in OG (section 2.6), American *The Major Syntactic Structures of English* is a collective effort. Some twenty collaborators were involved, beside the three principal author-editors: Robert P. Stockwell (born 1925), Paul Schachter (1929), and Barbara Hall Partee (1940). By their initials, the work will often be referred to as SS&P (1973). As a "transformational ... grammar of English" (1973:iii), SS&P represents an unlikely phenomenon, a general NG 'grammar' of Modern English, rather than specific NG literature. SS&P refer to an "expectation that most of the information about the transformational analysis of the grammar of English that was available up through the summer of 1968 could be brought together and integrated in a single format" (1973:iii); 'information ... available' is reminiscent of OG's 'available evidence'; but 'integrated in a single format' rather of NG's 'in accordance with the associated theory' (see Chapter 1). SS&P (1973) would thus amount to a compromise between OG and NG – the very notion of which is a refutation of *A–Z*'s uncompromising juxtaposition of OG and NG.

However, in Part III *A–Z* charts point-by-point for Modern English grammar the relative 'failure' of the compromise, i.e. that SS&P prove staunchly *narrow* in comparison to the comprehensiveness achieved by the *open* grammars of OG. Moreover, SS&P themselves instantly admit as well that expecting a compromise to be possible was in fact "naive" (1973:iii); and juxtaposition already re-emerges, as the more mature view. Note that under *A–Z*'s juxtaposition of OG and NG, SS&P may be excellent NG precisely because it fails to compromise itself.

In fact, SS&P suggest a truly *narrow* approach to Modern English grammar by restricting themselves in their title to 'major' structures. For an *open* approach every structure is equally to be covered, each one being as important as the next. But just as a point of grammar may be pertinent or not according to a theory, so it is only in relation to a theory that structures can be *narrow*ed down to the more – or the less – major ones.

Still, SS&P do lay claim to a measure of comprehensiveness: "We believe the considerable survey that it [SS&P] represents ... will be quite useful to scholars and students of English and of transformational theory" (1973:v). Note 'of English': SS&P thus do make it into McKay's (1984) list of English reference grammars, selected on the basis of comprehensiveness. But McKay also admits that instead of genuinely comprehensive coverage, SS&P

(1973) really "covers only those aspects ... already ... studied within the ... [NG] framework" (1984:124); that is, points pertinent to NG theory. Gross (1979:859) seems to be nearer the mark, in a passage that it will do *A–Z*'s case for juxtaposition good to quote at some length:

> no linguist has been able to construct a ... [NG] grammar with the type of coverage that traditional grammars used to provide ... Jespersen 1909 [sic], Poutsma 1904–29, etc. The only recent step in this direction (Stockwell *et al.* 1973) is not a grammar; it is an attempt to integrate partial data.

Being NG, SS&P will effectively remain *narrow*, limited like Chomsky (1957) to the 'partial' evidence that is pertinent to however wide a range of NG-theoretical positions. It will be seen in Part III that in SS&P (1973) this is indeed something quite different from the genuinely comprehensive coverage provided by OG grammars.

[Biography: on Stockwell: Duncan-Rose and Venneman 1988; see sections II.2, II.4, also on Schachter and Partee]

3.3 Joseph E. Emonds (born 1940) *A Transformational Approach to English Syntax* (1976)

Paraphrasing the title of Emonds (1976) as 'an NG approach to Modern English grammar', J. E. Emonds falls squarely within NG. In fact, Emonds (1976) is seminal *narrow* literature: Emonds develops a major constraint on transformations, the Structure Preserving Constraint (see below). And Emonds (1976) has duly not been included in McKay's (1984) list of Modern English grammars with comprehensive coverage. However, the material in (1976) is not necessarily pertinent only to the theory of structure preservation: 'It is ... hoped that this book can serve ... even beyond the period of its theoretical immediacy" (1976:vii). Accordingly, Emonds does pretend to a kind of comprehensiveness; a major reason for the position accorded to Emonds (1976) in *A–Z* is that it takes SS&P for a model: "A comprehensive treatment of this sort has previously appeared only once (Stockwell, Schachter & Partee 1968)" (1976:vii; SS&P 1968 = 1973, cf. Emonds 1976:257).

It will be useful – to avoid much repetition in Part III – here to turn briefly to Emonds' *narrow* notion of structure preservation. Suppose we have a structure A + B + C (e.g. *John hates music*) which is related to a structure C + A + B (e.g. *music John hates*). NG might account for this by means of a transformation: A + B +

$C \Rightarrow C + A + B$. Emonds' breakthrough proposal is to radically *narrow* such transformations: they should essentially be possible only in independent sentences ('root clauses', illustrated above); but not in subclauses, say the bracketed one of $X + [A + B + C]$ (e.g. *let [John hate music]*, * *let [music John hate]*; * indicates an ungrammatical sentence – for discussion see section II.4). Beyond such 'root' transformations, transformations would only be possible if they are either minor 'local' ones; or major ones which preserve structure, and which give Emonds' theory its name (note again, as in section 3.2, the theory-bound status of notions like 'major' and 'minor'). By local transformations, two parts of a structure next to one another may exchange places: $A + B \Rightarrow B + A$: e.g. *enough money, money enough* (but $A + B + C \not\Rightarrow B + C + A$: *enough money for the train*, * *money for the train enough*).

The major constraint by which Emonds *narrows* transformations is that transformations may only *change* structures either in root clauses or locally, by exchanging neighbours; otherwise transformations do not change structure, but *preserve* it: say, $A_1 + B + C + A_2 \Rightarrow A_2 + B + C + A_1$. Illustration will readily become somewhat abstract, since a concomitant assumption is that A may be 'empty', $\emptyset$ (cf. also section z for 'zero'). But for concreteness suppose that A's are pronouns, including *it* and *you*. Then replacement of $A_1 = it$ by $A_2 = you$ preserves structure: *it may be easy to see you, you may be easy to see $\emptyset$* (cf. section H). Note that such a structure preserving transformation is not local (*it* and *you* are not next to one another); and that it *can* operate in subclauses: *let [it be easy to see him], let [him be easy to see $\emptyset$]*. Now suppose also that C is the adjective *easy*, i.e. $C \neq A$. Then replacement of $C = easy$ by $A_2 = you$ does not preserve structure, and hence is impossible: *it is easy to see you*, * *it is you to see $\emptyset$*.

In such ways, structure preservation is evidently a very significant constraint on transformations, with a vast range of potentially pertinent evidence (imagine the (im-)possibilities of transforming $A_1 + B + C + A_2 + D + A_3$; etc.). As such, Emonds makes a major contribution to effectively *narrow* NG, and by the same token "treat[s] systematically aspects of syntax particular to English" (1976:viii; as will be seen also in Part III of *A–Z*). But Emonds (1976) still remains primarily 'systematic': *narrow* NG, juxtaposed to purely cumulative, genuinely *open* investigations. [Biography: not found]

3.4 The NG literature 1955– ... (1986/1988)

The literature of NG is enormously extensive; and even for what *A–Z* has sampled, it will not do to attempt to give any kind of introductory survey here. The reader will obtain the bare information from the Bibliography. However, the fact that the last two subsections have dealt with attempted NG 'grammars' of 1973 and 1976 may suggest that *A–Z* concentrates on NG from the mid-1970s. It will be useful to dispel such an impression here. In fact, a look at the Bibliography will confirm that NG in *A–Z* ranges from (inevitably, Chomsky) 1955 to (by accident, Radford) 1988; but the sample was essentially closed off towards the end of 1986. The fact that the two NG 'grammars' date from the 1970s is merely due to the relative effective *open*ness of early NG.

It may also be appropriate to note here that the author's own attempts to contribute to the study of Modern English grammar are intended to belong to the NG literature; and some are thus included in the Bibliography. But it is hoped that in *A–Z* there is no consequent bias in favour of NG; as indeed the very undertaking of *A-Z* should confirm.

Part II
NG on OG

Newer narrow grammar on older open grammar

After the global introductions to OG and NG in Part I, the point-by-point juxtaposition of OG and NG accounts of Modern English grammar in Part III will constitute the core of *A–Z*. In further preparation, however, the preliminary considerations in Part I can well be extended by providing an appreciation of perceptions of OG within NG. These tend to deviate more or less sharply from juxtaposition of OG and NG as propounded by *A–Z*. Part II of *A–Z* addresses such more standard perceptions; and maintains that they are mistaken, so that juxtaposition stands. Following the practice initiated in Part I and maintained in Part III, we first probe Chomsky, then SS&P (1973) and Emonds (1976), and finally the NG literature.

II.1 On Chomsky on OG

As our interest is now in NG's perceptions of OG, we will not here go into Chomsky or his work by themselves beyond what is offered in Parts I and III. However, there is a practical problem even in saying anything about Chomsky's views on OG at all. Chomsky generally uses a blanket term 'traditional grammar', which might refer to virtually any approach to grammar from Aristotle (384–322 BC) or even Panini (?4th century BC) onwards. Chomsky never acknowledges English 'scholarly traditional' grammars, i.e. *A–Z*'s OG ones by Sweet, Poutsma, Kruisinga, Curme, Jespersen, and Quirk *et al.*, as an approach separate from other 'traditional grammar'. Hence one can hardly ever be certain that remarks of Chomsky's about 'traditional grammar' are to be applied to OG (very often they will not be: Chomsky's 'traditional grammar' can most often be located in the seventeenth century; cf. Chomsky 1966).

Nevertheless, for the purposes of *A–Z* it is important to get as close as possible to authoritative views of Chomsky on the relation of 'his' NG to OG. Fortunately there do appear to be some routes along which these can at least be approximated. First of all, in Part I we have already come across Chomsky's (1964:53) dismissive position on behalf of NG that comprehensiveness is neither serious nor significant; again, "I do not believe that seeking to account for 'all the facts' constitutes a reasonable goal" (1979:107). For *A–Z* Chomsky thus fundamentally juxtaposes NG to OG's goal of comprehensive coverage.

Furthermore, occasionally Chomsky does particularize "complete traditional grammar" (1964:16), or "traditional grammars ... of great scope like Jespersen's" (1979:109), or "traditional grammar, however compendious" (1980:43–4); where the references may well be taken to be to the comprehensive traditional grammars of OG in general. In fact, Chomsky has borne witness to his interest in Jespersen throughout his work (e.g. 1958/1962:124, 1986:8–9). Thus Jespersen is Chomsky's (1979:109) example of OG; there is no evidence that Chomsky has ever seriously investigated other OG. However, the point is again complicated by the fact that Chomsky is prepared to recognize two putatively distinct Jespersens: Jespersen the "philosopher" and Jespersen the "grammarian" (1979:156–7). Still, this section will survey aspects of Chomsky's views on Jespersen, where these represent the nearest thing to Chomsky's views on OG in general; otherwise, we will cautiously rely on general statements of Chomsky's about 'traditional grammar'.

As we have pointed out in Part I (implicitly following Chomsky 1986:2), there are two major conceptual shifts in the history of (Chomsky's) NG. The first conceptual shift was the Chomskyan revolution itself, and it established NG and its *narrow* programme by the late 1950s. The second conceptual shift, equally revolutionary but much more gradual, is the pursuit of NG as more effectively *narrow* grammar, from roughly 1968 onwards. Correspondingly, Chomsky's perceptions on the relation of NG to OG have shifted: from NG as a 'reconstruction' of OG (cf. 1958/1962:124) to OG and NG being "complementary" (1986:2). When it is still relatively *open* in practice, NG can perceive OG as a model to be reconstructed; as NG begins to effectuate its programmatic *narrow*ness, OG and NG come to be perceived as more independent, complementary approaches to grammar.

Chomsky's later perception, that OG and NG are complementary, is more easily compatible with the position that *A–Z* takes as its basis: juxtaposition. For Chomsky, the *narrow* concern of NG is with constraints that manifest themselves in all languages: universal features of points of Modern English grammar; features which Chomsky "doubt[s] that any traditional grammar, even the most comprehensive one, would trouble to note" (1979:61; cf. section R.4). Complementarily, Chomsky sees 'traditional grammar' as dealing with "exceptions" (1986:2), i.e. the particular features of each language separately. Note that non-natives would seem to be in a privileged position to observe such particular features in the foreign language they cover. In fact in OG Curme (cf. section 2.4) also acknowledges that "foreign scholars ... have sharp eyes for the *peculiarities* of our language" (1931:v; emphasis added).

However, *A–Z* contends that to the extent that OG is effectively comprehensive, there would be nothing left for NG to complement, i.e. to add to OG's coverage: the available evidence covered in OG should include the pertinent data of NG. For *A–Z*, the independence of OG and NG is thus in their being juxtaposed approaches, rather than in their being complementary in coverage. Specific evidence for *A–Z*'s position appears in Part III, section R for 'referential riddles': a pertinent point of Modern English grammar, which is Chomsky's (1986:3) purported example of where OG and NG should prove complementary; in fact, in section R, OG and NG appear to cover essentially similar evidence, but under juxtaposed approaches. With this we dismissively leave Chomsky's current view on OG and NG.

Before we turn to Chomsky's earlier view, NG reconstructing OG, we should say a few words about his schizophrenic interpretation of Jespersen: philosopher vs. (OG?) grammarian. The idea is basically that Jespersen the philosopher is *narrow*, Jespersen the grammarian *open* (1979:156–7). Naturally such a distinction comes more prominently to the fore when NG begins to be effectively *narrow*; there does not seem to be a dualistic view in Chomsky's earliest references to Jespersen. In fact, *A–Z* would be content to subscribe to the *open* view of only Jespersen the grammarian: it would be sufficient for our immediate purposes if Jespersen was at least *open* in his *MEG* juxtaposed to NG in Part III, whatever he might be like outside *MEG*. Still, the case for juxtaposition of OG and NG would be strengthened by a unitary view of Jespersen, as consistently *open*. And there are indeed some indications that even Chomsky's view of Jespersen the philosopher as *narrow* may be misguided.

It would take up too much space here to present an extensive study of Jespersen's vast output, or even of his two most philosophical works, *The Philosophy of Grammar* (1924) and *Analytic Syntax* (1936/1969). Chomsky restricts himself to the former. The latter is explicitly *open*: it is inductive, "I have everywhere started from sentences as occurring in actual living speech" (1969:90); and against constraints, Jespersen allows for "extensions" (1969:4). But what about Chomsky's interpretation of Jespersen's *Philosophy of Grammar* at least as *narrow*? Recall from section 2.5 Jespersen's (1924:48) avowed aversion of deduction. One might be prepared to ignore this on the argument that whatever Jespersen's aversions, there is no alternative to deduction in science. That is, any grammarian will, consciously or unawares, bring preconceptions to bear on his accounts of Modern English grammar, without which he would simply have no reference-points to organize his material at all. In fact, it may be that here we have a reason for the preponderance of non-natives in OG: attempting to be inductive, Jespersen – and Poutsma and Kruisinga – could proceed on the basis of a native language as an implicit frame of reference in approaching Modern English grammar.

We have now touched upon profound issues in the philosophy of science, with ramifications which extend far beyond the immediate concerns of *A–Z*. For practical purposes it is crucial that purported induction vs. deduction be seen as the juxtaposed aims of OG and NG; even if philosophical questions should hover over the extents to which, for Modern English grammar, these aims can be pursued in the purest fashions, whether by native or non-native grammarians. Part III of *A–Z* accordingly surveys evidence of the inductive and deductive practices in OG and NG respectively. Otherwise in the space available here we can do little more than bring Chomsky's *narrow* interpretation of Jespersen (1924) into disrepute.

Chomsky ascribes to Jespersen (1924) the view that users of language have a "notion of structure" (1975:4, 1986:8), which putatively can be associated with the universal constraints of NG; i.e. a *narrow* notion of structure. But for Jespersen there is actually a much less general "notion of *their* structure" (1924:19; emphasis added). The vital significance of 'their' is that it refers to "innumerable sentences heard and understood" (ibid.). This *open* number of 'innumerable' sentences is the basis on which Jespersen's notion of structure is supposed to develop: i.e. inductively. A *narrow* interpretation of Jespersen (1924) such as Chomsky's cannot be credited if it involves dropping Jespersen's crucial 'their' from his 'notion of ... structure'.

Let us now return, finally, to Chomsky's early perspective on OG, in which transformational NG is said to reconstruct OG: "transformational ideas are ... an important part of traditional grammar. E.g., Jespersen ... we will reconstruct as transformational" (1958/1962:124). Chomsky's examples (also 1964:29–30) include Jespersen's accounts of the relations between *the doctor's arrival/the doctor arrived*, and between *the barking dog/the dog barks*. These accounts were criticized by Nida (1951:143; see Nida 1960), a representative of 'structural' grammar which – in some respects like Kruisinga (see section 2.3) – only allows *narrow*ly formal accounts. Chomsky's trans-*form*-ational reconstruction of Jespersen apparently convinced Nida, who drops his criticisms of Jespersen in (1966). But eventually, Chomsky in turn retracts the transformational reconstruction: in more effectively *narrow* NG "transformations ... were gradually reduced", and this "represents a substantial break from earlier generative grammar, or from the traditional grammar on which it was in part modelled" (1981:7) (cf. also 3.1 and section v).

But what about Chomsky's conception itself, that early NG 'reconstructs' OG, or at least traditional grammar; was it correct at the time? Again, an answer is uncertain as long as Chomsky does not specify what 'traditional grammar' he has in mind. A notable instance is in one of Chomsky's most influential standard NG works, *Aspects of the Theory of Syntax* (1965; see section 3.1): "The investigation of generative grammar can profitably begin with a careful analysis of the kind of information presented in traditional grammars" (1965:63). Chomsky then presents a 'traditional' account of *sincerity may frighten the boy*: subject *sincerity* + auxiliary *may* + predicate *frighten the boy*. Chomsky does not cite any traditional grammar which actually has precisely such a tripartite account – hardly a 'careful analysis'. Certainly, the account is *not* typical of OG. Kruisinga (1932b:263ff.) for instance, would have an account with just two parts: subject *sincerity* + predicate *may frighten the boy*; and Jespersen (1927:203ff.) assumes an alternative tripartite account: subject *sincerity* + verb *may frighten* + object *the boy* (Quirk *et al.* keep things *open* by hovering between Kruisinga's two-part and Jespersen's three-part (but *not* Chomsky's 'traditional'!) approaches: 1972:35–6; 1985:45, 79; cf. also 1985:42, 45 for four-part analyses, 1985:50 for eight-part ones and beyond, etc.). Most OG goes implicitly along with Jespersen; for Jespersen there is in fact an interesting philosophy behind his account. Subject *sincerity* and object *the boy* should "in their relation to the verb stand on nearly the same footing", because a switch from object to subject is so common (1927:354); e.g. into subject *the boy* + verb *may be frightened* (see also section H for *it is hard to frighten the boy* (object) – '*the boy* (subject) *is hard to frighten*).

In all, and in so far as Chomsky's views on OG can be ascertained at all, *A–Z* tends towards dissent throughout. Early NG does not demonstrably reconstruct OG accounts. Comprehensive OG is not merely complementary to current NG in coverage.

And Jespersen 'the philosopher' is *open* rather than *narrow*, so that there is no split between Jespersen the OG grammarian and the 'NG' philosopher either. Chomsky's work need not lead one to give up, or even to modify, the juxtaposition of his NG to OG including Jespersen.

II.2 On Stockwell *et al.* on OG

Having obtained a fair perspective on SS&P (1973) with respect to juxtaposition of OG and NG in Part I, we here turn to SS&P's own perspectives on OG. In their collective work itself, SS&P include Jespersen's *MEG* among the references to one chapter (1973:66); and Poutsma's *GLME* among those to another (1973:674). In fact, they thus deal Poutsma one chapter short, since *GLME* also appears, without bibliographical acknowledgement, in a further chapter (1973:187; cf. section D.4).

Beyond SS&P, Partee (1965) uses OG – Jespersen and Curme – as starting points in 'traditional grammar' for developing her NG account of the subject and object relations in Modern English. This foreshadows the interest of 'relational' NG in OG; see section II.4. Partee (1965) is her doctoral dissertation, written under the supervision of Chomsky: cf. section II.1 on Chomsky's own (1965) NG 'reconstruction' of the 'traditional' subject. Schachter tends to use Jespersen as a source of genuine examples; which OG can be because under induction it bases itself firmly on observations. Representative is the following passage on the status of articles in constructions like *the kicking the dog*: "While articles ostensibly fail to occur ... Jespersen (1940[:118ff.]) cites numerous literary examples, from the fifteenth through the seventeenth centuries ... He notes, however, that 'modern native grammarians are unanimous in condemning this construction' (1940:118)" (1976:210; the quote is not quite accurate). Note another appearance of the (non-) native grammarian.

Neither Partee nor Schachter has remained within strictly orthodox NG, as we will briefly note at the end of section II.4. But perhaps the most interesting is the senior partner in the SS&P enterprise, Stockwell. Stockwell (born 1925) is one of the rare contributors to NG older in age than Chomsky himself (of 1928). In fact, Stockwell is a convert to NG, from an earlier approach more or less like Kruisinga's (section 2.4) and Nida's (section II.1). Once converted, Stockwell first follows Chomsky in expecting NG to reconstruct OG: "The linear ancestry of transformational grammar is to be found in traditional grammar ... Jespersen's grammar, for instance, is a mine of still unexploited richness, full of intuitively correct observations ... awaiting explicit formalization [i.e. NG reconstruction]" (1964:55–6). But it seems that the attempts at such reconstructions have disappointed Stockwell: "several schools of theoretical linguistics ... simply don't attempt to write grammars anymore. One can hardly imagine what a full grammar of English written within the ... [current NG] theory might look like" (1986:126). Because of NG's – duly also SS&P's! – failure to produce comprehensive coverage as in the 'full grammars' of OG, it sounds as if Stockwell has again been converted, now away from NG. At least, there is again evidence here for the juxtaposition of OG – with 'full grammars' – and (recent) NG – with such grammars being unimaginable.

II.3 On Emonds on OG

Emonds does not seem to have referred either directly or indirectly to any OG at all, either in (1976) or elsewhere. As in Part I, we may take this to indicate that Emonds is one of the most staunchly *narrow* grammarians of Modern English. Whether Emonds' consistent silence about OG is indeed due to an informed verdict on its juxtaposed incompatibility with NG cannot be ascertained, however. Cf. Emonds (1985:167) and section L.4 2 below.

II.4 On the NG 'literature' on OG

To a large extent, the Chomskyan revolution of 1957 was effectuated not so much by the publication of Chomsky's *Syntactic Structures* itself, but by its review by Robert Lees in the authoritative American journal *Language* (Newmeyer 1980:19, 35, 45–6). Significantly, Lees (1957:387) instantly relates NG to OG: "in a sense, transformational analysis is essentially a formalization of a long-accepted, traditional approach to grammatical relations. To cite only a single example, ... Otto Jespersen". Lees thus immediately established an NG perspective on OG: 'formalization' again amounts to Chomsky's view that NG reconstructs OG, where OG is practically taken to be represented (only) by Jespersen.

In broadest outline, therefore, it would be appropriate to refer to section II.1 for discussion of NG literature on OG: taking its origin in Lees, and Chomsky, the prevalent perspective is reconstruction; and attention tends to be restricted to Jespersen. Chomsky's own views are part of a veritable tradition: Gefen (1968), Reynolds (1969, 1971), and Jacobsen (1977) also variously study Jespersen in relation to NG, underplaying the possible implications of his position in OG. In all these studies, other OG is either not mentioned, or if it is, it is practically dismissed.

Thus in the case of Jacobsen, who at least precedes his discussion of "the main points of contact" (1977:45) between traditional and transformational-generative grammar with a relatively rare specification of what he means by 'traditional grammar'; Jacobsen promises both the tradition which started in ancient Greece, and (1977:61–2) (some) OG: Sweet, Jespersen, Poutsma, and Kruisinga. However, the actual discussion is only of "Jespersen, one of the greatest of the scholarly traditionalists [i.e. OG]" (1977:51–2); in this respect, Jacobsen is fully in line with Lees and Chomsky (see also below).

Similarly, although Gefen's (1968) title, 'Linguistic theory and language description in Jespersen', suggests juxtaposition of *narrow* theory to *open* description, Gefen fails to consider OG. Gefen rather attempts to relate Jespersen to 'structuralism' (the 'form-only' approach of Nida (see section II.1), and to some extent of Kruisinga's *Handbook* (see section 2.3)) and/or to NG. *A–Z* can concur with Gefen's (1968:403) conclusion that "Jespersen's importance lies in his descriptive achievements". This effectively juxtaposes Jespersen to both structuralism – Jespersen is "incomparably more comprehensive than any 'structuralist' grammar" (1968:389); and to NG – "transformationalist descriptive grammars have yet to see the light of day" (1968:399). But Gefen fails to mention Sweet, Poutsma, Kruisinga, Curme, and thus does not draw the apparently correct conclusion that descriptive achievements put Jespersen in line, not with either structuralism or NG, but with OG.

Much the same goes for Reynolds. Her (1971) title, 'What *did* Jespersen say?', seems to juxtapose her investigation to Chomsky's suggestion that NG complements OG by being "interested in what traditional grammars *don't say*" (1979:61; original emphasis). However, Reynolds actually finds herself forced to conclude that Jespersen should be seen as "an ancestor of Chomsky" (1969:267), since "he never did belong to any of the traditions within the mainstream of linguistic theory during his lifetime (1969:266). Note the obvious point that if Jespersen appears to have dissented from contemporary linguistic theory, i.e. from *narrow* approaches, this would be because his goals were in language description, i.e. *open*; which would line Jespersen up with OG (see also below; Reynolds (1969:128) juxtaposes Jespersen to OG, i.e. to three late nineteenth–early twentieth century 'schools': one including Sweet, Kruisinga, and Poutsma; another Curme (1969:37)).

Having surveyed the NG literature on Jespersen in particular,

A–Z is confirmed in its position that one should look at the relation between NG and OG in general. For instance, Ohlander (1980) discusses at least Sweet, alongside Jespersen: both as 'transformational grammarians'. This appropriation of Sweet and Jespersen to NG again conflicts with *A–Z*'s juxtaposition of them, as OG, to NG. It would take too much space here to attempt to parry Ohlander's challenge point by point. Rather, attention may here be drawn merely to Ohlander's conclusion: "The difference[s] between Sweet, Jespersen, and Chomsky do not, as a rule, pertain to the range of phenomena or facts actually observed by them" (1980:163). Ohlander will be seen to fail to even address the fundamental difference in 'range' between OG's available evidence and NG's pertinent facts. *A–Z* can thus maintain this difference as the basis of its juxtaposition of OG to NG.

However, Ohlander (1980) also touches upon another important issue that arises in juxtaposing OG and NG: grammatical and ungrammatical sentences. In section II.1 *A–Z* rejects Chomsky's presentation of OG and NG as complementary, covering language particular and universal points of grammar respectively. But OG and NG may also be perceived as complementary in that OG deals with (only) 'grammatical' facts, NG (also) with 'ungrammatical' ones. Being *narrow*, NG is inherently just as interested in what *cannot* be said as in what *can* be said. Recall from section 3.1 that Chomsky's revolution first addressed itself to "all of the grammatical sequences of L and none of the ungrammatical ones" (Chomsky 1957:13). For instance, the facts that *shut your mouth* is a good English sentence, but *mouth your shut* is not, may be equally pertinent to a constraint that NG will be eager to incorporate: that sentences cannot be transformed by simply exchanging the first and last words. Along these lines, NG abounds with ungrammatical sentences like *mouth your shut*, to show how NG constraints *narrow*ly exclude them. Such ungrammatical sentences are marked by *, an asterisk, which indicates that the example is not a straight fact, but an artificial one which could not occur: * *mouth your shut*. But note that what cannot occur cannot be observed either. That is, information about ungrammatical sentences can only be provided by introspection. Now recall from Chapter 2, Zandvoort (1961:23): "the foreign student ... has to rely on ... observation ... The native student has another source of information at his disposal, viz. introspection". Since ungrammatical sentences require native introspection, NG accounts are indeed predominantly produced by native grammarians: thus Chomsky, Stockwell *et al.*, and Emonds for English. By contrast, nonnatives are quite naturally prominent in making the observations of OG; from Chapter 2: Poutsma, Kruisinga, Jespersen, and Svartvik (one of Quirk's associates).

It is in fact sometimes claimed that OG and NG are complementary, in the sense that OG does not really cover ungrammatical evidence at all: "the standard reference grammars have traditionally dealt with language almost entirely in positive terms ... the asterisk notation for negative examples was an innovation of Chomskyan linguistics" (Sampson 1984:375). This is not true for native Sweet, for example: "* *the island was half*" (1891:14; cf. Ohlander 1980:141). Still, at least non-native grammarians in OG may be expected to be limited to grammatical evidence obtained by observation: "Non-natives are handicapped by having to work with affirmative data only" (Bolinger 1952/1965:284, with reference to Poutsma).

Even here, however, actually "Poutsma is fully prepared to ... use ... the (by now) familiar asterisk to mark ... ungrammatical products" (Meijs 1976:144); e.g. "* *That he would come was told me*" (1926:130). To Meijs' examples from (1926) one may add "* *The old is sometimes more valuable than the new*" (1914:409), "**he is who vexes me*" (1916:991), "* *a disobedient to his sovereign subject*" (1928:499), "* *He thinks to know it for certain*" (1929:767); i.e., in each of Poutsma's five volumes, asterisks are used. In contrast to Meijs' (1976:144) impression, ungrammatical facts indicated by * are to be found also in Kruisinga: e.g. "The plurals *men*, *women*, *children* do not occur in the post-genitive ... * *this attempt of the Chinamen's*" (1932a:66, footnote 1; cf. section G). Needless to say, a false picture about * in OG might appear from looking only at Jespersen, as NG tends to do: Jespersen does indeed not seem to mark sentences as ungrammatical by means of asterisks. On the other hand, Jespersen may well refer to negative evidence, in other ways: e.g. "while we have an ordinary object after *wish* (I wish you joy), this is impossible after *long* (I long for his arrival)" (1940:170); i.e. * *I long his arrival*. So too Curme (1931:80): "we never say [i.e.*] '*The king of Englands* now have less power than formerly'" (cf. again section G). In Quirk *et al.* * regularly "indicates an unacceptable structure" (1972:xi), or more succinctly * is identified as "unacceptable" (1985:x); in both *GCE* and *CGoEL* * is relatively frequent. It is undeniable, and quite natural, that in practice OG is more austere in giving ungrammatical evidence than is NG, as will frequently be seen in Part III. However, *A–Z* maintains that there is no fundamental difference between OG and NG in this respect: in principle, NG cannot be claimed to 'complement' OG by adding ungrammatical evidence to exclusively grammatical facts in OG.

Let us finally consider implications for the juxtaposition of OG and NG that arise in connection with developments in NG. As Chomsky changes his perspective on OG and NG – from reconstruction to complementary (see section II.1) – when NG effectuates *narrow*ness, it is of considerable interest to observe the roles accorded to OG in alternative NG, which more or less independently of Chomsky remains relatively *open*. Around 1968 Chomsky was confronted with developments of the idea that in NG all constructions that are *semantically* related should also be *grammatically* related. *A–Z* will use the term 'semantic NG' to refer somewhat roughly to such NG approaches as generative semantics, case grammar, etc. (cf. Newmeyer 1980:Ch. 4). To relate grammatically for instance *John killed Bill with a gun* and *John shot Bill dead* because they mean (approximately) the same thing, semantic NG allows transformations which can perform essentially any change on a structure, such as turning *kill with a gun* into *shoot dead*; effectively, transformations are thus kept *open* for anything. As Newmeyer (1980:167–8) pregnantly puts it, semantic NG opts "for pure description", and thus for comprehensive coverage, of "each and every fact about language".

With the above picture of semantic NG in mind, it is natural that semantic NG should not see itself as juxtaposed to OG, the earlier descriptive and comprehensive approach. Whereas Chomskyans relinquish the view that NG reconstructs OG when they effectuate *narrow* NG, semantic NG eagerly pursues such reconstruction. Thus Nilsen (1973:87–8) observes that *inter alia* Curme, Jespersen, Kruisinga, Poutsma, and Sweet "were well on their way towards developing a solid semantically based grammar [i.e. semantic OG] before attention was turned away by the ... transformationalists [i.e. by Chomskyan NG]": semantic NG redirects attention to 'solid' semantic OG. And Meijs (1976:150) similarly contends that the Great Tradition of (some) OG – Jespersen, Poutsma especially, and Kruisinga – is interesting because there is in NG "a steady trend towards more semantically-oriented ... grammar [i.e. semantic NG] ... , and therefore towards a position that is very close to the traditional one, in which ... semantic considerations played an important role". The affinity of OG and semantic NG is not entirely uncontroversial. To return to Jacobsen (1977) and Reynolds (1969), Jacobsen (1977:489–90) aligns Jespersen with semantic NG on the basis of Jespersen's dictum that "in syntax meaning is everything" (1931:291). But Reynolds (1969:256) believes that "Jespersen, if he were here, would warn against [semantic NG] overbalancing the scale towards semantics". Nevertheless, given the semantic NG perception of reconstructing

OG, the 'linguistic wars' between semantic NG and Chomskyan NG (Newmeyer 1980) parallel *A–Z*'s more peaceful juxtaposition of OG and Chomskyan NG.

The linguistic wars have been won by Chomskyan NG, and semantic NG is now practically defunct; as an attempt to span *A–Z*'s juxtaposition of OG and NG, semantic NG would have been moribund from the start. Many of its adherents have since adopted 'relational grammar' (Newmeyer 1980:167, 244), for *A–Z* 'relational NG'. Relational NG makes "rather different assumptions" (Newmeyer 1980:167) than semantic NG, and it would not be appropriate simply to extend to relational NG the interpretation as relatively *open*. Still, relational NG *does* again claim affinity to OG; in fact, OG is notably appealed to in developing relational NG from Chomskyan NG. Relational NG takes its name from the assumption that grammatical accounts should be in terms of grammatical relations like those of subject, direct object, and indirect object; Chomsky (1965:69) wants to circumvent these in the interest of *narrow*ing NG accounts to categories like noun, verb, and sentence. Postal (1976:151) insists that traditional grammar has always been *open* to grammatical relations, and accordingly suggests that if NG is to remain true to its claim of reconstructing traditional grammar, it must therefore become relational NG.

Interestingly, Fiengo and Lasnik (1976:185) automatically interpret Postal (1976) as suggesting a reconstruction of Jespersen in particular; but they then point out that in fact Postal's relational NG differs significantly from Jespersen. For instance, Postal (1976) takes *Mary* in *John gave Mary a book* to be 'direct object'; but *Mary* is 'indirect object' in Jespersen (1914:9); and in fact 'indirect object' consistently in OG (Sweet 1891:43; Poutsma 1928:212; Kruisinga 1932b:188; Curme 1931:96; Quirk *et al.* 1972:37; 1985:54; such unanimity is rare in OG). In spite of this rather salient point, the position of OG has continued to be perceived as fundamentally closer to relational NG than to Chomskyan *narrow* NG. "Relational Grammar ... agrees better with the insights of traditional grammar than does the ordinary transformational model" (Cole and Sadock, 1977:xi); "A ... reason for the immediate popularity of relational grammar was its ability to capture directly the descriptions of the great traditional grammarians in a way that standard transformational grammar could not. By and large, such linguists as Jespersen, Poutsma, Curme *et al.* talked about ... grammatical relations ... – hence relational grammarians felt they had more right to claim such persons as their direct predecessors than did the mainstream transformational grammarians" (Newmeyer 1980:243); and, "A precursor of relational grammar can be seen in Jespersen" (McCawley 1982:119). The exact position of OG with respect to relational NG may be established as relational NG fully develops itself.

Note that by now in discussing 'semantic NG' and 'relational NG', *A–Z* has strayed off the *narrow* course it has set itself, of orthodoxly Chomskyan NG. By much the same license one might now also expect expositions on the many other alternative approaches that have been developed. For instance those since SS&P (1973) adopted by Partee (e.g. 1976), Montague grammar; or by Schachter (e.g. 1976), daughter-dependency grammar. From there, one might go on to such developments in NG as lexical-functional grammar (Kaplan and Bresnan 1982); or Generalized Phrase Structure Grammar (Gazdar *et al.* 1985). And indeed there are also explicit opposites to NG like Functional Grammar (Dik 1978). Each of these, and their relations to OG, would however require separate study, much beyond what is germane to *A–Z*.

A–Z continues to focus on the juxtaposition of OG and, at least, current Chomskyan *narrow* NG. By now, it is indeed high time to provide some evidence for this juxtaposition, as in Part III we survey OG and NG accounts of points of Modern English grammar.

Part III

An *A–Z*

OG and NG accounts of 26 alphabetically ordered points of Modern English grammar

In Part III of *A–Z*, OG and NG accounts of Modern English grammar are juxtaposed in detail. With one point of Modern English grammar selected for each letter of the alphabet, 26 points are represented in two kinds of section: miniscules (small letters) indicate minor sections, e.g. 'b is for BE'; majuscules (capitals) indicate major sections, e.g. 'A is for *all*'. In minor sections, *A–Z* basically supplies a systematized presentation of the OG and NG accounts surveyed – commentary, speculations, and/or elaboration are kept minimal. In major sections, the juxtaposition of OG and NG is spelled out in more detail. Under majuscules, therefore, *A–Z* wants to muster full support for the claim that OG and NG are juxtaposed; under miniscules, *A–Z* hopes to enable and to entice the reader to become an ally, who more independently draws her own conclusions about the juxtaposition of OG and NG.

By systematically representing OG and NG accounts of Modern English grammar, *A–Z* should save the reader who wants to obtain a representative survey of grammatical literature some rather tedious hours searching through OG and NG for bits of information about a specific point. However, *A–Z* thus also denies the reader the considerable excitement that may be engendered by the 'discovery' of a more enlightening or insightful observation or description. In fact, *A–Z* would perform a most useful function if it merely lures the reader into progressing from majuscule sections through miniscule ones to completely independent explorations of the original literatures. Moreover, *A–Z* mainly represents accounts by selectively citing from OG and NG originals. To avoid Part III becoming a mere series of quotations strung together, anything remotely omissible has been avidly excised. Readers may therefore also want to turn to the originals if only to get the full stories.

Within a voluntary straight-jacket of alphabetical requirements, for one letter a plausible point of grammar will be more readily forthcoming than for another one. Ultimately, the selection is based on little more firm than accident and the author's personal preferences. But the alphabetical requirements are intended to prevent the worse evils of bias: the 26 points should amount to a fair cross-section of Modern English grammar by making it impossible to select only points which fit more easily the chosen perspective of juxtaposition. Nevertheless, 26 points remain only a selection from Modern English grammar at large. Moreover, since grammar is a tightly coherent phenomenon where things may hang closely together, a certain amount of overlap or interconnection between 'separate' points is inevitable.

A–Z aims to provide a framework for exploring more profitably OG and NG accounts of Modern English grammar, in that the reader will be better prepared for the respective contributions to the study of Modern English grammar that may be expected. But for the more serious student of Modern English grammar, *A–Z* cannot – and explicitly would not want to – replace the originals. Habitual reference to *both* OG *and* NG, and beyond them to any other framework, should precisely be encouraged by the way *A–Z* juxtaposes approaches and their contributions to Modern English grammar.

[Note that   *A–Z*'s subsidiary issue of (non-)nativeness figures in Part III in majuscule sections C, E, H, L, N, R, T and miniscule sections f, v, w, and y.]

A is for *all*

The English item *all* has a number of interesting properties. This section principally looks for accounts of one of these properties. Consider how *all* might be added to [1] if it is to relate to *the students*:

[1] *the students* must have left town

One rather natural possibility would be simply to put *all* immediately before *the students*:

[2] *all the students* must have left town

We will say that in [2] *all* takes the students as its 'target'; in example sentences italics identify *all* and its targets. Although we will learn about accounts of instances like [2] as we go along, *A–Z* will take as its point of departure the more notable possibility at this stage: to add *all* to [1] at some distance from *the students* and still have *all* take *the students* as its target:

[3] *the students* must *all* have left town

In [2] *all* takes an adjacent target; in [3] there is a distant target. What we want to know about accounts of *all*, in OG and in NG, includes whether they cover [3]; if so whether they relate [3] to [2] in some way, and if they do, how and why; and whether they allow *all* to take distant targets in yet more positions in [1], and why (not).

A.1 On OG on *all*

It would appear that the possibility illustrated in [3] has not attracted attention consistently in OG: instances of *all* with distant target are entirely absent from Sweet and Jespersen. One reason for OG to fail to be effectively *open* may be a historical orientation: Jespersen's *MEG* is subtitled 'on historical principles' (2.5),

47

and Sweet, too, traces developments from Old to Modern English (2.1). One such historical development is reinterpretation of examples like [3], *all* with distant target, as if they were like [2], *all* with adjacent target. This development seems to have shaped an OG perspective on *all*, also when it is not intended that its history determine description of Modern English. Even Kruisinga (1932a:262–3) in his handbook of *Present-Day* English states "When *all* refers to a noun (or pronoun) mentioned in the sentence [i.e. [3]], it may seem to be an adjunct to a following word [i.e. [2]]". To illustrate, Kruisinga suggests that the primary interpretation of [4] is as [4a]; only in a footnote does Kruisinga also admit [4b]:

[4] things are all wrong = [a] things are *all wrong*
[b] *things* are *all* wrong

The remarkable thing is that [4b], relegated to a footnote, is Kruisinga's single instance which corresponds exactly to [3]. Similarly, Jespersen (1914:456–7) is so preoccupied by the historical "transition ... to ... subjunct", i.e. from distant target to adjacent target, that he gives only examples of the latter; like [5], where adjacent target is the only possibility:

[5a] His Royal Highness was *all smiles* (*all* = subjunct)
[5b] * *His Royal Highness* was *all* smiles (*all* ≠ subjunct)
(cf. * *all his Royal Highness* was smiles)

Another notable feature of OG accounts of *all* is that some have *narrow*ly looked at its addition to pronouns rather than to nominal word-groups like *the students* in [1] or *things* in [4]. Recall Kruisinga's 'noun (or pronoun)' just cited for adjacent targets: the brackets suggest that pronouns are more readily distant targets for *all*. And notably enough, Kruisinga (1932b: 228–9; cf. also 1932a:260–1) does indeed *narrow* to pronouns his explicit discussion of the relations between *all* and its targets. *All* with adjacent pronominal target yields "only apparent syntactic groups"; [6a] "betrays its nature by" [6b]. But Kruisinga does not similarly discuss or illustrate nominals, i.e. whether in [2] we have separately *all* and *the students*, or a single group *all the students*:

[6a] *we all* agreed with you
[6b] *we* are *all* agreed with you

A *narrow* preoccupation even in OG with only pronouns as targets of *all* makes some sense, as the 'natural' possibility of [2] cannot strictly be observed for pronouns: *all* cannot immediately precede an adjacent pronominal target like *we*; cf. (*all*) *the students* in [1, 2]. Instead of [7a], a construction with *of* like [7b] may be used; or, *all* may immediately *follow* its target, as in [6a], or [7c]:

[7a] * all they must have left town
[7b] *all of them* must have left town
[7c] *they all* must have left town

Sweet provides another instance of pronominal preoccupations: although Sweet does not give any distant targets for *all*, he does observe that "The Old-English post-position . . . is still preserved . . . with pronouns" (1898:11):

[8] are *they all* gone?

Note again the historical orientation, 'Old-English'; and the *narrow* restriction to 'with pronouns'.

Since *all* necessarily shuns its natural position as in [7a] with pronominal targets, this may lead one to *all* and pronominal distant targets more easily as well: thus Kruisinga as in [6] above. In *GCE*, Quirk *et al.* (1972:141), cases of *all* after adjacent targets are both nominal [9a] and pronominal [9b]:

[9a] *the students all* passed their exams
[9b] *they all* passed their exams

Even in *GCE*, however, distant targets are again *narrow*ed to "cases of *pronominal* apposition" (1972:967; emphases added); e.g. [10] where *all* and, notably, its distant target *we* are both pronominal:

[10] *we*'ve *all* made up our minds

[10] is the single example of *all* with distant target in *GCE*. Only in *CGoEL* are distant targets given due recognition by Quirk *et al.*, for instance in their notable emendation of (1972:967): "cases of pronominal apposition" (1985:1399) now include [11], where only *all* is pronominal, but the distant target *the advisers* nominal:

[11] *the advisers* had *all* been carefully selected

So far we have seen OG to manifest itself in rather *narrow* fashion: historical developments, or positional peculiarities, shape OG's perspective, as if 'in accordance with a theory'; and duly, such OG is largely restricted to adjacent and/or pronominal targets of *all*. Only in *CGoEL* have we seen an OG account of *all* which is truly *open* in paying full attention to distant (nominal) targets, as in [3]. But in this respect, *CGoEL* is chronologically preceded by Poutsma, and by Curme.

Indeed, Poutsma is somewhat dauntingly extensive on *all*. For our purposes, the following seems fairly representative. Poutsma (1928:334–5) discusses alternations as between [2] and [3], e.g. [12]:

[12a] *all his children* have come
[12b] *his children* have *all* come

Poutsma initially suggests that in [12a] *all* = *his children* are in a kind of apposition (cf. Quirk *et al.*'s 'pronominal apposition' above), more or less as *my brother* = *Bill* in [13]:

[13] my brother Bill has come

In such cases as *the city of Westminster*, *the city* = *Westminster*, "Apposition ... varies with an *of*-construction". Thus Poutsma accounts for *of* as in [7b], or in *all of the students* (cf. [2]), *all of his children* (cf. [12a]). But apposition does not generally allow distance:

[14] * *Bill* has *my brother* come

Before turning to [12b], therefore, Poutsma first considers an alternative account of [12a]: *all* is also "semi-adverbial". In English, the semi-adverbial nature of *all* appears from its close analogy with *only*, "an indubitable adverbial modifier":

[15] only his children have come

Poutsma also derives evidence for adverbial *all* from Dutch, where *-e* may distinguish adjectives from adverbs:

[16] all the day = [a] *heel* de dag
             [b] de *heele* dag

As *all* can only take the position of adverbial *heel* (the adjectival position is for *whole*: *the whole day*), *all* may be taken to be adverbial like *heel*. Once *all* is thus identified as (semi-)adverbial, Poutsma then has an account for [12b] as well: adverbs generally "admit of being shifted". Compare the 'shift' of *all* from [12a] to distance in [12b] with the shift of an adverb like *only*:

[17a] only his children have come
[17b] his children have only come

Poutsma adds a condition to which we will return (but note already that a 'condition' is something *narrow*, again): to shift like an adverb, *all* should "modify ... the subject", i.e. take as its distant target only a subject. For the moment, note that adverbs also appear at the end of sentences, e.g. *too*:

[18] his children have come too

Thus Poutsma looks for *all* in this position as well:

[19a] *they* are good stories *all*
[19b] *'t* was silence *all*

Examples like [19b] are from poetry; otherwise, [19a] is the only example. Note that the distant targets are, once again, pronouns.

Curme's account of *all* (1931:30–1) is somewhat similar to the one given by Poutsma: only, *all* would be a "predicate appositive", rather than a plain appositive and/or (semi-)adverbial. A predicate appositive has "relations to both the subject and the ... verb", the latter like an adverb; for instance *sick* in [20], where identical subscripts represent 'related to':

[20] he_1 $came_2$ home $sick_{1+2}$

Similarly, in [21] *all* might be seen to relate both to the distant target *the others* ('all the others') and to the verb *killed* ('death was indiscriminate'):

[21] *the others*$_1$ were all_{1+2} $killed_2$

Unlike Poutsma's 'adverbial' *all*, *all* as a 'predicate appositive' does not directly account for *all* with adjacent target as well. Here Curme appeals once again to historical developments: *all* "developing towards ... attributive adjective", like *pitiable* in *the pitiable others*. But the nature of *all* as a predicate appositive should at least still account for "the word-order *all the others*", rather than * *the all others* (A–Z's * here represents Curme's "cannot stand"; cf. section II.4).

Now note that Curme initially agrees with Poutsma's condition that distant *all* be targeted 'to the subject'. But predicate appositives can also relate to objects:

[22] he *threw away*$_1$ the *bottle*$_2$ $empty_{1+2}$

Accordingly, Curme presently also allows *all* to take an object as target in [23a]:

[23a] I have *the letters all* together
[23b] I have *the letters* together *all*

Note that [23b] would emancipate OG from the effect of Poutsma's *narrow* account, that *all* shift from subjects, but not from objects. An interesting light on this issue is thrown by

CGoEL. Beside the appositional account amended from *GCE* [10–11], there is a lot of material on *all* in *CGoEL* which further broadly agrees with Poutsma. For instance (1985:381–2): *all* may be "postposed" ('shifted'), "[a]ccording to the rules for adverb placement" ('semi-adverbial'), "after a subject" (*narrow* condition):

[24] *the villages* have *all* been destroyed

But *CGoEL* (1985:1260) also notes marginal cases of shifting of *all* from a non-subject: [25], where ?* stands for "hardly":

[25] ?* several schools here, *which* I can *all* recommend

In the relevant clause of [25], the subject is *I*; the distant target of *all* is the object *which*. Perhaps the condition really is that the target precede the verb: usually the subject, but other constituents when these are *wh*-items like *which*. But it is not the purpose of *A–Z* to ponder the proper interpretation of [25].

Let us rather summarize the accounts of *all* that we have found in OG. These are not all optimally *open*. OG may be distracted from distant targets of *all* by history, or by pronominal targets: Sweet, and Jespersen. Kruisinga and *GCE* at least give instances of pronominal targets also with distant *all*; Kruisinga almost reluctantly admits one instance with nominal distant target – but he only analyses *all* with pronominal targets, on the basis of distant *all*. Curme accounts for *all* with distant targets in terms of 'predicate appositives', and thus foregoes a *narrow* restriction of targets to subjects. Poutsma and *CGoEL* do *narrow*ly restrict distant targets to subjects, although *open*ness reasserts itself when *CGoEL* gives one contrary example. Poutsma and *CGoEL* both also account for *all* in terms of apposition and/or adverbial positions: *CGoEL* uses both for distant targets; Poutsma uses apposition for adjacent targets, and has adverbial *all* account for distant targets, which he extends to adjacent targets, and to distant position of *all* at the very end of the sentence. It seems that Curme and *GCE*, and especially Poutsma and *CGoEL* provide the more notable, effectively *open* OG accounts of *all*.

A.2 On NG on *all*

Beside our two standard NG 'grammars' (no relevant material in Chomsky's work has come to hand), from the NG literature we will look here at Hogg (1977) and Culicover and Wilkins (1984) for NG accounts of *all*.

A–Z's older putatively 'comprehensive' NG grammar of English does not really get around to accounting for *all* with distant targets. SS&P (1973:159) do have examples like [26]; and they do point out the ambiguity with respect to target in [27] (cf. [4]):

[26] *they* are *all* dancers
[27] they are all his daughters = [a] *they* are *all* his daughters
                                    [b] they are *all his daughters*

But SS&P's actual rules – transformations 'T' – only account for *all the daughters*, derived by a rule 'T*all-the*' from *all of the daughters* through "erasing" of *of* (1973:149); i.e. by T*all-the*, *all of the* becomes *all the*; but strictly, *all (of) his* is thus not accounted for. Note also that the distant target of [26, 27a] is a pronoun, *they*, which is always without *the*, *the they; and to which T*all-the* thus cannot apply either. Rather, in the case of *all of them*, SS&P 'erase' *of* in the course of applying Tq(uantifier)-move(ment) (1973:151), by which "QUANTifiers marked [+SHIFT]" like *all* also move to the end of a subject: thus *all of them* becomes *they all*; and *all of the boys*, *the boys all*. With respect to distant targets, SS&P then only add tentatively: "Later positioning of these quantifiers appears to follow the rules for pre-verbal adverb placement" (1973:151). Note that 'appears' is rather *open*ly vague; and indeed SS&P's eventual account of distant *all* via adverbial placement would perhaps bear a certain similarity to Poutsma's or Quirk *et al.*'s OG accounts.

It should be added that SS&P (1973:407–8) provide an extension of their account of adjacent targets to *all* with co-ordinations as targets. They suggest that [28a] be derived from [28b] by an obligatory application of their Tq-move:

[28a]   *John and Bill and Harry all* passed
[28b]   * all John and Bill and Harry passed

SS&P's point about *all* in [28] involves analogy to *both*, which is possible in either *both John and Bill passed*, or *John and Bill both passed* after Tq-move of *both*; i.e. with *both* Tq-move is optional. We will see below that this again is a relatively *open* account, i.e. relative to Culicover and Wilkins 1984.

Next, Emonds (1976:239–41) does address *all* with distant targets directly. His examples are like [29]:

[29] (he said that) *my friends* may *all* be speaking German

In truly *narrow* fashion, Emonds first presents an argument that distant *all* should indeed be taken to have been shifted, i.e. to have earlier occupied a position adjacent to the target:

[30a] * both my friends may all be speaking Russian
[30b] * all my friends may both be speaking Russian

If *all* in [30] originates from the 'DET(erminer)' position adjacent to *my friends*, that position should not also be occupied by the analogous DET *both*; and conversely. In a similar vein, Emonds observes that when distant from its target, *all* should follow the *first* verb, 'AUX(iliary)' *may*; but *all* should not follow *be* or *speaking*:

[31a] * my friends may be all speaking Russian
[31b] * my friends may be speaking all Russian

Accordingly, Emonds has first a transformation that postpones DET like *all* to the end of its adjacent target, like SS&P's Tq-move; and then a second transformation that interchanges DET and AUX:

[32a] all   my friends may be speaking Russian
      DET target   AUX   (original)
[32b] my friends all   may be speaking Russian
      target   DET   AUX   (by Tq-move)
[32c] my friends may all be speaking Russian
      target   AUX DET   (DET-AUX interchange)

Note that in between [32a–b] and [32b–c], in each case only two adjacent constituents are interchanged: this means that the transformations involved are 'local' (section 3.3). In Emonds' *narrow* NG theory, local transformations can apply in both main and subclauses: hence our expository addition of *(he said that)* in [29]. The *narrow* locality that Emonds thus associates with the shifting of *all* is far removed from the *open* freedom that adverbials have; hence Emonds' NG duly juxtaposes to the OG accounts of *all* in Poutsma and *CGoEL*, as well as to the relatively *open* NG account anticipated by SS&P.

With Emonds (1976) effecting *A–Z*'s juxtaposition of OG and NG, let us now look at less effectively *narrow* NG, 'generative semantics' or semantic NG (see section II.4). Interestingly, within not-so-*narrow* semantic NG, Hogg (1977) gives an account of *all* which again relates *all* to adverb positioning, in particular of the negative adverb *not*. In Hogg's NG theory, adverbs may derive from 'higher predicates'. Consider [33], where the clause containing a lower predicate is bracketed:

[33a] [the students will probably leave]
[33b] that [the students will leave] is probable

Given the semantic similarity of [33a–b], in semantic NG [33a] will be derived from more or less [33b] by a 'lowering transformation'.

And such lowering also applies to *not*, and to *all*. First *not*:

[34] that [the students will leave] is not (cf. '. . . is not the case')

From [34] *not* may lower into the bracketed clause, in either of two different ways, [35]:

[35a] [no students will leave] (assume that *not* + *the* = *no*)
[35b] [the students will not leave]

Although actual derivations are much more complex than we represent here, the story about *all* is essentially the same: lowering *all* from [36a] leads to either [36b] or [36c]:

[36a] [the students will leave] all (cf. '. . . in all cases')
[36b] [all the students will leave]
[36c] [the students will all leave]

The essence of Hogg's semantic NG account thus is that "*all* may . . . appear in every position where a . . . negator [*not, no*] is grammatical" (1977:111); and that this accounts for [37] (cf. OG's [19]):

[37] * the students will go all
    (cf. * the students will go not)

All is misplaced in [37] just as *not* would be in the same position.

Lowering transformations are, by admission, hardly less than "magic" (Hogg 1977:2); i.e. they are impossible to *narrow*ly restrict. What should therefore at least come through from the above is that the quite different NG accounts of *all* by Emonds and by Hogg are both *narrow* in that they relate fairly directly to – by themselves less or more *narrow* – NG theories that they adhere to: structure preservation vs. semantic NG.

A similar point obtains for SS&P. Recall SS&P's derivation of [28a] from [28b] by obligatory Tq-move. But one generally accepted principle in more effectively *narrow* recent NG is to restrict rules to only optional ones. Thus Culicover and Wilkins (henceforth CulWil) (1984:83–4) suggest that Tq-move, which they call 'Q-float', cannot even exist, precisely because *optional* Q-float would allow both [38b] and, wrongly, [38a] (cf. [28]):

[38a] * all John, Fred, and Mary have left
[38b] *John, Fred, and Mary* have *all* left

In view of [38], CulWil propose to relate distant *all* to its target not by shifting, but by 'predication', answering remotely to Curme's OG notion of 'predicate appositive'. As in [20], predication can simply relate *all* to its target at a distance:

[39] the men have all left = *the men*$_i$ have *all*$_i$ left

There is an important, and somewhat complex, effect of subsuming distant targets under predication. In a transformational account, there must be a subject for *all* to have floated, or shifted, from; cf. Emonds' [32]. Now consider [40]:

[40] *the men* expect to *all* leave

In a *narrow* theory which does not allow lowering magic, *all* cannot have floated down from *the men* into *to leave*. Roughly, *to leave* therefore needs its 'own' subject, usually indicated PRO (for empty PROnoun, referring back to *the men*); from which *all* can then float without lowering:

[41] the men$_i$ expect [*PRO*$_i$ to all leave]
     (cf. the men expect [*the women* to *all* leave]

But CulWil's point is that this argument for a PRO in [41] does not stand if *all* can be related to its target by predication:

[42] *the men*$_i$ expect to *all*$_i$ leave

In [42] there is no more lowering magic than in [41]. All of this leads CulWil to a final subtle observation, on [43]:

[43a] the men all tried to fit into the car
[43b] the men tried to all fit into the car

Both of [43] can mean that the men tried to fit into the car as a group; but only [43a] can also mean that each of the men separately tried to fit into the car. Recall that in Curme's OG account by 'predicate appositives', *all* also relates to the verb. According to CulWil, the difference between [43a, b] follows under NG predication from both *all-try* and *all-try to fit* in [43a], vs. only *all-fit* in [43b].

Summarizing NG on *all* with distant targets, we find much what we should have expected. The nature of NG accounts is directly determined by theoretical concerns. A relatively *open* account of *all* with co-ordinations under a theory which allows obligatory transformations (SS&P) differs from a more *narrow* account when transformations may only be optional, i.e. by predication (CulWil). A semantic NG account by *open* lowering magic, where *all* originates from a higher sentence (Hogg), differs from a more soberly *narrow* one where *all* originates locally (Emonds). And perhaps most notably, in fairly early NG the issue of 'distant *all*' does not become pertinent, and is thus duly left aside by SS&P; whereas in more effectively *narrow* later NG, distant *all* does become pertinent, and accounts of it are therefore given, *narrow*ly designed in accordance with the respective NG theories (Emonds, CulWil).

A.3 Conclusions

On distant *all*, only some OG is perfectly *open*: historical developments or pronominal targets seem to have proven strong distractors. Moreover, there may seem to be 'echoes' of OG in NG: 'shift', *all* as adverb, *all* and predicate/-ation. Even so, *A–Z*'s thesis of juxtaposition of OG to *narrow* NG is in evidence here. That is, in OG omission of distant *all* can only be an unfortunate accident, as for instance the difference between *GCE* and *CGoEL* is there to prove. NG accounts, however, may clearly be seen to be more or less *open* or *narrow* as, in all cases, *narrow*ly determined by respective theories: optional and/or obligatory transformations; semantic NG vs. locality. As against this fundamental juxtaposition between OG and NG, any internal differences in OG or in NG, and any apparent echoes in NG from OG, are clearly mere coincidences.

A.4 Discussion and extensions

1 In an NG paper Verkuyl (1981) adopts the 'only one determiner hypothesis'. That is, in *all the children*, *all* and *the* cannot both be DETerminers, because there should be only one DET. "So a distinction is [to be] made between a DET *all* and a MOD[ifier] *all*" (1981:584):

[i] MOD DET noun   DET noun
    all   the   children   all   children

Verkuyl then observes that "this distinction comes out in Dutch at the morphological level":

[iia] *al* de kinderen   (*al* = MOD)
     all the children
[iib] * *al* kinderen   (*al* ≠ DET)
[iic] *alle* kinderen   (*alle* = DET)
     all   children
[iid] * *alle* de kinderen   (*alle* ≠ MOD)

• To which OG accounts does Verkuyl's NG account seem most similar? What would still be the essential differences?
2 In their introduction to NG, Keyser and Postal (1976) note the contrast between [iiia, b]:

[iiia] they are likely to all understand
[iiib] * they are difficult to all understand

For accounts of [iiib], cf. section H. Keyser and Postal (1976:6) then challenge "the reader to try and learn something about facts like those ... in the works of such encyclopedic grammarians as Curme, Jespersen, and Poutsma".

- Do Keyser and Postal here juxtapose 'encyclopedic' OG and NG in terms of more *open* and more *narrow* coverage?

Now consider the following excerpts from Poutsma's OG grammar (1916:1023; 1928:160; 1928:142, 145; cf. also section H):

All is usually shifted into the body of ... a complex predicate

a kind of complex predicate ... occurs with ... *likely*

in ... *This is difficult to describe adequately* ... the pronoun ... which is in the subjective relation to the nominal predicate [*this*], is in the objective relation to the following infinitive [*to describe*]

- To what extent does Poutsma on behalf of OG meet Keyser and Postal's challenge? Does this make OG more or less like NG than Keyser and Postal insinuate?

3 According to many NG accounts, auxiliaries are essentially verbs, just like lexical verbs. Thus Keyser and Postal (1976:295-6) suggest that *all* floats from the position at the head of the subject to positions to the left of any 'verbs'. Thus [iva] leads to [ivb], *all* to the left of *have*, or to [ivc], *all* to the left of *come*:

[iva] all the children   have   come
[ivb] the children all have   come
[ivc] the children   have all come

- Explain how Keyser and Postal's theory of floating to the left of any 'verb' forces them to countenance [v]:

[v] the fighters are now being systematically *all* destroyed by the defenders

- Would [v] have to be allowed by Emonds? Or by Hogg? What does this show about NG accounts?
- Can Poutsma or *CGoEL* account for [v]? What difference between OG and NG does this point up?

b is for BE

Consider [1a, b]:

[1a] the water walked down the street
[1b] the water was walking down the street

Both of [1a,b] are equally odd: *water* is not supposed to *walk*, but rather to *stream* for instance. In this sense, WALK is semantically the most important verb in [1a] – where WALK is on its own – as well as in [1b] – *walking* is more important than *was*. In [1b], *was*, a form of BE, only 'helps' WALK to appear as *walking*; in such cases, BE may be called an auxiliary verb (from the Latin for 'helper'); auxiliary or even AUX for short. In [2], however, BE is itself the only verb: there is no other verb for BE to be auxiliary to. In [2] BE may be called a copula (for the Latin for 'linker'), linking *the water* (subject) to *hot* (predicate):

[2] the water was hot

Beukema and Rigter (1984:36–7) suggest that it is "irrational" to distinguish between auxiliary and copula in grammatical accounts of BE: BE shows the same grammatical behaviour regardless. Consider for instance BE in *n*egation [3], *i*nversion [4], and *c*ode [5] (together with *e*mphasis, these are the so-called *nice*-properties); particularly in contradistinction to verbs like STREAM, where DO would appear:

[3a] * the water streamed not down the street
[3b] the water was not streaming down the street
[3c] the water was not hot
[4a] * streamed the water down the street
[4b] was the water streaming down the street
[4c] was the water hot
[5a] * the water streamed down the street, streamed it
[5b] the water was streaming down the street, was it
[5c] the water was hot, was it

Beukema and Rigter maintain that auxiliaries may be grammatically defined on the basis of *nice* behaviour as in [3b, 4b, 5b]; and
then BE is an auxiliary also in [3c, 4c, 5c], not a different kind of
thing, a copula. Beukema and Rigter therefore accuse some OG –
Quirk *et al.*'s *GCE* (1972) – of maintaining "traditional quirks of
classification" (1984:51; note the pun); and also some NG –
Wekker and Haegeman (1985) – of effectively reconstructing such
quirky classifications (1984:43; on NG 'reconstructing' OG, see
A–Z Part II).

It should be noted at this point that unification of auxiliary BE
and copula BE on the basis of *nice*-properties is a theoretical
decision, i.e. a *narrow* one; and hence it is not equally appropriate
to expect it in both OG and NG. At first, Beukema and Rigter
seem to accept as much: "In Quirk *et al.*, rules tend to be
observations about an inventory of grammatical structures, rather
than tools ... to separate grammatical structures from ungrammatical constructs" (1984:45; note the juxtaposition of *open*
observation to *narrow* separation; for (un-)grammatical, cf. section II.4). Nevertheless, they go on to insist that correct = *nice*
classification should be an issue even in OG, if there is to be any
classification at all: "If traditional quirks of classification cannot be
properly defended ..., a more rational classification should be
attempted" (1984:50–1). Accordingly, in this miniscule section
of *A–Z* 'b is for BE', the reader is presented with rudimentary
surveys of accounts of BE in OG and in NG, to be able to assess
whether traditional quirks of classification in OG juxtapose with
putatively more rational classification in NG; or the other way
around.

b.1 On OG on BE

Sweet distinguishes firmly between auxiliary BE and link-verb BE;
auxiliaries would give help, "The form-verbs used to modify the
English verb are called auxiliary verbs ... The chief auxiliaries are
be, ..." (1891:88); link verbs would conversely 'require help',
"many verbs ... are incapable of forming logical predicates by
themselves, and require the help of some other part of speech –
generally an adjective-word or noun-word ... Thus *he is* conveys
no sense whatever ... till some other word is added – *he is ready*,
he is a lawyer, he is here. We call such verbs link-verbs" (1891:94).
But it remains to be seen whether this is quirky, since Sweet does
not *define* auxiliaries by *nice*-properties, although he does refer to
n and *i*: "*be* and *have* do not take *do* in interrogative and negative
forms even when not used as auxiliaries: *is he ready?*" (1898:91).

Poutsma, too, defines auxiliaries independently of *nice*-properties: "Verbs which are used as substitutions for the inflections of tense, mood, voice, or aspect are ... auxiliaries" (1926:15; voice-substitution = '*be* taken', cf. section v for 'verbs of voice'); and on such a basis he can keep auxiliaries separate from copulas: "Verbs which are joined with a nominal or nominal equivalent to effect a predicating are called copulas ... e.g.: *He is idle, He is lazy*" (1926:5; *is* 'joined with nominal equivalent' *idle/lazy* = copula). But on top of that Poutsma then unifies auxiliaries and copulas, as 'verbs of incomplete predication', suggesting that they require help equally for complete predication: "the copulas and the auxiliaries have been called verbs of incomplete predication, the former requiring a nominal (or nominal equivalent) [e.g. *was hot*, [2]], the latter another verb in the shape of a participle [e.g. *was walking*, [1]] or an infinitive to form the predicate" (1926:17). Note that this allows Poutsma to circumvent a *narrow* effect of his auxiliary/copula distinction: "Some grammarians widen the range of auxiliaries ..., reckoning among them the copula ... *to be* ... in this grammar, the term auxiliary is rigidly employed in the strict sense defined above" (1926:17). Juxtaposed to 'widen', 'rigid' and 'strict' sound pretty *narrow*, but the cover term 'verb of incomplete predication' is in fact *open*ly wide.

Kruisinga does use *ni(ce)*-properties to define auxiliaries: "The verbs *can, may, shall* and *will* ... and a number of others ... show syntactic deviations ... they can take ... *not* ... without the verb *do*. Nor do they take this verb ... when other verbs cannot be used without it (as in ... sentences with inversion ...) ... For the reasons enumerated, it is necessary ... to treat these verbs separately; they are traditionally called *auxiliaries*" (1931:290; BE is then duly listed as another auxiliary). However, "The verb *to be* ... is to be looked upon as an auxiliary in some of its uses only" (1931:303); and Kruisinga then appears to rely on meaning in establishing non-auxiliary use of BE as a copula: "'John *is* quite tall' ... When the predicative verb does not express a meaning ... [t]he verb *be* ... is called a copula" (1932b:268–9).

Curme first distinguishes copula BE as a linker from auxiliaries: "There are four classes [of verb] – transitive, intransitive, linking, and auxiliary" (1935:63); "The copula *be* ... only links the predicate to the subject" (1935:66); "An auxiliary verb is one that ... helps other verbs, transitive, intransitive, or linking" (1935:69). Note that this is independent of *nice*-properties; although *n* and *i* are duly mentioned: "*do* ... is used ... with inverted word-order ... [and] when simple *not* is the negative ... however ... not in the case of the copula *be*, the tense auxiliaries, the modal auxiliaries" (1931:25). But Curme then still turns out to consider copulas also a type of auxiliary: "There are other common auxiliaries of quite a different type – the copulas. These ... link a predicate participle to the subject ... as auxiliaries of [progressive] aspect [= BE!] ... [or] as passive auxiliaries [= BE!]" (1935:69).

Jespersen again does define auxiliaries by *ni(ce)*-properties: "an 'auxiliary' ... is used negatively and interrogatively without *do*" (1931:11). But Jespersen does not ever seem to call BE an auxiliary on that basis. BE only appears to be explicitly classified as a copula: "*It was true* ... with *be*, which is practically devoid of meaning and only serves to connect subject and predicative, and is therefore called a *link verb* or *copula*" (1927:356).

For Quirk *et al.* on BE, cf. Beukema and Rigter (1984). *GCE* (1972:63–5) first elaborates on the definition of auxiliaries, including BE, by *nice*-properties. Their classification of BE also as a lexical verb is then quirky: "Note that ... BE ... can also be used as lexical verb" (1972:65). Much the same goes for *CGoEL* (*nice*-properties: 1985:121–7). If anything, the problem is exacerbated by exemplification of 'copula' BE where BE actually behaves *nicely* like an auxiliary: "The verb BE is a main verb (with a copular function ...) in ... *Is that building a hotel?*" (1985:129; Beukema and Rigter 1984 is not in *CGoEL*'s 1985 bibliography).

b.2 On NG on BE

Chomsky's original approach to BE is not to classify BE at all. Chomsky (1957:112) formulates transformational rules that effect *nice*-properties for modal auxiliaries, for *have*, and for *be*, without these having independently anything in common. Thus BE will show *nice* behaviour whatever its classification(s) might (not) be; when followed by a verb (1957:39) BE = *be* + *ing* (*be reading*); or *be* + *en* (*be taken*); when not followed by a verb (1957:67) BE = *be* + Predicate (*be my friend*). In particular, copular BE is explicitly *not* called a 'verb', to avoid BE ever being subject to the rules which effect *do* with verbs as in [3a, 4a, 5a] (1957:67).

Much the same still holds in Chomsky (1965), although now BE – and only BE – is classified as a copula (1965:72). Again the point remains that BE is *not* a 'verb'; in this case because then *President* in *be President* would incorrectly be defined as 'object-of' a verb rather than as 'predicate-of' a copula. Since Chomsky does not since then seem to have developed theories about *do* and/or about grammatical functions like object and predicate, Chomsky has not made any more fundamental proposals for classification of BE either.

In much subsequent NG, Chomsky's account of BE by non-classification has remained more or less standard. In particular SS&P (1973:601) note that its "adequacy ... as an account ... relevant to interrogative, negative, and emphatic transformations [i.e. *ni(c)e*-properties] has not been seriously challenged". Interestingly, SS&P then explicitly "leave open [in NG!] the question of whether this analysis represents a deep, or a deepest, structure" (ibid.). 'Deep or deepest structure' refers to whether BE joins modal auxiliaries in showing *nice*-properties by virtue of a transformation; or remains by itself with inherent *nice*-properties, as in Chomsky (1957). The former is roughly the unification adopted in Emonds (1976:206–17). For Emonds, in [6] BE is equally a 'main verb' (not 'auxiliary' vs. 'copula'); but in [7] BE has undergone structure-preserving Verb Raising, by which it becomes 'an auxiliary' (again, not auxiliary vs. copula) in showing *nice* behaviour:

[6a] John will be leaving
[6b] will John be leaving
[6c] John will be President
[6d] will John be president
[7a] John is leaving
[7b] is John leaving
[7c] John is President
[7d] is John President

As for NG literature, let us remain with Beukema and Rigter (1984) and its targets. Among the latter, Wekker and Haegeman (1985) attempt to incorporate "new ideas and insights" (1985:1–2) from 'EST', i.e. NG. With respect to BE Wekker and Haegeman state that "not only the auxiliaries *have* and *be* ... are involved in inversion, negation, and tag-formation [code], but also the lexical verbs *have* and *be*" (1985:50). For Beukema and Rigter this is not the new approach of NG; but "The traditional assumption is thus repeated" (1984:43): auxiliary BE vs. copula (= lexical) BE, in spite of *nic(e)*-properties. Instead, Beukema and Rigter insist that "The traditional stipulation ... that ... auxiliaries must be followed by a lexical verb, should be replaced by the observation that ... auxiliaries [are] ... followed by a ... predicate" (1984:39; note that contrary to *A–Z*'s juxtaposition of OG and NG, 'stipulation' – i.e. a condition – suggests *narrow* deduction in 'traditional' OG; and conversely, 'observation' suggests *open* induction in NG). Effectively, Beukema and Rigter take *is* in [7a] to be followed by a (verbal) predicate, *leaving*: hence BE is auxiliary; and in [7c] *is* is followed by a (nominal) predicate, *President*: hence BE is equally an auxiliary. Accordingly, in both [7c] and [7d] BE will show *nice* behaviour, as auxiliary.

b.3 Conclusions

The issue in section b is quirkily schizophrenic classifications of BE as alternately auxiliary and copula, contrary to unification of BE on the basis of its consistently *nice* behaviour. The summary accounts of OG and NG on BE in this miniscule section should suggest that juxtaposition of OG and NG manifests itself only rather deviously. That is, other than might be expected it is in NG rather than OG that the problem of classification is avoided by not classifying BE at all (Chomsky); OG submits to the somewhat *narrow* assumption that BE is to be given some classification. But the paradoxical effect seems to have been that most OG has indeed been *open* to a quirky classification of BE (Kruisinga, Jespersen, *GCE*, *CGoEL*). An *open* approach may also be maintained, however, by avoiding the truly *narrow* requirement of classification of BE on the basis of *nice*-properties. Thus, BE is unified if a copula is a type of auxiliary (Curme); or if both auxiliary and copula are verbs of incomplete predication (Poutsma). With OG optimally represented by Curme and Poutsma, or even when OG is quirkily represented, NG fundamentally juxtaposes to OG on BE: for NG classification of BE is necessarily a problem, given a *narrow* responsibility towards its consistency with respect to *nice*-properties; a problem to be overcome either by avoiding classification of BE (Chomsky); or by submitting any BE to Verb Raising (Emonds); or by classifying any BE as auxiliary (Beukema and Rigter); etc.

C is for complementation

Complementation is potentially a vast area of Modern English grammar. For its widest sense, consider a structure S = A + C and suppose that the presence of A in S entails the presence of C: then C may be said to complement A. For instance, S might be *fond of grammar* (in *they are fond of grammar*); as * *they are fond* is impossible, *fond* = A entails C = *of grammar*: C provides the complementation of A. In this section of *A–Z*, complementation is used in a much more specific sense. Essentially, the purpose of section C is to repeat in *A–Z* an investigation first carried out by Zandvoort (1961).

Zandvoort selects five verbs – *catch*, *conceive*, *fancy*, *find*, and *imagine* – and four patterns which might complement these verbs: cf. [1–4]; but see below for the likelihoods of complementations as in [1–4]:

[1] verb – pro/noun – infinitive
    (e.g. you may *find it do* her good)
[2] verb – pro/noun – *to*-infinitive
    (e.g. he *found it to contain* a necklace)
[3] verb – pro/noun – *ing* participle
    (e.g. we *found her standing* in the office)
[4] verb – pro/noun – *ed* participle
    (e.g. he *found his lady-love flown*)

Zandvoort then looks for OG accounts of these (five verbs × four patterns =) twenty points of Modern English grammar: in Poutsma, Jespersen, Kruisinga, and Curme (1961:19). In a doctoral dissertation supervised by Zandvoort, Van Ek (1966) considerably enlarges Zandvoort's investigation (1966:7–8), notably to some 300 verbs, again looking for OG accounts: in Poutsma, Curme, Kruisinga, and Jespersen (1966:12). *A–Z* maintains the twenty points of Zandvoort, but adds the OG accounts of Sweet (cf. Van Ek 1966:13), and Quirk *et al.* (1972, 1985) (too late for

Zandvoort and for Van Ek); as well as adding, of course, NG accounts.

To return to terminology, restricting the term 'complementation' to just [1–4] agrees with Van Ek (1966), who entitles them 'complementary structures of predication'; it also accords well with the term used in a seminal NG study of *inter alia* [1–4], Rosenbaum (1967): 'predicate complement constructions'. In section C, *A–Z* further reserves the term complementation (= predicate complement/complementary predication) to just Zandvoort's (1961) four patterns for just his five verbs.

Interestingly, Rosenbaum for NG is roughly contemporaneous with Van Ek on OG; but much more importantly, he also precedes *A–Z* in juxtaposing OG and NG. Rosenbaum (1967:109–14) extensively discusses the OG accounts, in particular of [2], in Poutsma and in Jespersen. But as he goes along, Rosenbaum repeatedly reaffirms his scepticism expressed at the beginning (1967:109) towards views as in Lees (1957), that NG reconstructs OG (see section II.4). For Rosenbaum, as for *A–Z*, the approaches of OG and NG are incompatible: "The traditional [i.e. OG] grammarians were extremely diligent [i.e. comprehensive]. They present much data that are quite relevant [i.e. pertinent] to ... a grammar for the complement system. But a traditional approach could not provide such a grammar" (1967:114) – only a *narrow* grammar based on an associated linguistic theory can distinguish relevant = pertinent data among the available evidence.

C.1 The *open* issue: coverage of complementation

Following Zandvoort (1961) and Van Ek (1966:7), let us first "ascertain to what extent existing grammars can be said to give adequate 'coverage' of the patterns"; i.e. of the twenty points of complementation. Note that coverage is the *open* issue about complementation: in the first instance, it may therefore be appropriately applied to OG grammars rather than to NG.

Accounts of the twenty points of complementation tend to be widely scattered throughout the various OG grammars; it would take too much space here to give a full survey. Rather, the reader who wants to go to the original works will find references in Van Ek (1966) and in the Appendix to this section. The Appendix may be briefly summarized as in [5] (S = Sweet, P = Poutsma, K = Kruisinga, C = Curme, J = Jespersen, Q72 = *GCE*, and Q85 = *CGoEL*; *1–4* = [1–4] above); and in [6]:

[5] Coverage of complementation – 20 points – in OG

	1	2	3	4
catch	J		PKCJQ72Q85	
conceive		PK	PK	
fancy		PK J Q85	PK J Q85	
find	SPKCJ	PKCJQ72Q85	PKCJQ72Q85	PK JQ72Q85
imagine		PKCJQ72Q85	PK JQ72Q85	P

[6] Scores on complementation in OG – out of 20 points

Poutsma	12
Kruisinga	11
Jespersen	10
Quirk *et al.* 1985	8
Quirk *et al.* 1972	6
Curme	5
Sweet	1

Two things will be noted about [6]. Firstly, the more comprehensive coverage here is provided by the non-native grammarians (*A–Z*'s subsidiary interest); in fact, native Sweet can barely be said to even begin to pioneer the *open* approach to complementation. Secondly, the OG grammars together cover thirteen points, so that none of the individual grammars would be entirely comprehensive on its own (the 'best' would be Poutsma with twelve out of thirteen = 92 per cent). In fact, Zandvoort complains that such results as in [5, 6] prove grammars to be "incomplete or even scrappy" (1961:24): only thirteen out of twenty = 65 per cent, the best individual grammar attaining only twelve out of twenty = 60 per cent. Needless to say, this should be destructive criticism of OG, whose *open* aim is to achieve comprehensive coverage.

However, it is possible to give a more positive interpretation of the results in [5, 6]. Van Ek (1966) also counts occurrences of [1–4] in a collection of authentic English, a 'corpus' of about 1,000,000 words. The figures for this corpus are given in [7]:

[7] Van Ek's (1966) observations of complementation in a
    1,000,000 word corpus

	1	2	3	4
catch				
conceive				
fancy			2	
find	1	1	53	18
imagine			11	

It might be suggested that an *open* approach, committed to observation, cannot 'reasonably' be expected to observe much beyond a 1,000,000 word corpus. Thus scores of OG on six reasonable points are given in [8]:

[8] Scores on complementation in OG – out of 6 'reasonable' points

Poutsma	6 (+6)
Kruisinga	6 (+5)
Jespersen	6 (+4)
Quirk *et al.* 1985	5 (+3)
Quirk *et al.* 1972	4 (+2)
Curme	3 (+2)
Sweet	1

Against reasonable expectations, OG together is fully comprehensive, and so are (non-native) Poutsma, Kruisinga, and Jespersen individually; moreover there is even wider than reasonable coverage.

If it now be thought that *A–Z* accuses Zandvoort (1961) of being unreasonable in calling OG 'incomplete or even scrappy', it should be noted that Zandvoort actually represents a rigidly consistent version of the *open* approach, which allows *A–Z* an eminent opportunity to juxtapose it to NG as a *narrow* approach. In fact Zandvoort himself was the author of what for a long time was probably the best-known grammar of Modern English: first published in 1945, it had gone through over twenty editions by 1975 (the later ones with the assistance of Van Ek). Some might even have expected that Zandvoort's *Handbook* should be a major representative of *A–Z*'s OG. However, this *Handbook* was actually a pedagogic grammar, and though *open* in spirit, Zandvoort (1945:preface) cogently disclaims for pedagogical reasons the comprehensiveness of 'pursuing every detail': as such, the *Handbook* does not belong to OG (incidentally, it scores on six points of complementation). To return to complementation and Zandvoort (1961), however, recall the use that was made of it in Chapter 2 and section II.4: Zandvoort (1961) firmly maintains the *open* position of an observer (as a non-native), and he thus wants the grammars to which he refers to "provide examples" (1961:23); he is not really satisfied with a mere rule. Van Ek (1966:16) *is* interested in whether a point is "mentioned and/or instanced"; but he also then relegates points "only mentioned, not instanced" by presenting them only between brackets (1966:21). Thus Kruisinga (1931:82) allows [3], pro/noun – *ing*, "after ... *to find, catch*", and then provides examples with *find* like [9]:

[9] he would wake up to *find the lamp* still *burning*

[9] is duly reported by Zandvoort (1961:20), and by Van Ek (1966:71); but Kruisinga's application of [3] also to *catch* is ignored by Zandvoort, who merely complains of "No examples in ... Kruisinga" (1961:22; cf. Van Ek 1966:41).

Another point is the basis for Zandvoort's interpretation of OG grammars as 'incomplete or even scrappy' because only thirteen out of twenty points are covered. It has already been suggested that collation with a corpus, [7], may put a different complexion on things: [8]. Beyond this, one may even wonder whether twenty out of twenty is not in fact an impossible score: for one or more of the five verbs, evidence of complementation by [1–4] might not be available because grammaticality is doubtful; for instance, '?' for [10]:

[10] ?I fancied *John go* there

Being committed to observation under *open* grammar, Zandvoort has to work with grammatical data only (cf. section II.4); un-grammatical data as in [10] are dismissed with a bland "Non-existent combinations apart" (1961:24). This largely reflects OG practice, where non-existent combinations of the five verbs and [1–4] are not given explicit recognition until Quirk *et al.*: for *catch* there is "no ... construction with infinitive complement" (1972:842), i.e. * *catch* in [1]. There seems to be no similar statement in *CGoEL* (1985), which accordingly resumes the more normal *open* practice of restraint in condemning unobserved (= unobservable?) phenomena; and in fact, Jespersen (1940:282) attests the pattern.

Finally, note that Zandvoort's insistence on exemplification of complementation points up that for OG it is sufficient to know *whether* the twenty points are covered, and of no fundamental concern *how* they are represented. In particular, representation of the pro/noun in [1–4] may be as subject of the following verb-form: verb – [subject – verb]; or as object of the preceding verb: verb – object – [verb] (cf. [14] below). These representations, in particular a choice between them in accordance with a theory of complementation, is the *narrow* issue of analysis to be taken up by NG (cf. Van Ek 1966:18). In fact, Rosenbaum (1967) dismisses such representations for OG, Poutsma, and Jespersen; although Rosenbaum takes Poutsma to align largely with verb – object – [verb], Jespersen with verb – [subject – verb], he juxtaposes such NG concerns to OG by pointing out that actually the choice between representations "was not simply the issue ... in traditional linguistic analysis" (1967:113).

Conversely, the *open* issue of *whether* the twenty points of complementation are covered is not really appropriate to NG. Nevertheless, for *A–Z* to point the juxtaposition between OG and

NG, it may be noted what scores NG attains. It seems as if in none of Chomsky's many writings, complementation of *catch, conceive, fancy, find,* and/or *imagine* has again been among the pertinent facts since Chomsky (1955/1975:268, 270–1, 297–8, 491). Chomsky prefers to use other verbs when presenting facts pertinent to discussing complementation. And what about the NG 'grammars', SS&P (1973) and Emonds (1976); and the NG literature? With the latter represented by Rosenbaum (1967:60–1, 121), NG scores are given in [11]:

[11] Scores on complementation in some NG – out of 20 points

Rosenbaum (1967)	6 (= *conceive, fancy, imagine*: pattern 2; *catch, find, imagine*: pattern 3)
Chomsky (1955)	3 (= *catch, find, imagine*: pattern 3)
SS&P (1973)	1 (= *imagine*: pattern 2)
Emonds 1976	0

It hardly needs pointing out that in general NG 'grammars', the scores are much lower than in NG literature specifically on complementation: SS&P (1973:570, 582, 771) and Emonds are not simply *open* to incorporating every point from the earlier NG literature; only when points are pertinent to Rosenbaum's specific NG do they stand a fair chance of being covered. Still, scores attained by OG grammars in [5, 6] are higher even than the one of Rosenbaum: comprehensive coverage of available evidence in OG yet exceeds coverage of pertinent facts in NG.

Finally, note that 'reasonable' scores as in [7, 8] are even lower for NG: two in Chomsky (1955) and in Rosenbaum (1967); none in both SS&P (1973) and Emonds (1976). As NG effects its *narrow* programme, there is no connection between being observed in a corpus and perceived pertinence. When told about the compilation of a(nother) 1,000,000 word corpus by W. Nelson Francis, to lay *open* for observation "the true facts of English grammar", Robert Lees reacted as NG would, suggesting introspection instead of observation (cf. section II.4): "You are a native speaker of English; in ten minutes you can produce more illustrations of any point in English grammar than you will find in many millions of words of random text" (Francis 1979:110; note the native!). With this we may switch to discussion of the *narrow* issue about complementation, in the next subsection.

C.2 The *narrow* issue: analysis of complementation

Consider complementation in [12] and the more or less synonymous [13a–c]:

[12]   I found John to sleep in the bathroom
[13a] I found that John sleeps in the bathroom
[13b] I found John, who sleeps in the bathroom
[13c] I found John asleep in the bathroom

Very roughly, one might say that [13a–c] might suggest that [12] be analysed along the lines of [14a–c] respectively (in [14b] *John* would be pronominalized, *who*, or left out, ____, respectively):

[14a] find [that John sleeps ...] → find [John to sleep ...]
[14b] find John [*John* sleeps ...] → find John [*John* to sleep ...]
[14c] find John [asleep ...] → find John [to sleep ...]

In section C.1 it has been put forward that analysis of complementation as in [14] is a *narrow* concern, such that choices among [14a–c] be made in accordance with an associated theory, as in NG. As Rosenbaum (1967:113) already observes, this juxtaposes to OG, where coverage of [12] rather than analyses [14] are the *open* issue. Still, that is not to say that analysis of complementation has not been considered at all in OG; in fact, OG coverage in [5, 6] is embedded in sometimes quite extensive discussion of analyses. Extensive discussion may even prevent optimally *open* "matter-of-fact treatments": "grammars ... burdened with grammatical theory ... tend to spread the material over ... many sections" (Van Ek 1966:18). Let us therefore briefly survey OG with respect to [14a–c]; keeping firmly in mind, however, that this should really prove an issue alien to the *open* nature of OG, as coverage is alien to NG in section C.1.

Sweet (1898:119) considers only one of Zandvoort's points of complementation: *find* – pro/noun – infinitive. Discussion of an apparently similar construction *I saw him come* as verb – object – object complement (1891:96) suggests analysis as in [14c].

Poutsma discusses most of his twelve points of complementation in sections on the 'accusative + infinitive' (1929:790ff.), or on participles that have "a similar function as the infinitive-construction in the accusative + infinitive" (1929:984ff.). On the one hand, Poutsma takes the pro/noun to be an object, and the infinitive or participle to be a separate predicative adjunct (1928:343): suggesting analysis [14c]; on the other hand, Poutsma (1929) presents a series of observations that in fact pro/noun – infinitive/participle resemble a single unit: rather suggesting [14a]. *A–Z*'s interpretation here differs from Rosenbaum's, who takes Poutsma to abide by [14c], but "for entirely the wrong reason" (1967:114); in OG reasons cannot be (right or) wrong, especially if coverage is as comprehensive as Poutsma's. In effect, we have an eminent case of juxtaposition here: Poutsma avoids a *narrow* choice between [14a] and [14c]; and he can thus *open*ly score highest on coverage in [6].

Kruisinga (1931:41, 151, 181) repeatedly insists that the pro/noun in complementation is only an "apparent object", but "not really an object at all, but the subject"; this points to analysis [14a]. For Curme (1931:120) verbs in [1–4] are followed by "two accusatives [which] together form logically a clause": again like analysis [14a]. Jespersen (1940:7–9) explicitly draws the comparison of [12] to [13a], and therefore firmly opts for [14a], calling the complement of the verb a single "nexus". Quirk *et al.* (1972:834) call complementations "non-finite clause objects with subjects", i.e. [14a]; however, Quirk *et al.* (1985) switch to something like Sweet's version of [14c]: verb – object – object complement; now expressly rejecting [14a]. The switch can be seen as another indication that the issue of analysis is definitely subordinate in OG: the important thing is that *CGoEL* (1985) is more comprehensive than *GCE* in [5–6].

It will be noted that in OG, only for Jespersen can one be truly confident about a choice among [14a–c] (for [14a]). Moreover, little true manifestation as there is in OG of [14a] and [14c], [14b] does not seem to have been intimated at all. In fact, [14b] is a relatively abstract analysis: it posits a *John* in a position where there is no *John* actually to be observed. As such, [14b] is alien to inductive OG, and would only be expected in NG, where *John* can be deductively posited on the basis of a theory. Indeed, [14b] is well-represented in NG: [14b] represents 'subject-to-object raising' as an analysis of complementation, in *A–Z*'s sense of [1–4] with five verbs. Subject-to-object raising is a transformation, and hence is standard in early NG, i.e. transformational NG (section 3.1 and Part II). The basic idea is that [14b] is transformationally derived from [14a], say as in [15] (verbal = infinitive/participle):

[15] verb-[pro/noun-verbal]⇒ verb-pro/noun-[_-verbal]

When the pro/noun is still part of the bracketed unit, it is its subject; when it is raised out of the brackets, it becomes the object of the preceding verb.

Subject-to-object raising would be motivated in NG essentially as in Rosenbaum (1967:60–1), under a theory about passivization as object-subject interchange. On the one hand, the equivalence of [16a, b] then suggests that *John* in [16a] be the subject of the bracketed clause; as in [14a]. On the other hand, the equivalence of [17a, b] conversely suggests that *John* in [17a] be the object to be interchanged with the subject *I*; as in [14b].

[16a] I found [John to occupy the bathroom]
[16b] I found [the bathroom to be occupied]
[17a] I found John [_ to occupy the bathroom]
[17b] John was found [_ to occupy the bathroom]

The essential idea of [15] then is to account for [16a] by the left-hand side of [15], before *subject*-to-object raising; and to account for [17a] by the right-hand side of [15], after subject-to-*object* raising. Subject-to-object raising, then, is essentially the analysis adopted by Rosenbaum (1967:60–1, 121), for *conceive, fancy*, and *imagine* complemented by pro/noun – *to*-infinitive, as in [2]; [15] is also adopted in SS&P (1973:559, 582, 592, 771) for *imagine* in [2].

Emonds (1976) does not cover any of Zandvoort's twenty cases of complementation specifically; cf. [11]. For Emonds (1976:77) it is sufficient to point out that any cases of complementation analysed by subject-to-object raising [15] would fall into the *narrow* range of transformations allowed by his NG theory of structure preservation: since verbs may have a pro/noun as object (*I found John*), putting a pro/noun into that position by subject-to-object raising preserves structure (cf. section 3.3). Beyond this, it is not pertinent for Emonds to cover specific cases of complementation. There is perfect juxtaposition between Poutsma for OG and Emonds for NG. Poutsma leaves *open* the analysis of complementation, but covers an extensive range of available evidence: twelve points in [5, 6]. To Emonds' *narrow* theory of transformations, analysis of complementation by structure-preserving subject-to-object raising is pertinent; rather than any facts, which are therefore taken for granted rather than extensively covered: no points in [11].

To wind up with Chomsky on complementation, it will be useful for the reader first to return to section II.4, on relational NG vs. Chomskyan NG. Subject-to-object raising is a label for [14] that refers to grammatical relations: subject, object. As such it is a kind of rule to which relational NG would *narrow* grammatical accounts: [15] = subject becomes object. In fact, subject-to-object raising is discussed most extensively in NG by Postal (1974); Postal (1976) duly goes on to become one of the most prominent originators of relational NG (section II.4). Conversely, Chomskyan NG retains from Chomsky (1965:69) *narrow* accounts exclusively in terms of categories like pro/noun, independently of grammatical relations. Accordingly, Chomsky himself came to reject accounts of passivization on the basis of the relational notion object (1973:233); and thus rejects the purported motivation for subject-to-object raising: subject/object interchange in both [16] and [17]. Quite naturally, therefore, Chomsky (1973:237) argues against [15], and in favour

of only essentially [14a]. The basic idea then is that *any* pro/noun
which immediately follows a verb should be liable to passivization:
such an account is effectively *narrow* in that a specification of the
pro/noun's grammatical relations is not allowed. In [16a] the pro/
noun *John* does follow the verb *find* immediately, and thus [17b]
can be accounted for by direct passivization from [16a]; without
any need for [15] to first raise the pro/noun as in [17a].

The *narrow* argument of Chomskyan NG against subject-to-
object raising, and for [14a], is reaffirmed in Chomsky (1981:38,
146). Chomsky (1981) presents a theory of *narrow* constraints (cf.
section 3.1). Among these is the Projection Principle, informally a
more *narrow* version of structure preservation; to the effect that
whereas Emonds takes structure to be preserved if structure A
changes into an independently possible structure B (cf. section
3.3), the Projection Principle requires structure A to remain
structure A. Consider [18]:

[18a] I found John
[18b] I found John to be absent

In [18a] *John* belongs to *found*: 'John is found'. In [18b] *John* does
not so belong to *found*: since rather 'John is absent', he cannot 'be
found'. Although this is inevitably a very rough representation,
John in [18a, b] is therefore to be differently analysed: as belong-
ing to *found* in [19a], but to *be absent* in [19b]:

[19a] I [found John]
[19b] I found [John to be absent]

By subject-to-object raising, the structure of [19b] would be
reinterpreted into the one of [19a]: this preserves structure for
Emonds, but not in the sense of the Projection Principle. Note
once again that, whereas Chomsky (1973, 1981) specifically address
the *narrow* issue of the analysis of complementation, none of
Zandvoort's twenty points are pertinent; and therefore Chomsky
is not *open* to covering them.

C.3 Conclusions

With respect to complementation in the sense of Zandvoort
(1961), one finds essentially the juxtaposition of OG and NG that
A–Z expects. In OG accounts, the appropriate issue is the one of
coverage: for how many of Zandvoort's twenty points is available
evidence cited? This is generally apparent from the fact that, with
an occasional exception in *GCE*, OG accounts have not committed themselves to non-existent complementation patterns.

More particularly, the *open* nature of OG is also evident from Poutsma's superior coverage; twelve points out of twenty amounts to double the number to be observed in a 1,000,000 word corpus; and moreover this correlates with his carefully *open* failure to commit himself to one analysis of complementation or another. Similarly, Quirk *et al.* are free to change from one analysis to another when they increase their coverage from six points in *GCE* to eight in *CGoEL* (although this still falls short of all non-native OG). In NG the situation is quite the converse. Even for NG literature specifically on complementation there is no compulsion to cover any more than six points out of twenty; Rosenbaum (1967). As for the NG standards, in an early work Chomsky may cover three points (1955/1975); but as *narrow*ness is effected more firmly, this reduces to none: in Chomsky (1973, 1981) as well as in Emonds (1976). Most notably, in NG coverage can be seen to correlate, not with availability of evidence, but with less or more *narrow* theory. As long as NG is committed to an inherently relational account of complementation by subject-to-object raising, Rosenbaum and SS&P cover some points, be it six or one. When Emonds refuses to commit himself to subject-to object raising, or when Chomsky rejects it, coverage dwindles to zero.

C.4 Discussion and extensions

1 *Find* complemented as in [1], *find* – pro/noun – infinitive, is covered only in earlier OG; it is the one point covered in earliest OG, Sweet (1891, 1898); but it is not covered in either recent OG, Quirk *et al.* (1972, 1985), or in NG. In fact, *find* – pro/noun – infinitive is not really observed in Van Ek's (1966) corpus either, although [7] suggests that it is. Actually, Van Ek (1966:68) cites his single instance [i] from the *Observer* of 18 July 1965, which did not otherwise constitute part of his corpus:

   [i] Outdoors you will *find Wren create* new green dimensions

   • Discuss the (in)adequacy of *A–Z*'s assumption that all OG and NG are concerned with 'Modern English'; and the (juxtaposed?) attitudes recent OG and NG might take towards [i].

2 Quirk *et al.* (1985) score higher than (1972) on complementation in [5, 6]; in their bibliographies, (1985:1664, 1648) includes both Zandvoort (1961) and Van Ek (1966); whereas (1972:1083–91) includes only the former.

   • What connections can be drawn between these two ways in which *GCE* and *CGoEL* differ?

3 Rosenbaum (1967:109, 119) twice misspells Jespersen as Jesper*son* (cf. section 2.5; in fairness to Rosenbaum, it should be admitted that he spells Jesper*sen* correctly about a dozen times); he misdirects the reader to Jespersen's *MEG* IV (1931) instead of *MEG* V (1940); and he refers to Poutsma (1904) rather than (1929).

● Which error would seem most serious, in view of *A–Z*'s juxtaposition of OG and NG?

4 Van Ek (1966:69) indicates that of his 53 instances of *find* in [3], *find* – pro/noun – *ing* participle, pro/noun is a reflexive pronoun in 28 cases (= 53 per cent) but "From the inventory of the grammars it appears that . . . [this] by far the commonest type . . . is not to be found in P[outsma], C[urme], J[espersen]" (1966:70); the type is not covered by Quirk *et al.* in *GCE* or *CGoEL* either. Consider, however, Kruisinga (1931:82):

> [ii] he *found himself hoping* that his statement would be laughed at
>
> [iii] he even *found himself envying* those old Treliss days

● Comment on the title of Zandvoort (1961), 'I found myself walking . . .', before Van Ek's investigation was carried out.

● (How) does (non-)coverage of *find* – reflexive pronoun – *ing* modify the picture of OG in [5, 6]?

According to Quirk *et al.* (1985:1207) *feel* – pro/noun – *ing* "occurs especially with a reflexive pronoun". Of Van Ek's (1966) six instances of *feel* – pro/noun – *ing*, none have a reflexive pronoun.

● How could the differences between Quirk *et al.* and Van Ek on *feel* or *find* – (reflexive) pro/noun – *ing* be accounted for?

5 Rosenbaum (1967:121) only applies subject-to-object raising to *conceive*, *fancy*, and *imagine* in [2], i.e. verb – pro/noun – *to*-infinitive. Consider Poutsma (1929:983):

> [iv] *She* could have been *imagined saying*, "There is a storm . . ."

[iv] is the only instance in OG for *conceive*, *fancy*, and *imagine* in [3] where the pro/noun is subjected to passivization.

● Discuss the coverage of negative data in OG (cf. section II.4), in view of the fact that no evidence is cited in OG for passivization of pro/noun in *conceive* or *fancy* – pro/noun – *ing*.

● Comment on what the implications of [iv] might be for Rosenbaum's NG.

● Why does(n't) [v] from Quirk *et al.* (1985:1203) have the same implications for NG as [iv]?

> [v] *Ann* was *caught reading* my diary

C is for complementation

Appendix: OG coverage of complementation: references

Sweet: *find* in (1): 1898:119.

Poutsma: *catch* in (3) 1929:990; *conceive* in (2) 1928:358; in (3) 1929:988; *fancy* in (2) 1929:796; in (3): 1929:988; *find* in (1) 1929:794; in (2) 1929:794; in (3) 1929:984; in (4) 1926:520; *imagine* in (2) 1929:806; in (3) 1929:988; in (4) 1929:808.

Kruisinga: *catch* in (3) 1931:82; *conceive* in (2) 1931:208; in (3) 1931:84; *fancy* in (2) 1931:211; in (3) 1931:84; *find* in (1) 1931:152; in (2) 1931:210; in (3) 1931:79; in (4) 1931:41; *imagine* in (2) 1931:210; in (3) 1931:84.

Curme: *catch* in (3) 1931:125; *find* in (1) 1931:125; in (2) 1931:125; in (3) 1931:121; (*image*, cf. Van Ek 1966:96: misprint for?) *imagine* in (2) 1931:249.

Jespersen: *catch* in (1) 1940:282 ("rare"); in (3) 1931:172; *fancy* in (2) 1940:282; in (3) 1940:474; *find* in (1) 1940:281; in (2) 1940:281; in (3) 1940:9; in (4) 1940:9; *imagine* in (2) 1940:282; in (3) 1940:147.

Quirk *et al.*: *catch* in (3) 1972:842, 1985:1206–7; *fancy* in (2) 1985:1181; in (3) 1985:1189–90; *find* in (2) 1972:838, 1985:1203; in (3) 1972:838, 1985:1206; in (4) 1972:842, 1985:1207; *imagine* in (2) 1972:842, 1985:1181; in (3) 1972:842, 1985:1189–90.

77

D is for DO SO for dependency

This section is about DO SO; but ultimately about two models of representing grammatical structures: 'dependency' and 'constituency'. *A–Z* cannot give anything like a full exposition of dependency and constituency. For a useful introduction, the reader is referred to Matthews (1981; especially Ch. 4). Dependency will here be roughly characterized as a relatively *narrow* model, constituency as a relatively *open* one. It should be clear at the outset, however, that a model of representing grammatical structure is in itself a theoretical issue, and thus arises necessarily only in NG; as long as OG achieves coverage of available evidence, it may be expected to proceed regardless of any model. That is precisely why we proceed via DO SO, which allows an indirect window onto dependency or constituency. Beyond that, a more conspicuous point of juxtaposition between NG and OG in this section will remain the relative firmness with which dependency and constituency can be established at all as models in either approach.

That is, for NG the matter is fairly straightforward. It is uncontroversial that early NG incorporates the constituency model. Only in (1970) has Chomsky introduced into constituency NG at least one *narrow* feature from dependency models: the requirement that structures have a 'head'. This is the so-called X-bar Convention (see below; and also sections G, j, T): we may say that Chomsky (1970) *narrow*s constituency towards dependency because he puts constituency 'behind bars'. This accords well with the general picture of NG that *A–Z* promotes: relatively *open* early NG = constituency; from which is gradually effectuated the *narrow* NG programme = constituency behind bars.

It is indicative of the *narrow* nature of NG – its firm theoretical orientation – that appropriate explication of dependency or constituency in NG may easily be obtained from the original sources cited in this section, or introductory expositions based on them. Concern is here therefore rather with OG. The point is not only that the theoretical issue of dependency or constituency is necessarily retrieved much more uncertainly from *open* OG as juxtaposed to *narrow* NG. It has also been claimed that traditional grammar, including Jespersen, essentially adopts dependency (McCawley 1973:235, 321). If dependency is indeed *narrow*, and if OG is largely traditional, then dependency in OG would controvert *A–Z*'s presentation of OG as *open*.

Let us therefore now first give an indication of dependency vs. constituency. By way of a first approximation: one may assume that a grammatical structure is a combination of just individual words; or that a structure is a combination of *both* words *and* groups of words. Consider [1]:

[1] her room upstairs

If structure is a combination of just words, then the representation of [1] can only be word + word + word, *her* + *room* + *upstairs*. If structure is a combination of (groups of) words, the representation may also be word + group of words, *her* + *room upstairs*; or group of words + word, *her room* + *upstairs*. The two kinds of representation are diagrammed in [2] and [3] respectively:

[2] words

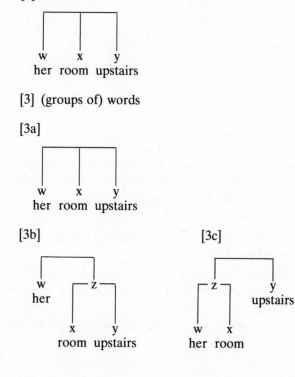

[3] (groups of) words

[3a]

[3b]   [3c]

Representation in terms of only words is formally encoded in dependency models; representation in terms of (groups of) words in constituency. Once again, this is only a first approximation. For now, let us say that [2] is a dependency structure, [3a–c] are constituency structures.

This will serve to convey some sense of how dependency may be said to be relatively *narrow*, and constituency to be relatively *open*: in the dependency model there is just the one structure for [1], viz. [2]; in the constituency model there is again [2] = [3a], but also two more structures, [3b, c]. For consideration of dependency or constituency in OG, this would be sufficient. What we will want to know is if OG does indeed appear traditional in maintaining the *narrow* range of representations like [2], contrary to *A–Z*'s conception of OG as *open*; as soon as representations as in [3b] or [3c] can be recognized in OG, however, OG is *open* to constituency, and *A–Z*'s conception of *open* OG may stand. In section D.2, evidence is presented that all OG may indeed be seen to be *open* to constituency in this way.

Still [2] and [3] are only about representations, and not yet about the truly proper issue for OG – comprehensive coverage, regardless of representation by dependency, constituency, or by whatever model. Coverage may well be brought in, however. Dependency *narrows* grammatical accounts to words; a dependency grammar, therefore, will not cover any evidence that a group of words, not a single word, is involved.

At least one such point of Modern English grammar arises for DO SO. Consider for instance [4]:

[4] David discussed dependency on Friday, and Diana did so too

It might be argued whether DO SO itself genuinely 'is' a group of words, as the spelling suggests; for instance, in this case of DO SO there is no passivization (this will also follow if SO, though a separate word, is by itself somehow not eligible for passivization):

[5a] dependency was discussed by David on Friday ...
[5b] * ... and so was done by Diana

However, DO SO may at least compellingly be seen to 'represent' a group of words, and not a single word:

[6a] David discussed dependency, and Diana did so too
[6b] * David discussed dependency, and Diana did so constituency

In [6a] *did so* can represent the group of words *discussed dependency* but in [6b] *did so* cannot represent the single word *discussed*. Prior to the general issue of dependency or constituency in OG and NG (*D* is for dependency?), this section will therefore look for grammatical accounts of DO SO in particular – *D* is for DO SO. Beside constituency as in [3b, c], we will want to establish whether accounts of DO SO involve just single words – dependency, (too) *narrow* – or groups of words – constituency, *open* (enough). Note that effective constituency in accounts of DO SO will readily explicate ungrammatical evidence, as in [6b]; cf. section II.4.

D.1 On NG on DO SO (and dependency)

Against dependency, then, [3b] or [3c] and DO SO are sufficient. This is therefore all that section D.2 will pursue for OG. For NG, however, it will be appropriate to complicate the picture in [2, 3] a little further, to be able to indicate how constituency is *narrow*ed in later NG, 'behind bars'. But let us first consider representative early NG, for instance Chomsky's (1957:27) analysis of [7a] as in [7b]:

[7a] the man hit the ball

[7b]

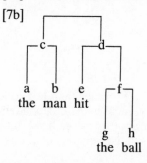

It will be seen that [7b] contains three indications of constituency: the groups of words c, *the man* (a 'Noun Phrase'); d, *hit the ball* (a 'Verb Phrase'); and f, *the ball* (another 'Noun Phrase'). Correspondingly, Chomsky (1957:65–6) indicates how groups of words would be invoked to account for (DO) SO. Thus, *so* would represent the group of words *hit the ball* if [7a] was continued . . . *and the woman did so too* (Chomsky separates *so* from *do*: *do* only 'supports' *so*, much as *do* supports *not* in *the man did not hit the ball*, etc.). Chomsky does not actually specify ungrammaticality if *so* is made to represent single words: * . . . *and the woman did so the goalpost*. Incidentally, Chomsky illustrates – rather than describes – *so* only when it represents the single word *arrive*: *John*

arrives and so do I; see below on the implications of a similar point in Jespersen.

Being based on representations as in [7b], accounts of DO SO firmly establish that early NG incorporates an *open* constituency model. To see how later NG *narrow*s constituency, we may return to [1], *her room upstairs*. In [1] the 'most important' word is *room*, for instance because *room* determines concord with the verb:

[8a] her *room* upstairs *is* cold (cf. * *are*)
[8b] her *rooms* upstairs *are* cold (cf. * *is*)

We may accordingly say that *room* is the 'head' of *her room upstairs*. A notable property of dependency structures is that they can always represent heads directly, for instance as in [9], where *room* is the head because it is associated directly with the 'top' of the diagram:

[9]

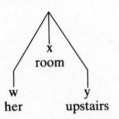

As soon as one uses slanting lines as in [9] rather than horizontal lines as in [2, 3] (note that we retain vertical lines!), dependency will necessarily represent one word or another as the head in this way. Now for constituency consider slanted versions of [3] as in [10]:

[10a]

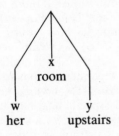

[10b]   [10c]

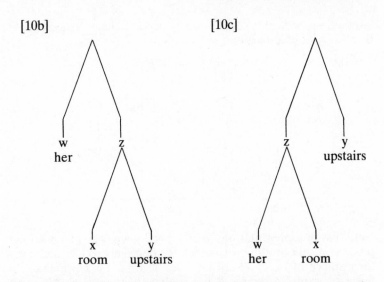

The important point about [10] is that there may not be heads: the tops of [10b, c] are not directly – by only a vertical line – associated with any word. In this sense, constituency is still *open*: after slanting, constituency allows structures to have a head, [10a], or not, [10b, c]; dependency *narrow*ly requires structures to have heads, [9].

The nearest things to heads that [10b, c] would have are *her* and *upstairs* respectively: these are at least relatively directly associated with the tops, without intervening *z*'s. However, concord in [8] suggests that such interpretations of [10b, c] are mistaken: *room* should be the head. Perversely, *room* is precisely the one word in *her room upstairs* that cannot be directly associated with the top in any constituency representation of *her room upstairs* which actually involves an intermediate group of words *z*: such a *z* will always intervene between *room* and the top, in both [10b] and [10c]. This is essentially the problem about constituency that the X-bar Convention may be seen to address – Chomsky maintains constituency, but he puts it 'behind bars', such that in spite of constituency the top of a representation may still be associated with each word.

To this end, each group of words *z* that constituency allows, but dependency does not, is in a sense *narrow*ed into a 'word', such as dependency does allow. For instance, if *x* is a word, and *z* is a group of words which contains *x*, then *z* may 'X-bar': X-bar is like a word, *x*; but not quite a word, bar. Unlike [10b, c] constituency behind bars now allows *room* to be the head of *her room upstairs* after all: say as in [11a] or [11b] respectively (where the tops might then be X-double-bar; etc.):

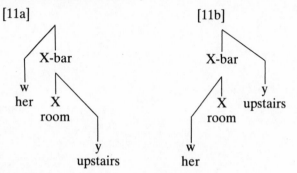

Note that in representations like [11] NG keeps *open* an essential property of the constituency model: the possibility to give accounts, for instance of DO SO (or of ONE, see section D.4 2/3 below), in terms of groups of words X-bar, rather than words *x*. Although Robinson (1970) proposes to incorporate dependency wholesale into NG, constituency behind bars has been the standard position since Chomsky (1970).

For instance, both SS&P (1973:5,21) and Emonds (1976:12–20) subscribe to X-bar Conventions. And Emonds (1976:178–9) accordingly accounts for *John told us that the game was canceled before we left, and Mary did so at the airport* in terms of *did so* (or alternatively just *so*) representing the group of words *tell us that the game was canceled*; like Chomsky (1957), Emonds does not explicate that just a single word cannot be represented in this way (* *... and Mary did so our opponents*, etc.). SS&P (1973) do not give any account of DO SO at all; as one may expect in NG if a point is not seen to be pertinent.

For our third NG account, in a major NG exposition of constituency behind bars like Jackendoff (1977), DO SO can hardly fail to be pertinent. Thus Jackendoff (1977:75) duly presents the negative evidence of * *John said at 6:00 that smoking was fun, but Susan did so at 5:00 that it was bad for you*; where *did so* is wrongly made to represent just *said*: the kind of evidence that one fails to find in OG at all, as we will now see.

D.2 On OG on dependency and DO SO

To be able to identify whether the model of structure in OG is as *narrow* as dependency, or *open* to constituency, one looks for pointers to [3b, c], here repeated for easier reference:

[3b]   [3c]

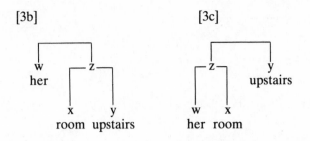

If accounts of points of Modern English grammar in OG can be seen to point to [3b] or [3c], then OG is not restricted to dependency, but *open* to constituency, as *A–Z* expects.

To begin with Sweet's *NEG*, then, one may easily see Sweet as pioneering constituency on behalf of OG: "I may call attention to the *new* method of organic analysis, which ... tries to analyse it [the sentence] into lesser *groups*, each with a definite structure of its own" (1891: xii; emphases added). If in traditional grammar there was indeed *narrow* dependency (McCawley 1973), then Sweet's 'new organic analysis' into *groups* sounds like a new departure, into *open* constituency. And indeed one may find it so. Sweet (1898:8) for instance discusses *three wise men*, "where *wise men* is equivalent to *sages* ... *three* ... come[s] before such groups". That is, representation of *three wise men* would be as in [12], parallel to [3b]; [12] is constituency, combination of a word *three* with a group of words *wise men*:

[12]

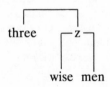

With Sweet having pioneered constituency, later OG may clearly be seen to follow Sweet's lead. Poutsma (1914:21) illustrates that "Sometimes a word-group ... serves to modify a word-group": *United Kingdom Tea Company*, where Poutsma's various underlinings indicate the representation of [13], a firm case of constituency, group of words + group of words:

[13]

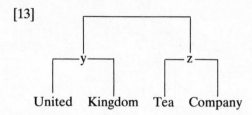

United   Kingdom   Tea   Company

Kruisinga also aligns explicitly with constituency: "A syntactic group is a combination of words" (1932b:177); and "It is ... very common for a member of a group to be a group in itself" (1932b:183). In fact, for Kruisinga it is so obvious that grammatical accounts have to be *open* to constituency that "it would serve little purpose to enumerate all these" (1932b:184); thus pertinent illustration cannot be given (but see [18] below). Curme (1931:129) states that "An adverb ... modifies not only ... a single word but often also a prepositional phrase ... as a whole". That is, Curme intends *entirely around it* to be represented as in [14], once more a case of [3b], word + group of words:

[14]

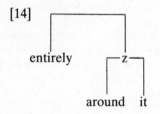

entirely

around   it

Jespersen (1914:363) discusses cases of two adjectives modifying a single noun: "broken *wooden boxes*" (original emphases). The idea is that of the two adjectives "one ... belongs closely to the substantive and forms one composite idea with it". *Broken wooden boxes* points to representation [15], i.e. constituency as in [3b]:

[15]

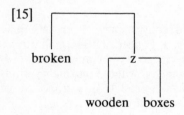

broken

wooden   boxes

Finally Quirk *et al.*'s (1972:918) discussion of *really quite unbeliev-ably*, and even more explicitly its bracketing as "[really [quite [unbelievably]]]" (1985:1323), directly correspond to another in-stance of constituency and [3b]:

[16]

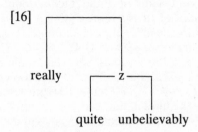

[12–16] leave no doubt that OG, from Sweet onwards through Quirk *et al.*, is *open* to constituency in general. Let us now address the primary issue for OG, of how this *open*ness is exploited in accounts of DO SO. Poutsma, Kruisinga, and Quirk *et al.* turn out to cover evidence from DO SO for groups of words.

Poutsma (1916:756–7): "*to do* ... together with *so* representing a preceding verb with its enlargements (objects and adverbial adjuncts)":

[17] I frequently thought of mentioning to you our Association, but feelings of delicacy prevented me from doing so

I.e. *doing so* represents the group of words *mentioning to you our Association*.

Kruisinga (1932a:224): "*So* accompanies ... *do* to refer to a preceding verb with its adjuncts":

[18] The Utopians set much store by Greek, but ... they did so chiefly on account of the knowledge ...

I.e. *did so* represents *set much store by Greek*. Note that Kruisinga uses constituency inductively, to describe [18]; rather than deduc-tively 'enumerate' all cases of constituency beforehand.

And in Quirk *et al.* (1985:875) "The combination of pro-forms *do so*, seen as a unit, acts as a substitute for a ... predication":

[19] As no one else has succeeded in *doing so*, I shall attempt to solve the mystery myself (= solving the mystery)

Cf. (1972:684–7), where the same points are made somewhat less clearly; cf. also (1985:877, 879) on [5b]. In [19] Quirk *et al.* are explicit about *doing so* representing *solving the mystery*.

Note that *do* and *so* themselves appear to be taken as a group of

words: 'together', Poutsma; 'accompanies', Kruisinga; 'a combination, a unit', Quirk *et al.* But at least DO SO is observed to represent
a group of words: not just a verb, but 'verb *with enlargements*',
Poutsma; 'verb *with adjuncts*', Kruisinga; 'predication' (i.e. verb +
objects), Quirk *et al.* However, none of these OG accounts
explicitly excludes the possibility of DO SO representing a single
verb on its own, and not its enlargements, adjuncts, or objects – as
one might expect in *open* accounts (see section II.4).

By contrast, Sweet, Curme, and Jespersen do not seem to have
admitted groups of words into their accounts of DO SO. For Sweet
(1891:132) "In *he likes it, and so do I*, . . . *so* is felt to be equivalent
. . . to a pronoun of reference – 'he likes it, and that (i.e. liking) do
I' ". Note that Sweet keeps *so* before *do* separate from *do*; and that
so is said to represent the word *liking* rather than the group of
words *liking it* (cf. on Jespersen below). For Curme, "the adverb
so is used . . . referring to the contents of the preceding proposition
. . . 'I'll send it tomorrow if I can arrange to do so' " (1931:100; cf.
1935:10). Again, *so* is kept separate from *do*. Moreover, the fairly
concrete issue of whether *do so* grammatically represents a word
send or a group of words *send it tomorrow* does not arise for
Curme at all; he rather takes *so* to represent more abstractly the
'contents' of the 'proposition', i.e. the meaning of 'I'll send it
tomorrow'.

Jespersen does not actually discuss DO SO, but rather *so . . . do*
(somewhat like Sweet 1891; Chomsky 1957): "it is often convenient
instead of repeating the same verb to use . . . *do* . . . 'He impressed
me as being a perfectly honest man. So he did me' " (1927:248).
The point here is that *did* and *so* are indeed separate in such cases,
because *he* intervenes. Moreover, *did* here does represent a single
verb, *impressed* on its own: 'So he impressed me'. What Jespersen
does not seem to have observed is that in the case of DO SO this is
impossible: * *he did me so too*, whereas *he did so too* is OK if DO
SO represents the group of words *impressed me as being a perfectly
honest man*.

D.3 Conclusions

In this section, *A–Z*'s representation of NG is fairly straightforward: Chomskyan NG never incorporates *narrow* dependency,
for instance because of DO SO; but NG does develop from
relatively *open* constituency to relatively *narrow* constituency
'behind bars'. This juxtaposes with OG, where the issue of
dependency or constituency is firstly significantly less clear. From
Sweet's new organic analysis onwards, OG may in principle be

open to constituency; but in practice, in accounts of DO SO, the apparently more traditional model of dependency seems to retain a hold: comprehensive coverage of evidence available from DO SO for groups of words, as in constituency, is not achieved by Sweet, by Curme, and by Jespersen. Nor does any OG cover negative evidence that DO SO does *not* represent just a single word, i.e. against dependency.

Nevertheless, Poutsma, Kruisinga, and Quirk *et al.* represent truly *open* OG: *open* constituency, to allow them to cover comprehensively the available evidence that DO SO represents groups of words.

D.4 Discussion and extensions

1 Consider the bracketings of [i] (Quirk *et al.* 1972:916):

[ia] his [brilliant (last book)]
[ib] his [last (brilliant book)]

- Represent the analyses of [i] in diagrams such as [2, 3].
- Do the analyses of [i] point to the dependency model or to the constituency model? Is *GCE* thus *open* or *narrow*?
2 Much the same points as elaborated in the main text for DO SO apply to ONE as well:

[iia] Curme is a well-known author of a grammar, and Jespersen is an even better-known one
[iib] * Curme is a well-known author of a grammar, and Chomsky is an even better-known one of books

In [iia] *one* can represent the group of words *author of a grammar*; in [iib] *one* cannot represent the single word *author*.
- Discuss whether *one* requires dependency or constituency, and why.

Consider the following OG accounts of *one*: one may "substitute ... *one* for the noun" (Sweet 1891:66); *one* can be "used as the substitute for a noun" (Poutsma 1916:1174); *one* is "used to refer to class-nouns" (Kruisinga 1932a:297); *one* "refers to some word already mentioned" (Jespersen 1914:247–8); *one* is a "substitute for a ... noun" (Quirk *et al.* 1972:222); *one* "is used as a substitute for a ... noun, or for an equivalent nominal expression" (Quirk *et al.* 1985:387).
- For each OG account of *one*, identify it as dependency or constituency. Which account best allows comprehensive coverage of the available evidence to be achieved?
3 In [ii] above, *one* does not occur on its own, but accompanied by

an even better-known; this *one* may be pluralized: '. . . Jespersen and Poutsma are even better-known ones'. There is a different *one* that does occur on its own, and that cannot be pluralized:

[iii] Curme wrote a grammar of English, and Jespersen wrote one (* ones) too

SS&P (1973:187) observe that in cases like [iii] "*one* is considered . . . [as] containing all the modifiers present", i.e. *one* represents *a grammar of English*, not just *a grammar* for instance. SS&P go on to observe that "This interpretation agrees with Poutsma's, who notes that . . . *one* 'represents a preceding noun with all its modifiers'" (the reference, which SS&P omit, is to 1916:1174).

- Can the interpretation of *one* as in [iii] be accounted for under dependency? Why (not)?
  The case of *one* in [iii] is a "problem" for SS&P, but rather "of course" for Poutsma.
- Comment on the juxtaposition between OG and NG as it emerges here.

E is for *e* (parasitic gaps)

In various types of construction, it may be appropriate to recognize the presence of a 'gap'. Consider the sentences of [1]:

[1a]   do you like him?
[1b] who do you like   ?

There is a relatively simple way of approaching [1]. It may be observed that a direct object regularly follows its verb: in [1a] *him* (direct object) follows *like* (verb); but in [1b] the direct object *who* somehow precedes its verb *like* (at a distance). Such an account may be seen to be an over-simplified one, however. Suppose that one infers from cases like [1a] that a direct object *has to* follow its verb; as [2] would confirm:

[2] * him do you like?

Accordingly, another way of approaching [1] is to say that, despite appearances, there actually *is* in [1b] a direct object that *does* follow the verb: this object would be a 'gap'. Thus in [3] the direct objects are italicized (we will represent a gap by *gap*; in NG this *gap* is called 'trace' or 'variable'):

[3a]   do you like *him*?
[3b] who do you like *gap*

If one wants to recognize *gaps*, they clearly cannot arise out of the blue:

[4] * do you like? = do you like *gap*

In fact, contrasts as between [3b] and [4] suggest that *gap* is possible only if another part of the construction 'licenses' *gap*. In [3b] *gap* is licensed because in a sense *who* identifies *gap*; but in [4] there is nothing like *who*. Hence *gap* in [4] is left unidentifiable; and the sentence is *. This is represented in [5]:

[5a] who do you like? = who do you like *gap*who
     (*gap*who is *gap* licensed by *who*)

[5b] * do you like? = do you like *gap*?
(*gap*? is *gap* left unidentified)

Conversely, one may also say that there *has to* be a *gap* somewhere in a construction if there is a *wh*-element like *who* to license such a *gap*:

[6a]   do you like him?
[6b] * who do you like him?

We can attribute the unacceptability of [6b] to a similar cause as the ungrammaticality of [7]:

[7] * do you like him it?

Verbs such as *like* can only take one direct object; either *him* or *it*, but not both. But if *who* has to license a *gap* then there are also two direct objects even in [6b]; cf. [8]:

[8a] * who do you like him *gap*who
[8b] * who do you like *gap*who him

In other words, with respect to cases like [4], * *gap* without *who*, and of [6b], * *wh*-element without *gap*, one may assume that there has to be a *one-to-one* relation between *wh*-elements and *gap*s, as in [1b] = [3b] = [5a].

It should be clear that once *gap*s are recognized, the one-to-one relation *wh-gap*wh is a *narrow* 'constraint' of the kind that NG should be after. The occurrence of *wh*-elements and of *gap*s would be strongly constrained by one-to-one, such that the impossibility of just a *gap* as in [4], or of just *who* as in [6b] is accounted for. Moreover, NG should by its nature be especially interested in 'empty' categories like *gap*s. Precisely because in the case of a *gap* there is nothing 'actually there', any constraints on *gap*s like one-to-one must be deeply inherent to human language; and as such they are of primary pertinence to NG as a *narrow* theory of what is human language (cf. Chomsky 1981:55; also *A–Z*'s section z) Conversely, since a *gap* cannot by definition be simply 'observed', OG's observations of available evidence might well be expected to forego *gap*s (but see below).

Still, of *A–Z*'s two NG 'grammars' of Modern English, SS&P (1973) do not yet adopt the kind of account in which one-to-one could apply. Rather SS&P have a version of the simpler account that we alluded to: they have a rule of 'WH-fronting' by which a direct object which follows its verb can be fronted if and only if the direct object contains a *wh*-element. Thus they start with sentences like [9], and then derive [10] from these by WH-fronting:

[9a]   do you like *him*? (= [1a])
[9b] * do you like *who*?
[10a] * *him* do you like? (= [2])
[10b]   *who* do you like? (= [1b])

Quite explicitly, in [10b] there is nothing like *gap* in the original position of *who* in [9b]; rather there is an instruction to "erase" this position (1973:619).

Emonds (1976:183) has a similar rule of WH-fronting, where the original position of the *wh*-element becomes "Ø". Still, for Emonds, WH-fronting is a rule of "substitution". That is, Emonds (1976:188ff.) adopts [11a] as a more abstract representation of [9b], and then derives [11b] by WH-fronting:

[11a] WH do you like *who*
[11b] *who* do you like Ø

Since any sentence has at most one element WH that can be substituted for, this comes quite close to one-to-one. Even more notably, in Emonds' NG theory the focus is on 'structure preservation' (section 3.3). Although Emonds does not put things in precisely these terms, the recognition of *gap*s clearly ensures that 'structure is preserved', viz. the regular structures where direct objects follow their verbs.

Although not yet in SS&P nor even quite in Emonds, once NG is effectively *narrow*ed by incorporating one-to-one, it also excludes licensing of *two* gaps by *one wh*-element:

[12a]   did you protect Bill   against himself?
[12b]   who did you protect Bill   against   ?
        = *who*   *gap*who (OK by 1-to-1)
[12c]   who did you protect   against himself?
        = *who*   *gap*who   (OK by 1-to-1)
[12d] * who did you protect   against   ?
        = *who*   *gap*who   *gap*who (* by 1-to-1)

It therefore stands to reason that it should cause a great deal of concern in NG when there appear to be exceptions to one-to-one, where unlike [12d] multiple gaps to a single *wh*-element are quite acceptable:

[13a]   did you buy the book without reading it   ?
[13b]   what did you buy   without reading   ?
        = *what*   *gap*what   *gap*what

In more recent NG, multiple *gap*s as in [13b] have duly become a boom area. The extra gap is usually represented by *e*, and called a 'parasitic gap'. In the case of [13b], the second *gap* is the parasitic one *e*, because it is at least marginally possible to retain the pronoun of [13a] in its stead; whereas the first *gap* has to be *gap*:

[14a]   what did you buy   without reading it   ?
         = *what*   *gap*what
[14b] * what did you buy the book without reading   ?
         = *what*   *gap*what

In [12b] represented as [15], therefore, '*e* is for parasitic *gap*':

[15]   what did you buy   without reading   ?
        = *what*   *gap*what   *e*what

The parasitic-gap boom in NG came later than SS&P (1973) and Emonds (1976); because one-to-one is not yet (firmly) integrated into their NG theories, multiple *gaps* have failed to be recognized as pertinent, and so SS&P and Emonds (1976; but cf. 1985, as in section E.4 4 below) do not say anything about parasitically acceptable multiple *gaps* either. Nor is it appropriate here to review the massive NG literature (including Chomsky; e.g. 1981) on multiple gaps since they did become relevant through one-to-one; but do note that *pertinence* is indeed the appropriate, *narrow*, NG reason for attention or not. Otherwise we will restrict ourselves to complementing SS&P and Emonds by Haegeman (1984) and Contreras (1984), who convey something of the flavour of various NG accounts of parasitic gaps. Moreover, Haegeman (1984) is in fact an outstanding example of the ways OG and NG can beneficially coexist – provided their juxtaposed natures are first given due recognition.

E.1 On NG on parasitic gaps

One NG approach to multiple gaps is to say that in a sense they still *narrow*ly conform to one-to-one. This involves a claim that two *gaps* to a single *wh*-element have to be as it were 'invisible' to one another. Consider a partial NG representation of [12a] given in [16a] (analyses like [16a], and the other ones in this section, are abundantly motivated in NG, and will here be taken as 'given'; [16b] represents [12d] and will be discussed directly):

[16a]   [16b]

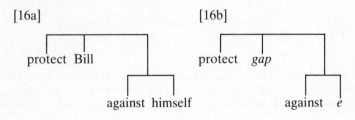

Let us say that a position B is visible from a position A if the first horizontal line above A is also above B (in NG this is one version of 'c-command'). Thus in [16a] *himself* is visible from *Bill*: the horizontal line over *Bill* is also over *himself* (the intervening horizontal over *himself* does not prevent the upper horizontal from also being over *himself*, though not immediately). But *Bill* is not visible from *himself*, because the first horizontal over *himself*, the lower one, is not over *Bill*. Metaphorically, we may now say about [16b] that because *e* is visible from *gap*, *gap* will see that *e* is licensed by *who*; and *gap* will not try to also be licensed by *who*, as this would violate one-to-one. So [16b] is illegitimate, and [12d] is *.

Now consider the structure of [13a] and [13b], with acceptable multiple gaps:

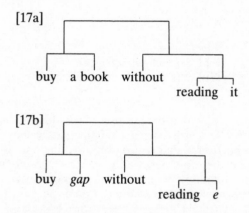

The crucial property of [17] is that here *e* is *not* visible from *gap*: the first horizontal over *gap* is not also over *e*. As in [16b], nor is *gap* visible from *e*. Since the two gaps are therefore invisible to one another, neither can see that the other is licensed by the same *what*; and so each will assume itself to be a *gap* to be licensed by *what*, without ('knowingly') violating one-to-one. This kind of account is a great boon to NG: the *narrow* constraint of one-to-one is maintained, but NG is still able to distinguish between un-grammatical multiple gaps as in [12d] and acceptable parasitic gaps as in [13b]: in [16] *e* is visible from *gap*; in [17] *e* is not visible from *gap*. Essentially, this is the kind of account of multiple gaps that Haegeman (1984) represents.

Under its metaphorical interpretation, in terms of visibility, the above NG account of parasitic gaps is not entirely consistent. So far we have looked at multiple gaps from the point of view of the gaps themselves, whether the gaps are visible to one another. But in fact, both gaps are visible anyway from the single *wh*-element. Consider the kind of position *wh*-elements have in NG, as in [18]; in [18a] WH corresponds to WH in [11a]:

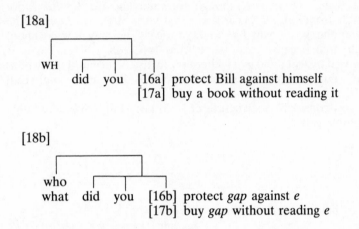

[18a]

WH

      did   you   [16a] protect Bill against himself
                    [17a] buy a book without reading it

[18b]

who
what   did   you   [16b] protect *gap* against *e*
                    [17b] buy *gap* without reading *e*

The notable property of [18] is that the position of *wh*-elements is so high up that anything else is visible from *wh*: immediately above *who* or *what* there is a horizontal that is also over anything else. In our terms, a *wh*-element therefore necessarily sees that it licenses two gaps, *gap* and *e*, in violation of one-to-one. This is one way of looking upon modifications of the NG account of parasitic gaps as in Contreras (1984).

The modification is effectively to have one-to-one *narrow*ly respected also from the point of view of the *wh*-element: for that purpose, in parasitic gap constructions a sort of second WH is recognized, an empty one; cf. the empty position corresponding to *which* in cases like [19]:

[19a]   the house which I bought
[19b]   the house   I bought
      = the house WH   I bought *gap*wh

Given an empty WH, the analysis of [13b] may now be given as in [20] ([20] retains pertinent features of NG representations, but otherwise deviates considerably for expository convenience):

[20]

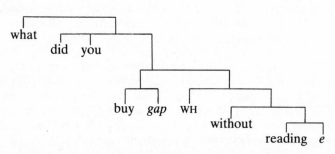

The constraint on [20] is now rather that the empty WH and *gap* be invisible to one another. As the reader may verify, this is satisfied in [20]: there is no horizontal immediately over one which is also over the other. Note that the empty WH is not a 'gap': no overt item could appear in its position. There are thus two one-to-one relations *wh – gap* in [20]: *what – gap*, and WH *– e*. (In addition, *what* will also license WH, and hence indirectly *e*; but since WH is no gap, the relation *what –* WH is independent of the one-to-one relations *wh – gap/e*, and thus independent of one-to-one.)

E.2 On OG on parasitic gaps (and on OG in NG)

It should be remembered that a lot more can be, and recently has been, said about NG accounts of parasitic gaps; particularly by Chomsky. But we will now return to Haegeman (1984), and via Haegeman to OG. Recall that Haegeman does not have an empty WH as in [20], but relies on the invisibility of *gap* and parasitic *e* to one another, so as to retain a measure of one-to-one. Haegeman points out that this accounts for a constraint on a subject *gap* and *e* parasitic on it:

[21a]   I   bought it without Bill seeing me
[21b] * who   bought it without Bill seeing   ?
     = *who gap*who   *e*who

[21c]

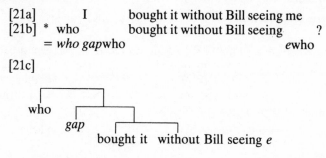

The problem in [21c] is that *e* is visible from *gap*: the first horizontal over *gap* is over *e*. Because in NG subjects occupy a fairly high position, other gaps will generally be visible from a gap in subject position, so that parasitic gaps *e* cannot satisfy one-to-one by being invisible to subject *gap*s.

This is where, in Haegeman (1984), OG comes into NG. Haegeman calls *gap* 'trace'; and she observes (1984:232) about parasitic gaps that: "traditional descriptivist grammarians [i.e. OG] of the early twentieth century also pointed them out. Moreover, in an area where judgments are often difficult and unclear, [in] their examples (all from attested sources) . . . [p]arasitic gaps are seen to occur . . . both by subject traces [*gaps*] and by object traces [*gaps*]". That is, OG presents authentic available evidence (cf. section 3.2) as in [13], that *e* can be parasitic on a *gap* which is a direct object; but also evidence in apparent opposition to [21b], that *gap* may be a subject and still have an *e* parasitic on it.

First, OG's accounts of object *gap* and *e*. Poutsma (1929:643): "the relative is in the objective relation to the verbs in both the relative and the adverbial clause". Among his many examples (also in 1916:1003–4) there are those of [22a] (with *wiles* erroneously as *whiles* in 1929!) and [22b]; to which *A–Z* adds *wh*-element, *gap*, and *e*:

[22a] wiles which modern statesmanship, even while it practises   ,
        which   *e*which
       condemns
              *gap*which

[22b] clarity   I could envy   without reaching
        which   *gap*which   *e*which

(Note that in [22b] we supply *which* as if there were an empty *wh*-element more or less like WH in [19].) Then Jespersen (1931:202): "The relative is sometimes the object at the same time of the verbs of both clauses". His examples include:

[23] a man whom if you know   , you must love
       whom   *e*whom   *gap*whom

Finally Kruisinga (1932b:380): "the antecedent serves as an element of the sub-clause in regard to both the predicative and another verb". Note that Kruisinga is inexplicit about whether *gap* and *e* are subject or object: they are merely 'elements'. But his example is of object *gap* and object *e*:

[24] that which their listeners have . . . felt   without being able
       which   *gap*which
      to shape
            *e*which

Next, OG's accounts of subject *gap* and parasitic *e*, which are recalcitrant to NG accounts if [21c] applies. Poutsma (1929:643): "Instances in which it [i.e. the *wh*-element: in [25] *who*, which could appear instead of *that*] is in the subjective relation to the verb in the relative clause appear to be less frequent":

[25] a villain ... that, unless you get rid of   ...,   will marry
        who   *e*who   *gap*who
... that young woman

And Jespersen (1931:202): "In the following cases the relative is seemingly the object of one and the subject of another verb":

[26] a letter ... which unless we get   back,   must ruin
        which   *e*which   *gap*which
them both

A characteristic fact about OG accounts is that there is no explicit discussion of any *narrow* constraint like one-to-one, nor any ungrammatical instances of multiple gaps like [12d] that would be accounted for by such a *narrow* constraint. One would expect such features to be reserved for NG (cf. section II.4); and indeed they do appear in recent NG, as section E.1 has shown. But long before that, there *is open* coverage in OG, evidence of multiple gaps which *are* possible; although only in OG 'of the early twentieth century' (Haegeman 1984:232); and only in non-native OG: viz. Poutsma, Jespersen, and Kruisinga – and notably not in the later twentieth century (native) *GCE* (1972) or even *CGoEL* (1985), in spite of the latter's post-dating the NG parasitic gap boom. Moreover, Poutsma and Jespersen are in fact explicit about a contrast between *gap* as object and *gap* as subject, if *e* is to be parasitic on them: Poutsma calls the latter 'less frequent', and Jespersen qualifies the possibility with a (very vague) 'seemingly'; Kruisinga does not even illustrate any *e* parasitic on subject *gap*: it may well have escaped his notice under the inexplicitness of 'element' rather than 'subject' and/or 'object'. It is possible to see here in various ways confirmation of the oddness of subject *gap* and parasitic *e*, which should be * in NG if [21c] applied.

However, it is here that in fact OG allows Haegeman to make a contribution to NG. She notes that in the case of object *gap* and parasitic *e*, OG examples have either *gap* before *e* [22b, 24], or *e* before *gap* [22a, 23]. Note that actually only Poutsma has both orders in one OG grammar: Jespersen has only *e* before *gap*, Kruisinga only *gap* before *e*; something that Haegeman does not mention. By contrast, in the recalcitrant case (for NG!) of subject *gap* and parasitic *e*, OG examples always have *e* before *gap*: [25, 26] (but in Jespersen's examples there is no contrast object –

subject here; nor does Kruisinga have instances of subject *gap*s in the first place). Note that in [25, 26] the first *gap* is indeed the parasitic one *e*, as can be seen along the lines of [14], as in [27]:

[27a] a letter which, unless we get *it* back, must ruin them both
[27b] * a letter which, unless we get   back, *it* must ruin them both

This is pertinent to NG. Haegeman suggests that in NG the OG feature 'subject *gap before e*' is precisely the *narrow* feature which prevents [21c] from applying, and thus makes [25, 26] acceptable. Consider the NG analysis of [26] in [28]:

[28]

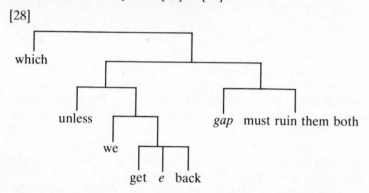

As Haegeman points out, the crucial difference between [28] and [21c] is that in [28] the first horizontal over *gap* is *not* also over *e*; although a subject is fairly high up in NG analyses, in [28] the preposed adverbial *unless we get e back* is even higher up than the subject. This allows parasitic gap *e* to be invisible even from *gap* in subject position, and thus allows one-to-one to be satisfied, because neither subject *gap* nor parasitic *e* can see in [28] that the other one is also licensed by *which*.

Note that in this case the NG account of gaps *e* parasitic on subject *gap*s seems to derive from their account in OG. Haegeman does present her point as if it has first been deduced quite independently in NG, in properly *narrow* fashion; and as if it is then merely "supported" (1984:232) by OG. But in fact OG does appear to have inspired NG here. Firstly, although Poutsma is among Haegeman's references, she avoids actually citing his subject–object contrast, or his telling examples; [22, 25]. By giving both, Poutsma is by far the most successful OG grammar on parasitic gaps, i.e. the most comprehensive one. Haegeman as it were 'underrepresents' OG by slighting Poutsma, and thus gives a slightly skewed impression of the originality of (her) NG in this area. Secondly, Haegeman's operative example is [29]:

[29] a note which, unless we send   back,   will ruin our
       which   *e*which   *gap*which
     relationship

Clearly, [29] is just a minimal variation on OG's original [26] from Jespersen, especially since all Haegeman's actual NG analyses of [29] retain *get* from Jespersen's [26] rather than *send* as in [29]! Still, it is then of course a matter internal to NG whether OG's *open* observations on *e* parasitic on subject *gap* are *narrow*ly pertinent to NG. They need not be so at all; but in Haegeman they prove to be, in terms of the (in)visibility contrasts between [21c] and [28].

E.3 Conclusions

OG can stand its own ground quite well in the area of multiple gaps which has recently been somewhat monopolized by NG. If NG can offer *narrow* explanations of parasitic gaps which are impossible, by virtue of constraints like one-to-one and visibility (c-command), OG can offer an *open*ly comprehensive range of evidence which may be pertinent to NG: multiple gaps fairly freely if *e* is parasitic on object *gap*; but if *e* is parasitic on subject *gap*, then only if *e* is invisible by preceding *gap*. The latter situation is indeed *open*ed up to NG from OG by Haegeman (1984). As Haegeman (1984) illustrates quite well, this is how OG may be of service to NG: the comprehensive evidence in OG is here "valuable" (1984:232) to NG if NG is so preoccupied with *narrow* constraints that it even overlooks actual possibilities which are pertinent to NG's *narrow* constraints; as [25, 26] are by [28]. As for Chomsky (1962:20) NG "should include [things] whether Jespersen does or not", so conversely Haegeman should take [25, 26] into consideration only as NG can *narrow*ly account for them, and not merely because OG includes them.

E.4 Discussion and extensions

1 One grammar of English from the early twentieth century that *A–Z* does not look at systematically (because it is in German) is by Wendt. Wendt (1914:171) notes cases where 'insertion of the (formal) main clause makes possible intertwinings (Latinisms)' (unauthorized translation). He cites from a periodical the authentic evidence of [i]:

[i] one of the letters was as follows, which Mr Westcott commenting upon, describes as unusual

● Identify *wh*-elements, *gap*s and/or parasitic *e* in [i].

- Comment on whether Wendt's is *open* and/or *narrow* grammar, in view of his characterization of [i] as 'possible' but also a 'Latinism'.
- Could Wendt's [i] have inspired Haegeman (1984) like Poutsma has done?

2 Quirk *et al.* (1985) have among their references a (1985) paper by Haegeman (see section v); and a paper from the same issue of the periodical that Haegeman (1984) appears in. But they fail (refuse?) to cover parasitic gaps as these appear in Haegeman (1984). Given this, discuss whether Quirk *et al.*'s *CGoEL* is 'comprehensive' as its title claims, or *open* as *A–Z* calls it. Also consider (other) OG grammars here.

3 In a satirical piece, Pullum (1986:287) satirizes facile claims about the relations between OG and NG:

> I found my old friend ... Brody ... arguing ... that [in NG] the governing category for x is the minimal category with a SUBJECT z distinct from x which contains both x and either the governor of x (if x is governed) or the governor of the minimal maximal category dominating x (if x is not governed), where z is accessible to x, z need not be an actual SUBJECT unless x is PRO or a lexical anaphor ... I think it is reasonable to see in Brody's formulation a refinement and sharpening of insights implicit in traditional grammar [i.e. OG].

- Although it may easily spoil jokes if you try to explain them, explain what Pullum attacks here: is Brody's NG formulation wrong, because it is (not) like OG? or should OG simply be left out?

Now consider an NG definition of c-command (= visibility) in [ii] (Haegeman 1984:229):

> [ii] Node A c-commands node B iff the branching node α_1 most immediately dominating A either dominates B or is immediately dominated by a node α_2 which dominates B, and α_2 is of the same category type as α_1.

Clearly [ii] is somewhat 'Brody-esque'; and Haegeman does not adopt it.

- Given the way OG is used in Haegeman (1984), do you think that Haegeman would, or should, reject or accept [ii] according as it (does not) capture 'insights implicit in OG'?

4 By one NG account "Parasitic gaps in *finite* adverbial [clauses] are correctly predicted to be less acceptable" (Emonds 1985:91; emphases added) than in non-finite ones. [iii] contains the

corresponding examples, with Emonds' judgements expressed by *:

[iiia] * I disliked the painting that the expert scrutinized before you described

[iiib] * which books should I make a list of while you are putting away?

[iiic] * which students can we criticize while you interview for jobs?

- What functions (subject, object, etc.) have any *gap*s and/or *e*'s in [iii]? How does this distinguish between the NG accounts of parasitic gaps by Haegeman (1984) and by Emonds (1985)? With which NG account do the OG accounts of Poutsma, Jespersen, and Kruisinga go along in this respect?
- Would you argue that OG shows Emonds' prediction, and hence his *narrow* NG, not to be 'correct' after all? Cf. [22a, 23–6]. Stuurman (1987:469) suggests that Emonds (1985) be interpreted as a sequel to Emonds (1976): "comprehensive ... descriptions, along with a theory of constraints".
- How could the fact that Emonds only deals with parasitic gaps in an "excursus" (1985:88–92) be constructed as evidence that Emonds (1985) is indeed, or not, *open* grammar?

f is for *for*

In English, some infinitive constructions with *to* may be accompanied by a *for*-construction. In [1], the infinitive construction is *to improve himself*, without or with the *for*-construction *for John* respectively:

[1a] Bill was eager to improve himself
[1b] Bill was eager for John to improve himself

In [1b] *John* acts as the subject of the infinitive construction; for one thing because *himself* is interpreted as 'Bill' in [1a], but as 'John' in [1b] (cf. section R). *For John* in [1b] may accordingly be said to illustrate the '*for* – subject' property of English *to*-infinitives.

A number of questions may be asked about *for* – subject. For instance, one might consider the alternative representations of sentences like [1b] as in [2a–c]:

[2a]

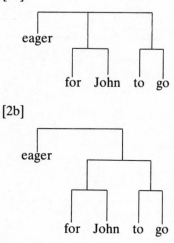

[2b]

[2c]

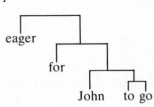

Representation as in [2a–c], and in particular some *narrow*ly determined choice between them, would be a primary issue only for NG; nevertheless, sometimes extensive considerations may also be found in OG (e.g. Poutsma 1928:183, 1929:823–4, 1926:774ff.; Kruisinga 1931:193ff.; Curme 1931:457; Jespersen 1940:308ff.). This miniscule section of *A–Z* does not take its point of departure in [2a–c], however. We will rather start from two other points about *for* – subject: a point about *for* – subject after verbs; and a point about *for* – subject after nouns. The information on OG and NG accounts of these points in sections f.1 and f.2 respectively should enable the reader to draw her own conclusions about juxtaposition of OG and NG in this area.

With respect to *for* – subject after verbs, consider [3]:

[3a] we're hoping to improve ourselves
[3b] * we're hoping John to improve himself
[3c] we're hoping for John to improve himself

If there is to be a subject for a *to*-infinitive after the verb *hope*, this subject requires *for*, as as it does after the adjective *eager* in [1]: *for John*, not plain *John*. [3a–c] represent the regular case as it applies after verbs. However, with certain verbs, *for* is not required; for instance *want* does allow a 'plain subject' *John* in [4a]:

[4a] we want John to improve himself
[4b] we want for John to improve himself

Even verbs like *want* may be observed to revert to *for* – subject, however: if the verb and the subject of the infinitive are *not* as in [4a] immediately next to one another. In [5], they are separated by *very much*:

[5a] * we want very much John to improve himself
[5b] we want very much for John to improve himself

For *for* – subject after verbs, we will sample OG and NG accounts of alternations as between [4] and [5].

f is for for

After nouns, in infinitives one again finds *for* – subject only, and no plain subjects:

[6a] a long time to stay awake
[6b] * a long time John to stay awake
[6c] a long time for John to stay awake

After nouns, however, the *for* – subject construction is not the only prepositional construction that may be observed, but also cases like [7a]; again the preposition is indispensable, [7b]:

[7a] a long time during which to stay awake
[7b] * a long time which to stay awake

The simplest, *open*, assumption is that prepositional constructions as in [6c] and [7a] may simply both be added to the same infinitive after a noun. From a *narrow* perspective, however, it is more natural to assume that the constructions *for John* from [6c] and *during which* from [7a] should somehow be impossible to combine:

[8a] ?a long time for John during which to stay awake
[8b] ?a long time during which for John to stay awake

For *for* – subject after nouns, we want to sample OG and NG accounts of the alternation between [6c] and [7a]; and perhaps combinations of [6c] and [7a] as in [8].

It may here at once be observed that Sweet does not account for any cases of *for* – subject at all. Sweet does use the construction, however: for instance, "For the author ... abruptly to address his readers would be uncolloquial" (1891:71), which is cited as one of his authentic examples of *for* – subject by Poutsma (1929:824).

f.1 On OG and NG on *for* – subject after verbs

Alternations between plain subject and *for* – subject after verbs are regularly in evidence in OG. For instance, in Poutsma (1929:800) [9a] cited from Sweet (1891:48); and (1929:817) [9b]:

[9a] I like boys to be quiet
[9b] you'd like better for us both to stay at home

From Kruisinga, [10a, b], (1931:188) and (1931:201) respectively:

[10a] they didn't want him to see the Procession
[10b] I wanted so for her to die

The two examples of [11] are both from Curme (1931:250):

[11a] you would like Captain Lay to lunch at the White House

[11b] Mrs. Roosevelt would like for you to lunch at the White House

[12a, b] are two examples in Jespersen, (1940:284, 301):

[12a] I like you to look at me
[12b] you'd like better for us both to stay home

Quirk *et al.* (1972:739) present the examples of [13], (1985:1062) the ones of [14]:

[13a] he wants me to leave
[13b] he wants for me to leave
[14a] he didn't like me to be alone at night
[14b] he didn't like for me to be alone at night

However, not all of [9–14] are equally to the point, for *A–Z*, with respect to [4] vs. [5]. Neither Curme nor Quirk *et al.* (the 'natives' in OG!) come to grips at all with the effect that distance of the infinitive from the verb may have. That is, for Curme [11a] is merely "older English": and for Quirk *et al.* [13b, 14b] are merely "AmE" (American English). Thus Poutsma, Kruisinga, and Jespersen remain. Interestingly, Poutsma and Jespersen have their eyes on the same example from George Eliot (they have used different editions, hence with or without *at*). Yet, between Poutsma, Kruisinga, and Jespersen there is still a notable difference. With respect to examples like [9b] Poutsma (1929:817) complains that "there is not, apparently, the least call for" *for*; and elsewhere that *for* "answers no useful purpose" (1926:778); as if in [9b] *for* not just *open*ly could, but actually *narrow*ly should, be absent just as in [9a]. Similarly, for Kruisinga (1931:202) [10a] is simply a "competitor" of [10b], as if *for* might be left out from the latter as from the former. Poutsma and Kruisinga illustrate, but fail to recognize the pertinence of distance; i.e. that the effect of *better* or *so* intervening is to make *for* indispensable. By contrast, Jespersen does recognize that in [12b] *for* "is evoked by something intervening between the verb and the infinitive", viz. *better*. On this point, Jespersen is alone in OG.

When one turns to NG, the alternation between plain subject and *for* – subject for infinitives after verbs does not seem to have been pertinent to Emonds (1976) at all. Other standard NG however, we may illustrate by [15] from SS&P (1973:520–1) and [16] from Chomsky (1981:19):

[15a] I hate you to do things like that
[15b] I hate very much for you to do things like that
[16a] the students want Bill to visit Paris
[16b] the students want very much for Bill to visit Paris

Much as in the case of Poutsma and Kruisinga in OG, SS&P in relatively early NG let the alternation between plain subject and *for* – subject in [15] pass by without any explicit recognition for the intervening *very much*; leaving the early NG account effectively *open* (cf. Part II). However, Chomsky (1981:69, 142) indicates how *very much* in [16] becomes particularly pertinent once the *narrow* concerns of NG are effectuated. Chomsky adopts the *narrow* position that every nominal like *Bill* in [16] must have 'Case', to be obtained from a verb or a preposition, under a *narrow* condition of 'adjacency'. That is, roughly (but see below) *Bill* must have either a verb or a preposition immediately to its left. In [16a] this is the case: *want* is a verb immediately to the left of *Bill*. In [16b] however, *want* cannot satisfy the *narrow* condition that *Bill* have a verb to its immediate left, because *very much* intervenes. This accounts for the appearance of *for* in [16b]: a meaningless item which only serves to provide *Bill* with a preposition to obtain Case from immediately to its left.

f.2 On OG and NG on *for* – subject after nouns

With respect to [6–8], OG accounts (except for Sweet) duly present examples like [6c, 7a] (respectively Poutsma 1929:825–6 and 1929:776–7; Kruisinga 1931:196 and 1931:175–6; Curme 1931:237 and 1931:237–8; Jespersen 1940:302 and 1940:273–6; Quirk *et al.* 1972:878–9 and 1972:879; Quirk *et al.* 1985:1266–7 and ibid.). Also the impossibility of [7b] is regularly observed (Poutsma 1929:776–7; Kruisinga 1931:176; Jespersen 1940:275; Quirk *et al.* 1985:1266). But OG accounts do not explicitly touch upon [8] at all; which suggests that the possibility of [8] is effectively left *open*, as one would expect in OG. Still, the way examples like [6c] and [7a] are sometimes put alongside of one another may suggest that [8] is not taken to be genuinely possible after all. One instance must suffice here. Curme (1931:237–8) first illustrates [7a] with [17a]; then introduces a "simpler form" like [6a], [17b]; and only then talks about cases where "the infinitive has a subject of its own introduced by *for*", [17c]; so, does *for* – subject appear *only* in the latter 'simpler form'?

[17a] an abundance of men from whom to select
[17b] an abundance of men to select from
[17c] an abundance of men for her to select from

Under the *narrow* approach of NG, one might expect accumulations of prepositional constructions as in [8] to be more peremptorily ruled out, preferably on the basis of some theory. Since such a theory lacks in SS&P (1973), they do not have any account of *for* – subject after nouns at all. Chomsky (1981) does develop a theory, viz. a version of [2c], to which [8] would seem pertinent; but still he also fails to touch upon *for* – subjects after nouns. Finally, Emonds (1976) does give an account of *for* – subject, on the basis of a theory that involves both of [2b, c]; in accordance with which Emonds accounts for the exclusion of [8], as well as of [7b].

To obtain appropriate effects from a *narrow* constraint on 'adjacency', Chomsky (1981:52–3) essentially opts for [2c] as the representation of *for* – subject, as in [18a]. Only, *for* is taken to be able to alternate with *during which* in [18b]; combination of [18a, b] would then yield [18c] as a representation of accumulated prepositional constructions:

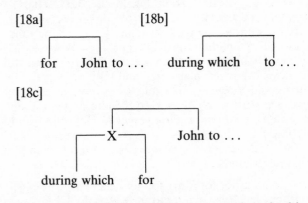

[18a]   [18b]

for   John to ...   during which   to ...

[18c]

X   John to ...

during which   for

However, for [18c] the question may now be raised in what sense *for* is 'adjacent', i.e. immediately to the left of *John*, to provide *John* with Case. In [18a] there is no 'intervening' X between *for* and *John*; in [18a] *for* thus counts as 'adjacent' to *John*. This accounts for any case of *for* – subject, like [6c] or [16b]. Alternatively, [18b] accounts for cases like [7a]. But in [18c], in between *for* and *John* there is now the additional combination X of *during which* plus *for*. This would mean that X rather than *for* counts as being 'adjacent' to *John*; and hence [8] is impossible, since *John* remains without Case. (The technical notion in NG for with or without X intervening is 'c-command'; cf. section E.)

Chomsky (1981:53) actually develops the point about X intervening for *during which* rather than for *for*; but it would easily be extended as indicated to *for* as well. Also Chomsky (1981) does not actually apply his *narrow* account explicitly to *for* – subject after nouns. Perhaps the reader is expected to go back to Chomsky (1977:98–9), where one does get illustration and/or discussion of cases like [6–8]. However, to pursue this here would not keep section f miniscule. We will therefore rather turn to Emonds (1976).

Emonds (1976:195–7) agrees with Chomsky that [2c] is basically the representation of infinitive constructions with *for* – subject; and that in [2c] *for* counts as an item immediately to the left of *John*. For Emonds, the significance of this is that therefore *for* and *John* may undergo a 'local' transformation, because *for* and *John* are next to one another (see section 3.3). In particular, [2c] may switch to [2b] by a local transformation: *for* – *John*⇒ *for+John*. Once given [2b], now suppose that the position of *for+John* may be left 'empty': then this position would allow another prepositional construction along similar lines as *for+John* to take its place by a 'structure preserving' transformation (again see 3.3). That is, *during+which* may occupy the position of *for+John*, thus replacing *for+John*, without changing structure [2b]. On the other hand, *John* or *which* on their own are not ... *+John* or ... *+which*; and these could thus not replace the *for+John* and still preserve structure [2b] intact; hence [6b] and [7b] are impossible. Moreover, nor could *during+which* join *for+John*, rather than replace it, because [2b] is only preserved if there is just the one construction: either *for+John* or *during+which*. Hence [8] would be *. Along these lines, Emonds (1976:192) therefore can – and, since it is pertinent, does – give *narrow* accounts for the examples [19b, c, d] that he presents:

[19a]   I found an usher for Mary to buy tickets from (cf. [6c])
= from *for–Mary* by [2c] to *for+Mary* by [2b]
through local transformation

[19b]   I found an usher from whom to buy tickets (cf. [7a])
= from *for+Mary* by [2b] to *from+whom* by [2b]
through structure preserving transformation

[19c] * I found an usher who to buy tickets from (cf. [7b])
= from *for+Mary* to *+who*

[19d] * I found an usher from whom for Mary to buy tickets (cf. [8])
= from *for+Mary* to *from+whom+for+Mary*

f.3 Conclusions

On infinitives after verbs, OG and NG clearly juxtapose in that the drive towards comprehensiveness ensures that all OG (but for its pioneer Sweet) covers alternations between plain subject and *for* – subject after verbs; by contrast the requirement of pertinence *narrowly* entails the absence of such alternations from Emonds

(1976). In that sense SS&P (1973) is *open* like OG, with alternation covered although no pertinence is apparent. Coverage *is* due to pertinence, however, in Chomsky (1981): i.e. due to a *narrow* account in terms of 'adjacency'. Again this juxtaposes to OG where no such *narrow* condition of 'adjacency' is recognized (although here in OG Jespersen is the exception that proves the rule).

On infinitives after nouns, juxtaposition of OG and NG rather appears in that OG tends to cover both *for* – subject and other prepositional constructions; but then leaves accumulation of constructions *open*, although there does not appear to be any available evidence for it; whereas NG does not cover either prepositional construction – let alone both – if it is not *narrow*ly pertinent (SS&P 1973); or on occasion NG (too) *narrow*ly does not cover either even if this would be pertinent (Chomsky 1981). In Emonds (1976) proper *narrow*ness ensures that accumulation of constructions is accounted for – and in truly *narrow* fashion rejected – in accordance with Emonds' theory of local and structure-preserving transformations.

G is for group genitives

Here's an old puzzle (also reported by Jespersen, 1942:287). Can the son of George's daughter be the daughter of George's son? Yes; and in two ways. Suppose we have two genealogies G, each with three generations g:

G1: g1 = George → g2 = daughter → g3 = (grand)son
G2: g1 = George → g2 = son → g3 = (grand)daughter

In G1, George's grand*son* = the *son* of George's daughter = the daughter of George's *son*; in G2 George's grand*daughter* = the *daughter* of George's son = the son of George's *daughter*. Grammatically, the puzzle revolves around the different relations that obtain: the son of [George's daughter] for G1, or [the son of George]'s daughter for G2; and [the daughter of George]'s son for G1, or the daughter of [George's son] for G2. That is, both *the son of George's daughter* and *the daughter of George's son* may be interpreted as containing either a plain genitive *George's*, or a 'group genitive': *[the son/daughter of George]'s*:

[1] George's grandson   = [a] the son of *George's* daughter
                          = [b] *[the daughter of George]'s* son
[2] George's granddaughter = [a] the daughter of *George's* son
                          = [b] *[the son of George]'s* daughter

Specifically, *[the son/daughter of George]'s* is a group genitive because *'s* is attached to the last element of a group of words, *[the son/daughter of George]*; rather than to the logically most important single word, either *son* or *daughter*.

If the reader is still, or perhaps by now, completely puzzled, this section is about OG and NG accounts of 'G for group genitives'. In an attempt to assist comprehension, in examples and quotations, the most important item in a group and the *'s* will be capitalized: thus [1] and [2] become [3] and [4]:

[3a] the son of GEORGE's daughter   (plain genitive)
[3b] the DAUGHTER of George's son   (group genitive)
[4a] the daughter of GEORGE's son   (plain genitive)
[4b] the SON of George's daughter   (group genitive)

Note that the contrast betweeen 's attached to a word, GEORGE, in the plain genitive, or 's attached to a group of words, *the SON/DAUGHTER of George* in the group genitive, strongly recalls an issue from section D (cf. also section j): dependency vs. constituency. Indeed, as in section D, both extensions of OG beyond *narrow* dependency, and the move in NG to put constituency *narrow*ly 'behind bars', will again be in evidence here.

G.1 On OG on group genitives

Apart from purely *open* coverage – what evidence of group genitives may actually be observed in Modern English – an issue that seems to have attracted much OG attention is the relations of group genitives to 'group plurals'. Is there also a group plural like the group genitive: ?*the SHOP on the corners* beside *the SHOP on the corner's owner*. Cf. the plain plural *the SHOPS on the corner*. And is there a combination of group genitive and (plain) plural: ?*the SHOPS on the corner's owner*. Note that once group genitives are in evidence, OG might be expected to assume both possibilities to be *open* too.

Let us begin with pure coverage, however. Sweet (1891:318) pioneers *open* inventories of types of group genitives that may be observed. In Sweet's inventory, 's may attach to a prepositional modifier, *of England*; or to a clausal modifier, *I saw yesterday*:

[5a] the KING of England's son
[5b] the MAN I saw yesterday's son

Poutsma (1914:33–4) reduces rather than expands this inventory, although he refers to Sweet (1891:318) as if for support. Poutsma actually only retains '[s] attached to a prepositional modifier, *of my happiness*:

[6] this DESTROYER of my happiness'[s] letter

And even [6] is denigrated as "grotesque", hardly a truly *open* approach such as Sweet pioneers. Kruisinga (1932a:37, 68) again recognizes group genitives with 's attached either to prepositional modifier, *of Wales*, or to clausal modifier, *I saw yesterday*; but he then does extend the inventory with a third type, 's attached to a numerical modifier like *the Second* in [7c]:

[7a] the PRINCE of Wales's recent tour
[7b] the MAN I saw yesterday's father
[7c] JAMES the Second's reign

Still, Kruisinga's approach is not entirely *open* either: except for the prepositional modifiers of [7a], group genitives are "extreme" and "verge on the ridiculous". Curme's (1931:80) inventory is again quite *narrow*, with only the group genitive with prepositional modifier, *of England*; no further types are observed at all:

[8] the KING of England's private property

A more effectively *open* approach to group genitives is again met with only in Jespersen. Jespersen (1942:281–98) extends Sweet's inventory to become fully comprehensive by including five different types: the modifier to which 's attaches may be prepositional, *of the world*; clausal, *who keeps below me*; numerical, *the Fourth*; adverbial, *else*; or adjectival, *apparent* (whether *else* is an adverbial or adjectival modifier does not seem clear; but it is not relevant here either):

[9a] the MAN of the world's responsibility
[9b] the MAN who keeps below me's saucepan
[9c] King HENRY the Fourth's reign
[9d] SOMEBODY else's wife
[9e] the HEIR apparent's eldest son

Nor does Jespersen express any more severe judgement than "colloquial" (1942:293). All the more notable in such an effectively *open* account is Jespersen's somewhat *narrow* approach with respect to the last type, adjectival modifier + 's: "This genitive can ... be used only in ... fixed groups ... It is not possible to say for instance, *the WOMEN present's opinion*" (1942:282; cf. section II.4).

In more recent OG, one again finds smaller inventories than Jespersen's. In Quirk *et al.* (1972:202; 1985:328–9) the inventory only contains the prepositional type, [10a] and the adverbial type, [10d]; Quirk *et al.* (1985:1344–5) add the numerical type, [10c]. Both (1972:921) and (1985:1345) practically exclude the clausal type as "not normally acceptable" = " ? " (1985:1282 is even more *narrow*ly censorious than " ? " about an additional clausal example: " * ? "):

[10a] the KING of Denmark's court
[10b] ?a MAN I know's car
[10c] ELIZABETH the Second's reign
[10d] SOMEBODY else's car

Coverage with respect to group genitives thus varies considerably from one OG grammar to another; and is really comprehensive only in Jespersen. Nor does OG consistently maintain an *open* approach when it looks from group genitives to group plurals, like COURT *martials*. Again Sweet sets a general direction: "The principle of group-inflection is not carried so far with the plural ending" (1891:319). Poutsma does not then take this up at all, but Kruisinga and Curme do develop the point. Curme (1931:80) *narrow*ly excludes group plurals: "we never say '*The* KING *of Englands* now have less political power than formerly'". Similarly, Kruisinga contrasts a plain plural like *the* QUEENS *of England* with a group genitive like *the* QUEEN *of England's*; and then insists on such a "different treatment" (1932a:63). This juxtaposes with the more genuinely *open* approach in – again – Jespersen, that genitive and plural may "show the same tendency of adding the ending to the last part", i.e. equally group genitives and group plurals; except that with plurals the tendency – almost ruefully – "could not be carried through to the same extent as with the genitive" (1942:298). Quirk *et al.* (1985:313) (but not yet 1972:174–5!) also keep *open* both COURT *martials* and COURTS *martial*.

There is a similar contrast of Kruisinga to Jespersen and Quirk *et al.* with respect to the point of whether group genitives and plurals can be combined, *?the* SHOPS *on the corner's owner*. Again Kruisinga's practically *narrow* answer is 'no': "The genitive suffix is *never* added to nouns with a plural suffix, no matter whether this is final or not. Thus ... such groups as *the* QUEENS *of England never* take a genitive suffix" (1932a:39; emphases on *never* added; cf. also G.4 4 on 1932a:66, footnote 1). That is, for Kruisinga, * *the* QUEENS *of England's influence on history*. By contrast, Jespersen does present a combination of plural and group genitive, SONS-*in-law's*; and merely comments that "the ... form is *probably never* used" (1942:288, emphasis added). Eventually, Quirk *et al.* throw the matter entirely *open*: they construct the example *the* TEACHERS *of music's room*, without any negative comment at all (1972:920–1; 1985:1345).

Of course, the manifestation of more or less *narrow* approaches in OG accounts of group genitives is something of a set-back for A–Z, if OG is to be juxtaposed to NG because the latter (only) is *narrow*. It may well be that we will have to let group genitives be one of those exceptions which proverbially prove the rule: *open* OG vs. *narrow* NG in general, but just not at this point. Besides, we will somewhat obstinately try for a less apologetic attitude as well.

For one thing, one might set up a parallel between OG and NG.

NG develops from programmatically to more effectively *narrow* (Parts I and II). Conversely, OG would only gradually achieve an effectively *open* approach to group genitives. However, in NG – at least Chomskyan NG – there is more or less steady progress towards more *narrow* positions (as section G.2 will also illustrate). Any developments in OG accounts of group genitives rather appear to be by individual fits and starts: from two types in Sweet back to one in Poutsma; then up to three in Kruisinga, and back again to two in Curme; then up to five in Jespersen, but once again back to three in Quirk *et al*. It would seem that there might thus have to be more or less individual origins for relative *narrow*ness of OG accounts as well.

Let us thus take on Curme's *narrow* approach to group genitives first of all. It is tempting to seek a somewhat paradoxical origin in Curme's (1931:80) resistance to a *narrow* dependency-like account of group genitives (see section D for dependency). Such an account is apparently "usually" given, as if "the inflectional genitive -*s* is placed at the end of the group KING *of England* because these words are felt as a unit with the force of a single word". This would be *narrow* dependency in the sense that a group of words is eliminated in favour of a word. However, Curme rejects this kind of account: "This conception . . . cannot . . . be the compelling force . . . , for we never say *the* KING *of Englands* . . . treating the group KING *of England* as one word, adding the plural -*s* at the end". That is, because Curme wants to keep the account of group genitives *open* beyond dependency, he resigns himself to a *narrow*ly exclusive position on group plurals, 'never'. But Curme's strategy of distinguishing between group genitives and group plurals, against dependency, does not appear to have inevitably as *narrow* effects as in Curme. Jespersen presents the one effectively *open* account of group genitives in OG; yet Jespersen can agree entirely with Curme: "it is not enough to point out that the words put in the group-genitive are felt to be closely connected in meaning: this . . . does not explain the difference between the genitive *the* QUEEN *of England's* and the plural *the* QUEENS *of England*" (1942:296–7). There is no dependency in Jespersen either; but neither paradoxical *narrow*ness.

Instead of individual origins, let us therefore attempt a more general one for *narrow* OG after all. It may be important that the attachment of 's, whether to a single word or to a group of words, involves the attachment of an item that cannot stand alone: *George's daughter*, but **'s daughter*. With syntax as the part of grammar that deals with combinations of independent elements, 's would thus be a point of Modern English accidence, or morphology.

Does an *open* approach to grammar then perhaps manifest itself primarily, if not exclusively, in syntax? Apparently not with Curme: his *Accidence* attempts "to describe fully" (1935:v), but his *Syntax* slightly more *narrow*ly only "to present a . . . rather full outline" (1931:v). But Curme has indeed not provided a really *open* account of group genitives either. In OG it is Sweet and Jespersen who make the most of the divisions of grammar – and it is they exactly who present the more effectively *open* accounts of group genitives as well. So perhaps there is some connection.

Sweet (1891:204) defines 'accidence' as the "part of grammar which concerns itself specially with forms"; in contrast to 'syntax' as the "part of grammar which ignores distinctions of form as much as possible". Similarly, for Jespersen (1924:40, 45; referred to in *MEG* 1914:1, 485; 1942:1), morphology is the part of grammar in which "we proceed from the form to the meaning"; and syntax is the "second main division of grammar", which takes "a different point of view, from the . . . meaning", rather than form. For both Sweet and Jespersen, syntax may thus have been the more natural environment for the *open* approach to prosper (cf. also section II.4); indeed, Sweet (1891:205) explicitly objects to "narrowing [!] the scope of syntax [!] too much".

Although both Sweet and Jespersen deal with group genitives in the relatively *narrow* formal parts of their OG grammars – *Accidence* and *Morphology* respectively – Jespersen's effectively *open* approach to group genitives does coincide with his suggestion that 's has a "syntactical . . . function" after all: being an "interposition" between two items (1942:297–8), rather than a truly morphological ending on a single item. Conversely for Kruisinga, who gives a more *narrow* OG account of group genitives. In section 2.3, *A–Z* already admits that alongside Kruisinga's *open* approach to Modern English grammar, the fifth edition of his *Handbook* (1931–1932) also pursues a *narrow* aim: a restriction of grammatical accounts to formal features only, i.e. to morphology. Kruisinga's formal approach takes immediate effect in the case of a point like group genitives. Consider 'plural genitives': the spelling is supposed to distinguish *queens'* from *queens* but there is no real formal difference between them. Under Kruisinga's formal approach, this means that "English has no genitive plural" (1932a:39). Once this formal theory has been adopted, Kruisinga then goes fully *narrow*: no group genitives of plurals should exist either; i.e. from *queens* vs. * *queens's* is deductively determined also * *QUEENS of England's*.

At any rate, in section G.1, somehow OG is for 'Otto's group genitives'. OG other than Jespersen does not take Sweet's *open* lead, but shows a persistent tendency towards relatively *narrow* approaches to group genitives. On top of more or less exclusive inventories of types of group genitives, there are terms of abuse like "grotesque" (Poutsma), or "ridiculous" (Kruisinga); and statements like "we never say" this (Curme), or that is "not normally acceptable" (Quirk *et al.*). This simply does not add up to an *open* approach such as *A–Z* expects to find in OG. Even if we can identify more or less firm indications as to why group genitives should have evoked *narrow* tendencies in OG, it remains the case that, for once, OG accounts of group genitives do not consistently qualify for juxtaposition to NG as significantly more *open*. Except for Jespersen.

G.2 On group genitives in NG

If OG can barely muster one effectively *open* account of group genitives such as Jespersen's in [9], it should be expected that NG eagerly rules out of *narrow* bounds all cases of group genitives. There is however a very early statement of Chomsky's on group genitives like [11] which is entirely *open*: "it is necessary to make a decision as to the grammaticalness of [[11]] ... etc. I have noted many such instances in normal conversation, and would thus be inclined to admit this possibility" (1955/1975:281):

[11] the MAN from Philadelphia's car

Note the *open* inductive basis: what Chomsky has 'noted' is 'thus a possibility'; instead of *narrow*ly letting the theory decide the status of group genitives. Still, such an *open* approach may be of little significance in early NG, here even prior to the Chomskyan revolution of 1957, if later NG does effectuate *narrow*ness.

Once NG genuinely gets going after 1957, we get a more effectively *narrow* approach in SS&P (1973), who use group genitives to illustrate "some kind of constraint imposed by the length of the potential genitive" (1973:712). Although SS&P admit that "our ... grammar, as it stands, provides no account of these constraints" (1973:710), they prefer to err on the *narrow* side by allowing an anticipated constraint already to assign * to their single example of group genitives (with clausal modifier), [12]:

[12] * the MAN who lives on the corner's books

Whether such examples may or may not be 'noted' is no longer pertinent.

Rather than such resolute *narrow*ness becoming at once entrenched in later NG however, developments of NG accounts of group genitives, like those in OG, rather seem to go in the 'wrong' direction. NG appears relatively *open* when it submits like Chomsky (1955) to the more compelling available evidence of group genitives, and merely attempts to specify a *narrow* dividing line between such instances, and those which even OG tends to simply ignore or at least to abuse; and to all of which SS&P would bluntly assign *.

A case in point is Emonds (1976). In truly *narrow* fashion, Emonds (1976:18–19) formulates a 'recursion constraint'. This constraint essentially entails that genitive 's may not be attached to prepositional or clausal modifiers (Emonds thus allows other types of modifiers; but this is presumably unintentional, since Emonds never adduces any example like [7c, 9c–e, 10c, d]). Let us thus represent the recursion constraint as [13]:

[13] * NOUN modifier's

This is genuinely *narrow*. However, Emonds then still defers to available evidence of group genitives like [14]:

[14] the KING of England's hat

Accordingly, Emonds readmits "free [= *open*!] recursion" by making one exception to [13], viz. if the modifier is prepositional, but does not "dominate . . . a lexical preposition". The idea is that in *the King of England*, *of* would not really mean anything, but only serve as a grammatical link between *King* and *England*. By contrast, in *the book about Chomsky*, *about is* 'lexical' because it does mean something, e.g. 'taking for its subject'. Hence the effect of Emonds' account is that both *the KING'S hat* and *the BOOK'S author* are (of course) possible as cases of plain genitives NOUN'S; so is [14] possible as group genitive NOUN modifier's, in spite of [13], because *of* in [14] is not lexical; and only [15] is *narrow*ly excluded by [13]:

[15] * the BOOK about Chomsky's author

Chomsky, SS&P, and Emonds being 'standard' NG, let us now also look at some NG literature on group genitives. Halitsky (1975:290) develops a *narrow* condition much like Emonds' recursion constraint, which eliminates any possibility of group genitives. Unlike Emonds, however, Halitsky then sticks to his *narrow* guns, and does not attempt to allow some group genitives in again by an *open* backdoor. Halitsky (1975:291) rather maintains a *narrow* regime of * for any group genitive, like SS&P; [16] ([s] indicates the 'empty' variant of genitive 's after another *s* (cf. [6])):

[16a] * the REBELLION of the peasants' [S] outcome
[16b] * the ASSASSINATION of Kennedy's effect on the country
[16c] * the INVASION of Cambodia by America's failure

Halitsky's *narrow*ness is then again depreciated by Hornstein (1977). Hornstein (1977:152, 155) accepts that group genitives with prepositional modifiers should *narrow*ly be excluded:

[17a] * the COVER of the book's color
[17b] * the KING from England's speech

But like Emonds, Hornstein takes exception to the *narrow* exclusion also of [18]; "it is acceptable" (1977:155):

[18] the KING of England's speech

Unlike Emonds, however, Hornstein does not take exceptionally acceptable group genitives like [18] to be due to something relatively *open* like 'free recursion' if there be a 'non-lexical' *of*. Hornstein rather appeals to the more *narrow* version of constituency in NG, constituency 'behind bars' (cf. section D). Under the X-bar Convention, it is possible to distinguish between modifiers which belong more, or belong less closely to the noun: *of . . .* belongs more closely to *King* than *from . . .* , as may be seen in the word-order: *the King of England from France,* * *the King from France of England.* It is as if the word-group X-bar *King of England* is like a single word *x* (cf. the dependency-like account of *King of England* as a single unit; which Curme and Jespersen reject); and this is precisely a *narrow* effect of dependency which the X-bar Convention grafts on to constituency in NG. Behind bars, 's may thus *narrow*ly attach to *x*, KING'S; *x* + modifier = X-bar KING *of England's*, [18]; but not beyond that to X-bar + modifier, * KING *(of England) from France's*, [17b].

It should be noted that Hornstein's re-admission of the available evidence for group genitives is therefore quite different from Emonds'. Emonds merely satisfies an *open* tendency to respect available evidence, as a specific exception, 'free recursion', to a *narrow* recursion constraint [13]. Hornstein, however, relies on a general *narrow* theory, constituency behind bars, which happens to have an *open* effect with respect to (only) some group genitives. Even if earlier NG excludes group genitives more radically (e.g. SS&P, Halitsky), the NG approach in Hornstein must still be seen as more effectively *narrow*, precisely because it no longer regulates the inclusion or exclusion of group genitives on the basis of a specific if unstated constraint on length, or of a specific exception of free recursion; but on the basis of straight deduction from a general *narrow* principle, the X-bar Convention.

G.3 Conclusions

OG and NG accounts of group genitives in Modern English present some intriguing features, from the point of view of juxtaposition. Honesty should compel us to admit that on this point, 'G is for a gamble'. The juxtaposition of OG and NG does not quite work out the way it 'should' in *A–Z*. Instead of being staunchly *open* and *narrow* respectively, the impression one might easily get from section G is that OG tends to take *narrow* depreciatory positions towards group genitives of various types; whereas NG will keep *open* certain possibilities when it might be expected to exclude them. Unless explanations, like the ostensibly morphological nature of 's in OG, or constituency behind bars in NG, can be established, it is precarious for *A–Z* to juxtapose OG and NG only as represented by Jespersen and Hornstein respectively as effectively *open* and *narrow* approaches to group genitives. Still, one thus at least finds that Jespersen juxtaposes to NG, rather than being its precursor (cf. Part II); and it is only by such juxtaposition that one can then see other OG and NG to fail in their respective purposes.

G.4 Discussion and extensions

1 Exemplification of group genitives has tended to be royalist; e.g. [5a, 7a, c, 8, 9c, 10a, c] in OG; and [14, 18] in NG.
 ● Comment on OG and/or NG discontinuities of which these examples would (not) be symptomatic.
2 Consider the examples of [ia–e] from Jespersen, [if–k] from Quirk *et al.*:
   [ia] God Almighty's storm
   [ib] the day before yesterday's paper
   [ic] the cellars where Mary Queen of Scots' Secretaries were put to the rack
   [id] Laplace's face, perfectly smooth, as a healthy man of fifty's, bespoke intelligence
   [ie] the old man who kep' the house's wife
   [if] the Museum of Modern Art's director
   [ig] the director of the museum's book
   [ih] the teacher of music's room
   [ii] the man in the car's ears
   [ij] a man of distinction's influence
   [ik] Elizabeth the Second's heir
 ● Discuss why all these examples contain group genitives.
 ● Distinguish the group genitives into types, on the basis of the type of modifier to which 's attaches.

- What difference(s) between Jespersen's and Quirk *et al.*'s accounts of group genitives appear(s) from these examples? Is the one OG grammar more *open* than the other?
3 Consider the following excerpts, one from OG (Quirk *et al.* 1972:194), the other from NG (Halitsky 1975:291):

> It is ... the noun head that determines the choice of genitive ... only those with the personal noun head ... can take the *-s* genitive irrespective of modification:
> [iia]   the DIRECTOR's books
> [iib] * the BOOKSHELF's books
> [iic]   the DIRECTOR of the museum's books
> [iid] * the BOOKSHELF of the museum's books

> we must distinguish carefully between the unacceptability of nominals like [iiia, b] ... In order to see why, consider [iva, b] ... Since [ivb] is just as unacceptable as [iiib], it might be argued that both ... are unacceptable due to ... *growth* appearing as the head ... But ... we cannot attribute the ill-formedness of [iiia] to any like restriction on the distribution of ... *assassination*:
> [iiia] * the ASSASSINATION of Kennedy's effect on the country
> [iiib] * the GROWTH of the corn's rapidity
> [iva]   the ASSASSINATION's effect on the country
> [ivb] * the GROWTH's rapidity

- Can it be identified which is the OG account, and which the NG account? How and/or why (not)?
- What should one make of the fact that no such passage can be found in the later Quirk *et al.* grammar, *CGoEL* (1985)?
4 OG tends to be relatively more *narrow* about group genitives than *A–Z* expects. Consider again Kruisinga (1932a:66): "instead of saying * *this attempt of the Chinamen's* we can say *this attempt of the Chinamen*".
- Why does Kruisinga want to exclude *the Chinamen's*?
Jespersen (1942:282) excludes *the women present's opinions* because *the women present* is not 'a fixed group'.
- Is this consistent with Jespersen's refusal to explain possible group genitives on the basis of units 'closely connected in meaning'? What alternative account of * *the women present's* would Kruisinga give? And Hornstein?
Sampson (1984:375) insists that the use of negative evidence, and of the * to indicate such evidence, is an innovation of NG (see section II.4).

- In what sense does Kruisinga (1932a:66) suggest that Sampson's views be modified?
5 SS&P (1973:674) include Poutsma (1929) in the Bibliography to their Chapter 11, on Genitives. This is one of the rare references of SS&P to OG (see section II.2). But in fact, Poutsma (1929) does not have any account of genitives at all; Poutsma's accounts are in (1914).
- What does SS&P's error with respect to Poutsma (1914/1929) suggest about continuity or juxtaposition between OG and NG?
- Would, or should, SS&P's account of group genitives have looked different if they had taken more seriously Poutsma's account, i.e. (1914) instead of (1929)?
6 Sweet (1891:319) makes the cogent suggestion that even if 's attaches to the head noun itself, rather than to a modifier, one may still have a group genitive. That is, in *the old king's son*, "we may regard the *-s* as inflecting not *king*, but the whole group *the-old-king*".
- What does Sweet's spelling with hyphens suggest about constituency, (groups of) words, or dependency, (just) words?
Consider now Poutsma's (1914:33) representation of Sweet's example as "the *old King's* son".
- What difference(s) between Sweet's and Poutsma's accounts of *the old King's son* becomes apparent here?
With respect to his example [8] Curme (1931:80) talks about "the group *king of England*" as well as "the group *the King of England*". Similarly, Kruisinga (1932a:39) hovers between the groups *the queens of England* and *queens of England*.
- Which of Curme's and Kruisinga's groups are similar to Sweet's, which to Poutsma's?
Finally, Hornstein (1977:54) analyses *the King of England* as in [v] (N for noun; cf. section D):

[v]

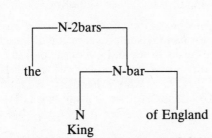

- In what way(s) does an analysis as in [v] (not) represent the insights about groups of Sweet, Poutsma, Curme, and/or Kruisinga? How does this reflect on the juxtaposition of OG and NG?

H is for *'hard to handle'*

Sentence [1] illustrates the point of Modern English grammar that is at issue in *A–Z*'s section H:

[1] Harry is hard to handle

A number of English adjectives like *hard* have a particular effect on a following infinitival construction: in [1] *to handle*. *Handle* by itself is a 'transitive verb', i.e. a verb which has to take a direct object; in [2] *handle* thus needs the direct object *the horse*:

[2a]   Harry has handled the horse skilfully
[2b] * Harry has handled   skilfully

However, in an infinitive that follows *hard*, the situation may be reversed: in [3] the direct object *the horse* is impossible:

[3a] * Harry is hard to handle the horse skilfully
[3b]   Harry is hard to handle   skilfully

The effect of *hard* on *handle* in [3] is reminiscent of the effect that passive forms (BE, *-ed* participle) have on *handle*:

[4a] * Harry was handled the horse skilfully
[4b]   Harry was handled   skilfully

In [4] the passive forms invert the effect of the active forms in [2]: now a direct object for *handle* is impossible. But although [1] and [3b] lack the passive forms of BE and *-ed* participle, like passives they also disallow a direct object: moreover, [1] and [3b] imply, as [4b] explicates, that it is *Harry* who 'is handled'. Adapting a term from Sweet (1891:116; 1898:120), we will say that in [1] and [3b] there is a 'passival' infinitive: passive in meaning, but active in form.

An adjective like *hard*, then, somehow allows a passival infinitive construction: a transitive verb like *handle* may appear without its otherwise obligatory object. More specifically, in [1] and [3b] *hard*

124

causes the direct object of the infinitive to be 'represented' elsewhere in the sentence, by *Harry*.

Consider now a sermon that Chomsky has preached, and that takes for its text a sentence like [1], viz. *John is easy to please:* with a passive infinitive *to please*, the object of transitive *please* being represented by *John*. For 'observational adequacy' read: coverage, i.e. the *open* approach; for 'descriptive adequacy' read: in accordance with an associated linguistic theory, i.e. the *narrow* approach:

> Suppose that ... sentences [like [1]] ... are observed ... A grammar that achieves ... observational adequacy would ... merely note this fact in one way or another ... To achieve ... descriptive adequacy, however, a grammar would have to assign structural descriptions indicating that *John* ... is the object of *please* [and *Harry* the object of *handle* in [1]] ... The transformational model does ... make grammars available that can achieve ... descriptive adequacy (Chomsky 1964:34)

In this section '*H* for *hard to handle*', we will follow Chomsky (1964) in looking for observational adequacy in OG: does OG cover *open*ly (= 'in one way or another') [1] and related facts about passival infinitives that Chomsky lists (brought together below as [5a–h])? And does NG juxtapose to OG in rather exploiting this point of Modern English grammar for descriptive adequacy which is *narrow* (= deductively 'make available'; vs. 'be available' in OG)?

In [5], *A–Z* summarizes Chomsky (1964). [5a] repeats [1] for convenience; [5b, c] illustrate the basic passival property of [5a], viz. that *Harry* represents what would otherwise be the object of *handle*; [5d, e] complicate [5a] by the addition of nominal *a ... man* to *hard*, or by the addition of *for* – subject to the passival infinitive *to handle* (cf. section f); [5f, g] show that *Harry* may not only represent a missing direct object in the infinitive, but also a complement of a preposition: *with (Harry)*, *by (Harry)*; [5g] also shows that in addition to being passival, the infinitive may be a straight passive in form, *be helped*; finally [5h] identifies possibilities in relative clauses: with *who is hard to handle* [5h] is a relative counterpart of [5a] with passival active infinitive, and with *who it is hard to handle* – with *it* – [5h] is a relative counterpart of [5c] with straight active infinitive.

[5a] Harry is hard to handle
[5b] to handle Harry is hard
[5c] it is hard to handle Harry
[5d] Harry is a hard man to handle

[5e] Harry is hard for us to handle
[5f] Harry is hard to haggle with
[5g] Harry is hard to be helped by
[5h] Harry is a human who (it) is hard to handle

H.1 On OG on *'hard to handle'*

'Observational adequacy' with respect to [5a–h] varies in OG. Table H.1 gives an initial survey: + means that the point in question is observed for *hard* itself, (+) indicates that the point is observed for another adjective like *hard*: Chomsky's (1964) *easy*, or *difficult*, etc.; for ½ see [6–10] and discussion below.

Table H.1 Coverage of 8 points from Chomsky (1964) for *hard* etc. in OG

	S	P	C	K	J	GCE	CGoEL
5a passival		+	+	+	+	+	+
5b active		+		(+)	(+)	+	+
5c active + *it*		+	½	(+)	(+)	+	+
5d + nominal					+		(+)
5e + *for*−subject		(+)	½				(+)
5f + preposition		(+)		+	(+)	(+)	(+)
5g passive + prep		½			½		
5h relatives		(+)		(+)	½		

Let us fill in some details of Table H.1. Firstly, [6–10] give examples with *hard*, + or ½, as they appear in individual OG grammars (to save space, (+) will not be exemplified extensively). Note that, but for OG's pioneer Sweet, all OG covers *A–Z*'s starting point, passival infinitives after *hard* [5a]. Sweet does not cover the points about *hard* at all. Nevertheless, Sweet (1891:116; 1898:119) pioneers OG by observing passival infinitives alongside genuinely passive ones: *the house is to let, the house is to be let*; cf. Poutsma and Jespersen on [5g].

[6] Poutsma (1926:364, 458)
 [a] the Gods are hard to reconcile
[e]/[b] to do this is especially hard for those who . . .
 [c] 't is hard to say, if greater want of skill appear in writing or in judging ill
 [g] she is harder to be understood [passive; no prep: ½]
 [i] poor Rebecca felt it hard to bear (beyond [5]: missing object of *bear* ≠ subject; = overt object of *felt*: *it*)

[7] Kruisinga (1932a:151)
    [a] whether the change ministers to ... comfort ... is hard to say
    [c] a more heinous offence against the State, short of actual treason, it is hard to imagine

[8] Curme (1931:191, 256)
    [a] the work is hard to translate
    [c] it was hard for me to understand him [ignore *for me*: ½]
    [e] it was hard for me to understand him [= 5c + *for*−subject: ½]

[9] Jespersen (1927:216–19)
    [a] the Gods are hard to reconcile [cf. [6a]]
    [d] the Boers are a hard nut to crack
    [f] those who are hardest to come at
    [g] things were hard to be distinguished [passive; no prep: ½]
    [h] those who are hardest to come at [but no cases with *it*: ½]
    [i] that made my position harder than ever to endure (beyond [5], like [6i]: missing object of *endure* ≠ subject; = overt object of *made*: *my position*)]

[10] *GCE* (1972:827), *CGoEL* (1985:1229)
    [a] he is hard to convince [1985: *he = Bob*]
    [b] to convince him is hard [1985: *him = Bob*]
    [c] it is hard to convince him [1985: *him = Bob*]

And now for some discussion. Poutsma (1926:363ff., 457ff.) discusses [5a–c] extensively for *difficult* rather than *hard*; he illustrates [5e] for *impossible* and [5f] again for *difficult*. With respect to [5h] Poutsma stands out among OG for his explicit statement that in relative clauses "The construction with ... *it* is ... the rule, that without ... *it* being, however, fairly common" (1926:365). Perhaps even more notably, Poutsma also extends Sweet's pioneering observation about passive infinitives alongside passival ones to *hard* in [6g]. Note that [6g] is thus only ½ of [5g]: in [5g] the infinitive is passive on top of being passival; in [6g] the infinitive is passive instead of passival. [6g] is thus an observation about infinitives after *hard* that extends beyond what Chomsky (1964) adduces. Similarly, in [5a] the *Harry* which represents the missing object of passival *to handle* is a subject; but Poutsma also illustrates in [6i] that the missing object may be represented by another (overt) object elsewhere. Again Poutsma's coverage here extends beyond Chomsky's 'observationally adequate' [5a–h].

Kruisinga's examples [7a, c] have a curious property: they both involve what Poutsma (1926:364–5) – but not Kruisinga himself – calls more or less exceptional cases of "Front position of the logical object of the infinitive ... when this object is represented by a lengthy word-group". Thus [7a] might be simplified to *this is hard to say*; and [7c] (which is also one of Poutsma's 'exceptional' examples!) to *it is hard to imagine this*. A similar complication adheres to Kruisinga's coverage of [5h]. Kruisinga (1932a:151–2) illustrates a relative clause with passival infinitive, i.e. without *it*, *which is not easy to make*; but he then claims that "In relative clauses ... front position of the object makes *it* obligatory": as if *which it is not easy to make* only is possible, but * *which is not easy to make*. Although Kruisinga effectively does cover both cases of [5h], the putatively 'obligatory *it*' somewhat detracts from his effective *open*ness.

Curme's [8] do not seem to require any comment. Jespersen's (1940:271ff.) elaborate illustration and discussion of [5a–c] is for *difficult* rather than *hard* – as in Poutsma. Generally, for Jespersen much the same applies as for Poutsma. He too extends his observations beyond Chomsky's 'adequate' [5a–h], additionally covering the genuine passive for the passival infinitive in [9g]; and an overt object, instead of subject, representing the missing object of a passival infinitive in [9i].

Finally, it is interesting to see an increase in 'observational adequacy' in Quirk *et al.* from *GCE* to *CGoEL*: [5d, e] are illustrated for *difficult* and *easy* (1985:1220, 1229). Moreover, *CGoEL* also comes closer to coverage as in Poutsma and Jespersen in going beyond Chomsky (1964) to observe the representation of a missing object by an overt object: *Mary finds the violin difficult to play* (1985:1220): missing object of passival *to play* = object of *finds*: *the violin*. If *CGoEL* is thus on its way to earning its title of being *Comprehensive*, it still does not match Poutsma or even Jespersen on [5g] and [5h]. On the other hand, *CGoEL* (1985:1229) distinguishes itself from other OG (but cf. *GCE* 1972:827 on *easy*) in making a negative observation in support of the interpretation of the infinitive after *hard* as passival, i.e. missing an object. Consider [11]; on * see section II.4:

[11a]   Mary arrives
[11b]   * Mary arrives Bob
[11c]   * Bob is hard to arrive

Just as *arrives* in [11a] cannot take a direct object *Bob* in [11b], so in [11c] *arrive* cannot appear as a passival infinitive after *hard* so that *Bob* would represent a missing object for *arrive*.

We may now sum up the 'observational adequacy' of OG with respect to '*H* is for *hard to handle*'. As a glance at Table H.1 shows, and as the subsequent discussion should confirm, coverage of [5] is adequately comprehensive in OG grammars together; and even in one individual OG grammar by itself: Poutsma's. Some OG grammars fall more or less dramatically short of observational adequacy, but other grammars extend their observations beyond [5]. Thus Poutsma especially, and Jespersen (two non-natives!), and next *CGoEL*, are the more comprehensive, more *open* grammars on this point. The question now arises, if OG is to be juxtaposed to NG, whether this is all? Does OG 'merely' provide comprehensive coverage without any 'descriptive adequacy'? The one case in which it seems that the answer is a plain 'yes' is Curme. In spite of his seemingly telling examples in [8], Curme nowhere describes the infinitive of [8a] as 'passival', with a missing object represented by *the work*. Recall that even Sweet (1891:116; 1898:119) indicates the point about passival infinitives, if not for those following *hard*.

Now consider other OG grammars that cover *hard to handle* more or less extensively. Poutsma (1929:457) describes carefully that a case like [6a] represents an "infinitive with passive meaning in the active voice", because [6a] is "felt to be a condensed form" of [6b, c]. In Kruisinga's (1932a:151) description, [7a] is one of the instances where "the subjects ... might also be considered as the objects of the [infinitive] verbs" (note the *narrow* limitation to 'subjects', vs. Poutsma's [6i], Jespersen's [9i], and *CGoEL*'s similar case with *difficult*); and for Kruisinga [7c] shows that the subject "would become object ... if we inserted *it*". Jespersen (1940:270–6) describes in extensive detail cases like [9a] where the infinitive is "retroactive", i.e. "referring back to a preceding item which is normally its object" (note 'preceding item' generally, rather than Kruisinga's 'subject' specifically). Jespersen even has a notation to indicate the passival nature of retroactive infinitives, as in [12]: S = subject, O = object, p = *to*, I = infinitive:

[12a] Harry is hard to handle (= [1, 5a])
[12b] S(O)*   p I*

The raised stars indicate that I takes O (I is active transitive *handle*), but that O is missing, being represented by S; I is passival. Finally Quirk *et al.* (1972:827; 1985:1229) also describe that in [10a] "the subject ... is ... the ... object of the infinitive", because [10b, c] are analogous constructions (note the *narrow* restriction once again to 'subject'; only 1985:1220 specifies beforehand that this restriction is "For illustrative purposes" only).

At this point it is crucial to note that even if OG thus quite generally describes the passival nature of infinitives like *to handle* after *hard* as in [5a], this does still not by itself amount to what Chomsky (1964) would call 'descriptive adequacy'. The point is that 'descriptive adequacy' depends on an associated linguistic theory which *narrow*ly "assigns" descriptions rather than leaving these descriptions to arise haphazardly, *open*ly "in one way or another" (1964:34). To take a case in point. Jespersen's notation gives an exact enough description in [12b] of what goes on in [12a]; and Jespersen would similarly represent [13a] as in [13b]. However, there is no theory to prevent Jespersen from an inadequate description of [13a] also as in [13c]:

[13a] that made my position harder to endure (cf. [9i])
[13b] S   O(O*)   p I*
[13c] S(O*)   O   p I*

Given *open* availability of [13c], description as in [13b] is quite sufficient for OG, but not 'descriptively adequate' for NG. Although this point does not become as perspicuously clear in the case of the more verbal, less formalized descriptions of *hard to handle* in OG other than Jespersen, the same distinction between accidental description and descriptive adequacy applies. In spite of a fair amount of description in OG, we find as *A–Z* expects that OG achieves observational adequacy, rather than descriptive adequacy as Chomsky (1964) sets these for '*H* is for *hard to handle*'.

H.2 On NG on '*hard to handle*'

The ability of adjectives like *hard* to allow passive infinitives to occur has been a constantly pertinent point of Modern English grammar in NG: ever "Since the origins of work in generative grammar, considerable attention has been given to such constructions" (Chomsky 1981: 308). For *hard to handle* we therefore do not have to go to NG literature beyond SS&P (1973), Emonds (1976), and – especially – Chomsky. Indeed *hard to handle* affords a notable view of the character of NG, as Chomsky proceeds to give (at least) four different accounts of this point. This is inherent to the deductive approach of NG: as the theory changes, to effectuate the *narrow* programme, earlier accounts of the same facts have to be revised so as yet again to be in *narrow* accordance with a current theory. In this particular case, the point is reinforced by the fact that Chomsky (1981) explores an account of *hard to handle* that approximates to the one that Chomsky (1964) relies on for adjectives which do *not* allow passive infinitives.

In fact, a prominent feature in NG is that accounts of *hard (to handle)* tend to be directed towards the contrast to *happy* in [14] ([1], [3a], and [11c] repeated for convenience):

[1]   Harry is hard to handle
[3a]   * Harry is hard to handle the horse skilfully
[11c] * Bob is hard to arrive
[14a] * Harry is happy to handle
[14b]   Harry is happy to handle the horse skilfully
[14c]   Bob is happy to arrive

Specifically, unlike *hard*, *happy* cannot be followed by a passival infinitive where an object is missing, [14a]; but conversely, *happy* can be followed by a straight transitive infinitive, with object present, [14b]; or by an intransitive infinitive, [14c]. Cases like *hard* vs. *happy* are already "famous examples" for SS&P (1973: 579).

But the first – and since most famous – such pair to be discussed in NG is Chomsky's (1964:34–5, 60–1) *easy* vs. *eager*, with the same set of properties: for an account, Chomsky refers to Miller and Chomsky (1963:476–80). There the basic idea is that *happy to handle Harry* is a single unit, 'Adj'; whereas *hard to handle Harry* are two separate units: 'Adj' *hard*, and infinitive *to handle Harry*. Then the transformational model of NG makes available an account by which *Harry* may come to be missing from an infinitive and be represented elsewhere because *Harry* may be 'moved' by a transformation; but such a movement of *Harry* is under a *narrow* condition that it does *not* take place out of an 'Adj'. Cf. [15], where the position to which *Harry* may (not) move, ... , corresponds to *it* in [5c]:

[15a]

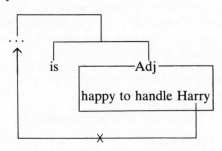

[15b]

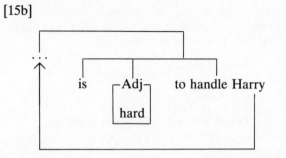

The point about [15b] for Chomsky (1964:34) is that in a transformational model such an account is made available and hence
descriptively adequate: *(it) is hard to handle Harry* is transformed
into *Harry is hard to handle*; the *narrow* feature consists of the
built-in condition that *to handle Harry* not be part of 'Adj'.

SS&P (1973:579–80) and Emonds (1976:77–8) essentially take
over the account of [15b] for [16] – which represents "adjectives
like *easy, difficult, hard, . . .* " – and [17] respectively:

[16a] John is easy to please
[16c] it is easy to please John
[17c] it is hard to lift John onto the horse
[17f] the horse is hard to lift John onto

For SS&P, [16c] is transformed into [16a] by [15b] as 'object-to-
subject raising'; for Emonds by transformation [15b] there is
'subject replacement by object raising' in [17f] from out of the
infinitive of [17c]. In both cases note the – in NG duly – *narrow*
restriction to subjects for items representing the missing objects,
counter to OG observations like [6i, 9i]. Otherwise, the more
notable *narrow* account is here perhaps Emonds' (cf. section 3.3).
In particular, Emonds points out the *narrow* property of [15b] that
it accords with his theory of structure preservation: replacement of
the nominal subject *it* in [17c] by the nominal object *the horse* in
[17f] preserves the subject as a nominal structure. Thus, "The
value of the [structure preserving] constraint is that it explains . . .
why English does not have" [18a]:

[18a] * it has this task been easy to finish
[18b]   it has   been easy to finish this task

[18a] would be transformed from [18b] by putting the nominal *this
task* into a new position: since this changes the structure in a way
that [17f] does not, [18a] must be *.

On the other hand, Emonds is careful not to commit himself firmly to subject replacement as the NG account of *hard to handle*: for Emonds it is sufficient that *if* the account is by subject replacement, then structure preservation would distinguish between [17, 18]. The fact is that by 1976 the effectuation of *narrow* NG has already begun to affect the account of *hard to handle* in [15b], specifically in Chomsky's own work. The details of Chomsky's reasons for progressing, from one NG account of *hard to handle* to another, duly deduce *narrow*ly from the current overall NG theories – and are thus inevitably quite complex. The reader may want to go to the originals for the full stories. Here we will rather drastically (over-)simplify. However, the simplifications are intended to be true to the originals in that they convey something of the sense in which the series of Chomsky's accounts represents a steady increase in effective *narrow*ness.

Recall, then, firstly that the *narrow* property of [15b] is intended to be that movement out of infinitives is restricted, to infinitives *not* part of 'Adj'. Chomsky's subsequent accounts of *hard to handle* further restrict movement out of *any* infinitive, irrespective of 'Adj'. One *narrow* approach is to allow movement out of an infinitive only from its subject position as in [19] (on *for* cf. section f):

[19a]   it   would be unwise for Harry to marry Sue
[19b]   Harry would be unwise   to marry Sue
[19c] * Sue   would be unwise for Harry to marry

Chomsky (1973:264) assimilates *hard to handle* to [19] by allowing *Harry* first to move *within* the infinitive, to the subject position; and only then to move *out of* the infinitive, from the subject position. A rough indication of such an account is given in [20]; note that [20] is *narrow* because of the abstract intermediate structure [20b], which transforms into [20c] as [19a] into [19b]:

[20a] ...   is hard ...   to handle Harry
[20b] ...   is hard Harry to handle
[20c] Harry is hard   to handle

Although [20] is more *narrow* than *open* movement from anywhere out of an infinitive, the question now arises whether the movement within the infinitive that it presupposes should still be *open*. Such movement is excluded elsewhere (unless there are passive forms; cf. [4b]); e.g. [21b]:

[21a]   Harry handled the horse
[21b] * the horse handled

A next step would thus be an account which is yet more *narrow* by excluding movement to the subject position everywhere, also in infinitives as from [20a] to [20b]. Now there is a possibility, in infinitives *and* more generally, for movement of *wh*-items (cf. also section f):

[22a] the decision   to make an appointment
[22b] the decision what to make

Moreover, in some cases a *wh*-item may be dropped, leaving an apparently passival infinitive with missing object:

[23a] the decision [to make the decision]
[23b] the decision [which to make]
[23c] the decision   to make

Adapting [22, 23] to *hard to handle*, Chomsky's (1977:103) account therefore looks essentially as in [24]:

[24a] Harry is hard   to handle Harry
[24b] Harry is hard who to handle
[24c] Harry is hard   to handle

Note that there is now no longer any movement out of the infinitive; but only *narrow*ly within the infinitive the quite general transformation of *wh*-movement.

If [15b, 20, 24] thus represent increasingly *narrow* accounts of *hard to handle*, the ultimate step would be not to allow any movements, either out of or even within an infinitive, at all. This is a step that Chomsky (1981:312) indeed explores. The idea then is that *hard to handle* is a "complex adjective", roughly the 'Adj' of 1964 in [15a], except that *Harry* is not part of the adjective. The account of passival *hard to handle* then becomes something like [25], notably parallel to [26] as the contemporary analysis of genuine passives:

[25a] ...   is [$_{Adj}$ hard to handle] Harry
[25b] Harry is   hard to handle
[26a] ...   is [$_{Adj}$ handled] Harry skilfully
[26b] Harry is   handled   skilfully

H.3 Conclusions

OG and NG clearly juxtapose in their approaches to *hard to handle*. OG has been seen to pursue and attain its essential goal, Chomsky's (1964) observational adequacy. Any amount of description in OG still leaves the account of *hard to handle* fundamentally *open* so that descriptive adequacy is not really to the point. On the

other hand, for NG, observational adequacy is no real consideration. In simplifying NG to the succession of [15b, 20, 24, 25]
in section H.2, one ignores a wide array of observations about
hard to handle which are pertinent to Chomsky's more subtle
arguments for the various accounts that he considers. But this
is appropriate since what is truly representative for NG is the
fate of the single observation about *hard to handle*, its passival
character, in work spanning some twenty years: Chomsky (1964;
1973; 1977; 1981). In OG this would be mere repetitiveness,
since there is no contribution to observational adequacy – no
increased coverage. In NG, it is essential that the same observation return again and again, as long as the theory changes in
effectuating *narrow*ness: with every change, the account of *hard
to handle* has to be redesigned to maintain (if not to increase)
descriptive adequacy – to accord again with the current version
of the theory.

H.4 Discussion and extensions

1 Jespersen (1927:217) and (1940:270) both cite [9d], but each
   from a putatively different source. The latter source is identified by
   Jespersen (1949:13) as page 548 of a 1925 edition of Galsworthy's
   Forsyte Saga; the former source is left unidentifiable.
● If Jespersen's (1927:217) source for [9d] is erroneous, and
   (1940:270) is correct, does this make a difference for Jespersen's
   'observational adequacy'?
2 Consider the instances with *difficult* in [i] from Poutsma
   (1928:142):

   [ia] it is difficult to describe this adequately
   [ib] this it is difficult to describe adequately
   [ic] to describe this adequately is difficult
   [id] this is difficult to describe adequately

● Which of [ia–d] contain(s) (a) passival infinitive(s)?
● Poutsma discusses [ia–d] as "variations". Does this make for
   observational adequacy, description, and/or descriptive
   adequacy? Why?
● One may wonder whether [i] is an arbitrary choice, or also reports Poutsma's experience: 'difficult to describe adequately'.
   Indeed, according to Chomsky OG cannot attain 'descriptive
   adequacy': why not?
   Cases like [ib] are prominent in Kruisinga (cf. [7c]), exceptional in Poutsma, and apparently absent from both Jespersen
   and NG.

- Which OG grammarian is thus the more similar to NG, if any? Why (none)?
3 Consider [7c, a] from the main text and/or [ib, d] above. Since Kruisinga's observations about *hard to handle* involve such alternations, the description of *hard to handle* amounts to mere presence or absence of *it*.
- What essential property of all NG accounts considered in section H.2 does Kruisinga's account thus avoid? Does this make Kruisinga's account more *narrow* than NG? Why (not)?
- Would Kruisinga's account be 'structure preserving' as in Emonds' theory, if it was transferred to NG as *it*-insertion or as *it*-deletion?
4 Chomsky (1977:105) presents the instances of [ii]:

> [iia] the sonata is easy to play   on this violin
> [iib] the violin is easy to play sonatas on

- Indicate which of [iia–b] contain(s) (a) passival infinitive(s). There appear to be no observations in OG about alternations as in [ii]; cf. [iii] from Poutsma (1926:364):

> [iii] it is never easy to evoke an age with a single figure

An observation similar to [ii] is intimated, but not spelled out for [17] by Emonds (1976:77).
- What would the alternatives like [ii] be for [iii], and for [17]?
- What would the non-appearance of such alternatives imply for observational and/or descriptive adequacy in Poutsma; or in Emonds?

i is for *if not*

For miniscule section i of *A–Z*, a point of Modern English is put forward by Meijs (1984). Consider sentences as in [1]:

[1] he takes a narrow if not Chomskyan view

Out of context, it seems that *if not* in [1] is amenable to opposite interpretations: a 'downtoning' one as in [2], or an 'intensifying' one as in [3]:

[2] he takes a narrow, but not quite Chomskyan, view
[3] he takes a narrow, or perhaps even a Chomskyan, view

Beyond the volatility of *if not* itself, Meijs finds it "intriguing ... that apparently neither the ... [OG] grammarians – Jespersen, Poutsma, Kruisinga, Quirk *et al.* – nor dictionaries ... shed any light on the ambiguity of *if not*" (1984:93). A culpable failure to cover volatile *if not* would go straight to the heart of OG. In fact, Meijs (1984:92) points to an inherent problem for an *open* approach to grammar pursuing induction: the aim of comprehensive coverage leads to a "quest for primary data"; in which, however, "traditional grammarians ... basically ... had no choice but to wait and see what happened to come their way and attract their attention in the source materials". If OG covers available evidence comprehensively, there is still no guarantee that the evidence has been comprehensively available. In this section, *A–Z* will look to OG and NG for directions through Meijs' (1984:97) "*terra incognita*" of volatile *if not*: for *if not*, is '*i* really for *incognita*'; or perhaps for 'intractable', because of its volatility?

i.1 On OG on *if not*

Does OG indeed have a blind spot for volatile *if not*? Up to a point, Meijs (1984) is right, and the answer is basically 'yes'. There is simply no such *if not* in Sweet, Poutsma, Kruisinga, or *GCE* (on

CGoEL see section i.3 below). In Poutsma (1929:707), however, there is at least one similar case, with *if* if not with *if not*: would [4] be 'no better, but at least as well', or 'no better, not even as well'?

[4] we shall do no better, if as well, as in January

But Poutsma himself does not recognize any such uncertainty. Nor does Curme in the relatively many instances of *if not* that he has (1931:66, 339–40):

[5a] one of the finest poems . . ., if not the finest
[5b] one of the most spacious, if not the most spacious, of salons

Notably, Curme does not distinguish these from examples with *if* like Poutsma's, e.g. [6]:

[6] a . . . keen, if narrow, insight into affairs.

Again like Poutsma, Curme lets [5, 6] pass by without any comment on volatility. The only case in OG where one might want to recognize a hint at volatility is Jespersen (1940:379). Jespersen has examples of *if not* like [7]:

[7a] one word more shall make me chide thee, if not hate thee
[7b] an irregular, if not dissipated life

To these Jespersen adds the comment that "To introduce an incomplete clause . . . *if* [not *if not*!] very often approaches the meaning of 'even if, though' or 'though perhaps a little'". The point here is Jespersen's *or*: does it restate (cf. 'twelve or a dozen') or does it present an alternative (cf. 'twelve or thirteen')? If the latter, Jespersen would be on to volatility: is [6b] downtoning 'an irregular, though not dissipated life'; or intensifying 'an irregular, though perhaps a little dissipated life'? But one cannot really be certain that this is the interpretation that Jespersen intends. And in any case, Jespersen talks about *if* rather than *if not*.

If OG gives scant, if any, recognition to ambiguity of *if not*, should it give more? Recall that Meijs (1984:93) also expects dictionaries to note the volatility (and they apparently fail as well): OG might be excused if the volatility of *if not* is not necessarily a point of Modern English *grammar*. Note that Jespersen's *MEG* 'on historical principles' is an explicit reference to the largest English dictionary, *OED*: also subtitled 'on historical principles'.

Besides dictionaries, one may also look beyond *A–Z*'s OG grammars in English to for instance Krüger's massive grammar of Modern English in German. Krüger (1917:1664, 1687) has quite some examples of *if not* (interspersed with just *if*):

[8a] a keen, if not lasting, interest
[8b] the statues, if not good, are tolerable
[8c] in comfortable, if not flourishing, circumstances
[8d] excellent, if not abundant, fruit

All the more notably, Krüger holds that in [8c], *if* means "wenn auch" ('though'), rather than "wenn (sogar)" ('even'). That is, there would *not* be volatility: [8c] only conveys downtoning 'comfortable, though not flourishing'; the intensifying 'comfortable, even flourishing' Krüger reserves for [9], with an explicit *even*:

[9] comfortable, if not even flourishing, circumstances

There are references to Krüger (1914) in Poutsma (1929:832); to Krüger (1897ff.) in Jespersen (1931:xxi; 1949:20); and not surprisingly the Professor of German Curme (1931:v) refers to Krüger's entire work, including (1917). Correspondingly, Curme is relatively extensive among OG on *if not*, like Krüger; one wonders whether the more general trend in OG may be due to Krüger declaring volatility of *if not* 'forbidden country' rather than *terra incognita*: intractable in grammar – and reserved for the dictionary.

i.2 On NG on *if not*

As far as has been possible to ascertain, there is apparently just one (!) attempt to account for *if not* by NG; a transformational account in Kjellmer (1975). Kjellmer (1975:142) discusses a "proviso" and a "provision": the appropriately *narrow* conditions that should be imposed in NG on a transformational account of *if not* by "deletion of identical elements"; roughly as in [10], identical elements italicized in [10b] and deleted in [10c]:

[10a] he takes a narrow approach to grammar if he takes not a
        Chomskyan approach to grammar
[10b] he takes a narrow *approach to grammar* if *he takes* not *a*
        Chomskyan approach to grammar
[10c] he takes a narrow   if   not
        Chomskyan approach to grammar

Kjellmer (1975:143ff.) then goes on to discuss the volatility of *if not*, which for him notably appears from appearance of an additional *even* in two different positions (1975:145; cf. Krüger 1917): downtoning [11a] and intensifying [11b] respectively:

[11a] a narrow *even* if not Chomskyan approach to grammar
[11b] a narrow if not *even* Chomskyan approach to grammar

Given the nature of NG, however, it still appears that Kjellmer's account of the volatility of *if not* effectively leaves it grammatically unknown ground. That is, by effectively *narrow* NG, ambiguity of *if not* should now follow from an account in which differently positioned *even*'s are indiscriminately taken along in the transformation of deletion: both <u>even</u> *if not* and *if not* <u>even</u> leaving volatile *if not*. If the essential *narrow* restriction on Kjellmer's deletion is to deletion of *identical* elements, however, the *even*'s in [12] *cannot* be indiscriminately deleted, because they are *not* identical to anything else in [12a] and [12b] respectively:

[12a]   he takes a narrow *approach to grammar* even if *he takes* not *a* Chomskyan approach to grammar

[12b]   he takes a narrow *approach to grammar* if *he takes* not even *a* Chomskyan approach to grammar

In this way, from [12] Kjellmer's account only really extends to either [11a] or [11b]; but not to the purported ambiguity of [10c]. As it stands, volatile *if not* does not appear to be pertinent to *narrow* NG – and as such the ambiguity of *if not* might again be tractable in a dictionary, rather than in NG grammar.

i.3 Conclusions

If the volatility of *if not* is to be left to the dictionaries, OG is absolved of culpability: since Curme and Jespersen at least cover some instances of Meijs' *if not*, grammatical coverage is comprehensive in OG at large; and otherwise OG properly prefers (here) not to encroach on the dictionary. On the basis of this miniscule section of *A–Z*, the reader may now want to juxtapose OG and NG. If Curme and Jespersen in OG are to be exonerated, is it impertinent for Kjellmer (1975) to bring *narrow* NG and the ambiguity of *if not* together as he claims to do? It may at least be noted that Quirk *et al.* (1985:1146, 1654) refer to Kjellmer (1975), but still do not discuss [13] (1985:982) as volatile:

[13]   her manner was unwelcoming if not downright rude

A lot also depends on how seriously one should take Kjellmer as NG in the first place: his "*If* we adopt a transformational outlook" (1975:142; emphasis added) hardly suggests a firm, effective commitment to a *narrow* approach. Thus it is no surprise that Kjellmer's account of *if not* is in effect a new, extended version of Krüger's older account: both are essentially usurping the domain of the dictionary, rather than involved in pursuing juxtaposed NG and OG, respectively.

j is for Jespersen's junction

The alphabetical organization adopted in *A–Z* to avoid extreme biases is at the same time a strait-jacket for certain letters especially, for which few if any interesting points of Modern English grammar can readily be found. This applies for instance to *j*. *J* might have been used for *jury* ('the jury *has*/*have* returned') or for *just* (= 'only a short time ago'; still, *I have just arrived* vs. * *I have arrived only a short time ago*); but these are likely to remain somewhat feeble. In section w for *whom* for *who*, Jespersen's notion of 'primaries' plays a prominent role. Since 'primaries' are tied up with Jespersen's notion of 'junction', it seems just as well to devote a miniscule section *j* to 'Jespersen's junction'.

The point about junction is, once again, closely related to dependency. In section D (cf. also section G) it has been seen that Jespersen consistently exceeds a dependency-like *narrow* limitation to just words if comprehensiveness requires this. However, Jespersen's notion of junction ensures that – if no *narrow* consequences ensue – Jespersen talks in terms of words rather than groups of words.

Consider for instance *fat cattle*. This is a junction because a more important word is linked to a less important word: *cattle* ranks above *fat*. Accordingly, Jespersen assigns 'primary' rank to *cattle*, '1'; and 'secondary' rank to *fat*, '2'. Junction is then a combination of words of descending ranks: *fat cattle* = 2 1 = junction. Similarly, *very* is again one rank lower than *fat* in *very fat cattle*: 3 2 1, another junction. The point now is that in dependency fashion, Jespersen does not recognize *two* junctions here: *very fat* = 3 2; *very-fat cattle* = 2 1. Put differently, Jespersen is content to see the *word very* as a modifier of the *word fat*, and the *word fat* in turn as a modifier of the *word cattle* – as in dependency; whereas constituency would rather take the *group of words very fat* as a modifier of *cattle*.

Once again it is essential to recall from section D that the dependency element in Jespersen's junction is *not* an inviolable *narrow* restriction. For instance, Jespersen (1936/1969:110) describes the junction *not particularly well constructed plot*: 5 4 3 2 1; where "*constructed* qualifies *plot*" (instead of the group of words *not particularly well constructed* qualifying *plot*), "*well* qualifies *constructed*" (rather than the group of words *not particularly well* qualifying *constructed*), and so on. However, Jespersen (1936/1969:111) then instantly allows *certainly* in *certainly not very cleverly worded remark* to qualify the group of words *not very cleverly worded*, as in constituency: 3 2 (=5 4 3 2) 1, where '2(... 2)' does not descend in rank and thus goes beyond junction. What this section will nevertheless look for is Jespersen's junction, dependency in practice if not in principle, in OG and in NG.

j.1 On OG on Jespersen's junction

Let us first ascertain why dependency practice might be exercised even in an *open* approach such as OG. The reason probably is just terminological economy. That is, in a constituency approach, one would have to use the fairly laborious locution 'word or group of words' over and over again: *cattle* may be modified by a word, *fat*, or by a group of words, *very fat*, etc. Jespersen's junction allows one to simply say once and for all that *cattle* may be modified by a word like *fat* – and elsewhere again once and for all that *fat* in turn may be modified by a word like *very*. Along these lines, in OG Quirk *et al.* (1985:416–17) expressly state that they talk about adjectives – words – "For the sake of simplicity ... where, strictly speaking, we should refer ... to 'adjective phrase'". 'Strictly speaking' is against the *open* spirit of OG, and OG will prefer 'simplicity'. Although such an explicit appeal to economy is innovatory in OG (it even does not yet appear in Quirk *et al.* (1972)), still economy would also explain the appearance of Jespersen's junction in earlier OG, without explicit justification.

So let us see then whether Jespersen's junction does thus appear in OG. In the following excerpts capitalization is *A–Z*'s. Sweet (1891:16) states that "in *he is very strong, strong* is ... head-WORD to the adjunct-WORD *very*, which, again, may itself be a head-WORD, as in *he is not very strong*"; i.e. *not very strong* = 3 2 1, a junction. Similarly in Poutsma: "the adjective ... before its head-WORD ... modified by an adverbial adjunct ... as in *notoriously unstable support*" (1928:501), i.e. *notoriously unstable support* = 3 2 1, a junction (generally, Poutsma seems prepared to use the more verbose constituency terminology, e.g "word(-groups)",

1928:481). Curme (1931:62) refers explicitly to "Jespersen's influence" for a description of *exceedingly prompt action* as 3 2 1, a junction. Kruisinga, who devotes a large part of his *Handbook* to word-groups alongside words (1932b:177–261), appears to have consistently avoided anything like Jespersen's junction, even for terminological convenience. Finally, both *GCE* and *CGoEL* also judiciously circumvent the dependency implications of Jespersen's junction by illustrating with words rather than word-groups when they avail themselves of terminological economy, either implicitly (1972) or explicitly (1985:416–417).

The preceding survey of junction in OG – Sweet, Poutsma, Curme – passed over Jespersen's *MEG*. Since junction is Jespersen's own 'invention', there is abundant evidence of it in *MEG*: from Volume II's *very good wine* = III II I (1914:2–3) up to and including Volume VII's *not particularly well expressed thought* = 5 4 3 2 1 (1949:54). The more important cases here are, of course, those where Jespersen in fact goes *beyond* his own junction, in truly *open* fashion. For instance, Jespersen's discussion of *high good humour* again already in Volume II (1914:363), is represented as "21(21)" in (1936/1969:9), i.e. constituency: *high* modifies the word-GROUP *good humour*.

j.2 On NG on Jespersen's junction

If we now turn to NG, the point about terminological economy by junction does not really apply here. Since NG may restrict itself to what is pertinent on any occasion, words may be pertinent in one case, groups of words in another. For NG the point is of course again to effectively *narrow* accounts. If in the one case *cattle* may be modified by a word, the adjective *fat*, and in another case by a group of words, the adjective phrase *very fat*, then the way seems *open* for *cattle* to be modified by an arbitrary collection of things. Instead, NG once again relies on constituency 'behind bars' (see sections D, G) to *narrow* this range. That is, by the X-bar Convention of NG, for every word x there is a group of words X-bar. NG can therefore economically, but crucially *narrow*ly, say that *cattle* can only be modified by a group of words A-bar: under the X-bar Convention, the group of words A-bar may then be *very fat* or just *fat*, as long as the head word *A* is minimally present. Thus whereas Jespersen's junction allows economy by saying that in both *fat cattle* and *very fat cattle*, *cattle* as 1 is equally modified by just the word *fat* as 2, so constituency 'behind bars' allows NG to say that in both *fat cattle* and *very fat cattle*, *cattle* is equally modified by the group of words (*very*) *fat* as A-bar.

Single word word-groups are accordingly widely found throughout NG. Three examples will here suffice. In SS&P (1973:22) *students* is a word-group N-bar. For Emonds (1976:23) single proper nouns, pronouns, and lexical verbs are all phrases: *John* is NP (not just N), *she* is NP (not just pronoun), *eat* is VP (not just V), etc. And in Chomsky (1981:134), for instance, *stupid* is a word-group AP. However, given a *narrow* commitment to the principle of constituency 'behind bars', even NG will occasionally revert to economy by dependency-inspired terminology, apparently much like Quirk *et al.* (1985:416–17) for the sake of simplicity. Thus Emonds (1976:58) calls the same item *sensible* alternatively an AP (word-group; constituency 'behind bars') and an adjective (word; dependency).

j.3 Conclusions

If anywhere in *A–Z*, then in this section *j* should be for 'juxtaposition'. The readers may constitute the jury which decides (who decide) whether this juxtaposition has 'just' been shown even in so miniscule a section. We submit that it has. Terminologically, OG's economy tends to be by dependency: junction; NG's by constituency. More fundamentally, whereas OG does not *narrow* itself to single word junctions, this juxtaposes to NG which does *narrow*ly commit itself to the single word word-groups of constituency 'behind bars'.

K is for kataphoric *the*

There are relatively few words with initial *k* in English; none of these is readily associated with a point of Modern English grammar that will serve the purposes of *A–Z*. However, *k* can still be pressed into service for the point indicated in sentences [1, 2]:

[1]   I want to tell you about the boy
[2a] I want to tell you about the boy who lives next door
[2b] I want to tell you about the boy from upstairs
[2c] I want to tell you about the red-haired boy

Unless one imagines an elaborate context, [1] in isolation is an odd sentence, in particular as compared to those of [2]: somehow, the appearance of the definite article *the* is not quite natural in [1] (cf. '... a boy '); but *the* is unproblematic in each of [2a–c]. Apparently, *the* can be supported via material which follows *the*, and which lacks in [1]: *who lives next door* in [2a], *from upstairs* in [2b], *red-haired* in [2c].

Quirk *et al.* (1972:155) adopt for cases like *the* as in [2] the term 'cataphoric'. *Cataphoric* is derived from two Greek elements: *kata-* means something like 'down', i.e. 'further along (in the sentence)'; *-phoric* means 'bringing' or 'pointing'. The term cataphoric for 'pointing forwards' is not particularly well-established in English (it has apparently been coined in analogy with 'anaphoric', a term more generally used for 'pointing up', i.e. referring backwards); the authoritative dictionary *OED* only lists *cataphoric* in its *Supplement*, and refers to *kataphoric*, with a *k*. Hence *A–Z* will – somewhat deviously – use *K* for 'kataphoric'. There are various items that may be used kataphorically in English; but in section K we want to establish in particular to what extents OG and NG treat as a point of Modern English grammar the kataphoric property of *the*: the ability of *the* to refer forward, to anticipate later material, as illustrated in [2].

K.1 On OG on kataphoric *the*

Sweet (1898:55) initially recognizes a "purely grammatical function" for *the*, in which it is used "to refer back"; i.e. the anaphoric counterpart of kataphoric *the*. But Sweet (1898:57) then goes on to discuss [3]:

[3a] the man who was here yesterday (cf. [2a])
[3b] the front door, the hall door
[3c] the old horse (cf. [2c])

If in the case of [3c] "the speaker has two horses, and . . . adds *old* to show which of the two he means . . . [then] the article and the adjective share the function of identifying between them". For Sweet, therefore, only one of the functions of *the* is 'purely grammatical', viz. to refer backwards; the kataphoric function of *the* – to refer forward in the sense of sharing a function with material that follows – is thus *not* 'purely grammatical'. As such Sweet's account of *the* is not grammatically entirely *open* to kataphoric *the*; although it still covers [2a, c], as well as *the* anticipating kataphorically on a noun-modifier, *front* or *hall* in [3b].

In Poutsma's (1914:518) account of *the* there is also a gradation of functions. There is a "primary function of marking off or defining". But also, "the definite article has the secondary power of denoting . . . that the thing(s) we are speaking of, is (are) individualized or specialized . . . by (a) word(s) used for the purpose". This secondary function of *the* amounts to its kataphoric one. Consider [4]:

[4] the wine which he drank was sour (cf. [2a])

For Poutsma in [4] *which he drank* are specializing or individualizing words; and *the* refers forward in denoting their anticipated appearance. Interestingly, although the kataphoric function of *the* is thus made out to be only 'secondary', Poutsma still appears to assimilate to kataphoric *the* the cases where *the* seemingly – and for Sweet purely grammatically – rather refers back; as in [5]:

[5] I plucked a flower; this is *the* flower

In [5] *the* may seem to refer back to *a flower*; but for Poutsma, this *the* effectively refers forward, viz. to implied specifying or individualizing words: "i.e. 'the flower *that I plucked*'". In addition to kataphoric *the* anticipating clauses, [4a], Poutsma (1914:532–6) also acknowledges cases where kataphoric *the* denotes a subsequent prepositional word-group as in [2b], or adjective as in [2c]; as well as noun-modifiers, as in [3b].

Kruisinga assigns to the definite article *the* an – at times somewhat bewildering – variety of functions. Firstly, *the* may be used "deictically ... and anaphorically" (1932a:239). Anaphoric duly means referring backwards, "to a preceding mention of the idea" (1932a:147). For deictic functions, Kruisinga then lists four different possibilities, of which 'anticipatory' seems the one that would cover kataphoric. However, Kruisinga goes on to give examples like [2a] such as [6], where *the* is said to be 'determinative' (1932a:241), rather than anticipatory:

[6] the creatures who are excited by ... excitement (cf. [2a])

On top of this, Kruisinga (1932a:242) then declares that for *the* "the preceding ... functions [anticipatory, determinative] are not its essential and characteristic functions". The 'essential and characteristic' functions of *the* do however include the 'defining' one – and, "All nouns take the defining article when they are made definite by an adjunct or clause". Clauses that make nouns take the defining article are like [2a] and, again, [6]; adjuncts are illustrated by prepositional groups as in [2b], but may fairly be assumed to include also adjectives like [2c], etc. In terms of anticipatory, determinative, and/or defining functions, Kruisinga thus has an *open* range of accounts for kataphoric *the*.

For Curme (1931:511), *the* "has a twofold function: anaphoric *the*, pointing backward ... ; determinative *the*, pointing to a definite person or thing, described usually by a following genitive, adverb, prepositional phrase [like [2b]] or relative clause [like [2a]]". Note that Curme's 'usually' denies any inherent relation between *the* and following material. It would therefore not be appropriate to equate Curme's determinative entirely with kataphoric. Determinative *the* points in general; it does not specifically point forward. In comparison to other OG, Curme's account of *the* and material following it seems to be by a looser, more indirect association – a more *open* one – than kataphoric suggests. Indeed, Curme's adverb – e.g. *yonder* in [7] – does not appear elsewhere in OG for *the* to refer forward to (Curme's 'genitives', with *of*, do; as prepositional groups):

[7] the tree yonder

The authoritative treatment of *the* by Jespersen is not to be found in what *A–Z* takes to be his OG grammar, *MEG*. Jespersen died in 1943; the (last) volume of *MEG*, in which *the* is dealt with, appeared posthumously in 1949. Apart from a plan that Jespersen dictated, the sections on *the* were finished more or less independently by Niels Haislund. Interestingly, Haislund takes a *narrow* interpretation of Jespersen's plan. Haislund calls the plan a "theory" (1949:417); and he undertakes to treat *the* deductively "according to a theory". In all, Haislund's account is one in accordance with a theory, much as in NG. In effect, the theory is so *narrow* as to leave no place whatever for anything like kataphoric *the* in *MEG* (cf. section K.4 3 below on Hawkins 1978:13).

By contrast to Jespersen's plan/Haislund's theory, Haislund also refers to "only ... a fairly traditional exposition" in Jespersen (1933). Whether 'traditional' or not, Jespersen's (1933) authentic exposition is much more *open* than Haislund's would-be Jespersenian theory; specifically as regards kataphoric *the*. "*The* ... has really two distinct functions, that of determining in itself, and that of determining in connexion with a following word or words containing the essential specification. We therefore speak of the article of complete, and the article of incomplete determination" (1933:161). As the article of incomplete determination has a connection with (a) following word(s), it refers forward and amounts to kataphoric *the*. And indeed, Jespersen (1933:169) elaborates accordingly on the article of incomplete determination: "Under this category may be reckoned all combinations in which the substantive has an adjective [like [2c]] ... The clearest instances are, however, found when the supplementary determination follows after the substantive, thus with a prepositional group [like [2b]] and with a relative clause [like [2a]]". Where kataphoric *the* fails to become pertinent to Haislund's *narrow* interpretation of Jespersen's plan as a theory in *MEG* VII (1949), Jespersen's genuinely own exposition in (1933) is more truly OG in being systematically *open* to kataphoric *the*.

Finally in OG, Quirk *et al.* are the ones who actually use the term cataphoric (with initial *c*). *GCE* restricts the phenomenon to [2a, b]: "The cataphoric determiner [*the*] has forward reference to a postmodifying prepositional phrase [[2b]] or relative clause [[2a]]" (1972:155). *CGoEL* is more *open*ly comprehensive and adds [2c], even if somewhat reluctantly. "In practice ... the cataphoric use of the definite article is limited to ... postmodifiers [as in *GCE*: [2a, b]] ... In principle, however, there is no difference between postmodification and premodification [[2c]]" (1985:268). There is a curious inversion here; 'practice' – presumably the available evidence – is made out to be 'limited': more *narrow* than 'principle' – the more theoretical view of what kataphoric *the* can refer forward to.

K.2 On NG on kataphoric *the*

From OG accounts of kataphoric *the* in section K.1 it appears that *the* and the following material may 'share a function' (Sweet); that there is a 'connection' between them (Jespersen); and so on. This is particularly the case when *the* and the material to which kataphoric *the* refers forward are at some distance from each other, as in [2a, b]: these are the 'clearest instances' (Jespersen), or the ones to which kataphoric *the* is 'limited in practice' (*CGoEL*). It is precisely the tendency towards discontinuity between *the* and following material that appears to be pertinent to NG. Probably the most immediate way to achieve a *narrow* account of shared functions/connections/... would be to restrict these to items which are immediately next to one another. If there is some connection between k (say kataphoric *the*) and c (say a clause), then an account of $[k \ldots c]$ leaves *open* what the dots '...' can and cannot stand for. In $[\ldots k \ c]$ (or $[k \ c \ldots]$) this question does not thus arise, and the account of a connection between adjacent k and c can be more easily a *narrow* one. Only, k and c then need to be put asunder, by a 'transformation': $[k \ c \ldots] \Rightarrow [k \ldots c]$. Indeed, 'discontinuities' as in $[k \ldots c]$ are among the fundamental reasons for adopting transformational grammar as the first version of NG: cf. Chomsky (1957:41).

It is therefore to be expected that early, transformational NG at least will account for kataphoric *the* and following material first *narrow*ly next to one another; and only then separated transformationally. Quite generally, the idea is as in [8]; in [8a] the connection between *the* and the modifier can be accounted for; in [8b] the remaining + represents the kataphoric nature of *the*:

[8a] [*the* + modifier] − noun ⇒
[8b] [the +   ] − noun − modifier

That is, if one starts from [9a], transformation by [8] yields [9b] for [2a]:

[9a] [the + who lives next door] − boy ⇒ [9b]
[9b] [the +   ] − boy − who lives next door

Although neither Chomsky nor Emonds explicitly adduce kataphoric *the* as motivation, Chomsky (1965:129–31) and Emonds (1976:170) do in fact envisage transformational accounts of kataphoric *the* such as indicated in [8, 9] (transformation [8] is duly given a *narrow*, i.e. for him a structure-preserving, formulation by Emonds (1976:171)).

Perhaps the more interesting standard NG account here, however, is in SS&P (1973), who do consider both kataphoric *the* and transformational accounts such as in [8]. In particular, they acknowledge the approach in [8] as one possibility (1973:423–6) for what they call the *the* of "Definite description with relative clause" (1973:74). As the examples [10] make clear, this is *A–Z*'s kataphoric *the*:

[10a] the boy who gave me this book (cf. [2a])
[10b] the new teacher (cf. [2c])

[10b] shows *the* 'with relative clause' because *new* is taken to originate from such a relative clause via transformations: [the + who is new] teacher ⇒ (by [8]) the teacher who is new ⇒ the teacher new ⇒ the new teacher. SS&P then take up the possibility that *every the* is a kataphoric *the*: either with overt – full or transformationally reduced – relative clause; or "with deleted relative clauses" (1973:74). Notice that this seems to 'reconstruct' (cf. Part II) in NG the approach that in OG Poutsma intimates for [5].

The notable point about similarity between grammatical accounts of every *the* as kataphoric in both Poutsma's OG and in early NG is that it indicates that such accounts are equally *open* (cf. Part II). In fact SS&P maintain that such accounts are *too open* in that such accounts "would have to include non-linguistic material" (1973:77; cf. 1973:440); and thus cannot be *narrow*ly in accordance with an associated purely linguistic theory. That is, if there is only kataphoric *the*, then the account cannot be purely grammatical (cf. Sweet). Since SS&P do want to achieve a *narrow* grammar – "our more conservative frame of reference" (1973:440) – they ultimately decide that "All the syntax can . . . do is provide for . . . possibilities . . . and leave it to some sort of . . . semantic component . . . that these . . . be sorted out" (1973:449).

In other words, in SS&P (1973) one can follow quite closely a process by which NG effectuates its *narrow* programme. In early transformational accounts of kataphoric *the*, in which relative clauses quite freely change places as in [8], and/or freely delete as in Poutsma (1914), NG is relatively *open*. One may apply here Chomsky's (1965:234) dismissive "there is no particular difficulty in formulating . . . transformational rules that will have the desired properties". The very point about a *narrow* programme is that it looks for 'difficulties': as long as there is *no* difficulty and anything goes, there is no *narrow* account at all. Accordingly, SS&P come to take a *narrow* approach by which kataphoric *the* is simply no longer a point of Modern English grammar (but a 'non-linguistic' issue). In more effectively *narrow* NG, relative clauses should not freely move about and/or delete, and therefore kataphoric *the* comes to fall outside grammar in NG – and may be transferred to 'some sort of semantic component'. Note that kataphoric *the* thus loses its status as a pertinent point of Modern English grammar. The fact that points are pertinent only in relation to a specific linguistic theory means that in NG new points become pertinent as the theory changes; but equally it means that old points may cease to be pertinent and are therefore no longer covered in NG.

In effectively *narrow* current NG, kataphoric *the* does indeed appear not to be covered anymore at all. By the reverse side of the same coin, however, in NG which does not effectuate *narrow*ness, there is no need for kataphoric *the* to disappear behind the horizon in this way. For instance, Hawkins (1978:19) pleads for semantic – relatively *open* – NG (cf. section II.4). At least, Hawkins keeps NG still *open* enough for kataphoric *the* to remain highly pertinent: if kataphoric *the* is essentially a semantic matter, it is precisely in semantic NG that it may be accounted for. Thus, in [11] "there is something about the relative clause ... which makes ... *the* possible [as in [2a]]" (1978:131): kataphoric *the*:

[11] the woman he went out with last night

Interestingly, however, in Hawkins' semantic NG, the theory is that even kataphoric *the* in fact refers backwards, though indirectly: for instance, in [11], *the* is taken to refer backwards via the *he* in the relative clause, identified in the preceding context as 'Bill'. If every *the* (indirectly) refers backwards, then this is essentially the opposite of the accounts in Poutsma and early NG, where every *the* is kataphoric. That such opposite accounts can both be adopted once again indicates that if they are to be incorporated into grammar, then such grammar has to be *open* to the entire range of conceivable accounts: this is fundamentally true for OG, and apparently also for semantic NG.

K.3 Conclusions

Needless to say, in the *open* approach to Modern English grammar of OG, aimed at comprehensive coverage, it is inconceivable that a point like kataphoric *the* should cease to be covered, as has been seen to happen in much NG. This is the more salient respect in which OG and NG are juxtaposed to each other even when respective accounts appear to bear certain similarities to each other. On the other hand, in this section where '*K* is for kataphoric *the*', the juxtaposition is not just between OG in section K.1 and NG in section K.2. It also obtains in the contrasts between Jespersen (1933) – 'OG for *O*tto's *o*wn grammar' – and Jespersen

(1949) – 'NG for *N*iels' *n*eo-Jespersenian grammar'. Jespersen's (1933) exposition highlights kataphoric *the* as the article of incomplete determination; Jespersen's (1949) plan = Haislund's theory ignores kataphoric *the*, which is not pertinent to the theory. Similarly, within NG juxtaposition exists between relatively *open* NG – early transformational or later semantic NG – to which kataphoric *the* is pertinent; and current NG which has dropped kataphoric *the* from the more *narrow* roster of points of Modern English that are pertinent to a more effectively *narrow* approach to grammar.

K.4 Discussion and extensions

1 *A–Z* takes Quirk *et al.* (1972; 1985) to belong to OG. However, if Quirk *et al.* are genuinely *open*, they should also prove to be *open* to influences from NG. Consider the following two excerpts, one from OG (Quirk *et al.* 1985:268), one from NG (SS&P 1973:78):

A: anaphoric use of *the* does not always involve ... identical nouns ...

   [24] I saw *a boy* flying a kite ..., and *the little fellow* was almost pulled off the ground

   ... such examples ... require an apparatus considerably more complex than [identical nouns] ...

B: Some ... examples of indirect anaphora ...

   I lent Bill *a valuable book*, but ... *the cover* was filthy and *the paper* was torn

   ... There is ... no easy way to explain the ... occurrences of *the* by means of ellipsis ...

- Can it be identified which of A, B is from OG, which from NG? Why (not)?
- Would there be an 'easy way' of explaining [24] in A by ellipsis, i.e. by an implied relative clause? Which (OG and/or NG) account(s) would approach [24] in this way?
- If 'complex apparatus'/'no easy way' were a reason for not treating anaphoric *the* in grammar, would the account then be OG, or NG? Why?

2 The appearance of kataphoric *the* is perhaps most noticeable with proper nouns. For instance, *the Napoleon who lost the*

battle (Poutsma 1914:571), *the England that I know* (Chomsky 1965:217), *the Mr Brant about whom he has so often talked* (Kruisinga 1932a:242), *the Alice I like best* (SS&P 1973:448).

- Indicate in what sense(s) *the* is obviously kataphoric in the examples cited.
- Does the fact that OG and NG cover much the same ground in the examples cited show that they share some essential characteristic? Why (not)?
  For Poutsma (1914:571) the appearance of kataphoric *the* with proper nouns, in anticipation of a relative clause, "would seem to be indispensable"; for SS&P (1973:448) for *the* to appear with proper nouns "relativization is not only possible but necessary".
- Can a difference *open/narrow* be detected here? Why (not)?
  Poutsma also notes contrasts like '*the* London of the seventeenth century' vs. 'London of the last century'. Such contrasts do not appear to be covered by NG.
- Comment on the natures of OG and NG as they appear here. Jespersen (1933:170) cites *the England that he had left*. Jespersen (1949) has no such examples.
- How can the decrease in comprehensiveness be accounted for? Which account, (1933) or (1949), is the better one? Why?

3 Hawkins (1978:13) notes that Jespersen (1949) is based on Christopherson (1939) [sic: = -sen; cf. section 2.5]: both adopt the 'Familiarity' theory (cf. Jespersen 1949:404, i.e. Haislund writing). Hawkins then goes on to show that cases of kataphoric *the* "are all convincing counterexamples to . . . familiarity theory" (1978:130); and that thus "familiarity theory is much too restrictive" (1978:99). Indeed, Haislund does not admit cases of kataphoric *the* into Jespersen (1949).

- Comment on the natures of semantic NG in Hawkins (1978) and of Jespersen (1949) as they appear here. Which is *open*, which is *narrow*? Why?

L is for *let('s)*

In this section, *L* is for the form *let* in the positions where together with a subsequent *us* it may be abbreviated – technically: contracted – to *let's*; cf. [1]:

[1a] *let us* go
[1b] *let's* go

Let us (let's) thus say that the point of Modern English grammar at issue in this section involves 'contractors' *let* and *us/'s*. Seppänen (1977) presents a survey of properties by which contractor *let* distinguishes itself (notably from other instances of *let*); [2–4], [5–8], and [9–10] below are adapted from Seppänen's survey.

Firstly, contractor *let* cannot be *preceded* by a subject: [2]. On the other hand, contractor *let* may be *followed* by subjective forms, either in co-ordinations, [3], or in tags, [4]:

[2a]   *you* let us go
[2b] * *you* let's go
[3a] * let *we* go
[3b]   let you and *I* go
[3c]   let them go and *we* three stay here
[4a]   let us go, will you
[4b] * let's go, will you
[4c]   let's go, shall *we*

On a basis like [2–4], Seppänen suggests that in fact contractor *us/'s is* a subject of contractor *let*: if so, no additional subject can be added, hence * [2b]; the subjective forms *I* and *we* in [3b, c] are accounted for (but not * [3a]!); and [4c] amounts to regular repetition of the subject in tags (cf. '*they* like *you*, don't *they*/ * don't *you*').

If contractor *us/'s* is taken as the subject of contractor *let*, then contractor *let* may be seen to share a large number of properties with 'modal auxiliaries' like *will*, *would*, *may*, *might*, etc. Modal

154

auxiliaries can often be contracted with their subjects: *I will – I'll*, *he would – he'd*, etc. This might be extended to also include the notable ability of *let* to contract with *us* to *let's*. Also, modal auxiliaries may precede their subjects. Specifically, consider *may*: *you may live long* expresses 'possibility'; but *may you live long*, with inversion of subject and *may*, expresses a wish. Much the same applies – and must apply – to contractor *let* preceding contractor *us*; cf. [5]:

[5a] they let us go ('permission' ≠ 'wish')
[5b] let's go   ('wish')

Another point is that modal auxiliaries can be accompanied by other auxiliaries: perfective *have* (*will he have left*), progressive *be* (*can he be going*), and/or passive *be* (*would I be locked in*); again the same goes for contractors *let* and *us*:

[6a] let's have done with it
[6b] let's be going
[6c] let's be locked in

A further notable property of modal auxiliaries is that they allow verbs they are accompanied by to be left out – technically: ellipted; as in *he will go, and she may (not) go* ⇒ *he will go, and she may (not)* = ... *she may (not) [go]*. Such ellipsis is again also allowed after contractor *let's*:

[7] (Shall we go?) [a] Yes, let's   (= let's [go])
                   [b] No, let's not (= let's not [go])

Finally, there are two positions that *not* can appear in when a modal auxiliary precedes its subject: *may he not come, may not the work of the wicked prosper*. In the same way, *not* can either follow contractor *let* or its subject:

[8a] let's *not* come
[8b] let *not* the work of the wicked prosper

Although contractor *let* resembles modal auxiliaries in [5–8], there are a number of properties that are irreducibly unique to contractors *let* and *us/'s* together. Notably, there is the appearance of contractor *us* itself: *us* does not contract to *'s* except after contractor *let*: [2b]. Moreover, alongside the two negative patterns of [8], *let's* allows two exceptional patterns with *don't* in [9]:

[9a] *don't* let's go (cf. * don't may he go)
[9b] let's *don't* go (cf. * may he don't go)

Similarly, emphasis on contractor *let* may be reflected in the addition of *do*, either before contractor *let* or after; again there are no comparable patterns for modal auxiliaries:

[10a] *do* let's go (cf. * do may he go)
[10b] let's *do* go (cf. * may he do go)

Seppänen (1977) repeatedly complains that [2–10] are not comprehensively covered in accounts of contractors *let* and *us/'s*: point [5b] is "usually not recognized in grammars of English"; or "Most grammars of English fail to note the pattern" [8b] (1977: 520–1). The *open* issue of coverage, for *let's*, that this section will take up is therefore the extents to which OG and NG take cognizance of [2–10].

On the other hand, Seppänen also deplores that "a quick glance through a selection of existing grammars [cf. OG] ... [and] more modern approaches [cf. NG] ... suffices to show that, in most cases, the word *let* is not ... classified as a member of some subgroup of auxiliaries" (1977:515). Note that [8] for *n*egation, [5b] for *i*nversion, and [10] for *e*mphasis, involve three of the *nice*-properties by which auxiliaries may be *narrow*ly defined; cf. section b for BE (also section O for *ought*). In fact, as instances of 'code', the tag-questions of [4c] also pertain to the fourth *nice*-property; but unlike auxiliaries, *let* cannot be repeated in tags: * *let's go*, *let we*; instead in [4c] the tag contains *shall*. The *narrow* issue that Seppänen raises is whether OG and/or NG (should) account for properties of contractor *let* in accordance with its theoretical status as an auxiliary – and, we may add, the prior theoretical position with respect to *us/'s* as the subject of contractor *let*.

In sections L.1 and L.2, something hopefully somewhat more thorough than Seppänen's 'quick glance' at OG and NG accounts of *let's* should reveal patterns of *open* coverage and *narrow* classification, and/or their juxtaposition.

L.1 On OG on *let's*

For OG coverage of Seppänen's points about contractors *let* and *us/'s*, a useful point of departure is the survey of Table L.1.

L *is for* let('s)

Table L.1 Coverage of 15 points about *let* and *us/'s* in OG

		S	P	K	C	J	GCE	CGoEL	OG
2b	* you let's	(+)	(+)			(+)	(+)	(+)	5x(+)
3bc	let ... I/we		+	+	+	+	+	+	6x +
4c	shall we?					+		+	2x +
5b	'wish'								
6a	+have (perf)					+			1x +
6b	+be (prog)		+						1x +
6c	+be (pass)		+	+	(+)	+			3(4)x +
7a	let's [ ]						+	+	2x +
7b	let's not [ ]							+	1x +
8a	let's not	+	+		+	+	+	+	6x +
8b	let not		+	+		+		+	4x +
9a	don't let's	+	+	+	+	+	+	+	7x +
9b	let's don't			+	+	+		+	4x +
10a	do let's				+		+	+	3x +
10b	let's do			+					1x +

Before we expand on Table L.1, it may be pointed out that from the one empty row in Table L.1 for [5b], one should not hastily jump to the conclusion that OG fails in comprehensive coverage. Seppänen's point about [5b] is that contractor *let* expresses 'wish' *open*ly if and *narrow*ly only if there is inversion in that *let* precedes its subject *us/'s*. OG does regularly invoke similar notions in describing *let('s)*, as noted below. Here one instance will suffice: Curme (1931:394) describes *let us part*, etc. as "corresponding to ... expressions of will". Only, as in Curme, OG leaves this an *open* point, not explicitly restricted *narrow*ly to inversion.

On the other hand, the '(+)'s in the row for [2b] in Table L.1 may all perhaps be tendentious. That is, in none of the OG grammars is the most readily pertinent observation actually made in terms of negative evidence, a * (cf. section II.4). Sweet (1891:343) pioneers a more *open* approach to this point: "The shortening (-s) = *us* occurs only in *let's*. In early MnE (Modern English) it was more general". Poutsma (1916:708) also rather observes positively – in terms of actually available evidence – that "suppression of the *u* of *us* ... is ... now only met with in the admonitory [cf. [2b]: = 'wish'] *let's*, as in *let's go!*". Jespersen (1909:281; cf. also 1940:469) notes that "we have only *let's* ... in exhortations [cf. [2b]: = 'wish'] (*let's go*, etc. ...); otherwise *let us* is generally used (*let us know the time of your arrival* = inform us)"; note the *open*ly cautious 'generally'. Quirk *et al.* (1972:208) suggest that "*Us* has ... contraction to *'s* in *let's* (*Let's go*) but not where *let* = 'permit'"; but this is restated somewhat less *narrow*ly without any 'not' (= * ?) in (1985:1596) as just "contraction of *us*

157

in *let's*". Note that restrained use of ungrammatical evidence is an *open* feature (cf. section II.4).

Let us now give some substance to Table L.1 by citing some of the more notable examples to be found in OG; [11] for 3bc, [12] for 4c, etc., as indicated:

[11] 3bc
[11a] let my brothers and I ["etc."] (Poutsma 1916:710)
[11b] let you and I say a few words (Kruisinga 1932a:137)
[11c] let you and I cry quits (Curme 1931:44; cf. Jespersen 1940:470, 1949:236–7)
[11d] let's go and lunch at Prince's, you and I ... (Jespersen 1949:237; cf. Poutsma 1916:710)
[11e] let you and I do it (Quirk *et al.* 1972:211; 1985:338)

[12] 4c
[12a] let's go and lunch at Prince's, you and I, shall we (Jespersen 1949:237)
[12b] let's play another game, shall we (Quirk *et al.* 1985:813)

[13] 6a–c
[13a] let me have ordered what I would (Jespersen 1940:478)
[13b] let us not be for ever ... plotting (Poutsma 1928:118)
[13c] let them be ascertained (Kruisinga 1931:437; cf. Poutsma 1928:101, Jespersen 1940:478; in Curme 1931:443 *let* ≠ contractor: (+) in Table L.1)

[14] 7a–b
[14a] Shall we watch the game? Yes, let's (Quirk *et al.* 1972: 406; 1985:833, *shall = should*)
[14b] Should we watch the game? No, let's not (Quirk *et al.* 1985:833)

[15] 8a
[15a] let us not go (Sweet 1898:92; cf. Poutsma 1928:118, Jespersen 1940:470)
[15b] let's not do that (Curme 1931:433)
[15c] let's/let us not open the door (Quirk *et al.* 1972:405; cf. 1985:831)

[16] 8b
let not the traveller omit to visit ... (Poutsma 1928:118; cf. Kruisinga 1931:437, Jespersen 1940:443, Quirk *et al.* 1985:831)

[17] 9a
[17a] do not let us go (Sweet 1898:92; cf. Poutsma 1928:118, Jespersen 1940:443)

L *is for* let('s)

[17b] don't let's have any nonsense (Kruisinga 1931:426; cf.
        Quirk *et al*. 1972:405; 1985:831)
[17c] don't let us do that (Curme 1931:433; cf. Jespersen
        1940:443, 514)
[18] 9b
        let's don't go (Jespersen 1940:443; cf. Kruisinga 1931:418,
        Curme 1931:433, Quirk *et al*. 1985:831)
[19] 10a–b
[19a] Suppos'n we follow the brook . . . Oh, do let's (Curme
        1931:433; cf. Quirk *et al*. 1972:406; 1985:833)
[19b] let's don't talk of it . . . Let's do (Kruisinga 1931:418)

Clearly, Sweet only pioneers OG here, with three points out of
fifteen covered. On the other hand, with respect to Seppänen's
insistence that *let* be *narrow*ly classified as an auxiliary, Sweet
(1898:92) does state that in [17a] there is "anomalous heaping of
auxiliaries", i.e. the exceptional combination of auxiliary *do* with
another auxiliary (!) *let*.
    Following Sweet's lead, Poutsma (1926:163), Kruisinga (1932a:
138), and Curme (1931:432) classify contractor *let* as, respectively,
an auxiliary of mood, an auxiliary of modality, and again an
auxiliary of mood. In fact, Poutsma and Kruisinga, as well as
Jespersen – the three non-natives in OG (cf. Parts I and II) – also
touch upon the prior *narrow* assumption, that contractor *us/'s* is
somehow a subject; in each case referring to Dutch alternations
like *laat ons gaan* (*let us go*)/*laten we gaan* (*let we go*). For
Poutsma (1916:710), [11a] suggests that "after *let* . . . the pronoun
is understood to be in the subjective relation to the following
infinitive. Thus also in Dutch". Similarly, Kruisinga (1931:437)
cites Dutch cases resembling [11b] where a subjective form
indicates "clearly an auxiliary"; and thus for English [11b], too,
subjective forms "may be the result of the character of *let*, which is
an auxiliary of modality here" (1932a:138). Finally, Jespersen
(1940:470) comments on cases like [11c]: "As the pronoun is
virtually the subject, this . . . cannot be termed unnatural; in Dutch
it has become a fixed idiom".
    It will be noted that the Scandinavian Jespersen – unlike the
Dutchmen Poutsma and Kruisinga – does not draw from Dutch
(and/or English) the conclusion that contractor *let* is an auxiliary. And Seppänen (1977) seems to have remained within a
Scandinavian frame of reference. Jespersen is a major source
of Seppänen's examples, viz. [11c, 13a, 18]. But even though
Seppänen also follows Jespersen in referring to Dutch *laat/laten*,

he still does not include the Dutchmen Poutsma or Kruisinga in his 'quick glance through existing grammars'. A more leisurely look shows that Poutsma, especially, and Kruisinga come closer to Seppänen's *narrow* demand – *let* = modal, *us*/*'s* = subject – than any of the OG grammars that Seppänen does select, including Jespersen; and moreover, that both Poutsma and Kruisinga do *open*ly cover points that Seppänen (1977:520–1) thinks that OG usually fails on: *may* with inversion = 'wish' (Poutsma 1926:200; Kruisinga 1932b:334); and 8b (Poutsma 1928:118; Kruisinga 1931: 437).

To return to OG itself – rather than Seppänen's (mis)representation of OG – a few comments on individual grammars are now in order. Beyond the negative patterns of [8] and [9], Poutsma (1928:118) also covers a fifth pattern, which "appears to be very rare" and indeed is not included in the coverage of any other of *A–Z*'s OG grammars. In [20a] *not* appears after the infinitive, rather than after either contractor *us* as in 8a, cf. [20b], or after contractor *let* as in 8b, cf. [20c] (cf. also section O.4 2):

[20a] let us talk *not* of it
[20b] let us *not* talk of it
[20c] let *not* us talk of it

With respect to Curme, we should note that Table L.1 puts a '+' in the row for 10a on the basis of Curme's example [19a]. This follows Curme's own interpretation of [19a] as showing the appearance of "*do* before the *let*-form" (1931:433). However, [19a] in fact also shows the property of [7], viz. ellipsis:

[21] Suppos'n we follow the brook. Oh, do let's [follow the brook]

Curme fails to interpret [19a] as in [21], but it is not clear whether we should not perhaps still put at least '(+)' in the row for 7a in Table L.1. Note that Kruisinga's [19b] could similarly be taken to show ellipsis, viz. of *talk of it* – but such ellipsis would be after *do* rather than after *let's*.

For Jespersen, it may be noted that, although he does not get round to calling *let* an auxiliary in *MEG*, he does give notations like [22c] (1940:514):

[22a] let us take another chair
[22b] don't let us take that chair
[22c] v S V O

In [22c] S identifies *us* as subject (!); but also, small v represents *let* as a "lesser verb" (1940:6), in contrast to big V for just "verb".

Presumably a 'lesser verb' is something very much like an auxiliary after all. Note that Jespersen's single small v can apparently also represent both *don't* and *let* together; i.e. Sweet's 'anomalous heaping of auxiliaries'.

However, the most notable individual OG grammar in Table L.1 is probably *CGoEL*. On contractors *let* and *us*, *CGoEL* clearly deserves to call itself the *Comprehensive*. Quirk *et al.* (1985) improve on (1972)'s rather moderate six points out of fifteen, to overtake Jespersen, as yet leading with nine out of fifteen, and end up with ten out of fifteen. Moreover, Quirk *et al.* by (1985) cover two points in Table L.1 that other OG omits: 7a (but see the discussion of Curme's [19a] as [21]), and 7b. Poutsma on 6a, Kruisinga on 10b, and Jespersen on 6b only contribute one such unique point each (but cf. Poutsma on [20], uniquely).

Quirk *et al.* (1985:171) include Seppänen (1977) among their references. Whether or not the increased coverage of *CGoEL* is due to Seppänen at all, it may be noted that Quirk *et al.* re-affirm – contra Seppänen – their (1972) position that contractor *let* is *not* an auxiliary. In particular because contractor *let* is followed by objective *us* rather than subjective *we*, "*let* is totally unlike auxiliary verbs" (1985:148). In fact, Quirk *et al.*'s interpretation of subjective forms as in [11e] is that this is "hypercorrect" (1972: 210; 1985:338; cf. also section w on 'hypercorrect' *whom* for *who*) – rather than evidence of subject status. That is, [11e] is almost * even though it is observed. This is similar to the attitude that Poutsma takes towards [11a], with subjective *I* "instead of the grammatically correct objective" *me* (1928:710). It is clearly a rather less *open* attitude than the one that appears from Kruisinga's view that [11b] only "would *seem* to require" *me* (1932a:137, emphases added); or from Jespersen's defense against "traditional grammar" (1949:236) of *I* etc. in [11c, d], which "cannot be called unnatural" (1940:470).

L.2 On NG on *let's*

In a *narrow* approach to Modern English grammar, which searches for constraints on what is possible, contractors *let* and *us* are inherently unlikely to become pertinent. That is, only after contractor *let* does *us* contract to *'s*. As such, *let's* is a completely isolated exception to an otherwise quite general constraint against contraction of *us*. It would be perfectly consistent for NG to take the general constraint for granted; and in accordance with the constraint ignore a unique exception such as *let's* presents. In fact, *let's* does appear to have remained an extremely rare presence in

NG. Neither Chomsky nor Emonds (1976) among *A–Z*'s NG standards seem to have taken up *let's*. Perhaps even more tellingly, SS&P do make observations on *let's* – but only in a section on points of Modern English grammar "Not dealt with" (1973:636); in an *open* approach, making observations *equals* dealing with these points. One can see SS&P indulging their desire to provide a genuine – i.e. more or less comprehensive – grammar (cf. section 3.2) when they cover 4c, 8a, and 9a (1973:638) as in [23]: three points out of fifteen.

[23]   4c
[23a] let's start at once, shall we?
       8a
[23b] let's not start yet
       9a
[23c] ?don't let's start yet

But even this falls short of any but pioneering OG. The real point about SS&P's treatment of *let's* remains that they "do not have an analysis of these forms". That is, there is no account in accordance with a *narrow* linguistic theory to which examples with *let's* like [23] are pertinent.

Also in the NG literature at large, on specific points of Modern English grammar, *let's* is most conspicuous by its virtually complete absence. The single exceptions may well be two brief appearances in a question-and-answer exchange: Newmeyer (1971)–Costa (1972). Both papers adopt the 'semantic NG' version of NG (cf. section II.4); since this is relatively *open* NG, it is not surprising that *let's* should appear here. For Newmeyer (1971:393) the point about *let's* is the one of 4c, viz. *we* in tags:

[24]   4c
[24a] let's eat, shall we
[24b] let's eat, why don't we

For Newmeyer's (1971) semantic NG [24] is pertinent as the appearance of *we* in tags confirms that *we* is essentially the subject of both *let* and of *eat*; roughly as in [25a], which purports to be a remote representation of the meaning of [24]:

[25a] we let us [we eat]
[25b] we let us   eat
[25c]   let us   eat

From [25a] the two subjects *we* are then deleted: in [25b] the subject of *eat* because it is a non-finite clause (cf. we hope *for us* to eat ⇒ we hope to eat; cf. '*f* is for *for* + subject'); in [25c] the subject of *let* in analogy with 'imperative' sentences (e.g. *you behave yourselves, will you* ⇒ *behave yourselves, will you;* cf. section u for understood *you*, also section y). However, there is then a problem in [25a] before the latter deletion takes place: *we . . . us* would be expected to become *we . . . ourselves* (cf. section 'R for referential riddles'): [26] instead of, or at least alongside [25]:

[26a]   we let ourselves [we eat]
[26b]   we let ourselves   eat
[26c] *   let ourselves   eat

Newmeyer's NG account of [25] predicts [26] and in particular counter-factually [26c], rather than the actual [25c]; he asks, "Does anybody have a solution to this problem?"

In reply to Newmeyer's question, Costa (1972) suggests that in semantic NG a truer representation of the meaning of [24] would be remotely like [27a] rather than [25a]:

[27a] you let us [we go]
[27b] you let us   go
[27c]   let us   go

In [27a] *we* as the subject of *go* is now supposed to be able to be responsible for the appearance of *we* in the tags of [24]. On the other hand, the deletion of the subject *you* of *let* can now actually be identical with, rather than merely somehow analogous to, the deletion of *you* in imperatives. At least, [27] solves the problem of predicting [26]: *you* is not eligible for turning *us* into a reflexive (cf. * *you behave ourselves*). The fact that semantic NG can more or less freely switch from *we* in [24] to *you* in [26] gives another indication that semantic NG is relatively *open* (cf. section II.4).

Note that in both [25] and [27] it is *not us* that is taken as a subject – either of *let* or of *eat/go*. Correspondingly neither Newmeyer nor Costa classifies contractor *let* as an auxiliary. This confirms Seppänen's (1977) impression that the modern approach to Modern English grammar of NG will not identify contractor *let* as an auxiliary even if NG does at least pay attention to *let's*. In fact both Newmeyer and Costa seem to be taking for granted the quite standard assumption of semantic NG that there is no real distinction between auxiliary and lexical verb in the first place. Interestingly, an argument for this NG unification of auxiliaries and verbs (cf. section O) is derived by Huddleston (1978:49) from . . . the very contractor *let*.

Huddleston's point of departure is the phenomenon of 7, notably a point not covered in OG (but cf. Curme's [21]) until Quirk *et al.* (1972, 1985); viz. ellipsis as in [28]:

[28] 7
(Let's go and see John) [a]   Oh yes, do let's [go and see John]
                          [b] * Oh yes, do [let's go and see John]

However, unlike in Seppänen (1977), for Huddleston [28] does not
suggest that contractor *let* is similar to auxiliaries. Quite the
contrary. [28] is taken to show that *let('s)* is irregular, since it
cannot itself be deleted in [28b]: unlike both regular main verbs
(e.g. *go* in [7]), and auxiliaries (e.g. *do* from [19b]). In this way,
let's would then be counter-evidence to an NG theory that
distinguishes main verbs and auxiliaries as regular and irregular
respectively: alongside irregular non-deleting *let's*, deleting main
verbs and deleting auxiliaries would non-distinctly be 'regular'.

L.3 Conclusions

With respect to contractors *let* and *us*, juxtaposition of OG and
NG primarily appears from the rather dramatic contrast in the
extents to which points from Seppänen (1977) are covered in
either approach to Modern English grammar. After a pioneering
account with only minimal coverage in Sweet, coverage in OG
ranges between six and ten points out of fifteen in Table L.1;
whereas typical NG ignores *let's*; or if not, only covers one single
pertinent point or another: *we* in tags in the Newmeyer (1971)–
Costa (1972) exchange; ellipsis after *let* in Huddleston (1978). In
this respect, SS&P (1973) approximate NG more closely to OG
than anyone else: they cover three points; but none of these is seen
to be pertinent to any theoretical positions that SS&P adopt.

In particular, SS&P literally "leave *open* the question" (1973:
601; emphasis added) of whether a fundamental distinction should
be made between auxiliary and main verb. As such, the *narrow*
theoretical issue to which *let's* is pertinent *pace* Seppänen (1977) –
is contractor *let* an auxiliary? – does not really arise for SS&P. Nor
does it arise for Newmeyer–Costa, where no distinction between
auxiliaries and main verbs is recognized. And in Huddleston
(1978), *let's* is in fact enlisted as an argument for his *narrow*
position that auxiliaries and main verbs should be unified. By
contrast, in OG – especially earlier OG; prior to Quirk *et al.* – an
open attitude to main verb/auxiliary distinctions allows contractor
let to be freely classified as an auxiliary. Both in the *open* respect of
coverage and in the *narrow* respect of whether contractor *let*
should be assigned the status of auxiliary, OG and NG are
therefore essentially juxtaposed.

L.4 Discussion and extensions

1 The representation of [27] in the main text is a dramatically simplified one. Costa (1972) actually adduces a complex semantic NG representation which is somewhat more exactly represented as [i]:

[i] URGE – I – YOU [let – you – you and I [go – you and I]]

Transformations in semantic NG are supposed to be *open* enough to delete URGE – I – YOU; and to change *you and I* into *we/us* (cf. section m). This suggests once more that semantic NG is relatively *open*; cf. section II.4.

● Comment on the fact that *let's* makes appearances in OG, in early NG, and in semantic NG; but not in later Chomskyan NG.

2 Although Huddleston (1978) purports to take an NG approach, he does suggest that one should "consider ... a wider range of data"; and that one "needs constantly to be considering the properties of individual words" (1978:45). According to Newmeyer (1969:121, 147), it is "Traditional analyses [that] usually ... overemphasize the bizarre and otherwise ... 'degenerate' modals ... see Jespersen (1940)". Similarly, Emonds (1985:167) takes Huddleston to actually represent the "empiricist" = *open*, inductive approach, which Emonds – appropriately for *A–Z* – calls the "old road"; whereas NG represents a new approach.

● How would the fact that Huddleston covers *let's* – but Emonds does not – be interpretable as evidence for Huddleston following the 'old road' of OG = *open* grammar?

3 Jespersen (1936/1969:39) analyses [iia, b] as in [iic]; but Jespersen (1940:514) switches to [iiib] for [iiia] (cf. [22] in the main text); and Jespersen (1949:236) again returns to [iic]:

[iia] let   us go
[iib] let   's go
[iic] V O (S I)
[iiia] let us take another chair
[iiib] v S V   O

● Of [iic], [iiib], discuss which one would be more in line with Newmeyer (1971)–Costa (1972); which one more with Seppänen (1977); and which one more with Huddleston (1978).
Let's assume that Jespersen (1936 – 1940 – 1949) essentially allows for both analyses side-by-side (rather than changing his mind twice).

● How would [iic/iiib] represent an *open* approach? Discuss how in this respect SS&P (1973) would resemble OG.

4 Costa (1972:144) echoes Newmeyer (1971:394): ". . . does any-one have a solution to this problem?". Only, the problem for Costa is not Newmeyer's of [26] – which Costa purports to solve by means of [27] – but the alternation between [iva, b] (cf. [8a, 9a] respectively):

> [iva]   let's not go to Aunt Sissy's, Mummy
> [ivb] don't let's   go to Aunt Sissy's, Mummy

Note that [ivb] is already a 'problem' for Sweet (1898:92), viz. in so far as *anomalous* heaping of auxiliaries' is a problem.

- Comment on the juxtaposition between Sweet representing OG and Costa representing NG with respect to whether a 'solution' to a problem is something to be pursued.
- To what extent is [ivb] a 'problem' for Jespersen, who can subsume *don't* and *let* under a single v for smaller verb (cf. [22])? Is this an *open* feature?

For Costa's semantic NG, if [iva, b] mean the same thing, "=", they have to be syntactically related as well (see section II.4). For Costa the syntactic relation is by way of a transforma-tion of "neg-raising" (cf. section A for a semantic NG trans-formation of '*not*-lowering'), roughly transposing *not* from [va] to [vb] ([vc] then illustrates *do*-support for an isolated Neg *not*):

> [va]   let's not go
> [vb]   not let's   go
> [vc] don't let's   go

The problem about [v] is that such neg-raising would be conditional on contraction of *let* and *us* to *let's*; in Costa's view [ivb] '≠' [vi]: without contraction, [vi] can only mean 'don't allow us to go':

> [vi] don't let us go to Aunt Sissy's, Mummy

Now compare however [17a, c]; indeed, for Jespersen (1940: 443), [vi] would be "the idiomatic expression" corresponding to [iva], at least as much as [ivb]. In the *narrow* approach of NG, an account of a point of Modern English grammar is of no pertinence unless 'problems' arise, if necessary by brute force; in the *open* approach of OG no 'problem' can ever really arise. Comment on the different attitudes to [iva] and [vi] in OG and in NG, from this point of view.

5 Jespersen (1949:238) observes that subjective forms may also follow (at a distance) *let* when it is not contractor *let*:

> [viia] to persuade Richard to let us go . . . – we three, you
>   know (cf. * to persuade Richard to let's go)

[viib] he is willing to let us be friends, at least, Linton and I
(cf. * he is willing to let's be friends)

- Discuss the implications that [vii] would have for – or against –
Seppänen's interpretation of contractor *us* as the subject of
contractor *let*; and of contractor *let* in turn as an auxiliary.
6 Seppänen (1977) mainly cites from Jespersen (1940), *MEG* V;
his one quotation from Jespersen (1949), *MEG* VII, is a
misquote: *deceitful* (Seppänen 1977:522) for *dutiful* in [viii]
(Jespersen 1949:236–7):

[viii] don't let you and I talk of being dutiful

In particular, Seppänen does not give recognition to Jespersen's
(1949:237) reference to his native "colloquial Danish-Norwegian",
alongside of non-native Dutch:

[ixa] lad vi det ('let we this')
[ixb] lad os det ('let us this')

In Scandinavian [ix] there is no difference in *lad* accompanying
the choice between subjective *vi* and objective *os*; whereas
in Dutch there is such a difference, between *laten* and *laat*
respectively:

[xa]   laten we gaan ('let+*en* we go')
[xb] * laat we   gaan
[xc] * laten ons gaan
[xd]   laat ons gaan ('let us go')

Jespersen's greater familiarity with Scandinavian than with
Dutch also appears from his erroneous Dutch example *lat hem
nu toonen*; which (a) should be *laat hem* ... ; and (b) should be
laat hen ... if it is to be equivalent to *laten ze* ... , as Jespersen
intends.
- Discuss the relations between [ix, x] and the fact that the
Dutchmen Poutsma and Kruisinga *do* and the Scandinavian
Jespersen does *not* draw the conclusion that Modern English *let*
is an auxiliary.

m is for *meet* for mutual relations

If Ann is the mother of Betty, then Betty cannot be the mother of Ann (unless there are two Betty's, grandmother and grand-daughter): if m = 'be the mother of ', then $AmB \neq BmA$. We may say that there is a 'mutual relation' m between A and B in those cases where $AmB = BmA$. For instance, if Martha is married to Martin, then also Martin is married to Martha. *Be married to* expresses a mutual relation m. Similarly, if firm A merges with firm B, then also firm B merges with firm A; *merge with* is again a mutual relation m. In this miniscule section m, we are interested in the mutual relation m especially as it is expressed by *meet*: if Mr Maxwell meets Miss Marple, then Miss Marple meets Mr Maxwell.

Given the basic property of mutual relations, $AmB = BmA$, in the case of *meet* [1a] is equivalent to [1b]. In addition, the mutual relation of *meet* can also be expressed as in [1c, d]:

[1a] Miss Marple	met Mr Maxwell at midnight
[1b] Mr Maxwell	met Miss Marple at midnight
[1c] Miss Marple and Mr Maxwell met each other	at midnight
[1d] Miss Marple and Mr Maxwell met	at midnight

In [1c, d] the order *Miss M and Mr M* may equally be inverted, to *Mr M and Miss M*; in [1c] *one another* may also be found for *each other* (cf. also sections R.4 1, 2). Apart from the general point that *meet* expresses a mutual relation m in each of [1a–d] separately, this section also inquires whether in accounts of *meet* and/or mutual relations, two or more of [1a–d] are related to each other (note that 'be related to' is in itself again an instance of m: if [1a] is related to [1d] then [1d] is related to [1a]; $[1b]m[1c] = [1c]m[1b]$; etc.).

m.1 On OG on *m(eet)*

In OG, *meet* itself makes a regular appearance: in Sweet, Poutsma, Curme, Jespersen, and *CGoEL*; but not in Kruisinga or in *GCE*.

In Sweet (1891:92–3), a mutual relation *m* is referred to as "the idea of reciprocity" or "reciprocal meaning"; and there would be a relation between [1c, d]. That is, [2d] results from [2c] with "pronoun ... dropped, and the idea of reciprocity ... implied in the verb itself":

[2c]   they fought each other
[2d] those two dogs always fight   when they meet

Interestingly, Sweet takes *meet* to be a poor example of *m*, in spite of its appearance in [2d]: "In such a verb as *meet*, the reciprocal meaning is less prominent [than in e.g. *fight*]".

There is no such hesitation about *meet* as *m* in Poutsma (1916:1067–71). In [3] *meet* illustrates the relation between [1c, d]; in addition, Poutsma covers a related instance [3e]. That is, in [3c] "*each other* is often called reciprocal"; in [3d], however, "The reciprocal idea is ... implied, so that it is not expressed by any special word"; and in [3e] "the reciprocal idea may also be expressed by ... *mutually ... mutual ... together*":

[3c] the two had never met each other before
[3d] the two brothers   met   as brothers who loved
         each other fondly ...
[3e]   ... yet meet together rarely

Note that [3d, e] are parts of a single example of Poutsma's ([3e] is slightly adapted). The point is that Poutsma's instances are apparently fairly carefully organized to have the mutual relation *m* indirectly represented in the context even when it is not directly expressed. In [3d], there is just *met* rather than directly *met each other*; but at least there is the indirect evidence of an *each other* further on, with *loved*. Similarly for *one another* in Poutsma's example 'they used to nod to one another when they met'.

In Kruisinga the relation would once again be between [1c, d]: "We ... find the simple verb as an alternative to the verb with ... *each other ... their hands touched*" (1932b:203; cf. [1d]; and [1c] for 'their hands touched each other'). But *meet* is not included among Kruisinga's examples of *m*.

Curme stands out among other OG dealing with *m* in that he explicitly dissociates himself from simply equating cases of [1c] and [1d]: "we use the ... reciprocal pronoun when we think of ... mutual relations ..., while we employ intransitive forms when the idea of an action pure and simple ... presents itself to our mind" (1931:439). Accordingly, [4c] $\neq$ [4d] ([4c] is also said to occur only "sometimes"):

[4c] they met each other at the gate (= mutual relation)
[4d] they met   at the gate (= action pure and simple)

Note that [4c] ≠ [4d] resembles Sweet's denial of reciprocity in *meet*; only, for Curme the point is a general one which would for instance equally apply to *fight* in [2], etc.

In Jespersen's account, however, [1c, d] are once again equated (1927:332). In particular, "Some verbs are frequently used intransitively in the same signification as if ... *each other* ... had been added as object ... Thus often *meet*". In addition, "Reciprocity is sometimes indicated by ... *together*". I.e. [5]:

[5d]   we met   occasionally
[5e] God send we may all meet together

Note that Jespersen does not actually exemplify *met each other*, by way of [5c].

Finally, Quirk *et al*. A notable point about *GCE* (1972) is its almost complete neglect of the mutual relation *m*, let alone of *meet* as *m*. There is not even any place for *each other* and/or *one another* in their chapter on pronouns (nor are 'reciprocal pronouns' given any specification when they appear: 1972:806; Quirk and Greenbaum (1974) – ostensibly a "shorter version" of *GCE* "careful to preserve the structure of the parent book" (1974:v) – notably inserts a section on reciprocal pronouns in the chapter on pronouns: 1974:104–5, vs. 1972:213).

The *GCE* (1972) neglect of *m* and of *meet* is abundantly made up for in *CGoEL* (1985). The emphasis seems to be again on a relation between [1c, d]: [6c] "=" [6d] because "With verbs like ... *meet* ..., which are reciprocal and symmetrical in character ..., the reciprocal pronoun is optional" (1985:364):

[6c] Anna and Bob met each other in Cairo
[6d] Anna and Bob met   in Cairo

Quirk *et al*. (1985:1169) also have examples of "verbs with mutual participation": [7a/b, c]; in [7c] *we* = 'you *and* I' (cf. 1985:955), as in [7d]:

[7a/b]   I have met you
[7c]   we have met
[7d]   you and I have met

Note that [7a/b, d] suggest that [6c, d] may also be related to [8a, b]; cf. [1], but *not* [2–5]:

[8a] Anna   met Bob   in Cairo
[8b]   Bob met   Anna in Cairo

Even more importantly, note also that – for the first time in OG – [6c, d] and [7d] illustrate the mutual relation of *meet* with co-ordinations: 'Anna *and* Bob', 'you *and* I'.

m.2 On NG on *m(eet)*

If *CGoEL* is the first OG account of *meet* as *m* which features co-ordination in [6], in NG *meet* has only, if at all, been pertinent to co-ordination. To set the scene, consider Sag *et al.* (1985:134, 168) commenting on, *inter alia*, [8] with co-ordination of 'Kim *and* Sandy':

[8] Kim and Sandy met

Recent transformational grammar has largely abandoned co-ordination as a topic of study ... Over twenty years ago, ... coordination was a key topic in the discussions that led to the widespread acceptance of transformational grammar ... the present paper improves on earlier generative treatments ... by broadening the coverage while at the same time stipulating less

Note that 'broadening coverage' is by itself an *open* enterprise ('stipulating less' is the *narrow* issue). More importantly, however, Sag *et al.* distinguish 'earlier generative treatments' of transformational grammar both 'twenty years ago' and more 'recent' from their 'present' approach: transformational NG vs. so-called Generalized Phrase Structure Grammar, respectively (cf. section II.4); the latter pursues effective *narrow*ness by not allowing *any* transformations.

The pertinence of [8] 'over twenty years ago' to transformational NG, notably to Lakoff and Peters (henceforth L&P) (1969), was in fact that *only* cases of *m* like [8] are *not* to be accounted for transformationally, i.e. by ellipsis. Consider [9a], which may be interpreted as [9b]; accordingly [9b] may be taken to be transformed into [9a] by ellipsis of [*left*] as in [9c] (1969:115):

[9a] John   and Mary left
[9b] John left and Mary left
[9c] John [left] and Mary left

However, [8] cannot be accounted for in this transformational way; cf. [10] (1969:114):

[10a] John   , Bill   , and Harry
      met in Vienna
[10b] * John met in Vienna , Bill met in Vienna , and Harry
       met in Vienna

171

[10c]   John [met in Vienna], Bill [met in Vienna], and Harry
         met in Vienna

Since [10b] is *, [10b] is not available as the source from which
[10a] can be transformationally derived via [10c].

It is in [9] vs. [10] that there is a 'key to the widespread
acceptance of transformational grammar' (Sag *et al.*): transformation as in [9] accounts for simple co-ordinations; the impossibility
of transformation in [10] accounts for the fact that in [8] co-
ordination is not thus simple, but expresses rather a mutual
relation *m*. In spite of their claim of 'broadening coverage',
without transformations Sag *et al.* (1985) no longer seem to
provide a grammatical account of the difference between [8, 9a].

Anyway, in the earlier *open*ly transformational days, according
to L&P (1969:113) "It has long been observed that there are ...
two types of conjunction [i.e. co-ordination], sentence conjunction
[with or without ellipsis, i.e. [9a, b]] and phrasal conjunction
[i.e. [8]] ... For example, Curme ... in his *Syntax* [i.e. 1931],
(p. 162)". Note the tendency in early, transformational NG to
claim ancestry in OG (cf. section II.4).

In particular, Curme (1931:162) indeed observes that "Sentences containing ... [co-ordinating] conjunctions ... are often
not an abridgment of two or more sentences, but a simple sentence
with elements ... connected by a conjunction: 'The King *and*
Queen are an amiable pair' ...". Abridgement is Curme's term for
ellipsis, i.e. * *The King [is an amiable pair] and the Queen is an
amiable pair*. There are similar observations elsewhere in OG.
Sweet (1891:141) talks about 'expanding' *Mr Smith and Professor
Green called* (i.e. S called and G called, separately); or not (i.e. S
and G called, together). Poutsma (1929:548) alludes to Sweet's
observation that in *Mrs* [sic] *Smith and Professor Green called*
"compound elements [i.e. S and G called, together] differ from
contracted sentences [i.e. S [called] and G called, separately]".
But note that none of these OG observations belong to section
m.1, because they do not involve *meet* (recall from m.1 that *meet* is
not associated with co-ordination in OG until *CGoEL*).

In NG, and L&P (1969), however, the "crucial examples"
(1969:114) for two kinds of co-ordination do involve *meet*, viz. in
[10], vs. [9]. Interestingly, alongside [10], L&P (1969:140–1)
object to NG reconstruction of the relation consistently recognized
in OG, between [1c, d]. That is, [11c] "would be derived from"
[11a+b]; but "we would like to point out the impossibility of
deriving ... [[11d]] from [[11c]] ... by the deletion of *each
other*":

[11a+b] John met Bill and Bill met John
[11c]   John   and Bill met   each other
[11d]   John   and Bill met

Note that the relation of [11d] to [11c] is standard in OG; but no OG also involves [11a+b] in this – because OG does not deal with *meet* and co-ordination – until Quirk *et al.* (1985:364).

In this miniscule section it would lead too far afield to specify in any detail why L&P (1969) take it to be impossible to derive [11d] from [11c]; but note that *any* 'impossibility' amounts to a *narrow* approach. Here it has to do with another transformation, 'conjunct movement'; which is rather supposed to derive [12] from [11d] – an idea that is again not met with in OG:

[11d] John and Bill met
[12a] John and   met   Bill
[12b] John and   met with Bill
[12c] John   met with Bill

Rather than elaborate on [12] itself, let us take it as a point of departure for a final look at *meet* and *m* in the NG standards. Chomsky (1973:235–6) discusses the relation between [11d] and [12c] by Conjunct Movement; and *narrow*ly deplores its "dubious status". Emonds (1976:93–4) also notes that "There are arguments against" Conjunct Movement; but that it can at least be made to conform to Emonds' structure-preserving constraint. He illustrates this point with *m = mix (with) (beer and chocolate don't mix well – beer doesn't mix well with chocolate)* – but, unlike Chomsky, not with *meet*. One of the arguments against Conjunct Movement is in fact spelled out by SS&P (1973:312). Conjunct Movement from [12a] to [12b] would "represent . . . a unique case of movement [of *Bill*] out of a conjoined structure [*John and Bill*]". Rather than *open*ly admit such a 'unique case', NG prefers to adopt a *narrow* constraint that prohibits any escape from a co-ordination (cf. section T), such as *Bill*'s in [12b]. Accordingly, SS&P (1973:300) forego Conjunct Movement; and adopt [11] without reservation: e.g. Algernon is similar to Reginald and R is similar to A ⇒ A and R are similar to one another ⇒ A and R are similar; only, SS&P do not specify its application to *meet*.

m.3 Conclusions

Quirk *et al.* include Lakoff and Peters (1969) among their references to NG in both *GCE* (1972) and *CGoEL* (1985); however, only in (1985) do they, on behalf of OG, *open*ly extend coverage to co-ordinations, in connection with *meet*. In the meantime, *pace* Sag *et al*. (1985), co-ordination and *meet/m narrow*ly disappear from NG itself. The reader will readily see that emergence vs. disappearance of co-ordination, *meet* and/or *m* is representative of the general juxtaposition between OG and NG.

N is for numerals-as-nouns

For *A–Z*'s section N it seems appropriate to look towards the *N*G approach to Modern English grammar for a point of departure. In one of NG's more conspicuously ubiquitous references (cf. section N.4 2 below), Jackendoff (1977) develops a particular theory of the ways in which word-classes can, and more especially in *narrow* fashion cannot, be distinguished from each other. The technical details need not concern us here; for theoretical reasons, Jackendoff allows no more (and no fewer) than ten word-classes: verbs, auxiliaries, nouns, articles, quantifiers, adjectives, adverbs, degree words, prepositions, and particles. The relevant point for *A–Z* at this stage is that Jackendoff clearly exemplifies a *narrow* approach: a theory is allowed to determine an upper limit on the number of grammatical possibilities. For instance, Jackendoff cannot let any 'available evidence' for *two, three, nine, nineteen, ninety*, etc. indicate that they belong to a separate word-class of 'numerals': this would extend beyond the 'preconceived' limits of just ten word-classes.

Given his *narrow* outlook, Jackendoff notes that 'numerals' behave in certain ways like quantifiers such as *some* or like nouns such as *dozen* (note that both quantifiers and nouns *are* admitted among the ten possible word-classes). For instance, they can all occur in the same position in certain constructions, e.g. [1]; but not together, [2]:

[1a]   he bought *twelve*   books ('numeral')
[1b]   he bought *some*   books (quantifier)
[1c]   he bought a *dozen*   books (noun)
[2a] * he bought twelve some books ('numeral' + quantifier)
[2b] * he bought a dozen twelve books (noun + 'numeral')
etc.

To maintain the *narrow* restriction to ten word-classes, Jackendoff therefore sets out to explain the excessive 'numerals' away as

175

really cases of either quantifiers or nouns. But which? Here Jackendoff claims that "evidence ... that numerals are nouns ... [rather than quantifiers] comes from a construction ... in which ['numerals'] are preceded by adjectives and by the ... *singular* article" (1977:128–9, original emphases). For instance [3]:

[3] a   nasty   nine   nights
     singular article adjective 'numeral' plural noun

The point about [3] is that in [1c] the noun *dozen* is also preceded by the singular article *a*; but in [1b] a singular article could not thus appear with the quantifier *some*:

[4] * he bought a (nasty) some books

Therefore, Jackendoff concludes that his *narrow* restriction of word-classes to just ten is validated in that instead of excessive 'numerals', words like *nine* can indeed be unified with nouns in [3], and hence in [1a] and everywhere. We will therefore refer to the construction exemplified in [3] as the '*n*umerals-as-*n*ouns' of section N. Numerals-as-nouns thus involve a singular article (*a*), an adjective (e.g. *nasty*), a 'numeral' (e.g. *nine*), and a plural noun (e.g. *nights*).

It will be noted that Jackendoff's interpretation that *a* in [3] unifies 'numerals' like *nine* with nouns depends on the assumption that *a* does indeed belong to *nine*. On the face of it, this seems entirely reasonable, to the extent that *a* cannot alternatively belong to *nights*: * *a nights*, where * is due to the conflict between *singular a* and *plural nights* (the same point applies to *a* in [1c]: *a dozen books*, but * *a books*). We will return to this point; but first something else.

For the moment what is of interest to *A–Z*'s juxtaposition of OG to NG is that Jackendoff – who represents NG – refers to the latter, as if NG 'reconstructs' OG (cf. Part II). For numerals-as-nouns Jackendoff notes that it is "a construction little noted in the [NG] literature (although it appears in Jespersen)" (ibid.; note that Jackendoff does not specify the reference: it should be to Jespersen 1914:110–14). This illustrates the usual tendency in NG to ignore any OG other than Jespersen (see Part II). It also points towards the reason for things to be covered – or not – in NG: pertinence to a theoretical position. Unless word-classes are restricted to a specific number, such as Jackendoff's ten, unification of numerals-as-nouns assumes little or no theoretical significance in NG: there is no *narrow* concern whether *nine* is a 'numeral', or a noun, or a quantifier, or whatever. Accordingly, numerals-as-nouns will be 'little noted in NG literature'. In fact, as

Jackendoff's particular restriction to ten word-classes does not appear to have found any wider acceptance, the construction of numerals-as-nouns has apparently *not* been noted in NG at all before, or even after, Jackendoff; neither in the 'literature' (but cf. section N.4 below), nor in the putatively more comprehensive NG 'grammars' of SS&P and Emonds. But of course the comprehensive coverage of OG should extend to numerals-as-nouns: Jackendoff's *'although* it appears in Jespersen' seems to belie NG's profound misunderstanding of Jespersen as OG (see Part II). On the other hand, since OG should not have any stake in *narrow*ly restricting the number of word-classes, it is not to be expected that OG should interpret cases of numerals-as-nouns like [3] as evidence that numerals are to be unified with nouns.

On the basis of the above, *A–Z* will proceed as follows for '*N* is for numerals-as-nouns'. Section N.1 will review OG on numerals-as-nouns. Primarily, it will redress Jackendoff's exclusive attention to Jespersen: for all OG, we will inquire whether it covers numerals-as-nouns. Secondly, it will then be of interest to see whether and how OG accounts for the appearance of singular *a* with a plural noun like *nights* – in particular how else OG accounts for *a* if it does not *narrow*ly unify 'numerals' with nouns. As for NG, it can be stated here and now that a typically *narrow* situation obtains: only Jackendoff (1977) has covered numerals-as-nouns, as only for Jackendoff (1977) is the point pertinent to grammar (but see section N.4 3). In conclusion, section N.2 summarizes the situation as another case of juxtaposition of OG and NG (as usual, discussion and extensions follow, in section N.3).

N.1 On OG on numerals-as-nouns

To begin with Sweet as *A–Z*'s earliest representative of OG, the specific construction of numerals-as-nouns does not seem to be covered by Sweet at all. However, in view of what subsequent OG has to say about numerals-as-nouns, it is of interest to note that Sweet denigrates *narrow* interpretations of plurals: "subjects in the plural which suggest ideas of singularity may take singular verbs, as in *forty yards is too much*" (1898:82). It is the 'idea of singularity' in *forty yards* that accounts for the singular verb *is*, rather than plural *are*; irrespective of the plural form *yard-s*. Note that this reveals as *narrow* Jackendoff's NG interpretation of numerals-as-nouns; viz. the 'conclusion' that in *a nasty nine nights a* belongs to *nine* because of * *a nights*. Sweet would apparently be *open* to accounting for *a* on the basis of an 'idea of singularity' in *nasty nine nights*. (Incidentally, note that Sweet does cover corresponding negative data: "* this books" (1891:34), an un-grammatical combination of singular *this* and plural *book-s*. This is (just) one instance where a contrast between OG and NG as ignorant of or obsessed by negative evidence, respectively (see II.4), would be an inadequate over-simplification).

In Poutsma's OG grammar, comprehensive coverage is duly achieved in the area of numerals-as-nouns (as in most others). For Jackendoff's numerals 'preceded by adjectives and by the singular article', Poutsma (1914:304–5) has "The indefinite article ... before a word-group, consisting of a numeral and a plural noun, denoting a certain unit, especially when this word-group is pre-ceded by an adjective". Note that Jackendoff *narrow*ly stipulates presence of an adjective like *nasty* in [3]; but Poutsma *open*ly allows the adjective to be absent (though 'especially' = predomi-nantly it is present). That is, Jackendoff's [4a] corresponds word-by-word to Poutsma's [4b]; but Jackendoff has no equivalent to [4c]:

[4a] a beautiful two   weeks
[4b] a single   four   years
[4c] a   twelve months

Moreover, the respective interpretations of [4a, b] contrast dia-metrically. Jackendoff wants to look upon [4a] as if *a* belongs to *two*, so that *two* 'is' a singular noun, and *a beautiful two* is a word-group where singular *a* and singular *two* agree. But in [4b] Poutsma in so many words takes *four years* to be a 'word-group'. This is indicated by the bracketings of [5]:

[5a] [a beautiful two] weeks
[5b] a single [four years]

For Poutsma the point about [5b] is that *four years* is a word-group 'denoting a [= one = singular] certain unit'; such that singular *a* is accounted for as agreeing with the 'idea of singularity' (Sweet) in *four years* – without numeral *four* 'being', let alone 'having to be', a noun. The 'singularity' of *four years* is actually nicely emphasized by the adjective *single* in [4b]. Moreover, Poutsma goes on to draw explicit attention to the fact that "the following quotation [= [6]] where the word-group is referred to by *one* ... shows that it is understood as a singular":

[6] the *first six months* will not rank as *one* of the most important of our time

Both in covering cases like [4c] without adjective, and in fully emancipating numerals alongside nouns, Poutsma clearly juxtaposes to Jackendoff as *open* vs. *narrow* respectively.

Curme and Kruisinga also cover the point of Modern English grammar of numerals-as-nouns: [7a, b] correspond to [3] as indicated:

[3]   a nasty   nine nights
[7a] a rather uncomfortable ten   minutes (Curme 1931:541)
[7b] a good   six   days   (Kruisinga 1932b:314)

For Curme "the plural form of the noun may acquire a oneness of meaning so that in spite of the plural form we use the noun as a singular" (1931:540). Kruisinga (1932b:302) states that "Plural nouns of measure are often construed as singulars".

Curme thus directly continues the OG tendency of accounting for numerals-as-nouns in terms of meaning: 'the idea of singularity' (Sweet) – 'denoting a certain unit' (Poutsma) – 'oneness of meaning' (Curme). Kruisinga apparently stands a little apart from this tradition when he avoids an account in semantic terms by talking about a plural being 'construed' as singular. A 'construction' fits in better with Kruisinga's putatively more formal approach (see section 2.3) than an 'idea'. Actually, however, Kruisinga's formal construction ignores the role of the adjective (cf. [4]); as well as the formally essential question of whether 'numeral' + noun constitutes a word-group (cf. [5]). In fact, as for the reason to formally 'construe' singulars as plurals (or vice versa), it appears that for Kruisinga, too, it is essentially semantic: "The use of the number form naturally depends on the meaning" (1932b:303).

Even Kruisinga essentially extends the OG approach pioneered by Sweet, in another sense as well. Sweet only discusses the combination of plural subjects with singular verbs; and Kruisinga in turn also takes cases of singular *a* with plural nouns like [7b] as "details" (1932b:301), to be included in the coverage of plural subject – singular verb. In fact, Kruisinga's first example of plural construed as singular is an (unacknowledged) example of Sweet's: *thirty yards is a good distance* (Sweet 1898:82; Kruisinga 1932b: 302).

Given a firmly established tradition of OG covering numerals-as-nouns, it may be asked how the more recent Quirk *et al.* grammars carry on this tradition. Remarkably, they really don't. Neither *GCE* (1972) nor *CGoEL* (1985) genuinely covers this point of Modern English grammar. It is true that a somewhat intricate flow chart in the former (1972:143) might be interpreted as allowing *another – two – months*; but as the same chart then also allows * *these – other – month*, this is not adequate at all. The flow chart as such duly does not return in *CGoEL*, which more perspicuously presents the example of *another three weeks*, as well

179

as *another two rooms*. In addition, the reader is explicitly invited to "Note that when it is followed by a plural cardinal number [= 'numeral'], *another* takes a plural noun as head" (1985:262). But the latter note also seems to widen the gap between Quirk *et al.*'s coverage and the one this section is after: interpreted as [8a] the example does not correspond to [3] as [8b] would:

[3]   a   nasty nine nights
[8a] another   three weeks
[8b] a(n)   other three weeks

In other words, Quirk *et al.* at best seem to cover singular *another* with a numeral and plural noun; but *not* singular *a(n)* with adjective, numeral, and plural noun. Conversely, Poutsma (1914: 304: *another fifty years*) and Curme (1931:541:*another two weeks*) do cover [8], in addition to [3].

And so does Jespersen (1914:112), with *another ten days, another two seconds, another 26 dogs*. As Jackendoff (1977:128–9) attempts to annex Jespersen to the NG literature, let us now look finally at the extent to which Jespersen actually represents OG. We have already seen that Jespersen's coverage of numerals-as-nouns is not at all unique among OG: they also appear in Poutsma, Curme, and Kruisinga. So what might still transfer Jespersen to NG would rather be the interpretation: [5a] or [5b]? In truly *open* fashion, Curme and Kruisinga do not commit themselves either way: in OG coverage is essential; interpretation, if any, only secondary. But we have seen that Poutsma does argue for [5b], i.e. a word-group consisting of a numeral and a plural noun. Jespersen is in essential agreement with Poutsma here, taking the numeral to be an 'adjunct' to the plural noun, so that they constitute a word-group (cf. '2 1' in section j): "the whole word-group being treated as a singular" (1914:111). Moreover, in line with other OG, the 'treatment' of plural as singular is again entirely semantic: Jespersen entitles the relevant chapter of *MEG* 'Meaning of Number', and the specific section 'Unification of Plurals'. Thus we get OG's [9a] in Jespersen rather than [9b] which Jackendoff would like NG to 'reconstruct' from OG:

[9a] a delightful [three weeks]
[9b] [a delightful three] weeks

In fact, with respect to the NG issue of the word-class that 'numerals' would belong to, Jespersen explicitly epitomizes the *open* attitude: "grammarians [*inter alia* NG] disagree as to the 'part of speech' [= word-class]; for us [OG] the question is of little importance, so long as we recognize [= cover] *a hundred*, etc." (1914:108).

Still, it would seem that a choice between [9a, b] (or [5a, b])
might be determined by drawing numerals-as-nouns – singular
article + plural noun – together with what Sweet already covers,
singular verb + plural subject. Note that especially Kruisinga
might be expected to do this, since he treats the singular article as
a 'detail' alongside the singular verb. But even Kruisinga does not
cover explicitly any example like either [10a] or [10b]:

[10a] ? a beautiful [three days] was spent in Spain
[10b] ?[a beautiful three] days were spent in Spain

Like Kruisinga for OG, Jackendoff fails to raise this issue on
behalf of NG, even though it seems obviously pertinent in the
latter case. Moreover, Jackendoff's OG source, Jespersen, comes
even closer to it than Kruisinga: "the whole plural word-group
[e.g. *three days*] being treated as a singular, as shown by the form
of the verb [e.g. *was*] or by a singular adjective [e.g. *a*], or *by both
in the same sentence*" (1914:111; emphases added). 'Both in the
same sentence' would be [10a]. Unfortunately Jespersen only
illustrates the two former, separate cases: singularity shown either
by the verb or by the article (as in Kruisinga); but not actually any
case like [10a] with both at the same time. Thus Poutsma remains
the one grammar in OG – and NG! – to approximate coverage of
this issue: viz. the singularity of *six months* assumed to be shown
both by a singular article *a and* by the pro-form *one* in sentence [6].

On the other hand, it is Jespersen who pays most attention to
the role of the adjective in the numerals-as-nouns construction.
This adjective is *open*ly optional – though preferable – for
Poutsma; but *narrow*ly obligatory for Jackendoff (cf. [4]). However, Jackendoff does not *narrow*ly attempt to account for the
putative obligatoriness of the adjective (and if it is optional, there
is nothing for Poutsma to account for). Once again Jespersen
essentially agrees with Poutsma, both being OG (but recall that
Kruisinga ignores the role of the adjective). For Jespersen "the
indefinite article is often [i.e. *not* always] a means for placing an
adjective, which would otherwise be differently interpreted: *an
honest fifteen runs* is not the same as *fifteen honest runs*" (1914:
112). But why should the adjective play a role in the numerals-as-
nouns construction at all? For Jespersen (1914:111) "One of the
reasons why . . . in English, is probably . . . that adjectives have no
numerical inflection". That is, "*a delightful three weeks* would be
felt to be too incongruous in a language in which *delightful* would
either have a distinctive sg [singular] or a distinctive pl [plural]
ending". However that may be, it leads Jespersen to observe that
the construction of numerals-as-nouns "is unparalleled in any

cognate language". It may be that the particularly English status of numerals-as-nouns is precisely why it has so consistently been observed by OG, specifically by its non-native contributors: Poutsma, Kruisinga, Jespersen (see section 2.4 on Curme as (non-) native who 'accordingly' also covers the point); but not by the natives Sweet and Quirk; whereas NG, whose theoretical point of departure imposes a restriction to more or less universal features, has in overwhelming majority ignored this English peculiarity.

N.2 Conclusions

There will hardly be any need to belabour the juxtaposition of OG and NG with respect to numerals-as-nouns. OG and NG here largely appear true to form, and their juxtaposition is accordingly almost perfect. Prompted perhaps by non-native unfamiliarity, OG covers the point quite regularly, even if it does not appear in the pioneering OG of (native) Sweet, nor – more oddly – in the most recent OG of (largely native) Quirk *et al.* By contrast, NG has almost consistently ignored this point, which – whether as a point particular to Modern English grammar or otherwise – easily remains non-pertinent to its theoretical restrictions.

The juxtaposition of OG and NG may seem to dissolve upon the single occasion when NG does cover numerals-as-nouns. This is duly when the construction appears to be pertinent to Jackendoff's theoretical concern to sweep 'numerals' under the carpet: viz. by unification with nouns; for which Jackendoff refers to OG, particularly to Jespersen. However, the juxtaposition actually still manifests itself here. The NG notion of pertinence puts the focus on the singular article *a* which, as it cannot be related to a plural noun, may be interpreted as identifying the 'numeral' as a singular noun. Although Jackendoff refers to OG – only Jespersen – his theoretical perspective makes him pass by the prevalent OG interpretation – pioneered by Sweet, but also in Jespersen: that numeral + plural noun convey an 'idea of singularity', by which the singular article can be accounted for semantically – and hence is after all not pertinent to the grammatical status of 'numerals': as numerals, as nouns, or whatever. Moreover, Jackendoff's exclusion of any other OG than Jespersen is symptomatic of NG's *narrow* ability to ignore evidence – available in OG – in favour of the semantic account: Poutsma's observation of concord with singular *one* in [6]. The *narrow* way in which NG, represented by Jackendoff (1977), (ab)uses OG represented by Jespersen is profoundly contrary to the *open* nature of OG itself; and thus only serves to reinforce the juxtaposition.

N.3 Discussion and extensions

1 OG and NG disagree as to the interpretation of numerals-as-nouns: [5b] or [5a]. The main text alerts to hints in OG (Kruisinga, Jespersen) that this issue might be decided by looking for available evidence for [10a, b]; but neither OG nor NG effectively cover such evidence. However, Juul (1975) presents many authentic examples along the lines of *both* [10a] *and* [10b], e.g. [ia, b] respectively:

[ia] an additional 20,000 pounds *is* to be spent
[ib] a further 500,000 copies *are* being printed

- Would the availability of both [1a, b] as evidence be more of an embarrassment to OG or to NG? Why (not)?

Poutsma (1914:299) prefaces his coverage of numerals-as-nouns (and of singular/plural anomalies in general) with the statement: "In many cases the available evidence is not sufficient to draw reliable conclusions from as to the generally prevailing practice".

- In what way(s) do [ia, b] confirm or deny Poutsma's statement?
- In what way(s) is Poutsma's statement (not) representative of the *open* approach to Modern English grammar? To what extent does Poutsma practice what he preaches here?

2 For Poutsma, in *a single four years* there is a 'word-group consisting of numeral and plural noun': *four years* (cf. [5b]). However, in *the first six months*, Poutsma's emphases in [6] suggest that *first six months* is the 'word-group referred to by *one*'.

- Discuss how Poutsma's two interpretations of numerals-as-nouns differ from each other. Are the two interpretations incompatible? Which interpretation is more similar to Jackendoff's NG one (cf. [5b]), if either?

Jackendoff (1977) is a standard reference in NG for constituency 'behind bars', the attempt to incorporate into NG the constraints of dependency (see sections D, G, j) by X-bar theory. Jackendoff's interpretation of *a beautiful two weeks* in [5b] could be stated as 'the word *two* modifies the word *weeks*, the words *a* and *beautiful* each in turn modify the word *two*'. As such, Jackendoff's interpretation could be construed as being constrained to *words*, not admitting word-groups, as in dependency. On the other hand, Poutsma's interpretation of numerals-as-nouns requires recognition of a *word-group four years* at least (and perhaps also the word-group *single four years*); and thus Poutsma extends beyond the constraints of dependency to constituency.

- Discuss if and how Poutsma's OG interpretation(s) and Jackendoff's NG one would be *open* and *narrow* respectively.
3 With respect to Jackendoff's NG account of numerals-as-nouns, De Jong (1983:105) notes that "even within this ... restricted framework it is not hard to present an alternative account". In particular, De Jong suggests that 'numerals' may be unified with either determiners (e.g. in *three weeks*) or adjectives (e.g. in *these three weeks*). Note that Jackendoff *does* admit both determiners and adjectives among his ten word-classes; and that thus De Jong indeed equally explains 'numerals' away, i.e. equally *narrow*ly. Under her alternative NG account of 'numerals', De Jong (1983:108) goes on to suggest that numerals-as-nouns are no longer pertinent as they are to Jackendoff; they may now be reinterpreted as in [ii]:

   [ii] a beautiful [three weeks]

   In [ii], *three weeks* is taken as a 'complex noun' (cf. *fortnight*, i.e. a *word*, not a word-group, unlike apparently similar [5b]); and *three* is therefore neither determiner nor adjective, and thus irrelevant to De Jong's account of numerals-as-determiners-or-adjectives.
- Discuss whether for De Jong's NG account of numerals-as-nouns it would be more appropriate than for Jackendoff's to say that it 'reconstructs' the prevalent OG account [5b].
   De Jong (1983:108) twice calls numerals-as-nouns "unusual".
- Would it be appropriate to equate 'unusual' with the NG notion of 'not pertinent'. Would an 'unusual' construction (have to) be part of OG's available evidence? Could the Dutch linguist De Jong's 'unusual' be equated with the Danish grammarian Jespersen's 'unparalleled'. Why (not)?
   Poutsma (1914:305) and Jespersen (1914:114) explicitly draw the comparison of 'numerals-as-nouns' to cases like *a fortnight*. Neither other OG nor Jackendoff (1977) and De Jong (1983) in NG do.
- Can you account for (non-)coverage of *a fortnight* in OG and/or NG?

O is for *ought* without *to*

Among the more notable features of Modern English grammar are the differences that can be observed between 'modals' like *will* and '(real) verbs' like *want* as in [1]:

[1a] they will   go
[1b] they want to go

One difference between 'modals' and 'verbs' is already apparent in [1]: 'modals' may be followed by a plain infinitive *go*, verbs by a *to*-infinitive *to go*; but not vice versa:

[2a] * they will to go
[2b] * they want   go

By and large, a number of other properties neatly correlate to the property of appearing without *to* (−*to*) or with *to* (+*to*). For instance, from among the *nice*-properties of section b (cf. also section L), respectively *not* or *don't* as *n*egatives in [3]; and *i*nversion with subject, or *do* before subject in questions [4]:

[3a]   they   will not   go
[3b] * they don't will   go
[3c] * they   want not to go
[3d]   they don't want   to go
[4a]   will   they   go
[4b] * do   they will   go
[4c] * want they   to go
[4d]   do   they want to go

Also, there is, respectively, no -*s* or an -*s* in the third person singular:

[5a]   he will   go
[5b] * he wills   go
[5c] * he want to go
[5d]   he wants to go

Given [1–5], it seems evident that some distinction between 'modals' and 'verbs' can be made in Modern English grammar.

However, things are not necessarily as clear-cut as [1–5] may suggest. Problems arise when an item like *ought* is considered; for instance [6]:

[6a] they ought to go (cf. [1]: +to)
[6b] he   ought to go (cf. [5]: no -*s*)

Ought as in [6b] may be seen to be intermediate between 'modal' and 'verb': like 'modals' *ought* takes no -*s*, but at the same time like 'verbs' *ought* is +*to*. Needless to say, the question now arises how *ought* behaves in negatives and questions (cf. [3, 4]). Does *ought* take *not* and invert like 'modals'?

[7a] ?they ought not to go
[7b] ?ought they to go

Or does *ought* take *don't* and *do* precede the subject, as with 'verbs'?

[8a] ?they don't ought to go
[8b] ?do they ought to go

With respect to a putative distinction between 'modals' and 'verbs', it will be seen that [7] are the more intriguing cases: if these exist, *ought* would here behave 'inconsistently': modal *not* vs. verbal +*to* in [7a]; modal inversion vs. verbal +*to* in [7b] (in [8] *ought* would consistently be a 'verb': *do(n't)* and +*to*). In section '*O* for *ought* without *to*' (−*to*), A–Z is interested in whether OG and/or NG allow modal consistency to assert itself, as in [9]: where verbal +*to* of [7] makes way for modal −*to*, alongside modal *not* or modal inversion:

[9a] ?they ought not   go
[9b] ?ought they   go

Note at the outset that OG should be *open* to covering cases like [7], if there is 'available evidence' for such inconsistencies; whereas NG might proclaim consistency by [9] if a 'preconceived' theoretical distinction between 'modals' and 'verbs' is the *narrow* issue.

0.1 On OG on *ought* without *to*

In OG, a strongly prevalent tendency is to cover evidence of *ought* manifesting verbal consistency. Poutsma (1926:596), Kruisinga (1931:428), Curme (1931:414), Jespersen (1940:512), *CGoEL* (1985:139) all contain examples along the lines of [10]:

[10a] he didn't ought to go
[10b] did he ought to go

Note that [10] differs from [8] in taking verbal *did(n't)*, rather than *do(n't)*, along with verbal +*to*, to be verbally consistent. But for the moment, *A–Z*'s interest is in modal consistency for *ought*: modal *not* in negatives, and/or inversion in questions, along with modal −*to* as in [9].

In OG, only Poutsma, Jespersen, and Quirk *et al.* seem to present evidence from Modern English for [9]. Poutsma (1926:407) appears to consider such *ought* −*to* as a kind of poetic licence: "*Ought* now almost regularly stands with . . . *to* . . . In the following quotations the absence of *to* is, apparently, required by the metre":

[11] how ought/I address thee, how ought/I revere thee

The source of [11] is a late nineteenth-century poem (by R. Browning, *Agamemnon*); note that Poutsma does not specify that [11] apparently illustrates modal consistency for *ought* in questions: *inversion* along with −*to*. For Jespersen (1940:207–8) modal −*to* with *ought* is ostensibly exceptional in sentences like [12], which is coded as "Amr", i.e. American, and dated 1914: *ought* "has regularly the *to*-infinitive; only exceptionally the bare infinitive [i.e. −*to*]":

[12] she ought not   remain

Again, Jespersen leaves it to the reader to note that [12] is a *negative* sentence with modal consistency: *not* alongside −*to*. Only in the grammars of Quirk *et al.* does OG make explicit the point about questions and negatives: "*Ought* regularly has . . . *to* . . . , but AmE [American English] occasionally has the bare infinitive [−*to*] in negative sentences and in questions" (1972:82):

[13a] you oughtn't   smoke so much
[13b] ought you   smoke so much

Similarly in *CGoEL* (1985:139); and *CGoEL* also presents a corresponding piece of ungrammatical evidence (cf. section II.4):

[14] we $\left\{ \begin{array}{c} \text{ought to} \\ \text{* ought} \end{array} \right\}$ give him another chance

Needless to say, the essential point about Poutsma and Jespersen as *open* grammars is that they do cover *ought* −*to*. Although Quirk *et al.*'s explicitness about consistently modal *ought only* in negatives and questions will be useful in many ways, there is no real gain here with respect to the extent that OG is *open*. Quite notably, however, Poutsma, Jespersen, and *GCE* agree again in that none sees occasion to interpret [11–13] as evidence for (or against?) a *narrow* distinction between 'modals' and 'verbs' (note that [14] is automatically consistent with both +*to* and * −*to*, viz. consistently verbal and consistently modal respectively; because in [14] the distinction only arises in that one place: +/−*to*). For the latter *narrow* issue, one naturally turns to NG, in section O.2.

However, it may be noted that the issue does come up in OG as well. Unlike in *GCE*, Quirk *et al.* in *CGoEL* take *ought* +*to* to belong to 'marginal modals', i.e. "whose status is in some degree intermediate between ... modal auxiliaries ... and full verbs" (1985:136; in *GCE*, Quirk *et al.* also have 'marginal modals', but *ought* is not included here yet: 1972:82–3). By contrast "*Ought* ... may be treated as a central [= consistent] modal if speakers construe it with the bare infinitive" (1985:38): with −*to* as in [13]. Earlier Kruisinga – who does not cover *ought* −*to* at all – already observes that unlike other 'modals', "*ought* ... resemble[s] full verbs in ... the use of ... *to*" (1931:503).

Before turning to NG on *ought* −*to* now, we should not leave OG without having noted that with respect to *ought* −*to* in Modern English, Sweet and more saliently Kruisinga and Curme should be said to more or less fail to be *open*: they do not seem to have been *open* to available evidence along the lines of [11–13]. In fact, Sweet is explicitly *narrow* in stating that "*ought* has only the supine [i.e. +*to*]" (1896:118); but perhaps this may be excused in the pioneer of OG. For Kruisinga, *ought* is, less rigidly perhaps, one of the "auxiliaries taking ... *to*" (1931:291–2). Curme actually does allow *ought* −*to*, but not in Modern English: "the infinitive is ... used ... [w]ith its simple form [−*to*] ... [a]fter ... in older English, sometimes *ought*" (1931:474–5); Curme's (1931:476) example is [15] from about 1435 (*A–Z* has modernized the spelling):

[15] I ought   love my neighbour

Note that [15] is neither a negative sentence nor a question; *I ought to love my neighbour* with +*to* would be equally consistent (verbally) as [15] is (modally).

O.2 On NG on *ought* without *to*

If we now turn to NG, we should expect that what here determines the account of *ought* +/−*to* will be the logic of the situation rather than the facts of the matter. That is, under a deductive approach, if a theoretical distinction between 'modals' and 'verbs' is pre-supposed, any evidence from *ought* that such a distinction is not always maintained consistently will be non-pertinent; and may hence be ignored with perfect justice. Put differently, if NG *narrow*ly proclaims a 'modal/verb' distinction, the pertinent facts are sharp contrasts between *will* and *want* as in [1–5], to the exclusion of inconsistencies as in [6b, 7]: *ought* a 'modal' with no −*s*, with *not*, or with inversion; but also a 'verb' with +*to*.

By and large, this is indeed the situation that obtains in *A–Z*'s NG standards. Although not really fully committed this way, Chomsky has always practically admitted a distinction between 'modals' and 'verbs': for instance "I will omit any discussion of their [= of 'modals'] status" (1981:140). Similarly, SS&P intend to "leave *open*" (1973:601; emphasis added) whether they should impose a distinction. To be on the safe side, so to speak, Chomsky and SS&P therefore ignore *ought*, primarily when it is inconsistent with the 'modal/verb' distinction as in [6b, 7]; but then also when it *is* consistent with it, as in [11–13], as a 'modal'; or as in [10], as a 'verb'.

In Emonds (1976), however, the situation is somewhat different: "In the analysis . . . being proposed, . . . modals and verbs do not form a syntactic class, nor do they undergo any rules in common" (1976:213). Still, Emonds does not quite take his firm commitment to a 'modal/verb' distinction to be manifested by +/−*to*. Rather, Emonds adopts a theoretical position which *narrow*s *all* infinitives to +*to*, even those that follow 'modals'. Only, this *to* "is regularly deleted in [this] context . . . ; some exceptional cases that point to the existence of an underlying *to* in this position are . . . *ought to* . . . " (1976:220). The NG logic of this will again be clear: a *narrow* requirement for all cases to be +*to* in the first instance makes the 'exceptional' +*to* after *ought* a highly pertinent one; which is thus duly covered. Equally obviously, Emonds is not required to pay similar attention to any tendency for *ought* (for him) perversely to shed the pertinent +*to* anywhere: *ought* −*to* is *not* pertinent, and thus not covered by Emonds (1976).

Conversely, of course, if NG adopts the *narrow* requirement that 'modals' and 'verbs' should be unified, then it will take cases where the distinction cannot be maintained to be the pertinent ones: that is, inconsistent cases of *ought* +*to*. If beyond the NG standards we now turn to NG 'literature', a clear instance is afforded when Pullum (1981) argues for the unification of 'modals' and 'verbs'. Pullum admits that "my discussion has focused mainly on . . . *ought*" (1981:459); in particular on inconsistent examples of *ought* like [16] (1981:437):

[16] oughtn't we to do something

The point about [16], for Pullum, is its very inconsistency: +*to* would identify *ought* as a 'verb',but −*n't* (= *not*) and inversion would identify *ought* at the same time as a 'modal'. On the basis of examples like [16], for Pullum the *narrow* exclusion of a 'modal/ verb' distinction is vindicated. But just by this token, manifest (counter-)examples of distinctions between 'modals' and 'verbs' like [1–5] cannot so be pertinent; nor can *ought* be when it is modally consistent: *ought* −*to*; which therefore does not figure at all in Pullum's account, in spite of its 'focus' on *ought*.

In itself, all of this is precisely as fundamentally legitimate under a *narrow* approach as it is to conversely concentrate on *will* vs. *want* and ignore *ought*. But Pullum (1981:459) goes on to extol his version of the *narrow* approach: "the ability of a theory to account for items that are slightly aberrant or irregular ... is precisely the sort of thing that should be used as a criterion for accepting or rejecting" the theory. It is not obvious that this can be assented to under a *narrow* approach. At least, Chomsky has argued instead that it is the *open* approach of 'traditional' grammar that should – and does – "provide a full list of exceptions" (1986:2); whereas NG should be concerned with deep-seated regularities within and across languages rather than with Pullum's items that are 'slightly aberrant or irregular' (cf. Part II; also Newmeyer 1969, cited in section L.4 2).

Perhaps the Pullum–Chomsky controversy apparent here is resolved under Emonds' (1985) account of 'modals'. Opposite to Emonds (1976), Emonds (1985) adopts a theory by which 'modals' are *not* really different from 'verbs'; but rather they are unified with 'verbs' – but as verbs with 'unique' properties. That is, the vast majority of 'verbs' is essentially regular (e.g. *walk-walked* is regular; *find-found* is not but is still like *bind-bound*, etc.). But 'modal verbs' are irregular in *unique* ways, what Emonds calls 'Unique Syntactic Behaviour' (1985:165). Note that Emonds thus allows NG to be pertinent to both Chomsky's regularities, 'verbs', and to Pullum's irregularities, 'modal verbs', under one and the same *narrow* approach. More specifically, Emonds will now, like Pullum, focus on the pertinent irregularity of *ought*: it is precisely its inconsistencies which constitute the *unique* behaviour of *ought*. Thus, "*ought* irregularly takes a following *to*" (1985:167). Once again, that *ought* may also be regularized, i.e. given consistent modal treatment, is not as such pertinent to unique syntactic behaviour (although it does not contradict it either): *ought* −*to* is not covered by Emonds (1985) either.

It will now be clear that both the theoretical position that 'modals' and 'verbs' *can* be distinguished, and the one that they can *not*, will generally entail that *ought* entirely, or at least as *ought −to*, remains non-pertinent to NG. Lest it should now be thought that *ought −to* is thus necessarily not pertinent to *any* conceivable *narrow* approach to Modern English grammar, we may turn to theories that do not address the (non-)distinction of 'modal' and 'verb' as such. For instance, recall from OG, notably Quirk *et al.*, that *ought* may be seen to appear *−to* in negative sentences and in questions. If *ought* behaves in a special way in such contexts, this may obviously be pertinent to some theory specifically about negatives and/or questions.

Along these lines, in a contribution to the NG literature, Falk (1984:505) notes that the switches from verbal *need* and *dare* to modal *need* and *dare* in negative and interrogative sentences presuppose a theory about such sentences to account for the switches. And Falk goes on to anticipate that it will be deduced from such a theory that *ought*, too, should switch from 'verb' (+*to*) to 'modal' (−*to*) in negatives and questions; he duly presents the examples of [17]:

[17a]   I ought to feed the hamster
[17b] * I ought   feed the hamster
[17c]   ?ought I to feed the hamster
[17d]   ?ought I   feed the hamster
[17e]   ??I ought not to feed the hamster
[17f]   ?I ought not   feed the hamster

Note that Falk allows a prospective theory already to determine that an inconsistent case like [17e], *not* vs. +*to*, is worse than a regularized one, [17f], with −*to*. In anticipation of a theory, [17] is "A puzzle" (ibid.) of a kind only a *narrow* approach to Modern English grammar can produce.

An attempt to contribute to the solution of this NG puzzle is made in Stuurman (1987), where it is suggested that the theoretical link between +/−*to* on the one hand, and negatives and questions on the other hand, be established via 'finiteness'. To begin with, it is noted that in some cases the presence or absence of *to* correlates with whether the preceding verb is non-finite or finite respectively:

[18a]   they saw Bill   cross the river
[18b] * they saw Bill to cross the river
[18c] * Bill was seen   cross the river
[18d]   Bill was seen to cross the river

In NG, [18] may be taken to be pertinent to a theoretical position that finite items like *saw* take −*to*, non-finite ones like *seen* +*to*.

Also, finite items can invert with the subject, *will* in [19]; or precede *not* in [20]; but not non-finite ones:

[19a]   John will   stay, and   Bill *will* be invited
[19b]   John won't stay, nor *will* Bill   be invited
[19c]   John will   stay, and   Bill   *be* invited
[19d] * John won't stay, nor *be* Bill   invited
[20a]   Bill   was not   invited
[20b] * Bill will *be*   not   invited
[20c] * Bill   not *was* invited
[20d]   Bill will   not *be* invited

As applied to *ought*, Stuurman's theoretical position thus looks essentially like [21]:

[21] *ought*
    before *not* → finite   → −*to*: [17f], * [17e]
    in inversion → finite   → −*to*: [17d], * [17c]
    otherwise   → nonfinite → +*to*: [17a], * [17b]

Needless to say, Stuurman's account of *ought* entails, finally, that the consistently modal instances of *ought* −*to* are the pertinent ones for NG; there the correlations that the NG theory of [21] *narrow*ly proclaims are manifested: *not* and −*to*, inversion and −*to*. Under Stuurman's account of *ought*, the evidence that NG will have to, and can, ignore is of inconsistency; although this is the evidence predominantly available in OG; and also the evidence that is pertinent to both Pullum's (1981) and Emonds' (1985) NG theories of unification of 'modals' and 'verbs'. The latter theoretical point is something that Stuurman's account, like SS&P (1973), simply remains neutral to.

O.3 Conclusions

The juxtaposition between accounts in OG and in NG of *ought* is fairly clear at least as regards their respective practices. Whereas the more comprehensive grammars of OG (in this case Poutsma, Jespersen, Quirk *et al.*) are more or less carefully *open* to alternations between *ought* +*to* and *ought* −*to*, NG will more *narrow*ly focus on one *ought* or the other only as befits theoretical preconceptions: Pullum (1981) and Emonds (1976, 1985) focus on *ought* +*to* inconsistent with *not* in negatives and with inversion in questions, given their theories of (non-)distinctions between 'modals' and 'verbs'; in Falk (1984) and Stuurman (1987) the focus is on *ought* −*to* in such negatives and questions, given a (prospective) theory (of finiteness).

It is true that in OG the *narrow* issue of (non-)distinction between 'modals' and 'verbs' also arises, in Kruisinga and in Quirk *et al.* (1985). Indeed it should be admitted that Kruisinga's is a relatively *narrow* approach in this case as he only covers the *ought* +*to* that 'resembles full verbs'. But the *open* approach of OG reasserts itself in Quirk *et al.* (1985), for whose 'marginal modal' *ought* +*to* the centrally modal alternative −*to* is covered as well.

On the other hand, if Pullum's insistence that NG should primarily account for irregularities like inconsistent *ought* +*to* amounted to a demand for *open*ness, this again would seriously impair *A−Z*'s juxtaposition of OG and NG. Of course, it would be perverse to insist that NG should *not* account for irregularities: Emonds (1976, 1985) are none the less NG if *ought* +*to* is pertinent to them. But alongside Emonds' theories for *ought* +*to*, finiteness as Stuurman's theoretical framework does allow NG to take *ought* −*to* to be pertinent instead. Ultimately, it is thus still the theories that determine whether and which regular and/or irregular items are pertinent to NG; rather than conversely, as Pullum suggests, coverage of (ir)regularities determining by itself the acceptance or rejection of NG theories. And this does juxtapose to OG, for which coverage does remain the only appropriate issue.

O.4 Discussion and extensions

1 There seems to be a tendency for *ought* to avoid inconsistent behaviour in 'tag-questions' (*c* for 'code' among the *nice*-properties; cf. section b): viz. verbal +*to* in the main sentence, but modal repetition in the tag. Langendoen (1970:15–16) reports that only 26 out of 46 (= 56.5 per cent) American informants approved [ia], the others preferring [ib] or [ic]:

[ia] you ought to smoke, oughtn't you
[ib] you ought to smoke, shouldn't you
[ic] you ought to smoke, hadn't you

By contrast, 35 out of 46 (= 76 per cent!) approved [ii], where *ought* is modally consistent: −*to* (!) and repeated in the tag:

[ii] you ought not   smoke, ought you

It is interesting to note the appearance of *ought* −*to* in a book whose preface makes the following statement (Langendoen 1970:ix):

The title of this book is the same as that used by . . . Jespersen . . . The books are, however, very different in content . . .

Jespersen's ... is a one-volume summary of his monumental seven-volume grammar of English [cf. section K], which manages to touch on just about every imaginable topic of English grammar. This book aims to be ... comprehensive, but [my book] simply attempts to discuss some basic properties of English grammar in the light of recent developments in the theory of language.

- Discuss whether Langendoen characterizes Jespersen as OG.
- Discuss whether Langendoen characterizes his own work as OG, NG, or something else.
  When it comes to actually accounting for *ought* +/−*to* 'in the light of theory', Langendoen (1970:186) has the following to offer: "according to traditional grammar, the constructions that follow the so-called modal ... verbs ... are ... unmarked [−*to*] infinitives ... there is one ... modal ... verb, *ought*, which takes an unmarked infinitive only when negated and not always even then".
- Discuss whether Langendoen's account of *ought* +/−*to* agrees with the position that he takes *vis-à-vis* OG/NG; and with his observations about *ought* +/−*to* in [i, ii].

2 In much OG (Poutsma 1926:596; Jespersen 1931:128; Curme 1935:254) there is evidence along the lines of [iii]:

[iiia] they hadn't ought to shirk the consequences
[iiib] his friends hadn't ought to let him out
[iiic] he hadn't ought to do it

Note that in [iii] *ought* after *hadn't* appears a participle, i.e. *non-finite*.

- Discuss whether [iii] would be amenable to Stuurman's (1987) theory of (non-)finiteness as applied to *ought* +/−*to*.
  In addition to examples like [iii], Jespersen (1931:128) and Curme (1931:414) present the examples of [iva, b] (both from the same author) and [ivc] respectively (cf. [20a] in section L):

[iva] they'd oughtn't hang a boy
[ivb] you'd oughtn't beat your little son
[ivc] do you claim he'd (= he had) oughtn't

According to Jespersen, [iv] represents "rare (and seemingly not quite natural) variants".

- Discuss whether OG and/or (which) NG should have covered [iv], given that it is 'rare' and/or 'unnatural'.
- Discuss whether [iv] is more or less amenable to Stuurman's (1987) theory of (non-)finiteness than [iii].

3 Jørgensen (1984) claims that examples like [v] show that *ought* is a past tense – and hence finite – also when +*to*:

[v] I suppose I ought to be ashamed of myself? – Yes, I suppose you did

If *ought* in [v] was indeed finite, +*to* would not be expected under Stuurman's NG theory of (non-)finiteness. However, Stuurman (1987:129) notes that *did* as in [v] is not evidence of finiteness for *ought*; cf. [vi]:

[vi] Do you deny going there? – No, I admit I did

Since *did* in [vi] does not show *going* to be finite (it isn't), *did* cannot show *ought* in [v] to be finite either. Stuurman then goes on to claim that in [v] past tense *did* is not due to any correspondence with 'past tense' *ought* (which he takes to be tenseless – hence non-finite – instead); but due to the 'unreal' meaning of *ought*: somebody who says 'I ought to be ashamed of myself' implies that she is *not* really ashamed at all. Now consider the observation in OG (Quirk *et al.* 1985:235) that cases of *ought* "often imply nonfulfilment of the obligation":

[vii] I ought to be working now ... but I'm not

- Discuss whether Stuurman's NG account of [v] 'reconstructs' Quirk *et al.*'s OG account (see Part II).
  Poutsma (1928:68) includes "non-fulfilment" among the meanings of *ought*; Jespersen (1931:121) cites the meanings of *ought* as "duty, rightness, shortcoming, advisability, or strong probability".
- Discuss which of Jespersen's meanings for *ought*, if any, correspond(s) to non-fulfilment and/or unreal.
- Given an OG tradition of Poutsma, Jespersen, and *CGoEL* on *ought* meaning something like non-fulfilment, discuss whether NG 'ought to' cover this as a point of Modern English grammar. Curme (1931:414) presents the example of [viii] (cf. also Poutsma 1926:565, Jespersen 1940:512), and repeatedly calls it a "present" form:

[viii] he don't ought to go

- Discuss whether, and if so how, [viii] could be appealed to in OG and/or NG to decide whether *ought* is a 'present' or 'past' tense, 'tenseless', or whatever.

p is for 'preposition' *per*

To a larger extent than in many other languages, English vocabulary is 'hybrid'. Beside 'native' Germanic words like *freedom*, *king*, *friend*, there are many 'adopted' words like *liberty*, *royal*, *enemy*. Such adopted words may have been fully naturalized (*royal* becomes *royally* just like *free* becomes *freely*); but in some cases, foreign origins may still be recognizable. For instance, one item that is not of Germanic origin is the Latin preposition *per*, as in *per cent*, a Latinate phrase in English meaning 'in (a) hundred': 10 per cent = 'ten in (a) hundred'. As *per cent* = 'in (a) hundred' suggests, Latin had no articles such as *a* that appears in *a hundred*. And it seems that English *per* still retains its Latinate property of suppressing articles. Consider the instances of [1]:

[1a]   he sent the letter by   post
[1b]   he sent the letter by   the post
[1c]   he sent the letter per   post
[1d] * he sent the letter per the post

One of the most useful tools for more or less *narrow*ly determining the word-class that an item belongs to is co-occurrence vs. mutual exclusion. If an item P1 can occur in the same position as P2, it is likely to be of the same word-class as P2; but if P1 can appear together with P3, P1 and P3 are likely to be differently classified. Consider for instance *friend*, *enemy*, and *royal*. Both *friend* and *enemy* may occur in the position following *royal*: *my royal friend*, *my royal enemy*; this suggests that *royal* belongs to a different word-class than either *friend* or *enemy*. On the other hand, in the position following *royal*, *friend* and *enemy* exclude each other: * *my royal friend enemy*, * *my royal enemy friend*. Thus, *friend* and *enemy* are in the same word-class (nouns); and *royal* is in a different one (adjectives) (note that native or adopted makes no difference here).

Let us now consider the question of what word-class *per* would thus belong to. In Latin it was a preposition: and sure enough in English it is mutually exclusive with other prepositions as well; compare [2a, b] to [1a, c]:

[2a] * he sent the letter by per post
[2b] * he sent the letter per by post

[2] might be used to determine that *per* is, like *by*, a 'preposition' in Modern English as it was in Latin. However, for Modern English this classification is not the only evident possibility. On the basis of [1d], mutual exclusion of *per* and *the*, *per* might alternatively be said to belong to the same word-class as *the*, say 'determiners'. In *A–Z*'s miniscule section p, the point of Modern English grammar is the relation between *per* and determiners as it is (not) dealt with in OG and NG.

p.1 On OG on *per*

Almost all OG agrees in including *per* among the 'prepositions' of Modern English: Sweet (1891:476), Poutsma (1926:710), Curme (1931:565), Jespersen (1949:504), *GCE* (1972:301), *CGoEL* (1985:665). The notable exception is Kruisinga, who does not seem to recognize *per* in Modern English at all. Sweet and Curme do not really improve all that much on Kruisinga's non-coverage, in particular because they do not have any observations about the effect that *per* apparently has on determiners.

Poutsma (1914:530), however, at least notes that "the Latin *per* is frequently used in a sense similar to that of *a* [in [3b], (1929:529)]" (*a* being a determiner):

[3a] the production per head
[3b] so much   a   head

Note that Poutsma here takes *per* to be 'Latin' rather than (Modern) English; in (1926:806), *per* is 'Romance'. For Jespersen (1949:504) "The preposition *per* requires zero", i.e. no determiner (cf. section z) in [4a] alongside [4b] (1949:503):

[4a] a   shilling per   man
[4b] five shillings in the pound

There seems to be a subtle difference between Jespersen's *narrow* 'require' and Poutsma's more *open* 'is frequently used'. In fact it is notable that Poutsma is also careful to avoid *narrow*ly calling *per* in [3] a 'preposition'; in [3] it is just 'Latin *per*' without any classification; but 'similar to' a determiner. Conversely, when Poutsma says that "the half-naturalized *maugre, per, sans, versus* and *vice* may be included among the prepositions" (1926:710), he illustrates each of these items ... except *per* (which is here 'half-naturalized', rather than still 'Latin' or 'Romance'). It clearly looks as if Poutsma feels that the Latin classification of *per* as 'preposition' is not really applicable to any English cases; so that the *per* that does actually occur in English is not to be called a 'preposition'.

And this is, indeed, the position that OG may be seen to have adopted in Quirk *et al.*'s grammars. Both *GCE* (1972:301) and *CGoEL* (1985:665) list *per* among the English 'prepositions' (interestingly, *GCE* claims to present a "comprehensive list", but the *Comprehensive* adds to that list *like*, *near*, and the "foreign borrowings" *pro*, *qua*, *re*, *sans* – and more cautiously calls the longer list merely a "list of the most common ... prepositions"). Like Poutsma, however, Quirk *et al.* do not give any actual examples of *per* as an English 'preposition'. Rather, in cases like [5]:

[5] three times $\left\{ \begin{array}{c} a \\ per \end{array} \right\}$ decade

GCE and *CGoEL* agree that we have evidence of "the determiners *a* ... and (less commonly) *per*" (1972:142; 1985:261). In actual Modern English examples, for Quirk *et al.* *per* is a – be it less common – 'determiner', *not* a (common) 'preposition'.

p.2 On NG on *per*

As far as it has been possible to ascertain, no NG has paid any attention to *per* in Modern English, neither to *per* on its own, nor to *per* in connection with determiners. Apparently, so far *per* has not yet been seen to be pertinent to any theoretical position of NG, whether as a 'preposition' or as a 'determiner'.

Perhaps it is instructive to refer here to Sturm's (1986) NG account of *per* in Dutch, a very similar case to English *per*. Sturm's point of departure is that some Dutch 'prepositions', including *per*, may suppress determiners. Yet these cannot be considered to be 'determiners', because determiners *may* co-occur with these 'prepositions' as well: i.e. P1-N or P1-Det-N. Hence P1 $\neq$ Det. However, Sturm immediately contradicts this for P1 = *per*, which he goes on to admit actually may *not* co-occur with Determiners: *per*-N (cf. [1c]), but * *per*-Det-N (cf. [1d]). Not surprisingly amid such contradictory views, *per* and its relation to determiners remains for Sturm on behalf of NG "a mystery" (1986:290; unauthorized translation from the Dutch).

p.3 Conclusions

Until the range of possible solutions can be seen to be restricted by virtue of a *narrow* theoretical position, the mystery of *per* is not amenable to NG accounts; and thus not pertinent. Until then, and even by then (if ever), there can be no doubt about the juxtaposition of NG to OG: OG almost always includes *per* in its coverage; although – if not because – it ignores the mystery by avoiding to commit itself to any *narrow* classification of *per*.

Q is for quasi-questions

Suppose someone wants to report an invitation. She might write something like [1]:

[1] she asked: "Can you come?"

The quotation marks in [1] indicate that [1] is to be taken as containing a literal report of the invitation as it was made. However, one often reports less directly, and then one may write something like [2] instead of [1]:

[2a] she asked whether I could come
[2b] she asked if   I could come

Corresponding to the literal report of [1], [2] contains a modified report by means of a 'quasi-question' Q: the modifications in Q involve pronoun (*I* for *you*); tense (*could* for *can*); inversion (*I could* for *can I*); and the addition of *whether* or *if*. Now consider what happens in the case of statements. A literal report of a statement parallel to [1] would be [3a]; a corresponding indirect modified report, by means of a 'semi-statement' S parallel to the quasi-question Q of [2], would be [3b]:

[3a] she said: "You can come."
[3b] she said that I could come

The semi-statement S of [3b] shares with the quasi-question Q of [2] the changed pronoun (*I*), changed tense (*could*), and lack of inversion (*I could*, not *could I*). Thus a quasi-question Q appears to be primarily characterized, *vis-à-vis* a semi-statement S, by the presence of either *whether* or *if*, rather than *that*. In this section of *A–Z*, *Q* is therefore for Q: *whether*–Q (a quasi-question characterized by introductory *whether*), and *if*–Q.

The positions in which semi-statements S may occur overlap with the positions of *whether*–Q and *if*–Q. For instance, the position as complement (cf. section C) after the verb *know* in [4]:

[4a] I didn't know that   I could come
[4b] I didn't know whether I could come
[4c] I didn't know if   I could come

To represent OG and NG accounts of *whether*–Q and *if*–Q, let us take our cue (pun intended) from [4]. We first identify a number of positions that *that*–S may appear in; and then use these positions as a grid to probe for accounts of *whether*–Q and *if*–Q. From among the positions for *that*–S, *A–Z* selects (arbitrarily; and see section Q.4 2) the five in [5a–e]: *that*–S as complement after a verb (verb+S); after a noun (noun+S); after a preposition (prep+S); and *that*–S initially (S=init), specifically in the position of subject (S=subj):

[5a] I didn't *know that* I could come [= [4a]] :verb+S
[5b] her *hope that* I could come was false   :noun+S
[5c] I heard nothing *except that* I could come :prep+S
[5d] *that* I could come I didn't know   :S=init
[5e] *that* I could come was very pleasant   :S=subj

In [5] and henceforth in section Q, in examples the items that identify what type is at issue are italicized. Corresponding to [5a–e], *A–Z* calibrates accounts of *whether*–Q and *if*–Q with a five-point grid: (a) verb+Q, (b) noun+Q, (c) prep+Q, (d) Q=init, and (e) Q= subj.

Q.1 On OG on quasi-questions

We begin representation of OG accounts of *whether*–Q and/or *if*–Q with the first point of our grid: quasi-questions as complements after verbs, verb+Q. All OG grammars but one recognize both *whether*–Q and *if*–Q in this position; the examples in [6] are from Sweet (1891:130); cf. Jespersen (1927:42–3), Poutsma (1929:627–8), Curme (1931:245), Quirk *et al.* (1972:737; 1985:1053):

[6a] I do not *know*   *whether* it is true or not (verb+*whether*–Q)
[6b] I   *wonder if*   it is true   (verb+*if*–Q)

The only exception here is Kruisinga, who apparently recognizes only verb+*if*–Q (1932b:523).

If both verb+*whether*–Q and verb+*if*–Q are in fact recognized, however, the question arises of any disparity between them. Sweet does not allude to such disparity; for him, verb+*whether*–Q and verb+*if*–Q are entirely equivalent. One may however see a stylistic difference: [6a] with *whether*–Q is "slightly less familiar" (Poutsma); [6b] with *if*–Q is "colloquial" (Curme 1931:242).

Another salient point in OG is the relation of *if*–Q to other cases of *if*. Although from *if* onwards there is word-for-word identity with the *if*–Q of [6b], [7] does not correspond to a genuine direct question; [7] rather expresses a condition, 'in case it is true':

[7] I will not come if it is true

For Sweet, *if*–Q = *if*-conditional is a pure coincidence. Hence there is no disparity among verb+Q in this respect; *both whether*–Q *and if*–Q equally "must be distinguished" (1891:147) from conditionals. Poutsma basically accepts this pioneering OG approach: "Sweet rightly distinguishes [them]" (1926:820). And in Quirk *et al.* (1972:747; cf. 1985:1054), again, *if*–Q and *if*-conditional "have to be distinguished".

For some OG, however, there *is* a disparity among verb+Q here. Only for *if* does Jespersen (1926:42–3) point to "very natural ... combinations in which it is hardly possible to distinguish between a conditional and an interrogative":

[8] I hope you will *tell* me *if* you can come (verb+*if*–Q? *if*–conditional?)

Similarly, for Quirk *et al.* (1972:747; not 1985) in cases like [8] only with *if* there is "Something like a merger". For our purposes, the interesting point here is that as Jespersen and Quirk *et al.* recognize 'combination' or 'merger' of *if*–Q with *if*-conditionals only, there is thus disparity between *whether*–Q and *if*–Q in this respect. In fact, for Curme (1931:242) such disparity accounts for the stylistic differentiation of *whether*–Q and *if*–Q: "in the literary language we usually distinguish" Q and conditional; since *if* does not serve this purpose in cases like [8], one finds "the literary language ... preferring *whether*[–Q] to *if*[–Q] ... and reserving *if* for ... conditionals"; although alongside *whether*–Q, *if*–Q "is still widespread in colloquial language".

At this point it may be useful to summarize OG so far, i.e. on verb+Q; see [9]:

[9] OG on verb+Q

		style	(=conditional?)
Sweet	*whether*–Q		must be distinguished
	if–Q		must be distinguished
Jespersen	*whether*–Q		
	if–Q		combination
Poutsma	*whether*–Q	less familiar	rightly distinguished
	if–Q		rightly distinguished
Curme	*whether*–Q	literary..........(because)........	distinguished
	if–Q	colloquial.......(because)........	not distinguished
Kruisinga			
	if–Q		
GCE	*whether*–Q		
	if–Q		to be distinguished / merger
CGoEL	*whether*–Q		
	if–Q		necessary to distinguish

OG is generally more extensive on verb+Q than on any one of the other positions in [5]. Pioneering OG Sweet in fact *only* covers verb+Q. Where OG does consider other positions, disparity of *whether*–Q and *if*–Q preponderates in terms of evidence being available for the former but not for the latter. For instance, Curme (1931:242) has [10] for Q as complement after a noun, noun+Q:

[10] the *question whether* (not *if*) he should come (noun+ *whether*–Q)

For Poutsma, too, *if*–Q is "never used" as noun+Q (1929:627); but Poutsma does not appear to present evidence for noun+*whether* –Q such as [10], either; cf. (1929:626): "not often". And for Quirk *et al.* (1985:1054; not 1972) there is *whether*–Q vs. "?*" *if*–Q. Similarly for Q as complement after a preposition, prep+Q. Jespersen (1927:48) states that among examples of prep+Q there are "few with *whether* ... and none with *if*", e.g. [11]:

[11] brood *over whether* you're any good   (prep+*whether*–Q)

Accordingly, Poutsma (1929:625), Curme (1931:256), and Kruisinga (1932b:367) provide evidence for prep+*whether*–Q, but not for prep+*if*–Q; they make no explicit comment however. Only Quirk *et al.* (1985:1054; not 1972) again have prep+*whether*–Q vs. explicitly "?*" prep+*if*–Q.

Finally, quasi-questions in initial position, Q=init; specifically as subject, Q=subj. Kruisinga (1932b:365) again illustrates the latter for *whether*–Q without considering *if*–Q at all. But Jespersen

(1927:43) explicates that in fact in [12] "the use of *if* is hardly possible":

[12] *whether* he can come, I very much doubt
　　　(*whether*–Q=init)

More categorically, *if*–Q=init indeed is "never used" according to Poutsma (1929:627); or "is not used" for Curme (1931:242). This extends to cases of Q=subj: "*whether* has to be used" (Jespersen, 1927:41); "*Whether* (not *if*)" (Curme, ibid.); Quirk *et al.*, who ignore the more general Q=init, agree that *if*–Q "cannot occur in subject position" (1972:737), as in [13] (1985:1054):

[13a] *whether* she likes the present is not clear to me
　　　　(*whether*–Q=subj)
[13b] * *if* she likes the present is not clear to me
　　　　(* *if*–Q=subj)

It may be noted that for Q=init/Q=subj, Jespersen returns to *if*-conditionals, to exactly the opposite effect as for verb+Q, however. In the case of verb+Q, combination of *if*–Q and *if*-conditional as in [8] is 'very natural'; but by contrast combination is somehow 'hardly possible' in the case of Q=init; thus, the very reason why only *whether*–Q appears in [12, 13] would be that *if*–Q as in [13b] "would [too] easily be taken to be ... [a] condition".

We are now in a position to give global surveys of OG accounts of *whether*–Q and/or *if*–Q, as far as our five-point grid goes. In [14], + represents recognition of available evidence at the point concerned; a blank represents that the point is not considered; and a − represents acknowledged failure to uncover evidence. *Wh(ether*–Q) appears on the left, *if*(–Q) on the right.

[14]　*whether*–Q and *if*–Q in OG

	S		J		P		C		K		GCE		CGoEL	
	wh	if	wh	if	wh	if	wh	if	wh	if	wh	if	wh	if
verb+Q	+	+	+	+	+	+	+	+			+	+	+	+
noun+Q					−	+	−						+	−
prep+Q			+	−	+		+		+				+	−
Q=init			+	−	+	−	+	−	+					
Q=subj			+	−			+	−			+	−	+	−

It will be seen that [14] has a + at eleven points for *whether*–Q where it has a − for *if*–Q: there is one such point each in Poutsma and *GCE*, three each in Jespersen, Curme, and *CGoEL* (note the increase from *GCE* to *CGoEL*). These amount to the OG accounts of disparity between *whether*–Q and *if*–Q (possibly extended with the six points where [14] has + or − vs. blank; note that for Kruisinga *whether*–Q and *if*–Q would thus not overlap at all).

If we now raise the question of whether OG accounts represented in [14] are *open*, it is useful to first look at the left-hand side for *whether*–Q separately. Here, OG is indeed consistently *open*: there are +'s in each row representing 100 per cent coverage of available evidence for all five positions (note that only Curme scores 100 per cent on his own). In this perspective, each left-hand blank may in fact be taken to leave the point in question literally *open*; note that there is no − on the left-hand side in [14].

On the other hand it is less easy to take the right-hand side of [14] as straightforwardly *open*. The wayward aspect of [14] is that for *if*–Q it contains a − at twelve points, against only seven points with a +; where each − is readily interpreted as *narrow*: a restriction, limitation, constraint, etc. on *if*–Q. Thus in [14] OG concentrates on e*x*cluding *if*–Q rather than on *in*cluding available evidence. With twelve times − (out of 35 points), OG is 34 per cent *narrow* on the right of [14]. At all accounts, there is a considerable challenge from [14] for radical juxtaposition of OG and NG as *open* and *narrow* respectively: [14] would suggest that it might be a matter of degree, less or more *narrow* respectively. To meet this challenge in section Q.3, let us now first see to what extent NG is in fact (more) *narrow* on Q.

Q.2 On NG on quasi-questions

In NG, accounts of quasi-questions Q would be *narrow* if they essentially appear only to the extent that Q is pertinent to some theoretical position. In SS&P there is not really any such theoretical position for Q specifically; and they duly "do not deal with [Q] explicitly" (1973:656). SS&P do, however, want to establish that genuine questions are of a distinctive nature; and one of their pertinent arguments here is the very existence of Q distinctively characterized by *whether* or *if*. It thus behoves SS&P to illustrate Q once, as in [15]:

[15] he *asked* John $\left\{ \begin{array}{c} if \\ whether \end{array} \right\}$ he thought it would rain
(verb+*whether*–Q; verb+*if*–Q)

Note especially that no occasion arises for SS&P to pursue Q in other positions than the accidental one of verb+Q in [15]; nor do they (have to) consider disparity of *whether*–Q and *if*–Q.

Essentially the same *narrow* logic of theoretical pertinence applies to Emonds (1976); where it works out somewhat differently however, given other theoretical positions. Recall from section 3.3 that Emonds' theory is structure-preservation: movement should be restricted to positions which similar items could occupy anyway. Now consider [16b, c]: *there* cannot be made to introduce Q, but *where* can:

[16a]   the question *of whether* he lived there (prep+*whether*–Q)
[16b] * the question of there   he lived
[16c]   the question of where   he lived

Under Emonds' theory, movement of *there* in [16b] does apparently not preserve structure; but *where* in [16c] does. The pertinent point about [16a] is therefore that a *wh*-item, *wh-ether*, which independently introduces Q, represents a *wh*-position to which another *wh*-item, *wh-ere*, can move: as *wh*-to-*wh* (*wh-ere* to *wh-ether*) movement, [16c] accords with structure-preservation. Note that *if* is *not* a *wh*-item, and will thus not be pertinent to the structure-preserving nature of *wh*-movement as *wh-ether* is. Accordingly, Emonds (1976:189–90) indeed deals only with *whether*–Q: illustrating Q as in [16a] (1976:136; but cf. 1976:181) allows him to ignore *if*–Q, which will not occur as prep+Q.

In the larger 'standard' NG grammars, therefore, NG accounts of Q are *narrow* in the sense of having little concern with Q at all; much the same applies to Chomsky, for whom the point seems to have remained "in no way crucial" (1973:272). For their respective non-specific purposes, SS&P can just cite Q as evidence for the existence of 'questions' as a distinct category: and for this any available evidence, with *whether* and/or with *if*, will do; and Emonds (1976) can just use Q as evidence for a *wh*-position: and for this any *whether*–Q will do. But notably, since both SS&P and Emonds lack specific theories of Q, they are *not narrow* in the sense of imposing deductive restrictions on Q. Neither SS&P nor Emonds (1976) pay attention to any '−' such as make OG waywardly *narrow* in [14]. In NG a − contributes to *narrow*ness only if it is deductively pertinent to an associated theory; otherwise the more *narrow* approach is to ignore the point entirely. Accordingly, there seems to be no account of *whether*–Q and/or *if*–Q in Chomsky at all.

Correspondingly, in the more specific NG 'literature', restrictions on Q do deduce from theories adopted. A case in point is Yim (1984), who sets up his theory in such a way that *whether*–Q, but *not if*–Q, should appear in the same positions as 'noun-phrases', NPs, which we will here illustrate with *this*. In terms of our five-point grid, Yim essentially uses (c) and (d), noun+NP and prep+NP, to identify a non-NP and an NP position respectively:

[17c] * her *picture this* was beautiful   (* noun+NP)
        (cf. her picture *of* this was beautiful)
[17d] I heard nothing *except this*   (prep+NP)

Thus, like NP, *whether*–Q should not be able to appear as a complement after a noun, * noun+*whether*–Q (cf. 1984:192); but prep+*whether*–Q should be possible: hence [18] (1984:216):

[18] we were talking *about whether* we should help them or not
        (prep+*whether*–Q)

Note that Yim does not substantiate the pertinent restriction on noun+*whether*–Q; there is wayward available evidence for noun+ *whether*–Q in OG, e.g. [10]. And conversely for *if*–Q: contrary to NP, *if*–Q should appear as noun+*if*–Q, but not after prepositions, * prep+*if*–Q (cf. 1984:190–2). Notably, however, Yim does again not actually provide evidence (for * prep+*if*–Q, see OG, and cf. [11]; but in OG evidence for noun+*if*–Q, which Yim predicts, is not available; cf. [10]).

Thus, not only do restrictions on noun+*whether*–Q and prep+ *if*–Q deduce from Yim's theory in truly *narrow* fashion; Yim's neglecting to substantiate his deductions with pertinent facts also testifies to the *narrow* priority of theory over evidence. Let us now turn to Emonds (1985) for another instance of NG literature on Q. Emonds adopts, besides his (1976) structure-preservation, a 'unified theory of syntactic categories' to which *whether*–Q and *if*–Q will be pertinent if they can indeed be 'unified' with other categories. Emonds (1985:286) thus takes [19] as his point of departure, with (arbitrarily) verb+Q:

[19] Bill *asked* Mary *if* / *whether* a friend had put some books on
        a train (verb+*whether* / *if*–Q)

Given [19], *if*–Q might then be unified with *if*-conditionals (1985:287):

[20] you should relax if his friend has put those books on the
        train

The point now arises, however, whether *if*–Q [19] and *if*-conditional [20] are indeed in some sense ostensibly distinct, such that their unification even so represents a genuinely *narrow* approach. For this Emonds (1985:287) appeals to Q=init: conditionals would appear initially, quasi-questions would not:

[21a] * *if* his friend put those books on the train, you should inquire (* *if*–Q=init)
[21b] if his friend put those books on the table, you should relax

Along the same lines, [19] should have a *whether*-counterpart for Emonds' (1985) NG theory of unification to apply to: the *whether*-conditional of [22]:

[22] you should relax, whether his friend has put those books on the train or not

Moreover, unification of *whether* in [19] and [22] should again be *narrow* in relation to ostensible difference in [23] (1985:287–8):

[23a] * *whether* a friend had put some books on a train, Bill asked Mary   (* *whether*–Q=init)
[23b] whether or not his friend has put the books on the train, you should relax

Note that the * for [23a] contradicts available evidence for *whether*–Q=init in OG, e.g. [12].

So far, NG appears *narrow* with respect to Q either because NG ignores Q to the extent that they are not pertinent (SS&P 1973; Emonds 1976); or because NG deduces (but does not necessarily substantiate) pertinent facts from theories (Yim 1984; Emonds 1985). Before we now conclude that NG is thus consistently *narrow*, rather than just more *narrow* than OG in [14], an important qualification should be made. That is, in fact we have until now conveniently ignored some further facts about *whether*–Q and/or *if*–Q that appear in Yim (1984:251, n1) and Emonds (1985:286, n4) – even though these facts are *not* pertinent. For instance, Emonds elaborately illustrates disparity of *whether*–Q and *if*–Q as prep+Q (Yim's facts do not fit into the grid of [5]; but see section Q.4 1):

[24] debates *about whether/* *if* the weather is changing (prep+*whether*–Q; * prep+*if*–Q)

But such disparity among Q is in no apparent way pertinent to unification of *whether*–Q and/or *if*–Q with conditionals. If facts like [24] are included for completeness' sake alongside deductions from theories, then NG in Yim (1984) and Emonds (1985) is to that extent *open* – and as such again different from OG in degree rather than juxtaposed to OG in kind.

Let us now globally survey NG accounts of *whether*–Q and *if*–Q in appropriately parallel fashion to [14] for OG. In [25] Ø represents that the point is not theoretically pertinent; round brackets represent a point deduced but not substantiated; and + and/or Ø braced indicate that the appearance of Q at that specific point is arbitrary, and might have been elsewhere between the empty braces.

[25]   *whether*–Q and *if*–Q in NG

	Chomsky		SS&P		Emonds 76		Yim 84		Emonds 85	
	wh	*if*	*wh*	*if*	*wh*	*if*	*wh*	*if*	*wh*	*if*
verb+Q	Ø	Ø	{+	+}	{	}	Ø	Ø	+	+
noun+Q	Ø	Ø	{	}	{	}	(−	+)	Ø	Ø
prep+Q	Ø	Ø	{	}	{+	Ø}	+	(−)	+Ø	−Ø
Q=init	Ø	Ø	{	}	{	}	Ø	Ø	−	−

If we now raise the question whether NG in [25] is indeed *narrow*, it will firstly be noted that things like round brackets, braces, or Ø do not occur at all in [14] for OG: in OG there simply do not arise notions of facts deduced but not substantiated; or of facts arbitrarily selected; or of facts appropriately ignored if not pertinent. Unfortunately for *A–Z*, there is no absolute juxtaposition of NG to OG in this sense however, because of those cases where NG has a Ø accompanying + or −: at these points NG is *open* to some extent. Similarly, NG is *narrow* with a − at two points where OG has +: viz. the − (i.e. '(−)'!) in Yim (1984) for noun+*whether*–Q (vs. Poutsma, Curme with [10], and *CGoEL* in OG); and the − of Emonds (1985) for *whether*–Q=init (vs. Jespersen with [12], Poutsma, Curme, and Kruisinga in OG). But again, the significance of all this is reduced by one converse case: Yim (1984) deduces a +, be it a (+) in round brackets, where − appears in OG (Poutsma, Curme with [10], and *CGoEL*). Like [14], [25] again seems to present a situation where *open* or *narrow* is a matter of more-or-less in OG and NG, rather than of juxtaposition.

Q.3 Conclusions

Let's take stock. OG and NG accounts of quasi-questions with *whether* and/or *if* as represented above do not immediately juxtapose as *open* and *narrow* respectively. Firstly, going by [14, 25], OG is at best more *open*, NG at best more *narrow*, as a matter of degree rather than juxtaposed principle. Secondly, Emonds' (1985) 'unification' of Q and conditionals is reminiscent of OG accounts of 'combination' or 'merger' of *if*–Q and *if*-conditionals;

and would thus suggest NG 'reconstructing' OG (see section II.4) sooner than juxtaposition of NG to OG.

At worst *A–Z* might now fall back upon the excuse that Q represents an exception proving the otherwise quite general rule of juxtaposed OG and NG. But in fact it may be possible to do better than that. First reconsider the interpretation of OG on Q as *narrow* to some extent. This largely depends on the, undeniably many, points at which − appears in [14]. And each − does indeed represent an account which goes beyond the *open* approach defined as 'comprehensive coverage of available evidence': for a − no evidence is 'available' by definition. But note that this does not simplistically imply that each − therefore represents a *narrow* approach, defined in turn as 'account restricted to pertinent facts in accordance with a theory'. For actually no such theory can be found in OG. A − in OG is not pertinent in this sense; but is rather a point where the *open* approach has so far drawn only blanks.

In fact, the terminology behind some −'s in OG is revealing in this respect: in certain positions *if*–Q is 'not used' or 'never used', as if OG is *open* to possibilities which merely happen to remain unused. The same applies to Curme's account by which *whether*–Q may be 'preferred' to *if*–Q, and *if* be 'reserved' for conditionals: again, OG is thus *open* to the existence of *if*–Q, but its exploitation is taken not to be optimal. Under induction, a − in OG is a *possibility* for which no evidence has as yet become available (but no *); under deduction a − in NG is an *im*possibility for which no evidence will be admitted: * (cf. section II.4). In this sense, OG and NG are thus juxtaposed as *open* and *narrow* after all, only apparently having − in common. In fact the same juxtaposition applies to +: again in OG + is a possibility for which there also is available evidence; but in NG + is a pertinent fact even if evidence is lacking: Yim's (+) in [25].

Of course all this also reflects on the discrepancies between OG and NG, where [14] has a + and [25] a − or vice versa. These are natural discrepancies between inductive reports and deductive reasoning, each equally 'right' by the juxtaposed standards of *open* and *narrow* approaches respectively. And in fact we may now note that the ostensibly *open* inclusion of facts not pertinent in NG (Yim 1984, Emonds 1985) is explicitly *not* on a par with the really pertinent facts: in both Yim (1984) and Emonds (1985) they are relegated to footnotes. Under a truly *open* approach all evidence is equal, and there is duly no sense in which facts are thus relegated in OG.

Finally, consider the apparent similarity of OG's 'merger' and

NG's 'unification'. In fact these are also fundamentally juxtaposed. Merger or combination in OG are just descriptive terms which are *open* to switching from 'very natural' in one position (verb+Q) to 'hardly possible' in another position (Q=init). Unification is a *narrow*ly consistent theory which is to apply equally in all positions, even those where there is apparent differentiation (* Q=init vs. initial conditional). Thus the discrepancy between Emonds' (1985) * for Q=init in [23a] and the available evidence for *whether*–Q=init in OG's [12] is symptomatic of the juxtaposition between *open* merger and *narrow* unification. Looked at separately, OG and NG do not really present us with entirely *open* and *narrow* approaches to Q respectively. But the careful consideration that *A–Z* supplies of apparently more or less *narrow* or *open* features in OG and NG when the two approaches are put alongside one another reveals a fundamental level at which their juxtaposition as *open* and *narrow* in fact appears to be as consistent as anywhere else in *A–Z*.

Q.4 Discussion and extensions

1 Jespersen (1940:326) and Quirk *et al.* (1985:1054; not 1972) refer to a disparity between *whether*–Q and *if*–Q beyond the grid of [5]: only the former can be made infinitival, with *to*:

    [ia]   I don't know *whether to* see my doctor today
    [ib] * I don't know *if to* see my doctor today

There are similar facts in Yim (1984:192) and Emonds (1985: 286). No other OG seems to deal with *whether*-infinitives like [i]; nor do SS&P or Emonds (1976) in NG.

• Argue whether, and why (not), [i] is more appropriately expected in OG or in NG. Would you thus expect Yim and/or Emonds (1985) to have relegated [i] to footnotes? (Hint: would you expect infinitival status to be pertinent to NP-like distribution and/or unification, respectively?)

2 Beyond the positions identified in [5], another position that might be considered is complement after a copula: copu+Q. Consider [ii] from Curme (1931:185), [iii] from Kruisinga (1932b:373), and [iv] from Quirk *et al.* (1985:1054; not in 1972):

    [ii]   the first question ... *was whether*, or *if* ... he would do it
            (copu+*whether*–Q; copu+*if*–Q)
    [iii]   The question ... *is* not simply *whether* a knowledge of ancient Greece is necessary
            (copu+*whether*–Q)

[iva]   My main problem ... *is whether* I should ask for
        another loan
        (copu+*whether*–Q)
[ivb] * ?My main problem ... *is if* I should ask for another
        loan
        (*? copu+*if*–Q)

There appears to be no copu+Q in other OG or in the NG
reviewed in this section for Q.

- Discuss whether in [ii–iv] OG grammars differ in being more or
  less *open*.
- Discuss whether OG on copu+Q as in [ii–iv] vs. no copu+Q at
  all in NG amounts to juxtaposition of OG and NG as *open* vs.
  narrow.

3 Malone (1978) presents a survey – to 1978 – of NG on questions,
including Q. The survey goes over the ground in much more
extensive and theoretical detail than is possible here and
is recommended to the more persistent reader. We may note
here the following. Malone divides his survey into periods.
For his 'Early Period' of NG he notes "Extension of descriptive scope ... leads to formal complication" (1978:43);
'formal complication' being in conflict with the *narrow* aim of
restrictiveness.

- Discuss how Malone's characterization of early NG agrees with
  that of *A–Z* in Parts I and II: early NG is programmatically
  rather than effectively *narrow*.
  Malone also recognizes a (for him) 'Recent Period' of NG, for
  which it is "impossible to dub any one or few works ... as truly
  representative (let alone authoritative ...)" (1978:52); however, "The closest thing to an exception is Stockwell *et al.*
  1973" (1978:78). According to Malone, during his 'Recent NG'
  "simplification of a sort is achieved" and at the same time "there
  is an increase in the number of structures covered" (1978:58).
- Does Malone's characterization of his Recent NG make it closer
  to truly *narrow* NG than his Early NG? Why (not)? Because of
  the 'simplification'? And/or because of the 'increase in structures
  covered'?
- Does Malone's characterization of his Recent NG, and of SS&P
  (1973) as (almost) representative of it, agree with *A–Z*'s selection of SS&P as one of the few comprehensive NG grammars?
  Why (not)?

4 In connection with questions, Bolinger (1978:87) refers to ideas
"with a kind of obvious appeal that makes them rediscoverable
every few years when previous scholarship is overlooked".

Emonds (1985) does not refer to either Jespersen or Quirk *et al.*
(1972).

- Would NG 'unification' of quasi-questions Q and conditionals
  be 'rediscovery' when OG's 'combination' or 'merger' are
  overlooked? Why (not)? How does this affect *A–Z*'s juxtaposition of OG and NG?

R is for referential riddles

Like other languages, Modern English has words that can be used on their own to refer to entities. Thus *Mary* is a word that by itself refers to some specific female: one can be perfectly understood if one just says 'I saw Mary'. However, there are also words which do not thus by themselves refer to any specific entity. For instance, the personal pronoun *her* by itself refers to any female. Someone who just says 'I saw her' is likely to be asked who 'she' may be. One can make *her* more specific by accompanying it by a gesture of pointing. But one can also use *her* as a 'referential dependent', that is: as a word which depends on something else for its meaning (cf. also section K for kataphoric *the*). Thus in 'Where's Mary? I saw her', *her* may be referentially dependent on *Mary*. In line with much current linguistic practice, we will indicate referential dependence by identical subscripts: her_m is referentially dependent on $Mary_m$: $Mary_m$ is then called the antecedent of her_m.

One of the more notable properties of referential dependents is that they may be quite particular as to what can be used as an antecedent. Consider for instance [1]:

[1a] $Mary_m$ hoped that Susan would introduce her_m
[1b] * Mary   hoped that $Susan_s$ would introduce her_s

In [1] *her* can be her_m referentially dependent on $Mary_m$; but not her_s referentially dependent on $Susan_s$. If $Susan_s$ were to be an antecedent, then instead of a personal pronoun *her* one would have to use as its referential dependent a reflexive pronoun like *herself* (which in turn rejects *Mary* as antecedent):

[2a] * $Mary_m$ hoped that Susan would introduce $herself_m$
[2b]   Mary   hoped that $Susan_s$ would introduce $herself_s$

The area of referential dependents such as personal and reflexive pronouns is an important one for *A–Z* because among others the founding father of NG, Noam Chomsky himself, has suggested that this is an area where NG identifies and provides for gaps left by OG. In section II.1 we anticipated on section R to address, and in particular to reject, the view that OG and (current, effectively *narrow*) NG thus 'complement' each other. Note that the issue in [1, 2] is very much one of restrictions: the *im*possibility for *her* to be referentially dependent on *Susan*; the *im*possibility for *herself* to be referentially dependent on *Mary*. According to Chomsky (1986), in this area riddled with restrictions, a *narrow* approach as in NG should therefore lead to more comprehensive coverage than the *open* approach. As will be obvious, this is a(nother) serious challenge to the *A–Z* tenet that juxtaposition of OG and NG manifests itself in the comprehensiveness of the former, such that OG includes all the pertinent facts of NG – and much more – among its available evidence. This section R aims to explore the extent to which Chomsky's challenge can be met.

Let us first look at Chomsky's challenge in more of its particulars. His (1986:3) starting point is a more subtle version of the phenomenon illustrated in [1, 2]. In [3a] the personal pronoun *them* cannot be referentially dependent on *the men*; a referential dependent on *the men* would have to be reflexive, as in [3b]:

[3a] * the men$_m$ expected to see them$_m$
[3b]   the men$_m$ expected to see themselves$_m$

But in certain contexts the situation may be exactly the reverse. For instance, in [4] the [bracketed] instances of [3] are preceded by *I wonder who*: now only *them* may be referentially dependent on *the men*, *themselves* may not:

[4]   I wonder who [3a, b]
[4a]   I wonder who [the men$_m$ expected to see them$_m$]
[4b] * I wonder who [the men$_m$ expected to see themselves$_m$]

We will refer to the inversion from [3] to [4], from [a] = * but [b] = OK to [a] = OK but [b] = *, as the phenomenon of 'referential riddle'. With respect to instances of 'referential riddle' like [3, 4], Chomsky then claims that "It is doubtful that even the most compendious traditional grammar notes such simple facts" (1986:4). If this were true, then *A–Z*'s juxtaposition of 'compendious' OG to NG in terms of comprehensiveness must also be 'doubtful'.

Before one can adequately allay Chomsky's doubts as to coverage of 'simple' cases like [3, 4] in OG, one may first address the issue of whether [3, 4] indeed represent equally 'simple' facts. Note that in [3] one deals with a case of two verbs, *expected* and *to see*; let us accordingly say that [3] has a complexity (more familiar terms are: subordination; or embedding) of degree-2. By contrast,

[4] has three verbs, *wonder, expected,* and *to see,* i.e. complexity is higher: degree-3. A really 'simple' fact would then rather be a case of degree-1, with a single verb, like [5]:

[5a] * the men$_m$ saw them$_m$
[5b]   the men$_m$ saw themselves$_m$

Note that in the simplest case, degree-1 in [5], the situation is such that referential dependence on *the men* is impossible for personal pronouns: * them$_m$. In [3] this also obtains for degree-2 complexity: still * them$_m$. Then at complexity of degree-3 in [4] one gets 'referential riddle': now for *the men* referential dependence of the reflexive is out, * themselves$_m$; but them$_m$ is in. We conclude that an account of referential dependence that extends to 'referential riddle', i.e. that covers both *themselves*/* them and them/* themselves,* must go beyond 'simple facts' to some degree of complexity. In sections R.1 and R.2 we will now identify the extents to which OG and/or NG achieve coverage of both the simple and the more complex facts of referential dependence; and of the 'referential riddle' that Chomsky takes OG to fail in.

R.1 On OG on referential dependents

The earliest account of referential dependents in OG is the one of Sweet (1891:77). Consider Sweet's example [6a]:

[6a] he thinks too much of himself
[6b] he$_h$ thinks too much of himself$_h$

Sweet describes *himself* in [6a] as "a repetition of the logical subject of the verb". Translating into our terms, *himself* is thus referentially dependent on *he*; as indicated by subscripts in [6b]. Note that Sweet thus covers the kind of evidence that may be available for the simplest case: degree-1 with a single verb, *thinks.* The other side of the coin in the simplest case is the impossibility of referentially dependent personal pronoun, * him$_h$ instead of *himself$_h$*. In the *open* spirit, Sweet is chary of direct and immutable statements of this sort of restriction by such means as a * (see section II.4). However, Sweet does describe the reflexive pronoun in [6a] as "corresponding to the ordinary personal pronoun". 'Corresponding' may here apparently be taken to mean 'taking the place of' (cf. Poutsma 1916:836, discussed below), since Sweet goes on to specify that "A reflexive pronoun is a personal pronoun standing in ... relation to a verb ... being at the same time a repetition of the logical subject of the verb". That is, in [6], the referential dependent *himself* relates to the verb (i.e. 'is thought of') and represents the subject (i.e. = 'he'); and thus is reflexive, ousting the personal pronoun *him*.

This interpretation of Sweet's account of a simple case like [6] is reinforced when one turns to more complex cases, e.g. degree-2. The example of [7a] is Sweet's own; [7b–d] represent the referential dependencies involved:

[7a]   John told him to give himself plenty of time
[7b]   John$_j$ told him$_h$ to give himself$_h$ plenty of time
[7c] * John$_j$ told him$_h$ to give himself$_j$ plenty of time
[7d] * John$_j$ told him$_j$ to give himself$_j$ plenty of time

In particular, in [7a] "the reflexive pronoun *himself* ... refers us back to the logical subject of *give*, namely *him*", as [7b] indicates. But Sweet goes on to specify that what in [7a] "the reflexive pronoun refers back to ... is ... not the grammatical subject in the sentence"; i.e. *himself* can explicitly *not* be interpreted as referentially dependent on *John* as in [7c, d] (note that in [7d] the problem is at complexity of degree-1: on either side of the single verb *told*, *him* cannot be referentially dependent on *John*).

Thus, Sweet designs his examples in such a way that 'referential riddle' already occurs at degree-2: at degree-1 *he*$_h$ ... *himself*$_h$ in [6], but at degree-2 * *John*$_j$ ... *himself*$_j$ in [7]. In Sweet's comments, 'referential riddle' is ascribed to an additional 'logical' subject at degree-2 in [7]. As Sweet explains, this logical subject can be recognized as italicized *he* in [8], "being equivalent to" [7]:

[8a] John told him that *he* should give himself ... time
[8b] John$_j$ told him$_h$ that *he*$_h$ should give himself$_h$ ... time

Interestingly, this is also the point about Chomsky's examples of complexity at degree-2 and degree-3. In [4a], here repeated for convenience as [9a], 'referential riddle' is also due to another logical subject: viz. *who*, which can be recognized as *he* in [9b] ([9b] is not perfectly grammatical, but that is irrelevant here):

[9a] I wonder who [the men$_m$ expected   to see them$_m$]
    (= [4a])
[9b] I wonder who$_w$ [the men$_m$ expected *he*$_w$ would see them$_m$]

By contrast, at degree-2 in Chomsky's example [3a] the corresponding logical subject is rather *the men*, and therefore the situation comes out as in [10]:

[10a] the men   expected   to see themselves (= [3b])
[10b] the men$_m$ expected *they*$_m$ would see themselves$_m$

Although occasionally in somewhat more cautiously *open* terms than *narrow*ly exclusive NG would favour, it seems fair to conclude here that there is no doubt at all that, on behalf of OG, Sweet already notes 'such simple facts' as referential dependence and 'referential riddle'. However, it is also fair to say that since Sweet's account, OG has not really independently come up with anything quite so extensive in this area: for once, the pioneer remains to be surpassed. In particular, it may be noted that Chomsky's prime (if not only) source for OG (cf. section II.1), Jespersen, does indeed not seem to cover 'referential riddle'. We will see that this is not true for other OG; and Chomsky should not condemn OG without looking beyond Jespersen. But first we may note here that Sweet's exemplary OG account is in fact explicitly *open*. That is, Sweet makes a point of applying 'referential riddle', the alternations between reflexive and personal pronouns due to additional logical subjects, to English only; for any other language, other possibilities are *open*. A case in point is Latin, for which Sweet (1891:77) observes that the phenomenon of 'referential riddle' need not occur: in Latin, a grammatical subject may take a reflexive as referential dependent at any degree of complexity, i.e. in spite of any additional verbs and their logical subjects. The notion that things may go one way in one language, but another way in a second language, is a typically *open* one.

If we now turn from Sweet to other OG accounts of referential dependence and/or 'referential riddle', we have already suggested that these do not contribute much to OG meeting the standards that Sweet (and Chomsky) set. For instance, Poutsma (1916:836) essentially just repeats Sweet; he usefully explicates 'referential riddle', however (see above): "The personal pronoun [*him*] takes the place of the reflective pronoun [*himself*]" in [11b], which is equivalent to [11c] (recall that thus 'takes the place of' paraphrases Sweet's original 'corresponding'):

[11a] he$_h$ defended himself$_h$
[11b] he$_h$ begged me to defend him$_h$
[11c] he$_h$ begged me that *I* would defend him$_h$

Kruisinga (1931:403) has an interesting pair of examples to illustrate "the apparently reflexive use of the simple [= personal] pronouns" (1932a:142); that is, the phenomenon of 'referential riddle': in [12a] there is complexity at degree-1 by the single verb (*had*) *pointed*, and hence the simple pronoun *him* cannot be referentially dependent on *he*; but in [13a] there are two verbs, *had* and *pointed* separated by an additional subject *the difficulty*, and therefore the simple pronoun now can be referentially dependent on *he*:

[12a]   he had pointed out the difficulty to him
[12b] * he$_h$ had pointed out the difficulty to him$_h$
[13a]   he had the difficulty pointed out to him
[13b] he$_h$ had *the difficulty* pointed out to him$_h$

Finally, Curme (1931:100; 1935:10–11) compares [14a] to [15a]; the point is that "The reflexive ... can refer only to the subject of the ... clause in which it stands ... Hence, if the pronoun [is] in a subordinate clause ... , a personal pronoun is used":

[14a] I believed him to be deceiving me
[14b] I$_i$ believed him$_h$ to be deceiving me$_i$
[15a] I believed him to be deceiving himself
[15b] I$_i$ believed him$_h$ to be deceiving himself$_h$

So far, OG has thus been seen to cover, more or less elaborately, such facts as Chomsky (1986) doubts that 'even the most compendious grammar notes'. This leaves us with Jespersen and Quirk *et al.* Jespersen (1949:162ff.) only covers reflexives at degree-1, e.g. [16a]:

[16a] she pulled herself together
[16b] she$_s$ pulled herself$_s$ together

Although somewhat more elaborate, the same is true for the earlier Quirk *et al.*, *GCE* (1972): "the reflexive pronouns are used to denote co-reference in contrast with non-co-referential objects" (1972:211). Consider [17a] interpreted as in [17b, c]:

[17a] he saw himself/him
[17b] he$_h$ saw himself$_h$/* him$_h$
[17c] he$_h$ saw him$_i$/* himself$_i$

The account of *GCE* does not extend beyond such simple facts of referential dependence; and in particular *GCE* does not achieve coverage of 'referential riddle' in more complex cases, unlike most earlier OG. This is amply made up for in the later *CGoEL* however. Quirk *et al.* go on from a discussion of [17] (1985:356) to observe that the "reflexive pronoun always corefers to the subject of its own clause, even though that subject may be 'understood'" (1985:357); their examples include [18a, b] which in Sweet's terms are 'equivalent' to [18c, d]:

[18a]   she asked John   to invite himself
[18b] * she asked John   to invite herself
[18c]   she$_s$ asked John$_j$ if *he$_j$* would invite himself$_j$
[18d] * she$_s$ asked John$_j$ if *he$_j$* would invite herself$_s$

We may now summarize OG accounts of referential dependents as in [19]:

[19]   Referential dependents in OG: a summary

	S	P	K	C	J	GCE	CGoEL
degree-1	+	+	+	+	+	+	+
degree-2	+	+	+	+			+
degree-3+							
riddle	+	+	+	+			+

What remains of Chomsky's challenge to the comprehensiveness of OG is thus only the apparent lack of any explicit discussion at the levels of degree-3 or higher. This would be a serious gap if 'referential riddle', the switch from reflexive to personal pronoun as referential dependent, only occurred between degree-2 and degree-3, as Chomsky's examples [3, 4] suggest. But OG amply shows that this is *not* the case. The crucial point is to achieve coverage of both degree-1 and degree-2; then coverage of 'referential riddle' is an almost automatic consequence. For degree-3 and up, one may then transfer +'s from degree-2 on the basis of the essential equivalence of what Sweet (1891:161, 164) calls "complexes" (degree-2) and "extended complexes" (degree-3+) (cf. Poutsma 1929:545; Kruisinga 1932b:361–2; Curme 1931:175–6; Quirk *et al.* 1972:721; 1985:989). If Chomsky wants to cast doubts on the comprehensiveness of OG's coverage then he should look for gaps elsewhere than among referential dependents; and he should also look at OG beyond Jespersen.

R.2 On NG on referential dependents

When one considers Chomsky's claim that the facts of referential dependents and 'referential riddle' in Modern English grammar "were ... not ... noticed until quite recently" (1986:3), this is wrong with respect to OG; where Sweet (1891:77) can hardly qualify as 'quite recent' after almost a full century. But Chomsky is right when one only looks at "the course of the study of ... generative grammar" (ibid.), i.e. the development of NG. Before NG became more effectively, rather than programmatically, *narrow* (see part II), 'referential riddle' was not obviously pertinent; hence it is absent from both of *A–Z*'s earlier standards of NG, SS&P (1973) and Emonds (1976).

In particular, neither SS&P nor Emonds deal with referential dependence beyond complexity of degree-1. For SS&P (1973:168) "reflexivization ... must be within the same simple ... sentence", i.e. reflexives appear as referential dependents at degree-1. But SS&P do not seem to similarly require degree-2 complexity, i.e. *not* the same sentence, for personal pronouns, to account for 'referential riddle' (see also 1973:207–10). The nearest that SS&P thus seem to come to 'referential riddle' is the pair of sentences [20a, 21a]; but the impossibility for *them* to depend on *he* in [21b] appears to be ascribed to the different numbers involved (*he* = singular, *them* = plural), not to the degree of complexity being too low:

[20a] the boy saw himself
[20b] the boy$_b$ saw himself$_b$
[21a] he saw them
[21b] he$_h$ saw them$_t$

Emonds' NG theory of structure preservation (see section 3.3) does not have implications with respect to a pertinent degree of complexity either: structure may be preserved at degree-2 exactly as at degree-1, etc. Accordingly, for Emonds (1976:88) "reflexives ... are ... a pronoun copy of the subject", i.e. referentially dependent on the subject; but Emonds does not (have to) raise the issue of whether the reflexive operates at degree-1 as in [22], or at higher degrees of complexity:

[22a] the witness   killed herself
[22b] the witness$_w$ killed herself$_w$

In effect, it is indeed 'in the course of the study of generative grammar' that referential dependents and 'referential riddle' came to be recognized as a natural area for NG to come into its own in. As we have already suggested, one way of looking at referential dependents is to note the extent to which they are riddled with restrictions. Only when NG became more effectively *narrow* was it adequately equipped to direct its attention to the restrictions which make up 'referential riddle'. Though Chomsky has since then adopted much more sophisticated versions of the relevant theoretical constraints, we will look here at an early version in Chomsky (1973) (cf. also section T): for an interesting point about Chomsky (1973) is that here NG can clearly be seen to rely on something reminiscent of Sweet's 'logical subjects'.

The basic idea is that Chomsky (1973:239) restricts the applica-tion of rules to small domains (cf. also section T); and specifically, that each separate subject – logical or grammatical – creates such a domain. This is the so-called 'Specified Subject Constraint' SSC. For instance, in [23] we have italicized the subjects, and then bracketed the domain that each subject creates:

[23a] Susan talked to Mary about Anne seeing Kate
[23b] *Susan* talked to Mary about *Anne* seeing Kate
[23c] [Susan talked to Mary about [Anne seeing Kate]]

Now suppose that there are rules about referential dependents as in [24]:

[24a] a personal pronoun cannot be referentially dependent
[24b] a reflexive pronoun must be referentially dependent

Recall that by SSC [24a, b] only apply within a domain: thus a personal pronoun may still be referentially dependent on an antecedent outside its domain in spite of [24a]; but a reflexive cannot occur except with an antecedent within its domain. As in [25] (cf. 1973:241):

[25a] Susan talked to Mary about Anne seeing her/herself
[25b] Susan$_s$ talked to Mary$_m$ about [*Anne*$_a$ seeing her$_s$]
[her$_m$]
[* her$_a$]
[* herself$_s$]
[* herself$_m$]
[herself$_a$]

And, as we have already hinted, it is in these terms that 'referential riddle' as in [3, 4] is also pertinent to NG, as in [26, 27]:

[26a] the men   expected to see them/themselves
[26b] the men$_m$ expected that [*they*$_t$ would see them$_t$/*$_m$]
[themselves*$_t$/$_m$]
[26c] the men$_m$ expected   [to see them$_t$/*$_m$]
[themselves*$_t$/$_m$]
[27a] I wonder who the men expected to see them/themselves
[27b] I wonder who$_w$ the men$_m$ expected that
[*they*$_w$ would see them*$_w$/$_m$]
[themselves$_w$/*$_m$]
[27c] I wonder who$_w$ the men$_m$ expected
[to see them*$_w$/$_m$]
[themselves$_w$/*$_m$]

Under the impetus of constraints such as SSC, facts – both simple and more or less complex – about referential dependents and 'referential riddle' have become a centrally pertinent issue in much current, more effectively *narrow* NG. It would be impossible to make a motivated choice, apart from Chomsky's own works, from the vast literature that has grown up. We will therefore not attempt to satisfy for R our general aim of presenting at least three accounts of each point of Modern English grammar in *A–Z*.

Rather, we will merely turn to one issue that juxtaposition of NG to OG puts forward. Recall that we have seen that Sweet (1891:77) characteristically leaves his exemplary OG account *open* in view of the differences between English and Latin observed. The question arises whether the *narrow* approach of NG can still accommodate the absence of 'referential riddle' in Latin, which the *open* approach of OG is rather designed to take account of.

One answer that NG can indeed accommodate the difference between English and Latin is given in Anderson (1982). In typical *narrow* fashion, Anderson first suggests that the Latin facts are more restricted than is observed in Sweet's *open* account. That is, Sweet does not attach importance to the fact that in his examples at degree-2 where Latin still allows a reflexive (and English does not: * [7c, d]), the second verb is in the 'subjunctive' (cf. section s). Paraphrasing somewhat Anderson's formulations, we might say that only a subjunctive verb can 'undo' the effect of a subject, i.e. prevent a subject from creating its own domain by SSC. Roughly as in [28], where English represents Latin and where *Bill* is a subject that might create a domain (hence * *himself$_j$*) if it was not for the subjunctive *defend* (hence *himself$_j$* is OK):

[28] [*John$_j$* asked that <u>Bill</u> <u>defend</u> himself$_j$/him$*_j$]

If in [28] there is just one domain, created by *John* and bracketed, then in Latin *himself* may be dependent on *John* (or on *Bill* as in English); conversely for *him*, which would not be referentially dependent on *John* (nor on *Bill*). That is, the relations between *John* and *him(self)* at degree-2 would be exactly as between *Bill* and *him(self)* at degree-1, without 'referential riddle'. According to Anderson's (1982:19) NG, this is exactly the situation as it obtains in Latin – but *narrow*ly restricted to subjunctive verbs.

R.3 Conclusions

One of the more notable facts about accounts of referential dependents in OG is the difference in coverage between Quirk *et al.*'s *GCE* (1972) and *CGoEL* (1985). In *GCE* coverage does not go beyond degree-1 complexity; and hence 'referential riddle', the switch from reflexive to personal pronoun as referential dependent, remains behind the horizon. But in *CGoEL*, degree-2 complexity, and hence 'referential riddle' are dealt with in some detail, in this case justifying *Comprehensive* in the title. It might be supposed that *CGoEL* represents Quirk *et al.*'s more careful study of earlier OG, which amply anticipates the more comprehensive coverage. But in fact there is some reason to suppose that Quirk *et al.*'s accounts of referential dependents actually follow more closely "developments in linguistic theory" (1985:v; cf. 1972:vi), in particular developments in NG. That is, like Quirk *et al.* (1972), earlier NG does not provide genuine coverage of referential dependents beyond degree-1 either. Only later NG has achieved the kind of effective *narrow*ness which allows full recognition of the pertinence to NG of referential dependents at degree-2, specifically of 'referential riddle'; and in Quirk *et al.* (1985) OG may be seen again to follow suit.

Whatever the exact relation between NG and OG in Quirk *et al.* (1972, 1985), however, we can in any case safely conclude that otherwise Chomsky's (1986) view of the relation between OG and NG is grossly inaccurate. There are no facts which (later) NG notes but (earlier) OG does not: ever since Sweet's (1891) comprehensive account, the facts, including 'referential riddle', have remained part of the tradition of OG. In the area of referential dependents, the juxtaposition between OG and NG does not – and according to *A–Z* cannot – appear from distinct sets of facts that OG and NG cover: OG and NG are not thus "complementary" (Chomsky 1986:2); but rather OG's available evidence includes NG's pertinent facts. What remain, of course, are the fundamentally juxtaposed approaches to such facts. For OG, at any stage of its development, it is essential to be *open* to noting the facts as they are in Modern English or in Latin, and thus to 'merely' meet Chomsky's challenge by comprehensive coverage. But there does not have to be an attempt to ascribe *narrow* necessity to these facts; Sweet's observations about the role of subjects in Modern English remain dispensable, as Latin is supposed to show. On the contrary, NG may be expected not to note the facts unless a more or less *narrow* theory of constraints makes them pertinent: SS&P (1973) and Emonds (1976) ignore 'referential riddle', but Chomsky's SSC leads to its 'rediscovery' (as compared to OG) in Modern English grammar by Chomsky (1973); and of its – *narrow*ly limited – absence in Latin by Anderson (1982).

R.4 Discussion and extensions

1 Besides personal pronouns (at degree-2 and beyond) and re-flexive pronouns (at degree-1 only), there are reciprocal pronouns which are also referential dependents: *each other*, *one another* (cf. also section m). To some extent, reciprocals agree with reflexives in operating at degree-1 in [ia] rather than degree-2 in [ib]:

[ia]   the men$_m$ like each other$_m$
[ib]   ?John promised the men$_m$ that [*he* would like each other$_m$]

For reciprocals, too, Chomsky (1979:61) "doubt[s] that any traditional grammar, even the most comprehensive one, would trouble to note that such sentences must be excluded" (1979: 61); and "no ... traditional grammar, however compendious, would point out these facts" (1980:43–4). Another challenge to the comprehensiveness of OG. However, there is an important difference between reflexives and reciprocals: there is no 'referential riddle'. That is, there is no possibility to express the intended meaning of [ib] by reverting to another set of pronouns, as reflexives switch to personal pronouns. In other words, beside [ib] there is no available evidence at all.

• Discuss whether OG should still cover [ib] if there is no corresponding available evidence.
   In fact, it is not clear at all that reciprocals are really similar to reflexives as [i] suggests, following Chomsky. For instance, SS&P (1973:168) subscribe to the view that "reciprocals do not have the restriction of occurrence within the same sentence"; i.e. are *not* restricted to degree-1: [ib] is essentially OK. They note that "reciprocals may not occur freely ... but have no solution".
• In view of the apparent uncertainty as to whether [ib] 'must be excluded', would you argue that NG is in a position to reproach OG for not covering the facts about reciprocals except at degree-1? Recall that OG in general holds to straightforward transfer from degree-1 to degree-2 to ... , without any riddles. According to Quirk *et al.* (1985:365; not 1972: cf. section m), reciprocals are items that hardly occur in spontaneous authentic Modern English at all.
• On the natural assumption that degree-2 cases are even rarer (to the point of non-occurrence?) than degree-1 cases, would you argue that OG should (not) only cover the available evidence of reciprocals, viz. at degree-1?
2 In addition to their reflexive function, pronouns in *-self* and *-selves* may also be 'emphatic'; e.g. in [ii]:

   [ii] they will do it themselves

Van der Leek (1980:144) suggests that the distinction between reflexive and emphatic functions may sometimes be difficult to make, such that "confusion regarding this matter has been [i.e. in OG], and still is [i.e. in NG], widespread". According to Van der Leek, there are two ways out of this confusion. Firstly, a 'comparative' approach. In Dutch, reflexives translate by a pronoun with *-zelf* added; and emphatics by only *zelf* (e.g. for [ii] *zelf*, * *henzelf*). Secondly, the theoretical claim that the distribution of reflexives and reciprocals is exactly the same, such that a case of a *-self* pronoun where a reciprocal could not occur would necessarily be emphatic (e.g. in [ii] * *they will do it each other*). Basically, Van der Leek associates the former, comparative approach with OG, viz. with Poutsma and Kruisinga (OG's two Dutchmen); and the latter approach with NG. She also concludes that only the NG approach yields "an accurate account" (1980:124), whereas (1980:128) the OG accounts are at best "remarkably sound" (in Poutsma) or even "much less reliable" (in Kruisinga).

- Discuss how Van der Leek's two approaches – language comparison or theory – agree with *A–Z*'s speculation (section II.1) that in OG language comparison may 'make up' for theory, to explain the predominance of non-native contributions to OG. Against Van der Leek's NG assumption that reciprocals and reflexives have identical distributions stands SS&P's (1973:168) NG assumption that they are not the same (see section R.4 1; SS&P 1973:210 disclaim any concern with emphatics).
- Would you argue that such different assumptions invalidate Van der Leek's tenet that the theoretical NG approach yields more 'accurate' accounts than the comparative OG approach?

3 As the careful reader may have noticed, much OG assumes that the antecedent of a reflexive pronoun must be a subject: "repetition of the logical *subject*" (Sweet 1891:77, emphasis added; cf. Poutsma 1916:836, Curme 1931:100 as cited in the main text). However, Jespersen (1949:170) observes that "The reflexive does not always refer to the subject"; in [iii] the antecedent is an object (cf. [25] in the text):

[iii] we left Jane$_j$ to herself$_j$

In Emonds (1976:88) a reflexive is again "a pronoun copy of the *subject*" (emphasis added; cf. SS&P 1973:207).

- Would you argue that it is more important for OG or for NG to recognize cases of non-subjects as antecedents of reflexives?

4 In an interview with a Dutch newspaper, Chomsky extends his challenge about facts 'not noted' from Modern English to Dutch. In [iv] the English represents Dutch:

[iva] Jan$_j$ saw him$_i$/*$_j$
[ivb] Jan$_j$ thinks that [Piet$_p$ likes him$_j$/*$_p$]

- Do you think that Dutch is like English or like Latin with respect to 'referential riddle'?
  According to Chomsky 'you will not find such facts in even the largest 10-volume traditional grammar' of Dutch. However, the 3-volume grammar of Den Hertog (1892–1896), contemporaneous with Sweet, contains a discussion very much like Sweet's, with examples like [iv] (1896:71).
- Den Hertog (1892:iii) advertises the 'extensiveness' of his grammar. Does this suggest that he represents OG for Dutch? If so, would you argue that for Dutch too, OG can meet Chomsky's challenge?

s is for subjunctives

In *A–Z* the grammars of Modern English by Quirk *et al.* (1972, 1985) figure as the more recent, post-Second World War, representatives of OG. We have frequently had occasion to note that coverage in *GCE* (1972) is extended in *CGoEL* (1985), as *Comprehensive* in the latter's title entitles one to expect. Occasionally the difference is of another order however: not extension but revision. For instance, the so-called 'subjunctive' is first "not an important category in contemporary English" (1972:76); but later "the subjunctive in modern English ... is not so unimportant as is sometimes suggested" (1985:155). Note that 'not important' (1972) suggests some preconceived standard of importance, much as the *narrow* notion of '(not) major' depends on an associated linguistic theory (sections 3.2, 3). With 'not so unimportant' Quirk *et al.* (1985) thus retract their (1972) lapse into *narrow*ness.

One sense in which Quirk *et al.* (1985) take a more *open* approach to subjunctives appears in their recognition of a wider range of available evidence. In (1972:76), subjunctives are in evidence *only* when "there is lack of ... concord between subject and ... verb in the 3rd person singular present"; i.e. absence of verbal *-s*. That is, [1a] contains an evident subjunctive because of its contrast to [1b] with concord; but for [1c] no such evidential contrast can be available, as the verb shirks *-s* with *you* (cf. * 'you eats'):

[1a] they insist that he *eat* meat (subjunctive)
[1b] they insist that he eat*s* meat (not subjunctive)
[1c] they insist that you eat meat (?)

However, in (1985:157) "the absence of DO-support, as well as absence of ... *-s* ... is a criterion distinguishing the ... subjunctive", as in [2] (for DO-support, cf. *n* of *n*egation among the *nice*-properties of section b; also sections L and O):

[2a] they insist that you   *not* eat meat   (subjunctive)
[2b] they insist that you *do* not eat meat   (not subjunctive)

In other words, *CGoEL* is again *open* to the little evidence for subjunctives available from positive sentences – absence of *-s*; but also *open* to the consistent evidence for subjunctives available from negative sentences – absence of *do*. Negative subjunctives do not appear at all in *GCE*; but at *six* points in *CGoEL* (1985:157; but also 122, 134, 149, 777, 1012). For *A–Z*, such a subjunctive 'not so unimportant as is sometimes suggested' – note the iteration of *s* – spells the subject of (miniscule) section s: subjunctives evidenced not by the absence of *-s*, but by negation with *not* instead of *do(es) not*.

s.1 On OG on subjunctives

In the *open* approach of OG a notion '(not) important' should not really arise: everything for which there is any evidence available, however much or little or of whatever kind, is in principle equally to be covered. With respect to subjunctives, the effect of this seems to have been that OG has taken absence of *-s* as sufficient evidence, and has thus not been drawn towards systematically pursuing further evidence, e.g. from *not* without *do*. Thus Sweet pioneers OG in (1891:107), "The only regular inflection by which the subjunctive is distinguished ... in English is that of the third person singular present, which drops the *s*". In addition Sweet notes that "In ... *be* ... further distinctions are made: ... *I am, he is* ... subjunctive *I be, he be* ...". But Sweet has no negative subjunctives at all. In much the same spirit, Poutsma (1926:163). However, among the latter's multitude of examples, there is almost inevitably some accidental evidence for negative subjunctives, viz. (1926:189), an example from the nineteenth century:

[3] make what noise you will ... , so it *be not* treason

But note that even in [3] the subjunctive is evident from the form *be* (italicized) rather than from the negative (*not* only half-italicized): *be* vs. *is* but not *be not* vs. * *do(es) not be*; with *be* a distinction as regards DO-support does not arise (cf. section b).

Similar points can be made about Kruisinga's single example (1932a:450) of a negative subjunctive, [4]; about Jespersen's examples in [5] (1949:627, 639–40); and Curme's in [6] (1931:416, 424): *be* vs. *is, have* vs. *has,* not vs. * *do(es) not be/have*:

[4] doubt whether the critic *be not* a ... superfluous
     phenomenon

229

[5a] if it *be not* merely a sense of honour
[5b] God grant that he *be not* deceived
[5c] closing it carefully that the precious stone *be not* lost
[6a] I think it *be* (now *is*) *not* so
[6b] if experience *have not* taught you this

Note 'now *is*' in [6a]: Curme's examples in [6] are as early as 1605 and 1578, respectively (harking back to (much) before the twentieth century is a notorious and persistent problem in OG only circumvented by Kruisinga and Quirk *et al.*; but which *A–Z* generally ignores).

Curme (1935:330) also presents, as a "DO-form", the subjunctive *do take*, *with* DO-support; and indeed Curme (1931:407) cites [7] (which is not identified as a subjunctive, though); and Jespersen (1949:627) has [8] (from Shakespeare!):

[7] if he *do not* send for me
[8] if hee *doe not* mightilie grace himselfe on thee

However, Curme (1931:401) and Jespersen (1949:629, 641) also have [9, 10]: examples of negative subjunctives of other verbs than *be* and *have*, and still *without* DO-support (though in Jespersen again from the sixteenth/seventeenth centuries):

[9]   pray God it *last not* long
[10a] if my memory *fayle not*
[10b] if this *satisfie not*
[10c] though it *doe not* always so

Note, however, that even [9, 10] are all cases of 3rd person singular, i.e. distinguished by absence of -*s* as much as by absence of *do*.

Finally, we turn to Quirk *et al.*, first used in this section as point of departure, but here representing OG. As we have seen, *GCE* reverts to the failure of Sweet to cover any negative subjunctives, but now by a relatively *narrow* notion of '(not) important'. This is amply compensated for in *CGoEL*: in addition to [2a], there are the examples of [11]: all negative subjunctives of verbs other than *be*, *have*; and without *do* (1985:134/156, 777, 1012):

[11a] it is important/essential that this mission *not fail*
[11b] it is important that he *not stay*
[11c] I requested that they *not* interrupt me
[11d] they removed the prisoner in order that he *not disturb* the proceedings

Note especially that [11c], like [2a], is evidently a subjunctive *only* by virtue of the absence of *do*; i.e. there is no concomitant absence of -*s*, which *they* shirks anyway. Moreover, at one point in Quirk *et al.* (1985) (out of six on negative subjunctives), "There is ... *normally* no DO-support for subjunctive verbs" (1985:134, emphasis added); as if earlier OG's [7, 8] (vs. SS&P's * [18] in NG below) are also *open*ly let in; but no actual evidence is given.

Worthy of notice is also the sequence of *not* and subjunctive in Quirk *et al.* (1985), as compared to other OG (and NG below). In [9, 10] the order is 'subjunctive-*not*'; in [2, 11] '*not*-subjunctive'. This may represent a change that has occurred in English: cf. notably [10a], *fayle not* from the late sixteenth century (Spenser); vs. [11a], *not fail* from the late twentieth. The order is also 'subjunctive *be-not*' in [3–6]. Here again Quirk *et al.* deviate, but less sharply: "With all verbs except BE ... *not* before the subjunctive ... In the case of *be, not* ... either before or after the verb" (1985:156); [12a] thus agrees with the earlier OG evidence, but [12b] rather agrees with *CGoEL*'s own evidence for other verbs in [2a, 11]:

[12a] the Senate has decreed that such students *be not* exempted
[12b] the Senate has decreed that such students *not be* exempted

s.2 On NG on subjunctives

In NG, the *narrow* approach manifests itself in an evident tendency to try and spirit the subjunctive of Modern English away: the most *narrow* view of any phenomenon is that it really does not exist at all. The trick then consists of claiming that the subjunctive is 'really' a case of some other point of Modern English grammar, with which it can be unified (cf. also sections N, Q). Thus in *A–Z*'s standards the subjunctive is 'really' an imperative (Chomsky 1973, SS&P 1973), or 'really' an infinitive (Emonds 1976); and in the NG literature, the subjunctive is 'really' a modal auxiliary (Roberts 1985). The interesting point for us is that to all these various *narrow* unifications, negative subjunctives appear to be pertinent (Chomsky 1973:236 adumbrates an approach combining those of SS&P and Roberts; but he does not develop this at all).

The point can be clearly seen in Emonds: "the present subjunctive in English ... [and] infinitival *for* clauses ... have ... similar internal structure ... vis-à-vis ... the position of *not*" (1976:198; on *for* see section f); i.e. subjunctive '=' infinitive because of (inter alia) [13]:

[13a] for her not to know this is crucial
         (infinitive: *not* before *know*)
[13b] that she *not*   *know* this is crucial
         (subjunctive: *not* before *know*)

In fact, Emonds *narrow*ly imposes strict identity on infinitives/ subjunctives, with respect to *not*. In particular, since *not* always precedes infinitive *be*, *not* after subjunctive *be* is explicitly also excluded (1976:214): [14] (but cf. [12]):

[14a] * she requests that they *be not* examined
[14b] she requests that they *not be* examined

Note that in neither [13] nor [14] does the absence of DO-support uniquely identify subjunctives: in [13] there is also absence of *-s* (cf. [9, 10]); in [14] *be* instead of *are* (cf. [3–6, 12]).

In Roberts (1985:40–1) the same point applies, except that here the subjunctive is 'really' a case of "an empty modal", let us say Ø (cf. section z for 'zero'); and, "We can see that ... from the position of ... negation, which precedes the verb". Thus, along-side a full modal like *will* in [15a], we have an empty modal in [15b], i.e. [15c]:

[15a] I suggest that he will not be there by 8
[15b] I suggest that he   *not be* there by 8
[15c] I suggest that he Ø   *not be* there by 8

Accordingly, since [16a, 17a] are *, Roberts therefore also ex-cludes [16b, 17b]:

[16a] * I require that he will be not there by 8
[16b] * I require that he   *be not* there by 8   (= * Ø be not)
[17a] * I require that he will have not left before
[17b] * I require that he   *have not* left before (= * Ø have not)

By contrast to [15–17] for Modern English, Roberts notes that "In Middle and Early Modern English ... we find the verb and *not* in the reverse order in subjunctives"; e.g. *that he come not*, now *that he not come*: this agrees with the difference between earlier and later OG in [9, 10] vs. [11], respectively. Note however that both Emonds and Roberts disagree with OG on the status of *be not*: * in [14b, 16b]; but OK in Quirk *et al.*'s [12a] as in earlier OG's [3–6] (cf. also *have not* in [6b] vs. * *have not* in [17b]).

If we now finally turn to SS&P, the matter is here somewhat more complex than in other NG that *A–Z* looks at for *s* for subjunctives. That is, Emonds and Roberts *narrow*ly insist on identity between subjunctives and, respectively, infinitives and modals, so that subjunctives may be said not to exist separately. But SS&P want to rely on imperatives (cf. section u) to usurp the subjunctive; and then the problem cannot be avoided that impera-tives do allow DO-support (cf. also section y): *do come, don't run*

(1973:668). Rather than rely on evidence like [7, 8] in OG, SS&P *narrow*ly decree that DO-support not apply to subjunctives: "it is necessary ... to exclude such sentences as" [18a] (1973:665), or [18b] (1973:667; cf. [7, 8] in OG):

[18a] * I insist that John does not be given that
[18b] * I insist that John do   not come so often

In fact "our assumption that subjunctives are just ... imperatives ... may be something of an oversimplification" (1973:665). To nevertheless maintain the desirably *narrow* (over-)simplification, SS&P assume that imperatives and subjunctives are both charac- terized by an abstract feature SJC (for 'SubJunCtive'), which can be supported by *do*. But to prevent DO-support, then "In subjunc- tives, it is necessary that SJC be deleted" (1973:665; note the subjunctive *be*). SS&P's (over-)simplification thus effectively amounts to first transferring a subjunctive value SJC from subjunc- tives to imperatives; and then removing this SJC value from actual subjunctives! All the same, from this (too) *narrow* (over-) simplification, SS&P's systematic exploration of pertinent negative subjunctives arises, including [18] and also [19]; note especially that in [19b] *you* shirks *-s*, and absence of *-s* does not apply so that it is *A–Z*'s single NG example of a subjunctive only evidenced by absence of DO-support (cf. [2a, 11c]):

[19a] I insist that John *not come* so often
[19b] I insist that you   *not leave* as early as John

s.3 Conclusions

The juxtaposition between OG and NG with respect to subjunc- tives resides essentially in the more or less accidental appearance of negative subjunctives among the available evidence of OG; as opposed to their systematic exploration in NG, as pertinent to (over-)simplifications *narrow*ly eliminating subjunctives as a separate phenomenon: i.e. the juxtaposition of *open* and *narrow* approaches to Modern English grammar. In this juxtaposition Quirk *et al.* (1972) side with the latter, *narrow* approach: negative subjunctives are 'not important' and hence ignored.

In Quirk *et al.* (1985) the *open* approach reasserts itself with something like a vengeance. The subjunctive is now 'not so unimportant'; but notably *not* now 'important', i.e. not major = *narrow*. Not only does *CGoEL* cover negative subjunctives at least as systematically as any NG. They also allow the sequence '*not*-subjunctive *be*' that Emonds (1976) and Roberts (1985) exclude in NG. And, even more significantly, Quirk *et al.* do not attempt the *narrow* interpretation of subjunctives as 'really' something else. On the contrary. Quirk *et al.* (1985:149–50) apply in some detail the *open* notions of a "scale" or "gradience", under the *open* "guiding principle ... [that g]rammar is to some extent an indeterminate system" (1985:90); 'determinacy' is the *narrow* notion of grammar within strict constraints. Thus, by taking a number of criteria, including (absence of) DO-support, Quirk *et al.* (1985) on behalf of OG confirm the separate status, in a scale of gradience, of both subjunctives and imperatives (vs. NG in SS&P); of both subjunctives and infinitives (vs. NG in Emonds); and of both subjunctives and modal auxiliaries (vs. NG in Roberts).

T is for *though*

Consider the two sentences [1a, b], in particular the different word-orders in the subclauses: *though ... hard workers* vs. *hard workers though ...* :

[1a] *though* they are *hard workers*, they are poor
[1b] *hard workers though* they are, they are poor

It seems that in [1] *hard workers* is as it were 'transposed' between end position in the subclause in [1a] and front position in [1b], since only the one position or the other may be occupied, but not both; [1, 2] are parallel, but combinations of [1a, 2b] in [3a] or [1b, 2a] in [3b] are impossible:

[2a]		though they are active	, they are poor
[2b]	active	though they are	, they are poor
[3a]	* active	though they are hard workers,	they are poor
[3b]	* hard workers though they are active		, they are poor

In both [3a, b] *hard workers* appears to oust *active* by transposition. Moreover, of the structure *hard workers*, one cannot transpose one part but not the other:

[4a]	*	workers though they are hard	, they are poor
[4b]	* hard	though they are	workers, they are poor

Let us use *T* for transposed phrases, e.g. *hard workers* or *active*; *t* is for items like *though* around which transposition can take place. Now [1a, 2a] can be accounted for as *t ... T*, and [1b, 2b] as *T t ...*; but * *T t ... T*, either in the sense of [3] or of [4].

Of the two variants, *t ... T* and *T t ...*, it is *T t ...* with front position of *T* which is perhaps the more notable one. It is stylistically the more marked version. Moreover, transposition is not observed to put *T* in front of almost any other *t* but *though*; cf. *because, when, if*, etc.:

[5a]   if they are hard workers, they are not honest
[5b] * hard workers if they are   , they are not honest

One would therefore want to ascertain the precise extents of the possibilities in *T t* ... : what is found as *t* after *T* other than *though*; and what is found as *T* before *t* other than *hard workers* or *active*. In this section we will look at such aspects of *T t* ... , as they variously appear in OG accounts (section T.1) and in NG (section T.2).

T.1 On OG on *T t(hough)* ...

We may begin the discussion of *T t* ... by identifying a 'standard' OG account. Individual OG grammars may then be represented in relation to this point of departure. Two aspects of such a standard OG account would be [6, 7] with respect to the extents of *t* and *T* respectively:

[6] in *T t* ... , *t = though, as, that,* ...
[7] in *T t* ... , in *T* one finds absence of the article

We will look at [6, 7] one by one.

Starting from *t = though*, [6] extends *t* at least to *as* and *that*. For instance, in his discussion of "*though* ... placed in immediate succession to ... front position", Poutsma (1929:709) mentions that "In this function, *though* varies with *as*", as in [8] (1929:710):

[8] rich *as* he is, ... (*rich = T, as = t: T t* ...)

And Curme (1931:339) in turn equates *as* and *that*:

[9] Whig *as* (... = *that*) he was, ... (*Whig = T, as/that = t: T t* ...)

Although they may be less explicit about [6], essentially equivalent accounts are given in Kruisinga (1932a:370), *GCE* (1972:749), and *CGoEL* (1985:1097–8).

What then about *t* in Sweet and Jespersen? Their accounts are subsumed by [6] as the standard OG account of *t* in *T t* ... , by virtue of the dots in [6], '... '. These dots actually identify [6] as OG: they leave *open* the exact extent of *t*. OG will in principle observe what actually manifests itself: *T* may be found followed by *though*, or *as*, or *that*. But the dots serve to keep [5] *open* to accommodating further possibilities as they might be observed: OG will rarely *narrow* itself by excluding other *t* as impossibilities (cf. section II.4), for instance as for *if* in [5]. Although usually staunchly *open*, Poutsma seems to be exceptionally *narrow* in thus excluding possibilities: "*if* does not ... admit of being placed after the principal word of the predicate", [5b] (1929:710); and *though* belongs to [6] "to the exclusion of" *although* (1929:708), cf. [10]:

[10] (*) hard workers *although* they are, ...
(* = Poutsma's apparent judgement)

However, OG reasserts itself when Jespersen (1940:362) duly *open*s *t* up again even for *although*: "[R. L.] Stevenson [1850–1894] here also uses *although*", e.g. [11]:

[11] terrible *although* it was, ... (*terrible* = T, *although* = t: *T t* ...)

The dots allow for *although* to be accordingly added to [6].

Conversely, Sweet pioneers OG, in this case the OG account of *t* in [6], with only *as* and *though*: "*Such* sentences *as* 'big as he is, ...'" (1898:26, emphases added), where the italicized words imply the dots of [6], as yet specified for only *as*; the dots then turn out to accommodate at least also *though* (1898:109; [15a] below), and leave any other *t* *open*. Eventually, the principled *open*-mindedness of OG towards *t* is evocatively expressed in *CGoEL* (but not yet in *GCE*): Quirk *et al.* (1985:921) are carefully non-committal about [6] by stating about *t*'s that "There are *two or three* ... which are exceptional in that they can occur noninitially [i.e. after *T*]" (emphasis added). OG has consistently remained *open*, instantiating two members of *t* (Sweet), two or three (*CGoEL*), or three (Poutsma, Kruisinga, Curme, *GCE*), or four (Jespersen), or ...: [6].

Let us now turn to *T* in OG, i.e. [7]. The point about [7] may be illustrated as in [12]:

[12a]   though he may be a hard worker, he is
        poor
        (*though* = t, a hard worker = T: *t* ... *T*)
[12b] *   though he may be   hard worker, he is
        poor
[12c]   hard worker   though he may be   , he is
        poor
        (*hard worker* = T, though = t: *T t* ...)

That is, although *T* of *t* ... *T* in [12a, b] must contain an article, *a*, one observes absence of article in *T* of *T t* ... , [12c] (this complicates 'transposition'; it may rather be transposition *plus* loss of article). The OG account of [12] in [7] may be variously expressed. Poutsma (1914:647) observes "the suppression of the indefinite article before a ... noun ... followed by ... *that* or ... *as*"; Kruisinga (1932a:369–70) discusses "plain noun ... with front position ... in a ... clause with *as* or *though* ... also ... *vain fool that I was*"; and in Curme (1931:513) "A noun is often without an article ... in abridged clauses: *Child* though he was, ... ". Note that only Kruisinga gives his full account of *T t* ... in one place: absence of article, 'plain nouns', in *T* before *as*, and *though*, and *that*. Poutsma only relates [7] directly to *that* and *as*; extending it indirectly to *though* elsewhere, where in such cases "*though* varies with *as*" (1929:709). Similarly, Curme also relates [7] to *that* and *as* indirectly: his term 'abridged clause' is applied to '*gentle creature that she was*', '*dear kind soul as she is*' (1931:315), where *T* before *t* is also without article.

It seems fair to say that OG accounts of [7] are intended to represent absence of article in *T* of *T t* ... , irrespective of choice of *t*, in Poutsma and Curme as much as in Kruisinga. There is no such account, however, in Sweet or in Quirk *et al.* (1972, 1985); as it happens the most predominantly native OG grammars of Modern English (cf. section T.4 4 below). One will, of course, excuse the absence of [7] in Sweet on the general grounds of his pioneering OG. In particular, Sweet's four examples of *T t* ... all happen to contain adjectives as *T* (cf. [15a] below); whereas the question of absence or presence of article only arises with nouns. No such extenuating circumstances seem to readily apply to Quirk *et al.*: both *GCE* and *CGoEL* have at least the already accumulated evidence of [7] in Poutsma, Kruisinga, and Curme available (and *CGoEL* includes in its Bibliography pertinent NG literature: Radford 1980). In fact cases like [7] even occur, but still go unnoticed, in both Quirk grammars: '*fool that he was*', actually glossed as 'since he was *a fool*' (1972:750), or as 'even though he was *a fool*' (1985:1098, emphases added). Quirk *et al.* seem obstinately blind to [7], the absence of *a* in *T*.

In the case of Jespersen, the situation with respect to [7] is even more complicated. Perhaps [7] has less appeal for Jespersen than for other OG because Jespersen has a relative hoard of examples like [13], where article is *not* absent in *T* of *T t* ... ([13b] is also cited by Poutsma (1929:710); when Poutsma elsewhere adopts [7] (1914:647), cases like [13b] are apparently overlooked, however):

[13a] excellent a woman as she is   (1914:365, 1926:176)
[13b] big a puzzle as it was   (1914:365, 1926:176)
[13c] bright a girl as you are   (1914:509)

As Jespersen suggests, it still seems that in [13] something is absent, although other than the article; for instance the *so* of [14b] that is lacking illegitimately in [14a] but correctly in [13a]:

[14a] * though she is   excellent a woman, ...
[14b]   though she is so excellent a woman, ...

It will be seen in section T.2 below that the relation between absence of *a* in [12] and of *so* in [13, 14] may be quite pertinent for NG. Meanwhile, for Jespersen, examples like [13] may have confirmed that OG should leave presence or absence of article in *T* of *T t* ... as *open* as possible. That is, in a somewhat reluctant kind of appendix to an extensive survey of cases of "no indefinite article", Jespersen (1927:392) seems to both acknowledge and dismiss [7] in one breath: "For *beast that I am!* and *villain as the man was* see ... [elsewhere]", where 'elsewhere' [7] is however beyond the horizon. By not firmly committing himself to [7] in this way, Jespersen may have wanted to leave room for cases like [13].

At the same time, Jespersen commits himself much more firmly than any other OG to an aspect of *T* in *T t* ... beyond [7]: the functions that *T* may have in its clause. In practice, *T t* ... is represented in OG much the most frequently by cases where *T* functions as complement (cf. section C) to a copula verb like *be*; although terminology varies, the most common OG term, which we will adopt, is 'predicative' complement. Thus [15a] contains a predicative adjective (cf. *active* in [2]), [15b] a predicative noun (cf. *hard workers* in [1]; on BE as 'copula' see section b):

[15a] *humble* though it be   (Sweet 1898:109)
        be copula: *humble* = predicative
[15b] *orphan* though she was   (Poutsma 1929:709)
        was copula: *orphan* = predicative

[15] is pioneered by Sweet: his four examples of *T t* ... all involve predicative adjectives; later OG always illustrates more or less abundantly both predicative adjectives as *T* like [15a] and predicative nouns as *T* like [15b]. In comparison, OG generally gives few examples of *T* with adverbial function, viz. (excluding Jespersen discussed below) two examples like [16a] with *t* = *though* and seven like [16b] with *t* = *as*:

[16a] *greatly* though I admire her
        (*CGoEL* 1985:1098; cf. Kruisinga 1932b:420)
[16b] *rashly* as she acted
        (Curme 1931:334; cf. Poutsma 1929:710 twice; Kruisinga 1932b:449 three times; *GCE* 1972:750 = *CGoEL* 1985:1098)

Let's represent these OG accounts of the functions of *T*, so far predicative P and occasionally adverbial A, as in [17]:

[17] in *T t* . . . , *T*'s function = P, (A)

Jespersen's account is much more *open* than [17]. To begin with, to the total of nine examples of adverbial *T* = A elsewhere in OG, Jespersen on his own adds over fifteen (!) (1927:176–7; 1940:362). And Jespersen is practically unique among OG in adding that apart from *T* = P and *T* = A, also "an object may be preposed followed by *as*" (1927:177), single-handedly giving eight (!) examples like [18] (also 1940:362):

[18] *hot tears* as I have wept

(one accidental example like [18] in Kruisinga (1932b:449) goes unobserved among illustrations of *as* with "front position of adverb", i.e. like [16b]). If we represent object as O, then Jespersen's account of the functions of *T* [19] would clearly approximate more closely than [17] the OG aim of comprehensiveness:

[19] in *T t* . . . , *T*'s function = P, A, O

T.2 On NG on *T t(hough)* . . .

NG was originally best known as 'transformational' grammar, but is now rather called 'generative' grammar. As will be recalled from Parts I and II, this roughly reflects two phases in NG. Initially, NG's interest was primarily in 'transformations', which change a basic structure into a derived structure, and would thus allow the range of basic structures to be *narrow*ed. More recently, the restrictions on transformations themselves have in turn become so *narrow* that structures are again looked at in their own right. For the purposes of this section, it will be helpful to be able to refer to an earlier 'transformational' phase of NG, and to a later 'structural' phase of NG respectively. Concurrently, Chomsky changed his views on OG, from transformational NG 'reconstructing' OG to structural NG 'complementing' OG (see Part II).

T t . . . has attracted relatively little attention in NG. Under OG compulsion towards *open* comprehensiveness, all OG must – and does – have some account of *T t* . . . at least. But there need not be any NG accounts of *T t* . . . at all, unless *T t* . . . is pertinent to some specific NG theory. In fact, there is no *T t* . . . whatever in SS&P (1973). The NG accounts that there are, however, do duly reflect the developments from transformational NG to structural NG. Until the late 1970s, our informal notion of 'transposition' was readily reconstructed in NG as a transformation (cf. [20] below): e.g. Ross (1967), Chomsky (1973), Emonds (1976). After roughly

1980, something like 'absence of article', [7] of OG, raises questions about the structure of *T* itself, e.g. Culicover (1982). Recall that Chomsky and Emonds are, with SS&P, *A–Z*'s standard NG; Ross (1967) and Culicover (1982) here represent 'the NG literature'.

To begin with transformational NG accounts, then, *T t* ... would be derived by *T*-transposition [20] from basic *t* ... *T*:

[20] *t* ... *T* ⇒ *T t* ...
    e.g. [a] *though* Dick is *handsome* ⇒ [b] *handsome though* Dick is

From the NG perspective of *narrow* constraints, a question that arises with respect to [20] is whether [20] can transpose *T* in front of *t* from anywhere, as the dots '...' in [20] *open*ly suggest (cf. the discussion of the dots in [6] above); or whether this can be *narrow*ed. This is the issue in both Ross (1967) and Chomsky (1973): quite typically for NG, from different degrees of theoretical *narrow*ness deduce different looks at pertinent facts, however.

Ross (1967) is seminal NG: one of the earliest works where constraints come prominently to the fore to effectuate *narrow* NG; for instance, the constraint operative in [21] (cf. Ross 1967:223):

[21a]   though Dick is strong and *handsome*
[21b] * *handsome* though Dick is strong and

In [20], *T* = *handsome* is readily transposed in front of *t* = *though*; but in [21] transposition of *T* = *handsome* in front of *t* = *though* by [20] goes wrong. Ross observes that this may be ascribed to the fact that in [21a] *handsome* is actually part of a 'co-ordinate' structure, with *and*. Let us say that in a construction like *strong and handsome* in [21a], *and* is a 'jailor'; and the construction is a 'prison' out of which no escape is possible for *T* = *handsome*, not even by force of [20] (cf. section m). This is represented in [22], where the bracketed construction [...] is a prison because of jailor *and* italicized:

[22a]   though Dick is [strong *and* handsome]
[22b] * handsome though Dick is [strong *and*   ]

Ross identifies a number of constructions where a jailor may effect imprisonment. Another one is illustrated in [23, 24]:

[23a]   though I believe [that Dick is handsome]
[23b]   handsome though I believe [that Dick is   ]
[24a]   though I believe [the *claim* that Dick is handsome]

241

[24b] * handsome though I believe [the *claim* that Dick is
        ]

In the bracketed construction of [23], Ross appoints no jailor; and *T* = *handsome* is free to transpose by [20]. But in [24] the noun *claim* does function as a jailor, and *T* = *handsome* has to remain imprisoned.

However, Chomsky (1973:253, n32) suggests that a construction by itself, rather than with a jailor, may already be a prison for *T* in *T*-transposition [20]:

[25a]   though they told me [that Tom is handsome]
[25b] * handsome though they told me [that Tom is   ]

([23] would now be analysed differently than indicated, such that *T* = *handsome* would no more transpose out of a construction than in [20]). Accordingly, Ross (1967) and Chomsky (1973) have different judgements about transposition of *T* out of constructions without jailors: [23b] is OK for Ross but [25b] is * for Chomsky. Similarly, transposition of *T* = *handsome* out of five constructions [26b] is still fine for Ross because there are no jailors; but *T* out of two constructions [27b] would be * for Chomsky:

[26a]   though everyone expects [me to try [to force
        Bill [to make [Mom agree [that Dick is handsome]]]]]],
        . . .
[26b]   handsome though everyone expects [me to try [to force
        Bill [to make [Mom agree [that Dick is   ]]]]]],
        . . .
[27a]   though my friends suggested [that Mary
        thinks [that Tom is handsome]]
[27b] * handsome though my friends suggested [that Mary
        thinks [that Tom is   ]]

Clearly, the *open*ness of OG does not accord at all with a *narrow* concept like imprisonment, with or without jailors. In OG, the need for specific accounts of *T*-transposition out of constructions, beyond [20], does not arise. In fact, the only illustration, let alone explicit discussion, seems to be [28b] from Jespersen (1940:362):

[28a] though he was beginning [to feel sure of her]
[28b] sure of her though he was beginning [to feel]

Back in NG, for Emonds (1976:57–60) the issue is not whether *T* may transpose out of prisons, with or without jailors; but another *narrow* one, viz. why *T* may transpose at all. Under Emonds' NG theory (see section 3.3), for *T*-transposition to preserve structure there should be a basic structure $T_1 t \ldots T_2$; but such a structure does not seem to occur; cf. [3, 4]. Accordingly, Emonds' account of *T t* ... is not by [20], but by a highly specific 'local' transformation exchanging *t* and adjectival *T* next to one another. That is, the derivation of [31b] is from [29b], not directly by [20], but via [30b]. From [29] to [30] *T* is 'fronted', a possibility by itself, given [30a]; however, such fronting is not allowed in a structure with initial *t*; hence [30b, c] are *. Next, [30b] – but not [30c] – is then saved by local '*though*-inversion', which allows *t = though*, but *narrow*ly no other *t*, to become non-initial, so that [31b], but not [31c], is good after all:

[29a]			he usually is sensible
[29b]	though		he usually is sensible
[29c]	if		he usually is sensible
[30a]		sensible	he usually is
[30b]	* though	sensible	he usually is
[30c]	* if	sensible	he usually is
[31b]	sensible though		he usually is
[31c]	* sensible if		he usually is

Note how Emonds' account of *T t* ... is actually *narrow*. The general theory of structure-preserving transformations is too *narrow* to allow *T t* ... at all in the first place. Hence *T t* ... can only be a minor phenomenon by a local transformation exchanging only *t = though* with only *T* = adjective; no *t = as, that*; no *T* = adverb (cf. [16]), no *T* = noun (cf. [15b]). Since 'absence of article' [7] only arises with *T* = noun, it remains beyond Emonds' horizon, as in Sweet. But note that Emonds keeps his horizon *narrow* on NG purpose, viz. pertinence; whereas Sweet keeps his horizon *open*, for later OG.

On the other hand, when NG becomes predominantly interested in the structure of *T* itself, *narrow* constraints on *t* and *T* in turn disappear behind the horizon. Thus Culicover (1982:15) does acknowledge *t = as, that, though*; and *T* = adjective, adverb, noun. Conversely, 'absence of article' becomes a pertinent fact for structural NG. In fact, the contrasts between *genius, a genius* in [32] are Culicover's (1982:1–2) point of departure:

[32a]	though John is a genius, ...
[32b]	* though John is genius, ...
[32c]	* a genius though John is , ...
[32d]	genius though John is , ...

Note that in the *narrow* perspective of [32], the article *a* not just *is* absent from *T* in *T t* ..., [32d]; but it *must* be absent, [32c].

243

In more recent NG, structures are *narrow*ed down to just a few types, by disregarding specific categories. For instance, as a noun (N) may combine with an article into a Noun Phrase (NP), so an adjective (A) may combine with a degree adverb into an Adjective Phrase (AP). Thus both *a + genius* and *very + tall* would have the same structure [33a]; only, 'Specifier of X' and 'X-bar' are manifested variably, [33b, c] (this is an informal representation of 'X-bar' theory in NG as a powerful means of *narrow* unification; cf. sections D and G):

[33a] XP = Specifier of X + X-bar
[33b] NP = Specifier of N + N-bar
    e.g.   article *a*   + *genius*   = a genius
[33c] AP = Specifier of A + A-bar
    e.g.   adverb *very* + *tall*   = very tall

Culicover's application of [33] to [32] is to suggest (1982:8) that in *t ... T*, *T* = XP: i.e. *a genius* in [32a], * *genius* in [32b]; but in *T t ...*, *T* = X-bar: i.e. *genius* in [32d], * *a genius* in [32c]. But as [33] thus *narrow*s down the structure of *T* to either XP or X-bar, it will apply to X = A (AP and A-bar) as much as to X = N: *T* = XP in *t ... T*, i.e. *very tall*; *T* = X-bar in *T t ...*, i.e. *tall*. Culicover submits that this is precisely the case:

[34a]   though John is very tall   ($t ... T$: T = AP)
[34c] * very tall though John is   ($T t ...$: $T \neq$ AP)
[34d]   tall though John is   ($T t ...$: T = A-bar)

In essence, therefore, Culicover (1982) accounts for *T* in structural NG as in [35] (cf. [7] of OG)

[35] in *T t ...*, *T* = X-bar: there must be suppression of Specifier of X

Note that [34] is not entirely parallel to [32]: whereas in [32b] X-bar *genius* is impossible, in [34b] X-bar *tall* does appear to be possible:

[34b]   though John is   tall

This accounts readily for the neglect of 'suppression of adverb' in OG; between [34c, b] there does not appear to be any of difference in *T*, whether transposed or not: for OG there is therefore nothing to account for. It is only when NG *narrow*s down accounts as in [33], [35] that [34c] becomes a pertinent fact. Recall however that there is at least one instance where OG does appear to be aware of something more general than just 'absence of article': Jespersen's *(so) excellent a woman*, [13a, 14]. It may now be seen that in fact in both *genius* and *excellent a woman* there is equally suppression; viz. either suppression of Specifier of N *a*, or suppression of Specifier of A *so* (cf. Stuurman 1985).

T.3 Conclusions

There are clearly juxtaposed *open* and *narrow* accounts of *T t* . . . in OG and NG, with no real common ground between them. Even superficial agreement is fundamental disagreement when looked at carefully. Thus when the accounts of both Sweet in OG and Emonds in NG are of only adjectives as *T*. In Sweet's OG this is an accident of as yet limited observation, *open* to extensions to nouns, adverbs, etc. in later OG. For Emonds, however, *though*-adjective inversion is a fundamental NG attempt to *narrow* transformations, here to a local one. We see the same juxtaposition in the respective accounts of *t*: *as, though,* . . . for Sweet; only *though* for Emonds. Similarly, absence of article in *T* by [7] of OG may be subsumed by suppression of Specifier [35] of NG. But this would ignore the difference: in OG an article is *observed* to be absent, in NG a Specifier *has* to be suppressed. And in an example like [13a], *excellent a woman as* . . ., the presence of article *a* in *T* can suggest for OG, at least for Jespersen, caution with regard to even the minimal *narrow*ness of [7]; conversely its interpretation in NG would be the more generally *narrow* [35] for [7]: unified suppression of *any* Specifier. Beyond all this, NG concerns like those of Ross (1967) and Chomsky (1973), with impossible cases of *T*-transposition out of constructions/prisons, are entirely alien to, and hence practically absent from, OG. At no point in its development, either transformational or structural, does NG provide accounts of *T t* . . . that seem to have been remotely like either 'reconstructions' of OG, or 'complements' to OG. The fundamental juxtaposition between *open* and *narrow* accounts overrides anything else.

T.4 Discussion and extensions

1 As the main text observes, Poutsma (1929:709) excludes *although* as *t* in *T t* . . .; but Jespersen cites an example from Stevenson's *The Black Arrow*, and [11] from *The Dynamiter*. These are not included in Poutsma's (1926:835–46) list of Books Quoted From. But other books by Stevenson *are* in this list (1926:845). There are no additions to the list in Poutsma's (1928, 1929) volumes. Meijs (1984:92) (cf. section i) suggests that induction entailed a (*narrow*?) limitation before the days of the computer:

in making their observations, OG grammarians like Poutsma and Jespersen still "had ... to wait and see what happened to come their way and attract their attention".

- Does the difference between Poutsma and Jespersen on *although* confirm Meijs' suggestion? And what can be said about [6] in this connection?

2 In much NG literature there are examples of *T t* ... where *t* = *though* and *T* = verbal; e.g. [i] (Andrews 1982:313):

[ia]   though Andy will attack Mal on
       Tuesday
[ib] attack Mal on Tuesday though Andy will

A–Z ignores instances like [i] in the main text, to save space; there are no examples like [i] in OG before *GCE* (1972:750) and *CGoEL* (1985:1098), which both have [ii]:

[ii] fail though I did

- Discuss the (in)adequacy of *A–Z* taking 'Modern English' to be English throughout the twentieth century, in view of the apparently recent emergence of [i, ii], at least in grammatical accounts.
Andrews (1982:313) suggests that instances like [i, ii] show that *attack Mal on Tuesday* and *fail* are VPs, and that *will* and *did* are not part of VP.
- Discuss the claim that *attack Mal on Tuesday* and *fail* are/are not VPs, in view of [35]. Could they be V-bar's, and *will* or *did* Specifiers of V? (cf. [33])

3 Outside Jespersen, five (out of nine!) OG examples of *T* = A involve *much*, for instance, with *t* = *though*, [iii] from Kruisinga (1932b:420):

[iii] much though he loved the University

Consider the (un)grammaticality of the counterparts of [iii] with respect to transposition, e.g. [iv]:

[iva] * though he loved the University   much
[ivb]   though he loved the University very much

- In view of the contrasts between [iii, iv], discuss the OG account of 'absence' in *T* of [7], vs. the NG one of [35].

4 With respect to absence of article, [7] or [35], there is comparison to other languages in both OG and NG. "Dutch and English practice are uniform as to the suppression of the indefinite article before a predicative noun that is followed by ... *that* or ... *as*" (Poutsma 1914:647). "It would be easy to adduce

parallels to the cases of nouns without an article in many other languages" (Kruisinga 1932a:378). Similarly, Culicover (1982:22) refers to French, where X-bar rather than XP is observed even outside *T* of *T t* . . .: *je suis linguiste* ('I am [a] linguist').

- Discuss *A–Z*'s subsidiary issue, the apparent correlations between (non)nativeness, OG and NG, in this connection (see also the main text above).

u is for understood *you*

In a grammar of Modern English that purports "to agree with Chomsky (1965)", the *narrow* approach is duly espoused as follows: "Our book is not intended solely to be a compendium of facts about the English language. More facts than what we include here can be found in reference grammars" (Celce-Murcia and Larsen-Freeman, henceforth CM&LF, 1983: 4–5). CM&LF's NG is the model of Chomsky (1965): it is indicative of the less effective *narrow*ness of such relatively early NG (cf. Part II) that CM&LF use 'not solely' rather than plain 'not' to disavow an *open* 'compendium'. Rather than NG attempting a comprehensive compendium of facts as in OG, CM&LF take the (in 1965) prevalent view that NG *narrow*ly 'reconstructs the insights' (see part II) that are seen to be incorporated into OG accounts. For instance, with respect to imperatives: "The transformationalists' [= (early) NG] account of imperatives is ... in agreement with that of the traditional grammarians [= (*inter alia*) OG] such as Jespersen ..., who suggested that all imperatives have an understood *you*. However, by using transformational rules we can make Jespersen's intuition explicit and give syntactic arguments in support of it" (CM&LF 1983:140). The reference is to a re-print of Jespersen (1933), the one-volume derivative of Jespersen's (1909–1949) contribution to OG, *MEG* (cf. section K). In this section, we take miniscule u to be for '*understood you*'. This is a concept that may arise in various places in Modern English grammar; cf. for instance section y. However, following CM&LF (1983), we here pursue briefly accounts of imperatives to see whether, firstly, Jespersen's 'understood *you*' is indeed a traditional OG notion in presenting the facts of Modern English imperatives; and secondly, whether NG can indeed be considered to reconstruct OG insights by giving arguments for them.

One of the NG arguments for an understood *you* in imperatives that CM&LF refer to is the appearance of reflexive *yourself*/*yourselves* in imperatives: [1a, b], but not [1c–h] (cf. section R):

[1a]   shave yourself
[1b]   shave yourselves
[1c] * shave myself
[1d] * shave himself
[1e] * shave herself
[1f] * shave itself
[1g] * shave ourselves
[1h] * shave themselves

The same point applies to sentences with an actual *you* as subject:

[2a]   you shaved yourself
[2b]   you shaved yourselves
[2c] * you shaved myself
[2d] * you shaved himself
        etc.

A second point that CM&LF allude to is that *you* rather than other pronouns appears in tag-questions to imperatives: [3]; again as it does in tags to sentences with actual *you* as subject, [4]:

[3a]   go away, will you
[3b] * go away, will he
        etc.
[4a]   you didn't go away, did you
[4b] * you didn't go away, did he
        etc.

On the basis of such facts as in [1–4], CM&LF (1983:140) posit a transformational rule of *you*-deletion, as in [5]; but there are no similar rules of *I-*, *he-*, etc. deletion:

[5] *you* + Imperative ⇒ Imperative (with 'understood *you*')

In presenting OG and NG accounts of 'understood *you*', we will follow CM&LF's arguments, and their explication along the lines of [5].

u.1 On OG on understood *you*

An essential feature of CM&LF's NG in [5] is that it accounts for imperatives by means of 'deletion' of *you*: that is, it takes *you* to be basically present, unless it is transformationally removed but still 'understood'. An immediately notable point about much OG from this perspective is that it rather looks at things in precisely the opposite way. In an imperative like *go away* in [6a], without actual reflexive or actual tag, there is no 'available evidence' of any *you*. Hence the more orthodox *open* approach is to take plain imperatives as given; but to allow addition of a subject exactly if and when *you* is in actual evidence. Thus Sweet (1898:12), Poutsma (1926:200), Jespersen (1927:222), and Quirk *et al.* (1985:828; not 1972) all talk about a subject and/or pronoun *you* being "added" to an imperative like [6a] in cases like [6b]:

[6a]   go away
[6b] you go away

Kruisinga (1931:140) takes the same view, expressed as "The imperative may have its subject *you* prefixed to it"; and he goes on to suggest that "sentences are hardly imperatives when there is a subject" (1932b:293). That is, sentences like [6a] are imperatives precisely because there is no subject at all; rather than a deleted one understood.

Curme's and Quirk *et al.*'s (1972) positions with respect to deletion (NG) or addition (OG) in imperatives are not entirely clear. In a case like [7a] Curme allows the subject *you* to "stand" (1935:229), suggesting perhaps that in [7b] the subject *you* would be deleted.

[7a] Norah, you go
[7b] Norah,   go

Similarly, for Quirk *et al.* (1972:403) the "subject *you* is retained" in [8a], 'retention' being an apparent counterpart of deletion in [8b]:

[8a] you be quiet
[8b]   be quiet

But the only place where OG clearly suggests deletion is – *pace* CM&LF, indeed – Jespersen; instead of addition as in (1927), in (1931:251) he has: "it is possible that to the actual speech-instinct the imperative is nothing but a kind of abbreviated ... sentence: *Have an egg = Will you have a egg*".

[9a] will you have an egg
[9b]   have an egg

Sweet (1891:175) has an apparently similar example: [10a] "=" [10b]; but here the '=' represents "meaning", not abbreviation, i.e. deletion:

[10a] will you be quiet
[10b]   be quiet

And in this context (cf. also 1940:472), Jespersen does also refer to the "usual practice of tacking on a question with *will you* to an imperative", as in [11]:

[11] stop that noise, will you

However, Jespersen does *not* use *you* in tags as an 'argument' for understood *you* deleted by abbreviation. Nor does Jespersen commit himself to abbreviation in the first place: such a view is something that is *open*ly 'possible', but not necessary, as Jespersen (1927) as well as other OG shows.

Finally, under the more traditional view of OG that *you* may be added to imperatives, rather than deleted, there is no reason to look for any 'arguments' at all: there is simply the available evidence of *you* itself in cases like [6b], vs. [6a]. Hence, until Jespersen (1931) there is no real discussion in OG of tags for imperatives. On the other hand, there are some reflexives, viz. italicized in [12a] (Poutsma 1926:201), [12b] (Curme 1931:431), [12c] (Kruisinga 1931:139):

[12a] don't you, any of you, worry *yourselves* about that
[12b] you amuse *yourself*
[12c] now boys, enjoy *yourselves*

Note in particular that only in the last example does the reflexive appear without an actual *you* also being in evidence. Note also that, so far, OG offers a comprehensive account of imperatives with and without *you* only by putting several grammars together: Poutsma, Curme, and Kruisinga in [12] for reflexives; Jespersen in [11] for tags.

In the latter respect, Quirk *et al.* serve to integrate earlier OG. It is "implied in the meaning ... that the omitted subject of the imperative verb is ... *you*" (1972:403; almost identically in 1985:828). Note that this is thus a matter of 'meaning'; and not grammatical 'omission' = deletion by a transformational rule like [5]. And Quirk *et al.* then cite as 'confirmation' or 'demonstration' (subtly different, more *open* terms than CM&LF's NG 'arguments'?) both the phenomenon of subject *you* in tags; and the one of *your*-reflexives:

[13a] be quiet, will you
[13b] behave yourself
[13c] behave yourselves
[13d] * behave myself
       etc.

u.2 On NG on understood *you*

For their comprehensive coverage of facts about imperatives, Quirk *et al.* (1972, 1985) could have relied on earlier OG. But the systematicity of their account probably owes more to contemporaneous NG: as CM&LF suggest, accounts of understood *you* by transformational deletion are indeed so common in NG as to be found in all of *A–Z*'s three standards, and have accordingly fostered systematic attention to reflexives and/or tags, for 'arguments'. It is interesting to see this already in the very earliest NG, even preceding the Chomskyan revolution of 1957. Chomsky (1955/1975:553) already suggests that "In imperatives the noun phrase subject ... [is] dropped" by [5]; he adduces the reflexive argument, "since we have [14a] but not [14b], we see that the noun phrase subject must be *you*" (1955/1975:554):

[14a]   look at yourself
[14b] * look at myself
         etc.

This is complemented by Emonds (1976:244) who recognizes [5] as "Deletion of the subject NP *you* in subjectless imperatives" and illustrates this with tags:

[15] help me, won't you

It may be noted that in neither Chomsky (1955/1975) nor Emonds (1976) is the NG account very effectively *narrow*, however: Chomsky admits that to achieve a truly *narrow* account it may be necessary to look for "some better analysis" (1955/1975:556) than [5]; and Emonds, too, leaves as a "fruitful direction for research" (1976:248) the extent to which the theory of structure-preservation (see section 3.3) may be involved in restricting deletions like by [5].

SS&P seem to take the *narrow*ness of their account of imperatives much more seriously than do either Chomsky or Emonds. That is, they too have a transformational rule of *you*-deletion along the lines of [5] (1973:670). And they refer to both types of argument: "The reflexive in imperatives is *yourself/yourselves*" and "Tagged imperatives have *you*" (1973:640).

[16a]   look at yourself
[16b] * look at myself
[17a]   go home, will you
[17b] * go home, will he

About *you*-deletion SS&P then proudly admit that "it is quite clear that this will not account for all the data"; nevertheless they take *you*-deletion to be "the nearest approximation to a correct, though *limited*, generalization that can be made at present" (1973:647; emphasis added). What is essential for SS&P is that their NG be seen to be *narrow*, 'limited'; but not to provide comprehensive coverage of 'all the data' (a *narrow* puritan might even object to SS&P's '*though* limited'; instead of, e.g., 'because limited'). But note that even SS&P take *you*-deletion to approximate *narrow*ness only 'at present'. It seems fair to say that in more recent NG a more effectively *narrow* account of imperatives has failed to emerge, and *you*-deletion has thus lost much of the immediate pertinence that it still had in *A–Z*'s standard NG.

u.3 Conclusions

There is (too) little reason to accept CM&LF's (1983) suggestion that NG accounts of imperatives by *you*-deletion reconstruct the traditional approach as represented by OG. OG tends much more predominantly towards the opposite view, with *you*-addition. Even Jespersen's (1931) account by 'abbreviation', including *you*-deletion, is just one possibility, alongside *you*-addition in Jespersen (1927). This does not mean that OG fails to cover the 'arguments' for *you*-deletion: reflexives and tags appear separately in earlier OG, and together in Quirk *et al.* (1972, 1985).

Moreover, it is probably significant that for NG accounts which do reconstruct (minority) OG with *you*-deletion one can go back as far as Chomsky (1955/1975). *You*-deletion is hardly an effectively *narrow* account: one cannot readily conceive of a linguistic theory which allows *you*-deletion but not equally *I*-deletion, etc.; and why not even *the boy next door who made his girlfriend pregnant*-deletion? The more NG came into its own by effectively *narrow*ing its accounts, the more it grew away from OG; and the more it also grew away from imperatives, which are no longer pertinent if something like *you*-deletion has become theoretically (highly) suspect. NG on *understood* you juxtaposes to, rather than reconstructs, OG: either by *narrow*ly imposing *you*-deletion on all subject-less imperatives rather than *open*ly taking *you* to be added when evidence for *you* is directly available; or even more *narrow*ly by ignoring imperatives as no longer pertinent, whereas OG maintains *open* comprehensiveness on understood *you*, reflexives, and tags.

v is for 'verbs of voice'

In spite of evident differences, there are still senses in which sentences like [1, 2] might be said to be somehow related:

[1] man invented war
[2] war was invented by man

One relation between [1, 2] is that if the former cannot be interchanged as in [3], then the latter cannot be interchanged conversely as in [4] either:

[3] * war invented man
[4] * man was invented by war

Widely accepted terminology identifies [1–4] as matters of syntactic 'voice': [1, 3] are (attempted) instances of 'active voice', [2, 4] of 'passive voice'. Among the first points of Modern English grammar that were accounted for in NG was precisely the one of 'voice' in this sense: essentially, the passive voice was said to be the result of transforming the active voice, so that the ungrammaticality of both [3] and [4] only needed to be accounted for *narrow*ly once. Details need not concern us here, but active-into-passive transformations were one of the most important factors contributing to the initial success of the Chomskyan revolution (cf. Lakoff 1971:149). 'Voice' has since then remained in NG one of the more extensively accounted for points of Modern English grammar, as in one way or another it remained pertinent to successive versions of NG theory; and we would have to use a large majuscule V for 'vast' rather than look for a miniscule section in this area.

However, we can still reduce the issue of 'voice' to more nearly miniscule proportions in two ways. Firstly, in [2, 4] passive voice involves the appearance of a form of *be*; the question thus arises whether alongside [5], in [6] there is also a case of passive voice:

[5] the Danes invaded England
[6] England got invaded by the Danes

In [6], a form of *get* appears rather than *be* as in [2]. *Be* and *get* differ as 'auxiliaries' and 'verbs', for instance with respect to whether *do* appears in negatives (cf. section 'b is for BE', also sections L and O: *n* for negation, from among the *nice* properties):

[7a]   war was not invented by man
[7b] * war did not be invented by man
[8a] * England got not invaded by the Danes
[8b]   England did not get invaded by the Danes

For miniscule v, *A–Z* will rather look at 'verbs of voice' like *get* in [6]; than at by far the most widely discussed case, with auxiliary *be*.

Secondly, *A–Z* keeps its section on 'verbs of voice' miniscule by generally referring the reader to the surveys that the vast amounts of work on active-and-passive have elicited: for instance, Robson (1972:18–50) for NG supplemented by Stein (1979) for mainly OG. In fact, Stein (1979:120) already anticipates juxtaposition of OG and NG: NG "gives us less information on ... the passive in English than any traditional grammar", i.e. than OG. OG is *open* in the sense of including 'much information', and juxtaposes to NG with *narrow*ly 'less information'. In particular, in NG *A–Z*'s 'verbs of voice' "such as *become* and *get* ... are not generally included" (1979:121). Let us now, as briefly as possible to remain miniscule, specify somewhat accounts in OG and in NG of 'verbs of voice'.

v.1 On OG on 'verbs of voice'

In dealing with OG accounts of 'verbs of voice' we can take our direction from Stein's survey of "accounts of the passive ... in all the comprehensive [!] standard grammar books from Kruisinga [1925] to Quirk *et al.* [1972]" (1979:20); that is – roughly – of OG. Stein sees "a rather interesting development" (1979:21) when she finds two 'verbs of voice' in Kruisinga (1925), *become, get*; three in Poutsma (1926:13–14), *become, get, grow*; three also in Curme (1931:445–7), *become, get, stand*; and six in Jespersen (1931: 108–12), *become, get, grow, rest, sit, stand*. "We thus have a very clear development from a 'narrow' [!] interpretation of the passive to a ... 'wide' one" (1979:22). One need merely replace 'wide' by *open* to see the chronological increase from two 'verbs of voice' through three to six as the effectuation of OG's aim of comprehensive coverage.

In fact, one can even extend Stein's line further back in time and note that Sweet (1891:112) barely pioneers OG by not including any 'verb of voice'; but only *be* passives. And Kruisinga's (1931–1932) final contribution to *A–Z*'s OG indeed includes one more 'verb of voice' than (1925): beside *become*, *get*, also *come* as in 'come undone' (1931:38–9).

However, closer looks at OG unfortunately do not always yield quite the neatly clear increase of *open*ness that Stein intimates. In fact, Poutsma (1926:99) also recognizes *stand* as a fourth 'verb of voice' so that Curme (1931) and Kruisinga (1931) are later but also more *narrow* by one 'verb of voice'. Similarly, Stein ignores Curme (1935:218–19), who after Jespersen's (1931) six 'verbs of voice' goes back to three: *become*, *get*, and *come* in 'come untied'; but this is still more *open* in adding one 'verb-of-voice' to Curme (1931). However, Quirk *et al.* definitely go more *narrow*; just two 'verbs of voice' in (1972:802–3): *get* is the "only serious contender" of *be*, and "is often equivalent to *become*"; and in (1985:160–2) just *get* remains as the "only serious contender" (but cf. 1985:162 on *become* and, beyond 1972, *grow* and *seem* being, like *get*, "pseudo-passive"). Given *A–Z*'s interpretation of OG as *open*, a miniscule section on 'verbs of voice' can merely apply here Stein's observation that in comparison with "the older standard grammars", i.e. Kruisinga, Poutsma, and Jespersen (with the notable omission of Curme), "the grammars by ... Quirk *et al.* ... are *surprisingly* brief on the subject" (1979:125; emphasis added).

OG on 'verbs of voice' can now be summarized as in [9]:

[9] OG on 'verbs of voice'

	S	P	K	J	C	GCE	CGoEL
become, e.g. the stream became dammed up		+	+	+	+	+	
come, e.g. it came untied		+		+			
get, e.g. you may get fired at		+	+	+	+	+	+
grow, e.g. curiosity grew aroused		+		+			
rest, e.g. you may rest assured of that				+			
sit, e.g. Michael sat corrected				+			
stand, e.g. the meeting stands adjourned		+		+	+		
	0	4	3	6	4	2	1

Another point that remains unnoticed when Stein (1979) ignores Curme (1935) is the latter's regret that the 'verb of voice' *become* "has been overlooked by grammarians" (1935:219). Curme here subscribes to the *open* approach by commending "Poutsma's large English grammar", which does cover *become*; and he could have cited other OG as well. It may be noted that Curme goes on to suggest that "The Dutch scholar [Poutsma] quotes ... interesting ... examples, ... but he does not describe their peculiar character" (ibid.). In general Curme believes that "foreign scholars ... have sharp eyes for the peculiarities of our language" (1931:v). It is not clear whether Curme (1935:219) intends 'peculiar' to mean either 'strange' or 'specific'. In either case he seems to regret that his non-native model's *open*ly comprehensive observations should not be matched by descriptions; but if the latter require a *narrow* approach, perhaps the juxtaposition is inevitable (cf. Parts I & II; also section H).

v.2 On NG on 'verbs of voice'

If, following Stein (1979:22), accounts are the more *narrow* the fewer 'verbs of voice' they recognize, then NG will be optimally *narrow* if not even *be* is taken to identify a passive. Actually, NG is at least more *narrow* than OG in generally recognizing only *be* for passives: very few NG accounts address 'verbs of voice' beyond *be* at all (cf. Sweet in OG); and if they do, it is only *get* (cf. Quirk *et al*. 1985 in OG). The reason why even *get* should rarely appear in NG is given by Chomsky as early as 1955 (1955/1975:455–6): "there are 'passives' ... with *get* instead of *be* ... But our ... purpose is not to present a complete picture". We take this as the first of *A–Z*'s three NG accounts for v, viz. the standard *narrow* one: like *get*, 'verbs of voice' will not *open*ly appear for completeness' sake; but only if they can *narrow*ly be seen to be theoretically pertinent. Thus, in SS&P (1973:575), too, there is a '*get*-passive', "though the rule is not provided in this grammar". *A–Z*'s NG standards have not needed to (re)turn to 'verbs of voice' as pertinent at all: neither Chomsky elsewhere, nor SS&P (1973); nor in fact Emonds (1976).

For two more NG accounts of 'verbs of voice', at least of *get*, we thus have to go beyond the standards to the NG 'literature'. Let us first take Stein (1979:122) for our guide. In Stein's perception, passive – even with *be* – is eliminated from NG as it becomes *less narrow*: "a passiveless grammar is the consequential development and outcome of a theory which in its beginnings neglected the semantic level of language, and then had to incorporate it more and more". 'Neglecting' semantics, i.e. meaning, in the beginning is an early NG attempt to be *narrow*; 'incorporating meaning more and more' is thus a contrary NG development towards *open*ness. In particular, according to Stein, "Oppositions, such as ... between *be* and *get* passives, cannot be investigated solely in theory" (1979:122). That is, consideration of *get* as a 'verb of voice' may accompany the abandonment of the approach to grammar *narrow*ly in accordance with theory; and hence to abandonment of *narrow* NG proper. Although Stein does not use the actual label, she thus confirms *A–Z*'s view of 'generative semantics' (see section II.4): viz. as a development towards *open* 'semantic NG' by incorporating meaning; here the 'verb of voice' *get* is seen to play a role in such a development.

Stein cites Hasegawa (1968) and Lakoff (1971) as NG literature on *get* as 'verb of voice' pertinent to the development towards *open* semantic NG. This seems correct for Lakoff (1971), on whom thus see Stein (1979); but it bears witness to a serious misunderstanding of the nature of Hasegawa's work (also evident in Robson 1972:19). *A–Z* prefers to look at 'passiveless grammar' in Hasegawa (1968) as the outcome of the opposite development, viz. effecting NG's proper *narrow*ness: excluding not only 'verbs of voice' but also *be* as identifying passives. Hasegawa (1968) may be seen as a very early (if not the first) instance of NG effecting *narrow*ness by eliminating *be* from passives – intriguingly with the 'verb of voice' *get* thus playing the opposite role to the one it had in *open* semantic NG.

Note that Robson's survey of NG on passives is as early as 1972. One of the more specific instances that Chomsky (1981) gives of developments towards effectively *narrow* NG is indeed the elimination of passives since then: "In early work in generative grammar it was assumed ... that there are rules such as 'passive' ... In subsequent work, ... largely ... of the past ten years, ... in accordance with the sound methodological principle of reducing the range and variety of possible grammars to the minimum, ... 'rules' are decomposed into ... more ... fundamental elements" (1981:7). 'Reducing range and variation' is the aim of effecting *narrow* NG; 'decomposition of rules' is the tool. Now all of this is precisely what Hasegawa (1968) already proposes (but more than ten years before 1981; and he is not cited by Chomsky 1981). Hasegawa already takes it to be "possible to dispense with the special 'passive' transformation" (1968:242); instead, already "these putative transformations can ... be broken down into a few elementary operations" (1968:235). *A–Z* can do justice to Hasegawa's as a very progressive account of 'verbs of voice' in the interest of effecting *narrow* NG – and thus juxtaposing NG to OG. By way of our second NG account of 'verbs of voice' – beside

Chomsky 1955/1975 – we will now roughly indicate the kind of role *get* plays in Hasegawa's own paper; and, as our third NG account, we will then confirm Hasegawa's progressiveness by specifying an element of his account that essentially appears again in Haegeman (1985) (but she does not cite Hasegawa 1968 either).

Now recall that *be* and *get* in putative passives differ with respect to, for instance, DO-support: [7, 8]. Consideration of *get* alongside *be* accordingly leads Hasegawa to 'break down' (or to 'decompose') passive sentences into either *be* or *get* on the one hand, and something more 'elementary' (or 'fundamental') on the other: the passive participle, which in comparison to variable *be*/*get* is a more constant factor. Thus in *be killed* and *get killed*, *be* ≠ *get*; and it is constant *killed* that is the elementary part.

Now consider [10]:

[10a] Bill had John killed
[10b] Bill got John killed
     (a, b = 'Bill organized that John be killed')

As their common paraphrase indicates, both [10a] and [10b] contain a kind of reduced sentence *John killed* (corresponding to '(that) John be killed'), which is indeed passive – without either *be* or *get* being apparently necessary (see especially [10a]). The essential idea of Hasegawa then is that so-called passives involve instances of a very general process of deleting identical material: e.g. (*John wants Bill to go*, but) *John* wants *John* to go ⇒ *John wants to go* (cf. section f; also section L). Applied to cases like [10] such deletion yields [11]:

[11a] Bill got [Bill killed] ⇒ Bill got killed
[11b] Bill was [Bill killed] ⇒ Bill was killed

Hasegawa's NG account of so-called passive sentences allows a general process of deletion to be pertinent, rather than highly specifically either *be* or 'verbs of voice' like *get*; by virtue of interpreting such sentences as actually containing a sentence-within-sentence, bracketed in [11]: it is these sentence-within-sentences which are 'passive'. It is exactly this property that one meets again in Haegeman (1985). Only, Haegeman does not rely on Hasegawa's deletion, but on an – equally general – process of movement, e.g. [12]:

[12a] – got [Bill killed] ⇒ Bill got [– killed] (Bill got killed)
[12b] – was [Bill killed] ⇒ Bill was [– killed] (Bill was killed)

In fact, [12] can be seen as an (even) more *narrow* reinterpretation of [11]. Haegeman operates with a *narrow* one-to-one constraint on relations between meanings of verbs and 'participants' (the so-called *theta*-criterion, 1985:58). This works out differently for movement than for deletion. Let us say that in [10] there are two verbs and two participants: 'Bill + organizes', and 'killed + John'. In the same way, in [11] *Bill* would have two roles to play: both 'Bill + organizes' and 'killed + Bill'. But actually, this is *not* what *get* as a 'verb of voice' implies: rather [11a] only means 'killed + Bill, accidentally'. That is, there is just a single participant; and since in [12] there is just a single *Bill*, whereas in [11] there are two, [12] thus fits more *narrowly*: *Bill* can indeed only participate once, viz. in one-to-one relation to its original verb, 'killed'.

v.3 Conclusions

Juxtaposition between OG as *open* and NG as *narrow* with respect to 'verbs of voice' emerges when OG is seen to aim at a large number of 'verbs of voice', and NG to aim at a low number. OG, which includes at least *be* as identifying passives, juxtaposes to NG which excludes even *be* from passives, as in Hasegawa (1968) and in Haegeman (1985). In fact, most OG is *open* to passives beyond *be*; and includes at least *get*, or even up to six 'verbs of voice'. This also juxtaposes to NG, where recognition of *get*, if at all (and never any other 'verb of voice'), leads to *narrow* exclusion of both *be* and *get* from passives, in Hasegawa (1968) and Haegeman (1985).

Juxtaposition is obscured when Quirk *et al.* seem to pursue an increasingly more *narrow* number of 'verbs of voice'; and also when *open* semantic NG's recognition of *get* as 'verb of voice' appears to lead to passiveless grammars. However, to keep section v on 'verbs of voice' at all miniscule, these complications have not been gone into; it is left to the reader to see whether and how they can be reconciled to the fundamental juxtaposition of OG and NG that in section v we have found to be in evidence once again.

w is for *whom* for *who*

Pyles and Algeo (1970:31) note that "Sir Winston Churchill ... wrote of *faithful service to whomsoever holds the talisman*"; their point is "Sir Winston's choice of *whom(soever)* where schoolgrammars prescribe *who(soever)*". That is, as the subject of *holds* one would expect a subjective form with *who*, rather than objective form *whom*; cf. '*he* holds, * *him* holds'. In its miniscule section w, *A–Z* looks at OG and at NG accounts of objective *whom* for subjective *who*; as reputably found in Churchill's writings, for instance.

w.1 On OG on *whom* for *who*

If OG was simply *open*, it would merely faithfully record evidence of *who* and/or *whom* for *who* as available, without any preference for one or the other. However, one finds that OG does not actually maintain such dispassionate *open*ness. Sweet seems to recognize neither *whom* for *who*, nor in fact *who* itself in such cases. But now consider Poutsma (1916:945): "Sometimes we find *whom* where the grammar would require *who*". If grammar 'requires' *who* where one 'finds' *whom*, then one may use Poutsma's own definitional dictum (see Chapter 1) about 'wresting available evidence [*whom*] into harmony with some pre-conceived theory [*who*]'; i.e. a 'requirement' is *narrow*, something that 'above all one should avoid'. In fact, Poutsma (1916:957) goes so far as to present [1], where * is Poutsma's own (it represents a source where [1] is first made up and then rejected as "faulty"; note the use of * in OG: cf. section II.4):

[1] * that is the man whom I heard was ill
       (cf. ... the man *who* was ill)

However, *open*ness duly reasserts itself when Poutsma records authentic examples like Churchill's, i.e. available evidence: he does not (want to? dare to?) assign * to, for instance [2]:

[2] one whom all the world knew was so wronged
(cf. one *who* was so wronged)

Very similar situations obtain in other OG. Kruisinga objects to *whom* for *who* as "artificial" (1932a:175), or as "taught in the schools" (1932b:426; note the contradiction with Pyles and Algeo's *who* that 'school grammars prescribe'); Kruisinga still cites ample available evidence like [2] however (1932a:175–6; 1932b:426). Curme (1931:232) similarly states that "*whom* is incorrectly used for *who*" where "grammatical function demands" [cf. Poutsma's 'require'] *who*; but Curme, too, does give available evidence like [2]. In fact, in OG, Quirk *et al.* alone are unmitigatedly *narrow* in only talking about instances like [3] as "hypercorrect deviant sentences" (1972:901; 1985:1299); with no evidence admitted that contradicts the *:

[3] * that is the man whom we thought was not coming
(cf. the man *who* was not coming)

If Quirk *et al.* are exceptionally *narrow* in OG on *whom* for *who*, then Jespersen is exceptional in the opposite sense. Jespersen observes that generally "It is admitted that *whom* [for *who*] is common" (1927:197), but still "All grammarians, English and foreign, agree that *who* is correct, and *whom* a gross error" (note the hint at (non-)nativeness; see below); by contrast Jespersen declares himself "for *whom*". Before we now extol Jespersen as the only representative of OG consistently *open* to *whom* for *who*, it should be noted that being in favour of *whom* is not a neutral attitude either; and in fact, Jespersen in turn disparages available evidence for *who* as in [4], which is said to be (partly) due to "the teaching of grammarians that *who* is correct" (1927:201; note the contradiction with Kruisinga's *whom* 'taught in schools'):

[4] George Demple, who I fancied would sing
(cf. . . . *whom* I fancied would sing)

Jespersen's preference for *whom* is actually pertinent to a theory that he presents (neither Poutsma nor Curme do); viz. that in a sentence the subject is "primary" (1927:199), i.e. the grammatically most important part (cf. section j for Jespersen's junction). That is, in *who would sing*, *who* would be primary; and *would sing* secondary, and dispensable. For [4], let us represent this as [5]: the brackets in [5a] represent the dispensability of the secondary part *would sing*, yielding [5b]:

[5a] George Demple, whom I fancied (would sing)
[5b] George Demple, whom I fancied

The point then is that since in [5b] it is unobjectionable to have *whom* on its own as object of *fancied*, therefore Jespersen's theory would *narrow*ly 'require' (Poutsma) or 'demand' (Curme) that *whom* should be equally unobjectionable as the primary part of the longer object in [5a].

Paradoxically, Jespersen is most *open* to *whom* for *who* in OG because *whom narrow*ly accords with his theory of 'subjects as primaries'. On top of this, "*whom* is used because ... the speech instinct would be bewildered by the contiguity of ... as it were two subjects" (1927:199): *who* looks bewilderingly like a subject next to subjective *I* in [4], whereas objective *whom* next to subjective *I* in [5] would not be confusing in this way.

All in all, although OG *is* properly *open* to *whom* for *who* in Poutsma, Kruisinga, Curme, and Jespersen, there is in OG also a large amount of *narrow* condemnation (the former three), or commendation (Jespersen), of *whom* for *who*. Note also that OG's *open*ness does not appear in 'grammarians, English and foreign' alike; but only in the three non-natives, and in Curme as 'honorary' non-native (cf. section 2.4); in contrast to the natives' failure to cover *whom* for *who* at all (Sweet), or the blunt assignment to it of * (Quirk *et al.*).

w.2 On NG on *whom* for *who*

Although *A–Z* takes OG and NG to be juxtaposed as *open* vs. *narrow*, in (especially early) NG itself there is a strong tendency to represent OG and NG as two versions of essentially the same approach to grammar: NG putatively 'reconstructs' OG (see Part II). As OG and mainly Jespersen may in fact be seen to be to a large extent *narrow* on *whom* for *who*, one would thus expect NG to jump eagerly at the chance of – for once – indeed 'reconstructing' OG; be it an accidental feature of OG, by the side of *open* comprehensiveness on *whom* for *who* in Poutsma, Kruisinga, Curme; and also in Jespersen. And one can duly see NG accounts of *whom* for *who* as attempting to reconstruct aspects of Jespersen's accounts. There is, in typical *narrow* fashion, no – apparently non-pertinent – *whom* for *who* at all in any of *A–Z*'s NG standards. But in the NG literature Klima (1965:199) explicitly tries "To interpret [Jespersen's account] in terms of a generative grammar", i.e. of NG; Kayne (1980:80, n11) suggests that "Our [NG] analysis has something in common with that of Jespersen"; and Schreiber (1981) also cites Jespersen extensively before he accounts for *whom* for *who*, in a way that can be seen as a more recent = more *narrow* perspective on Klima's earlier NG reconstruction of

Jespersen. Let us now turn to some details of these three NG accounts of *whom* for *who*.

To begin with, Klima reminds one of OG, though of Kruisinga rather than Jespersen, in assigning a decisive influence on *whom* for *who* to the "resistance to the spread of *who* for *whom* ... transmitted by school grammars" (1965:210); and to "the 'grammatically correct' uses of *whom*, prescribed by the schools" (1965:212). More importantly, Klima devotes many pages (1965:197–210, 220–1) largely to expounding, extolling, and/or modifying Jespersen's views in order to arrive at a "formal [= NG] description ... that corresponds to [= reconstructs] Jespersen's intimations about the structure of sentences like *we feed the children whom we think are hungry*" (1965:203–4; cf. *children who we think are hungry*). These 'intimations' are Jespersen's theory that 'subjects are primaries'; but Klima (1965:201) decides *not* to reconstruct such a theory because it would incorrectly predict [6a] alongside [6b]; cf. [5]:

[6a]   * I fancied him (would sing)
          (cf. I fancied *he* would sing)
[6b]   I fancied him

Klima thus turns to Jespersen's secondary account of *whom* for *who*, the bewilderment imputed to two consecutive subjective forms *who-I* (note that in *I fancied he would sing* the subjective forms *I* and *he* are not contiguous): "the analysis I will present ... – but for other reasons than those suggested by Jespersen – is very much like ... his latter analysis" (1965:206). Note, however, that in a truly *narrow* approach it is precisely the 'reasons' for an analysis, i.e. its being in accordance with a theory, that are most significant; these Klima's NG explicitly does *not* 'reconstruct' from OG.

Klima's NG account of *whom* for *who* 'reconstructed' from Jespersen/OG, then, looks essentially as in [7] (1965:215):

[7]   *wh* – subjective ... ⇒ objective *wh* – subjective – ...
       e.g. [8a]   e.g. [8b]
[8a] *who*   *I*   fancied (would sing)
      = *wh*   = subjective
[8b] *whom*   *I*   fancied (would sing)
      = objective *wh* = subjective

Note that [7] eliminates contiguous subjective forms such as *who-I*, regardless of an additional (*would sing*). But [7] does not apply to '*I fancied he would sing*' for two reasons: *I* and *he* are not contiguous; and neither *I* nor *he* are *wh*-pronouns. The latter point means that [7] is actually (and 'excessively') more *narrow* than the OG account it is meant to 'reconstruct': Jespersen only specifies contiguity; and leaves *open* the nature of the pronouns, *wh* or other.

Kayne (1980:80), too, takes up the point that 'subjects-as-primaries' does not account for [6]; but Kayne still claims to be able to 'reconstruct' Jespersen's primary account rather than revert like Klima to Jespersen's secondary one. Kayne suggests that Jespersen's theory represented as *who (would sing)* be reinterpreted in NG terms, as in [9] where [9b] ilustrates '*wh*-movement':

[9a] (he   would sing)
[9b] (who would sing) ⇒ who (– would sing)

That is, a subject is part of its sentence unless as *wh*-item it is moved to outside of the sentence. The *narrow* interpretation of sentence is then as an impenetrable domain: *fancied* cannot trigger an objective form of *he* inside the sentence; hence [6a] = *I fancied (he would sing)*. But *fancied* can trigger objective form of *who* outside the sentence; hence [5a] = *whom I fancied (would sing)*. But note that Kayne's 'reconstruction' of Jespersen's primary account is again more *narrow* than the OG original: for Jespersen *all* subjects are primaries; for Kayne *only* moved *wh*-subjects. In its restriction to *wh*, Kayne's has quite properly more in common with Klima's *narrow* account than with Jespersen's relatively *open* one.

Finally, Schreiber (1981) accounts for *whom* for *who* by a rule that may be represented as [10], to bring out its similarity to [7]:

[10] *wh* – NP . . . = % ⇒ objective *wh* – NP . . .

In [10], NP ('noun phrase') stands for anything which could either be a subject or an object; it is equivalent to 'subjective' in [7] because an objective form contiguous to *wh* would never arise anyway. The % makes [10] into a 'variable' rule, % indicates that speakers vary as to whether or not they apply [10], and thus have *whom* for *who*, or just *who*. But the fundamental difference between [7] and [10] is in the status they are assigned. Klima looks for an account for *whom* for *who* in "a characteristic of the abstract system" (1965:200); i.e. [7] is part of his linguistic theory (a property that he also ascribes to Jespersen's primary account). But Schreiber (1981:187) rather takes [10] to be "an *ad hoc* rule . . . based entirely on a linear principle [i.e. on contiguity] and . . . nothing to do with . . . conditions which determine function". 'Conditions which determine function' are the *narrow* theory proper (e.g. Kayne's condition inside/outside a sentence, irrespective of linear contiguity); and [10] falls outside such a theory. The point is that at the time Klima was writing, NG theory was programmatically *narrow*, but still effectively *open* (see Parts I, II): if a rule like [7] is part of the abstract system, then why not a rule by which *who-I* in [8a] is changed to *who-me* rather than *whom-I* in [8b]?; etc. This sort of question still arises for [10], but no longer at the level of the abstract system, i.e. of the theory; which can accordingly be effectively *narrow*ed to the proper syntactic conditions. Note that Schreiber's account is thus the NG analogue to Poutsma's or Curme's in OG: the conditions of the theory 'determine', 'require', or 'demand' *who*, but something like [10] outside the theory still causes *whom* for *who*.

w.3 Conclusions

With respect to *whom* for *who*, juxtaposition closely competes with reconstruction as the proper perspective on the relations between OG and NG. With available evidence of *whom* for *who* covered in Poutsma, Kruisinga, Curme, and Jespersen, OG is in (non-native) majority *open*; by juxtaposition, the vast majority of NG accounts *narrow*ly ignores the point entirely. But so does Sweet in OG; and Quirk *et al.* in OG assign * to *whom* for *who*. Moreover, even Poutsma, Kruisinga, Curme, and Jespersen are *narrow* to the extent of registering (strong) likes and dislikes; and Jespersen even associates this with a theory: viz. of 'subjects as primaries', and/or an aversion to contiguous subjective forms. It is naturally in these *narrow* respects that NG accounts of *whom* for *who* may be seen to reconstruct OG.

However, even here a measure of juxtaposition may still be recognized: in NG Klima *narrow*s Jespersen's contiguity by super-imposing a restriction to *wh*-pronouns; Kayne *narrow*s Jespersen's 'subjects as primaries' to *wh*-moved subjects only; and finally, Schreiber again reconstructs Jespersen's contiguity more *narrow*ly by adding a restriction to *wh*. But Schreiber also recognizes that even such an account *narrow*ly reconstructed from OG is not proper to NG: a linear rule of contiguity only complements the properly *narrow* abstract system, to be *open* to *whom* for *who*. At this stage, therefore, NG reconstructing OG is complementary to NG proper; rather like Chomsky (1986) takes OG and NG to complement each other (see sections II.1 and R). But note that even here OG is thus comprehensive enough to accommodate both *open* and *narrow* aspects; and in this sense does not bear to be complemented. OG thus ultimately still juxtaposes to *narrow* NG which may be complemented; as by Schreiber's *ad hoc* rules reconstructed from OG.

x is for extraposition

There are only few words in English that start with x. However, the letter x itself has been put to various uses in grammars; for instance, Jespersen's concept of x-questions (1940:481; there are some incidental examples below) in OG; or the NG concept of X-bar structure (see e.g. sections D, G, j, T). Other possibilities are offered by the fact that 'x' is pronounced identically with *ex-*, the first syllable in many English words and grammatical terms. For its miniscule section x, *A–Z* exploits the latter possibility, in particular taking x to be for '(e)xtraposition'.

One common application of the term 'extraposition' is to pairs like [1]:

[1a] that John left is strange
[1b] it   is strange that John left

That is, [1a, b] are said to be the counterparts by extraposition: in [1a] *that John left* is at one extremity of the entire sentence; in [1b] *that John left* is replaced by *it*, and *that John left* itself deferred to the opposite extremity of the sentence. As with *(be) strange* in [1] in many cases such extraposition applies optionally, the clause *that John left* being possible at either extremity of the sentence, initially or finally. In other cases, however, extraposition applies obligatorily in such a way as to allow *that John left* only at the final extremity; for instance, with *seem*:

[2a] * that John left seems
[2b] it   seems that John left

There may also be circumstances under which extraposition does not merely affect the initial and final extremities of sentences: cases like *(be) strange* switch to obligatory extraposition when *that John left* would not otherwise be at either extremity of the sentence, but somewhere in the middle:

267

[3a] * is that John left strange
[3b]   is it   strange that John left
[4]   I think that John left
[5a] * I think that John left strange
[5b]   I think it   strange that John left

As opposed to extrapositions effecting interchanges *between* extremities ('from-x-to-x'), optionally in [1] or generally obligatory
as in [2], cases like [3] and [5] will be called 'extraposition *to*
extremities'; or x-to-x for short. In *A–Z*'s miniscule section x, it is
expedient to look at OG and NG only for examples, explanations,
and/or other expositions of x-to-x. Note that one may distinguish
between x-to-x in [3] and in [5]: with *it* a subject in [3], [3] would
show 'subject x-to-x'; but with *it* an object in [5], [5] would show
'object x-to-x' (cf. however section C for interpretation of *it* in [5]
also as a 'raised' subject).

x.1 On OG on x-to-x

In spite of an example of extraposition like [1b] (1898:119), there
is no real account of extraposition, optional or obligatory, let
alone of x-to-x, in Sweet at all. Otherwise, in OG, the prevalent
tendency seems to have been to be *open* only to something like
object x-to-x. This is to some extent at least the case in both
Curme's and Kruisinga's accounts of 'anticipatory *it*'. Curme's
rather vague (and at least in that sense *open*) account is about
cases "Where the construction is more or less complicated"
(1931:99–100); apparently, the complication may revolve around
object x-to-x as in [6c] (note that [6a, b] are not Curme's, but
A–Z's):

[6a]   I find refusal   of his request difficult
[6b] * I find to refuse him his request difficult
[6c]   I find it   difficult to refuse him his
          request

Nor is Kruisinga (1932a:148–9) much more explicit when he
suggests about 'anticipatory *it*' that "We find [= may find? must
find?] this *it* ... when a verb ... is construed with an object and
predicative adjunct". In [6c] *it* is Kruisinga's object, and *difficult*
his predicative adjunct; and *to refuse him his request* thus exemplifies object x-to-x, from within a sentence in [6b] to its extremity in
[6c].

The more notable OG accounts of object x-to-x are, however,
perhaps those of Jespersen, of Poutsma, and of Quirk *et al*. On
Jespersen see below. From Poutsma one may extract that "There

is ... occasion for the use of the anticipating ... *it* when the objective subordinate statement is ... divided in any way from ... the head sentence" (1928:210). We fasten on Poutsma's use of 'occasion' here. It is possible to interpret Poutsma as recognizing here that the 'occasion' for (i.e. cause of) extraposition may be the need to 'divide from the head sentence'; hedged in between *find* and *difficult* as parts of the head sentence in [6b], *to refuse him his request* is *not* divided from the head sentence; but at the extremity in [6c] it is so divided, i.e. by object x-to-x. Similarly, Poutsma (1928:207) recognizes that in cases like [6c] the effect of *difficult* is to provide an "element intervening between the verb and the objective ... infinitive-clause"; i.e. more or less again to keep the clause *to refuse him his request* at the extremity, by object x-to-x.

The interesting point about Quirk *et al.* on object x-to-x is, as in other sections of *A–Z*, the difference between *GCE* (1972) and *CGoEL* (1985). That is, in *GCE* there is no recognition of object x-to-x at all, but only of 'from-x-to-x': in cases like [6c] "clauses can [*not* must] undergo extraposition from the position of object" (1972:965). That this is inadequate, as [6b] shows, is only recognized in (1985:1393), where an entire set of examples like [6], including [6a, b], is given – the only such set in all OG; *CGoEL* is accordingly *open* to the fact that if an "object ... clause ... can undergo extraposition", in cases like [6] "it must [!] do so".

If in Curme, Kruisinga, Poutsma, and Quirk *et al.* (1985) – perhaps in order of excellence (and Jespersen is still to come!) – object x-to-x is more or less covered, and OG is thus *open*, this is not true to the same extent for subject x-to-x. Notably, in both *GCE* (1972:963–4) and *CGoEL* (1985:1391–2) Quirk *et al.* cover only cases where the subject is at the (initial) extremity anyway, and subject x-to-x thus does not arise (but only either optional or generally obligatory extraposition 'from-x-to-x', as in [1, 2] respectively). Much the same applies to all other OG, except (again) Poutsma and Jespersen.

Thus Poutsma (1928:137) has examples like [7c] (again [7a, b] are *A–Z*'s additions for explicatory purposes):

[7a] what does our way of dressing signify?
[7b] * what does how we dress   signify?
[7c] what does it   signify how we dress ...?

But [7c] passes by without any explicit comment from Poutsma intimating its x-to-x character; cf. *how we dress does not signify, it does not signify how we dress*, both possible with *how we dress* at either extremity. The only explicit comment in OG on instances like [7c] is Jespersen's, who notes that extraposition is x-to-x, i.e.

"necessarily when it is the subject of a question" (1927:25; note
that Jespersen's own example is of a 'nexus-question' like *does it
signify how we dress*; whereas *what* in [7c] makes [7c] into an 'x-
question': 1940:480–1). More generally, Jespersen (1927:25) refers
to extraposition "When for some reason or another it is not
convenient to put a . . . clause in the ordinary place of the subject,
object etc., . . . in the body of the sentence"; this is the appropriate
generalization across *both* subject x-to-x as in [7c] and object x-to-
x as in [6c] (and note Jespersen's *open* 'etc.'). Although of course
Jespersen's 'for some reason or another' is as vaguely *open* as one
can have it, he also recognizes the *narrow* objection to a clause 'in
the body of the sentence', i.e. rather than at its extremities.
Poutsma's *open* coverage of both subject x-to-x and object x-to-x
already compares favourably to other OG; but there can be no
disagreement that for x-to-x in general, Jespersen's is the really
successful *open* OG account.

x.2 On NG on x-to-x

There is a fairly strong tradition in NG that NG should, somehow,
'reconstruct' Jespersen, as if his significance was the extent to
which he anticipates NG, rather than juxtaposes to NG by contributing to OG. If Jespersen distinguished himself among (from?) OG in
his account of x-to-x, then one would thus expect NG's first concern
about extraposition to be reconstruction of Jespersen's account of
x-to-x. But this can hardly be seen to be the case at all (another
point against the entire notion of reconstruction, and in favour of
juxtaposition; see Part II). Extraposition has always been a stock
element in NG, from as early as Chomsky (1955/1975:496–7); but
Chomsky here only considers subjects in statements, i.e. already
at an extremity (the initial one) and thus ineligible for x-to-x. In
fact, one can interpret Chomsky's subsequent accounts of extraposition as exercises in *narrow*ly avoiding x-to-x.

Consider for instance Chomsky (1973:249), which introduces a
version of the 'Subject Condition', a seminal *narrow* constraint
which disallows any rule applying into or out of a subject.
Chomsky suggests that extraposition is pertinent to such a Subject
Condition, as in [8] where subjects are bracketed:

[8a]   [it]   amazed John that Mary
      saw this
[8b] what did [it]   amaze John that Mary
      saw?
[8c]   [that John saw this] amazed Mary
[8d] * what did [that John saw   ] amaze Mary?

Chomsky's intention is that [8d] is * because it violates the Subject Condition: in [8d], but not in [8b], *what* has been moved from the position of *this* out of a subject. But Chomsky thus fails to recognize that [8d] is already * because of x-to-x, as in [9] which is not pertinent to the Subject Condition at all:

[9a]   [it]   amazed John that Mary saw this
[9b]   did [it]   amaze   John that Mary saw this?
[9c]   [that John saw this] amazed Mary
[9d] * did [that John saw this] amaze   Mary?

(Note that in [8] there are Jespersen's 'x-questions', in [9] his 'nexus-questions'.)

Of course, [8, 9] do not disqualify the Subject Condition as part of *narrow* linguistic theory. We merely eliminate [8] as pertinent to the Subject Condition, because Chomsky neglects x-to-x in [9]. As much is apparent when the Subject Condition (in a more sophisticated form too complex to introduce in a miniscule section) returns in Chomsky (1981). Adapting Chomsky (1981:214), consider [10] (for *each other*, cf. section R.4 1, 2):

[10a]   they$_i$ think [it] is nice that pictures of each other$_i$ are for sale
[10b] * they$_i$ think he said   [that pictures of each other$_i$ are for sale]

The point about [10] is, roughly, that in [10a] extraposition prevents *each other* from being in a [...] inaccessible to *they*; whereas in [10b] there is no extraposition to such effect. For our purposes, note that in [10], unlike [8], Chomsky switches from subject of *(be) nice* to object of *said*: once again, this allows Chomsky to avoid recognizing the fact that in [10a] extraposition is x-to-x, i.e. serves the purpose of preventing *that . . .* in the body of the sentence; cf. * *they think [that pictures are for sale] is nice*, but OK *[that pictures are for sale] is nice*.

If there is something like an NG conspiracy to avoid x-to-x, then SS&P are virtual accessories. That is, SS&P only account for either optional or generally obligatory extraposition from subjects (1973:550, 578–9) and from objects (1973:553, 579). This is the more surprising because, for objects at least, SS&P (1973:521) do have examples like [11c] that illustrate object x-to-x, rather than 'from-x-to-x':

[11a]   I prefer for you to do that
[11b] * I prefer for you to do that very much
[11c]   I prefer it   very much for you to do that

x is for extraposition

As in the case of [6], it is *A–Z* rather than SS&P that adds [11a, b] to [11c], to identify x-to-x: in [11a, c], but not in [11b], *for you to do that* is at an extremity.

Lest it now be thought that OG and NG are simply juxtaposed in terms of recognizing x-to-x or not, respectively, we should now turn to Emonds (1976). Recall from section 3.3 that Emonds' NG theory is structure preservation. And indeed, extraposition can be seen to be pertinent to structure preservation. As [12a] is independently necessary anyway, the structure of [12a] is preserved when one goes from [12b] to [12c]:

[12a]   John made clear that Mary left
[12b] that Mary left was   clear
[12c]   it was   clear that Mary left

More particularly, extraposition is *not* possible if it does *not* preserve structure: English does not allow two post-verbal clauses as in [13a] (note that in [13a] *that John was late* is not at an extremity: hence*); and thus [13b] cannot be changed into [13c] by extraposition either:

[13a] *   Bill made clear that John was late that Mary left
[13b] that Mary left made clear that John was late
[13c] *   it made clear that John was late that Mary left

However, English does otherwise allow two post-verbal complements, of course; e.g. two 'noun phrases' (NPs) like *his father* and *a present* in [14]:

[14] John made his father a present

For Emonds' theory of structure preservation to account for contrasts between [12c] and [13c], [14] should *not* be the structure which [13c] 'preserves'; in other words, a clause should be different from an NP, so that extraposition of a clause to the position of an NP does, indeed, not preserve structure. Accordingly, Emonds (1976:127–33) sets out to show in considerable detail that clauses are indeed different from NPs. For Emonds clauses differ in particular from NPs in that NPs can, but clauses cannot, in our terms, be put freely in the body of the sentence (e.g. *his father* in [14]; this is also the point about the NPs *refusal of his request* and *our way of dressing* in the middle of [6a, 7a] above). Thus x-to-x may arise for clauses but not for NPs; for instance, object x-to-x as in [15], and subject x-to-x as in [16]. Note that Emonds himself presents the entire set of [15], without *A–Z*

272

having to add anything; in [16] Emonds takes [16c], x-to-x, for granted given * for [16b]:

[15a]   I take *this responsibility* upon myself
                    (NP)
[15b] * I take *to fix the lamp*   upon myself
                    (clause)
[15c]   I take it   upon myself *to fix the lamp*
         (x-to-x)
[16a]   why did *Mary's liking old records*   irritate him
                    (NP)
[16b] * why did *that Mary likes old records* irritate him
                    (clause)
[16c]   why did it   irritate him *that*
         Mary likes old records (x-to-x)

x.3 Conclusions

As befits a miniscule section x, we have been able to represent accounts of extraposition, especially in NG, only quite roughly, freely adapting things for expository convenience. It is left to the reader to fill out details and/or to go to the original presentations entirely. The conclusion should remain the same however.

With respect to x-to-x, extraposition which is obligatory to put clauses at the extremities of sentences, OG and NG are clearly juxtaposed as *open* and *narrow* respectively. That is, OG can be seen to pursue more or less successfully the *open* aim of covering evidence for x-to-x: object x-to-x in Curme, Kruisinga, Poutsma, *CGoEL* (not *GCE*), and pre-eminently Jespersen; subject x-to-x only in Poutsma and, again pre-eminently, Jespersen. But NG does not simply set out to reconstruct x-to-x from Jespersen. Rather, NG juxtaposes to Jespersen in that the appearance of x-to-x in NG depends directly on its *narrow* pertinence to theoretical concerns. Actual instances of x-to-x are thus (mis)-interpreted as pertinent to Chomsky's (1973) Subject Condition; or at least interpretation as x-to-x is avoided in SS&P (1973) and Chomsky (1981). Only in Emonds (1976) is x-to-x seen to be pertinent, to structure preservation: in particular the difference between x-to-x yielding clauses only at extremities of sentences, vs. appearance of NPs freely in the body of sentences; only under Emonds' structure preservation does a *narrow* account of x-to-x therefore ensue in NG.

y is for *why (not)*

In a 1963 paper, Bowman complains about the treatment accorded to sentences without subjects in "most grammars of English, including the more recent ones" (1963:23). Basically, Bowman objects to such sentences being indiscriminately treated as somehow all 'imperatives' (cf. section u). Sentences which, according to Bowman (1963:27), should *not* be identified with imperatives are "subjectless, simple-verb sentences which begin with *why* or *why not*"; for instance, [1]:

[1a] why say it
[1b] why not try again

But for *why (not)*, such sentences look like subjectless imperatives; e.g. [1a] and *say it*. However, for Bowman *why (not)* sentences differ from imperatives in two respects: firstly, an additional subject would not be "prefixed" (1963:23), * *you why say it* (vs. *you say it*); and secondly, any additional material is not uniquely determined: only *you* in imperatives, *(you) say it*; but variously *why (should one) say it*, *why (do I) not try again*, etc. Bowman's approach is neither OG nor NG (but more like 'American structuralism'; cf. Nida 1960, 1966; section II.1), and we do not want take up her own views here. But we can take them as *A–Z*'s point of departure in a miniscule section on y: accounts of *why* and/or *why not* sentences in Modern English in 'grammars', here OG, 'including the more recent ones', here NG.

y.1 On OG on *why (not)*

As one might optimally expect from the putatively comprehensive grammars of OG, they all cover both *why* and *why not* sentences: Sweet (1898:119), Poutsma (1926:436), Kruisinga (1931:144–5), Curme (1931:478), Jespersen (1940:324), Quirk *et al.* (1972:411, 1985:821). At the level of detail appropriate in a miniscule section of *A–Z*, three 'issues' may be recognized.

274

To begin with Bowman's complaint about forcing *why (not)* sentences into an imperative mould, this point only arises in OG at all for Kruisinga and for *CGoEL*. And in neither case does OG seem viciously guilty of Bowman's charge. Although Kruisinga does first entertain the possibility of classifying *why* sentences as "semi-imperative constructions" (1931:143–4), he rejects this once *why not* sentences are also taken into consideration: a *why* sentence is then seen to be "made negative by *not* . . . whereas . . . *do* is used . . . in the imperative" (1931:145). That is, *why say it* and imperative *say it* diverge when negative: 'why *not* say it', * 'why *don't* say it'; * '*not* say it', '*don't* say it'. As far as Quirk *et al.* are concerned, they may be seen to merely pay attention to the resemblance of *why (not)* sentences and imperatives in "illocutionary force", that is in meaning: both are "directives" (1985: 821). No specific claims about the grammatical identity of *why (not)* sentences and imperatives appear to be made.

Another point suggested by Bowman (1963) is the relation between *why (not)* sentences without subject and more conventionally 'complete' sentences with subject, e.g. *why (don't we) say it*. This point is taken up most elaborately in OG by Curme and by Jespersen. Quirk *et al.* call *why (not)* sentences "abbreviated" (1985:821; not 1972), but do not give any indication of the structure(s) before abbreviation. As for their "elliptical" constructions, Curme (1931:478) in [2] and Jespersen (1940:326) in [3] are more specific:

[2] why (should we) not go at once
[3] why (should you, don't we) do it at once

Note that Bowman's variability is in evidence here; e.g. *should we* vs. *should you* (moreover, one may wonder how 'ellipsis' from *don't we* is supposed to yield *not*; *vide* Kruisinga).

There is one further point about OG on *why (not)* that bears no relation to Bowman, but rather seems due to (unfortunate?) accident. Consider [4a] from Sweet (1898:119) and [4b] from Poutsma (1926:436):

[4a] why not go there yourself
[4b] why not go there myself

It turns out that [4b] is a 'mistake': Poutsma cites as his source Sweet, section 231, an error for section 2321; and more interestingly, Poutsma also confuses the reflexives, *myself* for *yourself*. This raises the question of the authenticity of [4b]: apparently there is no available evidence for *myself* in *why (not)* sentences; and one is left with Poutsma's evident (but non-native) intuition that the possibility of *myself* alongside (native) Sweet's *yourself* should be left open. Something similar is explicit in Jespersen (another non-native): Jespersen cites evidence for the authenticity of independent *why* sentence [5a] (1940:325); but when he considers the issue of *why* (*not*) sentences as dependent clauses, "Opinions differ as to the possibility of saying" made-up [5b] (1940:326):

[5a] why complain so bitterly now
[5b] I don't know why complain

Apart from evidently comprehensive coverage of *why* (*not*) sentences, the *open* nature of OG is perhaps most evident from Poutsma countenancing [4b] and Jespersen [5b].

y.2 On NG on *why* (*not*)

If *why* (*not*) sentences are consistently covered in all OG, juxtaposition to NG is already apparent from the fact that, although we may have overlooked something in the vast NG literature, only two NG accounts of *why* (*not*) sentences have come to our attention: from among *A–Z*'s NG standards, Emonds (1976: 244–5; with a faint echo in 1985:318, n29); from among the NG literature at large, Keyser and Postal (1976) (cf. section A.4 2).

To begin with the former. Its (intended) *narrow*ness is apparent from the fact that, by the side of *why* (*not*) sentences, Emonds begins by excluding any other interrogative adverbs, like *how*, *where*, etc., e.g. [6a]; this clearly juxtaposes to OG's available evidence for [6b] from Kruisinga (1931:144), or [6c] from Jespersen (1940:324) (cf. Poutsma 1926:436):

[6a] * how buy stock at this time
[6b] how preach at a creature on the bend of passion's rapids
[6c] how leave her there

*Narrow*ly, Emonds' reason for the exclusion of *how* in [6a] is that thus *why* (*not*) can become pertinent to Emonds' theory of structure preservation (section 3.3). The essential idea is that *why* (*not*) sentences involve deletion of *should one* (note that *should one* is another variation, beside ellipsis of *should we/you* in [2, 3]; in [6c] Jespersen assumes *should he*!):

[7a] why should one (not) buy stock at this time
[7b] why   (not) buy stock at this time

Should one-deletion as in [7] is not taken to be a structure-preserving process: [6a] would show that structures without *should one* are *not* necessary anyway (cf. *how should one buy stock at this time*). As we put forward in section 3.3, by Emonds' theory, *should one*-deletion could then still be either a 'local' or a 'root' process. A local rule should involve only two adjacent elements; but since *should* and *one* (= two elements) only delete in the presence of *why* (and putatively not *how*, etc.), a third element, the rule must thus be a (non-structure-preserving, non-local =) root one. This means that *should one*-deletion should quite *narrow*ly only take place in independent sentences; and Emonds duly rejects [8], analogous to [5b] which Jespersen keeps *open* since 'opinions differ':

[8]   * John asked me why not be more prudent

As for Keyser and Postal, their basic idea is that the account of *why (not)* sentences would be *narrow* if the account was "not unique" (1976:89). That is, a single account for two points of Modern English grammar would be more *narrow* than two separate accounts for two points, etc. (cf. sections N, Q, s for similar *narrow* unifications). In particular, Keyser and Postal therefore intend to deal with *why (not)* sentences in the same way as, *vide* Bowman, with imperatives. But note that for Keyser and Postal it is crucial that, vs. Bowman, imperatives and *why (not)* sentences *not* be a single point of grammar: one account for one point is not *narrow* in the intended way either. Rather, *why (not)* sentences and imperatives, as two separate points, should still *narrow*ly share a single account.

Keyser and Postal's single account then is in terms of understood *you* described by *you*-deletion (1976:202). Note that Keyser and Postal are thus *narrow* in only recognizing understood *you*, whereas OG and/or Emonds in NG put forward understood *(should) we/you/he/one*. As the reader of *A–Z*'s section u on understood *you* will appreciate, the attention of Keyser and Postal is thus drawn towards reflexives: as in the case of imperatives, if *why (not)* sentences arise only by *you*-deletion, they should be able to contain only *yourself, yourselves*, e.g. [9a]; in particular, Keyser and Postal (1976:90) take sentences like [9b] – which would suggest '*I*-deletion' – *narrow*ly to be "banned":

[9a]   why not devote yourself to charitable works
[9b]   * why not devote   myself to charitable works

Clearly, this heightens the interest of Poutsma's accidental [4b] with *myself* countenanced: [4b] *open* (but non-native; authentic?) vs. [9b] *narrow* (and native).

277

y is for why (not)

y.3 Conclusions

As far as Bowman's (1963) accusations of grammars more or less recent are concerned, there is not much to choose between older OG and newer NG: neither approach is hardened in the sins of identifying *why (not)* sentences with imperatives. Moreover, both approaches bear testimony to the variability of what is taken to be understood: *should we/you/he* and *don't we* in OG, *should one* and *you* in NG. Still, in other – more significant – respects, OG and NG strongly juxtapose, also on 'y for *why (not)*'. The juxtaposition is most evident in the *open* coverage of *why (not)* sentences in all OG grammars, for comprehensiveness' sake; vs. the *narrow* pertinence of *why (not)* sentences to only two versions of NG theory, Emonds (1976) and Keyser and Postal (1976). More specifically, NG *narrow*ly excludes facts that OG leaves *open*: *why (not)* sentences with *myself* as reflexive, as dependent clauses, or with *how* as alternative to *why (not)*.

z is for zero-plus-zero

A–Z's first point of Modern English grammar on which OG and NG are juxtaposed, in section A, is for *all*. In one sense, 'all' would stand for the comprehensiveness that *A–Z* takes to be essential as the purpose of OG. It would therefore be nice now to end up in section z with something that would similarly be appropriate to NG: given 'all' for OG, if we had 'nothing' for NG, their juxtaposition would appropriately be by 'all or nothing'. Indeed, according to its spiritual father, (current) NG is complementary to OG, being about what OG grammars "don't say" (Chomsky 1979:61; see section II.1); if OG says 'all', then 'nothing' is left for complementary NG. And in fact, one NG publication literally consists of 'nothing': viz. a blank part of a page (Fiengo and Lasnik 1972). For a small letter z, *A–Z* would be optimally miniscule by merely juxtaposing Fiengo and Lasnik's blank for 'nothing' in NG to OG's 'all': over 3,000 closely printed pages in the grammars of Poutsma and Jespersen, 1,600 pages in Quirk *et al.* (1985), etc. However, we will in addition pursue a more specific point of Modern English grammar as well: z is for 'zero-plus-zero'.

The concept of 'zero' in grammar is a complex one, and can assume various guises; for instance, the 'empty subject' or PRO of infinitives in sections A and f; the gaps in section E; the 'zero' (!) determiner in p; or the empty modal in s. Moreover, following Chomsky and Lasnik (1977), we may recognize *two* 'zeros' in [1b]: as [2b] indicates by means of $\emptyset$ and subscripts corresponding to [2a], one 'zero' corresponds to *that*, "the zero morpheme $\emptyset$" (1977:456); the other 'zero' corresponds to *she*, "[$_{NP}e$] – a category with null content" (1977:453; *e* is for 'empty'):

[1a] do you think that she left
[1b] who do you think left
[2a]   do you think that$_2$ she$_1$ left
[2b] who do you think $\emptyset_2$ $\emptyset_1$ left

In particular, Chomsky and Lasnik focus on a notable property of Modern English: if in [2b] one has $\emptyset_1$, then one *must* also have $\emptyset_2$, not *that$_2$*:

[1c] * who do you think that   left
[2c] * who do you think that$_2$ $\emptyset_1$ left

In its NG interpretation of [2b, c] we may refer to the contrast [1b, c] as a 'zero-plus-zero' phenomenon.

It is quite reasonable to expect OG and NG to differ with respect to the 'zeros' of [2b, c]. OG would not readily admit such 'zeros'; in the literal sense, in [1b, c] there is no available evidence of any 'zero'. It takes a theory, i.e. NG, about how similar [1a–c] should be, to deduce from [1a–c] the 'zeros' of [2b, c] alongside *that* or *she* in [2a]. Still, one could validly decide that NG's [2b, c] 'complement' OG only if OG actually fails to say anything about [1b] and/or [1c], in any terms, not necessarily 'zero'. More neutrally, for instance, we might refer to [1b, c] as a 'verb-plus-verb' phenomenon: *think* + *left*; but * *think/that/left*. In miniscule section z for 'zero', this is therefore the specific point of Modern English grammar that *A–Z* will pursue, in both OG and in NG.

z.1 On OG on 'zero-plus-zero' ·

Consider [3a–c], respectively from Jespersen (1927:210; cf. section w), from Curme (1931:246), and from Kruisinga (1932b:396):

[3a] George Demple, who I fancied would sing
[3b] discuss what I feel is the main issue
[3c] a corpse people don't know is there

OG examples like [3] (there are none in Sweet) share with [1b] the property of 'verb-plus-verb': *fancied* + *would* in [3a], *feel* + *is* in [3b], *know* + *is* in [3c]. But neither Curme nor Kruisinga display any awareness of a contrast between examples like [3] and ones like [1c], viz. with the verbs separated by *that*. By contrast, Jespersen (1927:198) presents an instance which conflicts with [1c] in supplying available evidence that *that can* (or once could) separate verbs: in [4] we have OK *wol* + *that* + *shal* instead of * *wol/that/shal*:

[4] avyse   whom that we wol that shal ben our justice
    consider who   we wish *that* shall be our judge

However, [4] is from Chaucer, and as such hardly 'Modern' English; moreover, Jespersen adds that "some [more Modern?] MSS. omit *that*", reinstating 'verb-plus-verb'.

There is OG, however, which covers both [1b] and [1c]. Firstly, Poutsma's (1926:616–7) examples where "*That* appears to be dispensed with almost regularly when . . . the relative is the subject of the . . . clause"; these include [5] with *determined* + *should*, not *determined/that/should*; and [6] with *asked* + *should*, not *asked/ that/should*:

[5] doubts which he determined should be . . . resolved
[6] to know what Helen would have asked should be done

Note that Poutsma only mentions 'relative as subject'. In [5] *which* is indeed a relative as subject of *should be resolved*: and the same goes for all of [3]. But in [6] Poutsma (unlike Curme, Kruisinga, or – except for [4] – Jespersen) also illustrates interrogative *what* as subject of *should be done*, as in [1b] interrogative *who* is subject of *left*.

Both relative and interrogative are finally explicit in Quirk *et al.* (1972, 1985). "When a Q-element [= interrogative; cf. 1972:394] is the subject of an indirect statement, the omission of the normally optional introductory *that* is obligatory" (1972:398; similarly 1985:1050): verb-plus-verb *think* + *did* are OK in [7a]; but * *think/that/did* in [7b]:

[7a]   who do you think   did it
[7b] * who do you think that did it

Also, in [8a, b] "When . . . a relative . . . is subject, . . . *that* . . . is obligatorily absent" (1972:900, similarly 1985:1050): *hopes* + *will* is OK, *hopes/that/will* is *:

[8a]   the poem which Tom hopes   will be written
[8b] * the poem which Tom hopes that will be written

Given OG's [3–8], especially the latter, NG which complements OG by covering what OG doesn't say should not address the obligatory absence of *that* between verbs, whether in terms of 'zero-plus-zero' or otherwise. Whether OG and NG are juxtaposed remains to be seen, when we have also looked at NG in section z.2. For the moment, we note that OG does not appeal to any 'zero'. For Poutsma, the point about [5, 6] concerns the parts *he determined, Helen would have asked* – for which there is, of course, available evidence in [5, 6]. About these parts, Poutsma observes that "*That* appears to be dispensed with almost regularly . . . when . . . suppression would leave a normally constructed sentence" (1926:616). That is, in [5a] *he determined* of [5] is suppressed; in [6a] *Helen would have asked* from [6]; but such suppressions would not have been possible with an additional *that* in [5b, 6b]:

[5]	doubts which he determined	should be resolved
[5a]	doubts which	should be resolved
[5b] *	doubts which	*that* should be resolved
[6]	to know what Helen would have asked	should be done
[6a]	to know what	should be done
[6b] *	to know what	*that* should be done

In rather the same *open* spirit, Quirk *et al.* (1985:1050; not 1972) assume that available evidence of *that* in [6–7] would be confusing: "*that* must be omitted, perhaps to prevent *that* from being initially misinterpreted as subject of the following verb". Cf. [9b, 10b], misinterpretations of [7, 8] which choose the 'wrong' *that*'s from [9a, 10a]; [9b, 10b] leave *who*, *which* unrelated to any appropriate gaps (for [9c, 10c] cf. section E):

[9a]		do you think (that) that did it
[9b]	who$_?$ do you think	that did it
[9c]	who$_i$ do you think	$\emptyset_i$ did it
[10a]		Tom hopes (that) that will be written
[10b]	that which$_?$ Tom hopes	that will be written
[10c]	that which$_i$ Tom hopes	$\emptyset_i$ will be written

z.2 On NG on 'zero-plus-zero'

In earlier NG, accounts of the 'zero-plus-zero'/'verb-plus-verb' phenomenon initially resemble OG. That is, in SS&P (1973) the phenomenon does not occur at all, as in Sweet; and in Emonds (1976:149–50) examples like [11], with *claimed + caused*, are not complemented by *claimed/that/caused*, with or without *, as in Curme or Kruisinga:

[11] the rain that John claimed caused the accidents

However, for SS&P and for Emonds the NG excuse applies that their theories are apparently not so *narrow* that obligatory absence of *that* is pertinent to them; no such excuse is valid in OG, where Sweet, Curme, and Kruisinga simply 'fail' (even if this may be condoned in a pioneer).

The first NG to which absent *that* is pertinent seems to be Perlmutter's (1971:100) theory that, for English at least, 'every sentence must have a subject'. Suppose that *that* indicates (*inter alia*) the presence of a sentence; and hence the need for a subject (cf. 1971:112). Thus [12a] contains a [bracketed] sentence because of *that*, and the sentence duly contains an underlined *subject*, in accordance with the theory. But in [12b] *that* also identifies a sentence, which now lacks a subject however, and hence is *. Finally, in [12c] there is no *that*, hence no need to recognize a sentence, and hence no subject is necessary, and everything is fine again.

[12a]   did he say that it happened
      =   did he say [that *it* happened]
[12b] * what did he say that happened
      = what did he say [that _ happened]
[12c]   what did he say happened
      = what did he say   happened

Note that Perlmutter's (1971) NG account still resembles OG in that it evades recognition of 'zeros': in Perlmutter's interpretation, the crucial point about [12c] is precisely that it contain just 'verb-plus-verb', and thus neither the position of *that* nor the position of the subject *it* at all.

However, in [12c] there is thus no gap $\emptyset$ for *what* to relate to either (cf. [9b, 10b]). As soon as NG *narrow*s itself by incorporating a one-to-one constraint on *wh*-items and gaps (cf. section E), a $\emptyset$ gap for *what* has to be recognized after all. Thus [12b], too, would have to have a subject, $\emptyset$ in the position of *it*; and its * no longer follows from a theory that 'every sentence must have a subject': because [12b] *would* have a subject, $\emptyset$.

From this perspective, it is not surprising that Chomsky and Lasnik (1977) reinterpret [12c] as [13c] with 'zero-plus-zero' (cf. [1, 2]): if every position of [13a] remains, and both *that* and *it* leave $\emptyset$s, then *what* can now properly relate to $\emptyset_1$ as its gap, as *what*$_1$ indicates, by *narrow* one-to-one:

[13a] did he say that it happened
      =   did he say that$_2$ it$_1$ happened
[13c] what did he say happened
      = what$_1$ did he say $\emptyset_2$ $\emptyset_1$ happened

But otherwise Chomsky and Lasnik's account of [12c, 13c] is still not effectively *narrow*: they have no general theory from which it follows that $\emptyset_2$ may not be replaced by *that*: in [13b] *what*$_1$ and $\emptyset_1$ are as properly related one-to-one, irrespective of *that*:

[13b] * what did he say that happened
      = what$_1$ did he say that$_2$ $\emptyset_1$ happened

When Chomsky and Lasnik (1977:451, 456) exclude [13b] by a purpose-built * *that*-$\emptyset$ "filter", this is not strictly pertinent to a *narrow* theory: things could just as well be the other way around, * $\emptyset$–$\emptyset$, and OK *that*-$\emptyset$.

More effectively *narrow* NG, by which the obligatory absence of *that is* pertinent to a general theory, is presented in Kayne (1981). For Kayne (1981:121), NG theory imposes requirements on *wh*-items and their gaps; not only that they be one-to-one, but also that the *wh*-item be sufficiently 'near' to its gap. Consider [14]:

[14a]   I know   that he left
[14b] * I know who that left
      = I know   who$_1$ that$_2$ $\emptyset_1$ left
[14c]   I know who left
      = I know   who$_1$ $\emptyset_1$ left

In [14b] *that* separates *who*$_1$ from its gap $\emptyset_1$ (technically, *that* prevents 'c-command'; cf. sections E, f); and hence [14b] is * (cf. also [5b, 6b]). But in [14c] *who*$_1$ is as near to $\emptyset_1$ as possible, and [14c] is OK. Note that for Kayne the point about [14] is thus '*wh*-plus-zero': * *who*/*that*/$\emptyset$. Under such theoretical assumptions now consider [15, 16]:

[15a]   who do you think left
      $\neq$ who$_1$ do you think $\emptyset_1$ left
      = who$_1$ do you think *wh*$_1$ $\emptyset_1$ left
[16a] * who do you think that left
      $\neq$ who$_1$ do you think   that $\emptyset_1$ left
      = who$_1$ do you think *wh*$_1$ that $\emptyset_1$ left

Clearly, if [14b] is * because *that* separates *who*$_1$ from $\emptyset_1$, then [15] should be at least as bad because *do you think* separates *who*$_1$ from $\emptyset_1$. The situation is saved however by the theory allowing for an intermediary abstract *wh* in the position of *who* in [14] (cf. again section E; *wh* is another 'zero', and in particular is not a *wh*-item and hence does not violate one-to-one, which still holds between *who*$_1$ and $\emptyset_1$); thus [15] is OK as '*wh*-plus-zero'. However, in [16] even the intermediary abstract *wh* is still not near enough to $\emptyset_1$, because again *that* intervenes: * *wh*/*that*/$\emptyset$.

z.3 Conclusions

In drawing a conclusion, the following statements about 'zero' in grammar may be juxtaposed. For OG, Jespersen 1936/1969:152–3) states that "The symbol 0 ... for something that is latent ... often ... is totally uncalled for ... Thus nothing is gained by saying that in *I believe he is ill* ... *that* is understood". On behalf of NG, for Chomsky (1981:55) "there is an intrinsic fascination in the study of properties of empty elements. These properties can hardly be determined inductively from observed overt phenomena, and therefore . . . to discover the nature of . . . human language . . . these elements offer particularly valuable insights". From 'nothing is gained' in OG to 'particularly valuable' in NG. But such juxtaposed approaches, OG's aversion from 'zero' under induction and NG's fascination with 'zero' under deduction, do not prevent both approaches from covering much the same ground; for section z, for instance, the obligatory absence of *that*: whether as 'verb-plus-verb', as 'zero-plus-zero', or however. What OG and NG say and don't say about this do not complement each other. What remains, in *A–Z*'s final section as throughout, is juxtaposition. For OG the point about the phenomenon is that available evidence be covered, somehow, anyhow; for NG the point had better not be covered unless in accordance with a specific theory to which it is pertinent; specifically under a theory about 'zeros' *narrow*ly constrained to being left sufficiently 'near' to what they relate to by one-to-one.

Bibliography

Aarts, F. (1975) 'The Great Tradition or grammars and Quirk's grammar', *Dutch Quarterly Review* 5:98–126.

Aarts, F. (1986) 'English grammars and the Dutch contribution: 1891–1985', in G. Leitner (ed.) *The English Reference Grammar*, Tübingen: Max Niemeyer, pp. 363–86.

Anderson, S. R. (1982) 'Types of dependency in anaphors: Icelandic (and other) reflexives', *Journal of Linguistic Research* 2–2:1–22.

Andrews, A. (1982) 'A note on the constituent structure of adverbials and auxiliaries', *Linguistic Inquiry* 13–2:313–17.

Beukema, F. H. and Rigter, G. H. (1984) 'The irrational dilemma', in J. L. Mackenzie and H. Wekker (eds) *English Language Research: The Dutch Contribution 1*, Amsterdam: Free University Press, pp. 33–52.

Bolinger, D. (1952) 'Linear modification', *Publications of the Modern Language Association*; reprinted in I. Abe and T. Kanekyio (eds) (1965) *Forms of English*, Tokyo: Nokuo.

Bolinger, D. (1975) *Aspects of Language*, New York: Harcourt Brace Jovanovich.

Bolinger, D. (1978) 'Yes-no questions are not alternative questions', in H. Hiz (ed.) (1978) *Questions*, Dordrecht: Reibel, pp. 87–105.

Bourgonje, B. and Dijkstra, A. (1982) '"Dutch" grammars of English', unpublished paper, University of Utrecht.

Bowman, E. (1963) 'The classification of imperative sentences in English', *Studies in Linguistics* 17:23–8.

Cattell, N. R. (1969) *The New English Grammar: A Descriptive Introduction,* Cambridge (Mass.): MIT Press.

Celce-Murcia, M. and Larsen-Freeman, D. (1983) *The Grammar Book*, Rowley (Mass.): Newbury House.

Chomsky, N. (1955) *The Logical Structure of Linguistic Theory*, New York: Plenum (published 1975).

Chomsky, N. (1957) *Syntactic Structures*, The Hague: Mouton.

Chomsky, N. (1958) 'A transformational approach to syntax', in A. A. Hill (ed.) (1962) *Proceedings of the Third Texas Conference on Problems of Linguistic Analysis in English, 1958*, Austin: The University of Texas. Reprinted in J. Fodor and J. Katz (eds) (1964) *The Structure of Language*, Englewood Cliffs: Prentice Hall.

Chomsky, N. (1962) Contributions to discussions, in A. A. Hill (ed.) (1962) *Proceedings of the Third Texas Conference on Problems of Linguistic Analysis in English*, Austin: The University of Texas.

Chomsky, N. (1964) *Current Issues in Linguistic Theory*, The Hague: Mouton.

Chomsky, N. (1965) *Aspects of the Theory of Syntax*, Cambridge (Mass.): MIT Press.

Chomsky, N. (1966) *Cartesian Linguistics. A Chapter in the History of Rationalist Thought*, New York: Harper & Row.

Chomsky, N. (1970) 'Remarks on nominalization', in R. A. Jacobs and P. S. Rosenbaum (eds) *Readings in English Transformational Grammar*, Waltham (Mass.): Ginn, pp. 184–221.

Chomsky, N. (1973) 'Conditions on transformations', in S. R. Anderson and P. Kiparsky (eds) *A Festschrift for Morris Halle*, New York: Holt Rinehart & Winston, pp. 232–86.

Chomsky, N. (1975) *Questions of Form and Interpretation*, Lisse: Peter de Ridder Press.

Chomsky, N. (1977) 'On wh-movement', in P. Culicover, T. Wasow and A. Akmajian (eds) *Formal Syntax*, New York: Academic Press, pp. 71–132.

Chomsky, N. (1979) *Language and Responsibility*, Hassocks: Harvester Press (ed. by M. Ronat).

Chomsky, N. (1980) *Rules and Representations*, New York: Columbia University Press.

Chomsky, N. (1981) *Lectures on Government and Binding*, Dordrecht: Foris.

Chomsky, N. (1986) 'Changing perspectives on knowledge and use of language', *Leuvense Bijdragen* 75:1–71.

Chomsky, N. and Lasnik H. (1977) 'Filters and control', *Linguistic Inquiry* 8–3:425–504.

Christophersen, P. (1939) *The Articles: A Study of their Theory and Use*, Copenhagen: Munksgaard.

Cole, P. and Sadock, J. (eds) (1977) *Syntax and Semantics 8:Grammatical Relations*, New York: Academic Press.

Collins, B. (1988) *The Early Career of Daniel Jones*, Ph.D. dissertation, University of Utrecht.

Contreras, H. (1984) 'A note on parasitic gaps', *Linguistic Inquiry* 15–4: 698–701.

Costa, R. M. (1972) 'Let's study *let's*', *Papers in Linguistics* 5:141–4.

Culicover, P. (1982) 'Though-attraction', distributed by the Indiana University Linguistic Club.

Culicover, P. and Wilkins, W. (1984) *Locality in Linguistic Theory*, New York: Academic Press.

Curme, G. O. (1931) *Syntax*, Boston: Heath. (= *A Grammar of the English Language* II)

Curme, G. O. (1935) *Parts of Speech and Accidence*, Boston: Heath. (= *A Grammar of the English Language* III)

De Jong, F. (1983) 'Numerals as determiners', in H. Bennis and W. U. S.

van Lessen Kloeke (eds) *Linguistics in the Netherlands 1983*, Dordrecht: Foris, pp. 105–14.

Den Hertog, C. H. (1892–1896) *Nederlandsche Spraakkunst*, Amsterdam: Versluys (Vol. I, 1892; Vol. II, 1892; Vol. III, 1896).

Dik, S. C. (1978) *Functional Grammar*, Amsterdam: North-Holland.

Duncan-Rose, C. and Vennemann, T. (eds) (1988) *On Language: Rhetorica, Phonologica, Syntactica. A Festschrift for Robert P. Stockwell from his Friends and Colleagues*, London: Routledge.

Emonds, J. E. (1976) *A Transformational Approach to English Syntax*, New York: Academic Press.

Emonds, J. E. (1985) *A Unified Theory of Syntactic Categories*, Dordrecht: Foris.

Falk, Y. (1984) 'The English auxiliary system: a lexical-functional approach', *Language* 60:483–509.

Fiengo, R. and Lasnik, H. (1972) 'On nonrecoverable deletion in syntax', *Linguistic Inquiry* 3–4:528.

Fiengo, R. and Lasnik, H. (1976) 'Some issues in the theory of transformations', *Linguistic Inquiry* 7–1:182–91.

Francis, W. N. (1979) 'Problems of assembling and computerizing large corpora', in H. Bergenholtz and B. Schaeder (eds) *Empirische Textwissenschaft: Aufbau und Aufwertung von Text-Corpora*, Königstein: Scriptor, pp. 110–23.

Gazdar, G., Klein, E., Pullum, G., and Sag, I. (1985) *Generalized Phrase Structure Grammar*, Oxford: Blackwell.

Gefen, R. (1968) 'Linguistic theory and language description in Jespersen', *Lingua* 19:386–404.

Grattan, J. H. G. (1926) 'Review of E. Kruisinga, *A Handbook of Present-Day English II*' (fourth edition), *The Review of English Studies* 2:243–4.

Greenbaum, S., Leech, G., and Svartvik, J. (eds) (1979) *Studies in English Linguistics*, London: Longman.

Gross, M. (1979) 'On the failure of generative grammar', *Language* 55–4:859–85.

Haegeman, L. (1984) 'Parasitic gaps and adverbial clauses', *Journal of Linguistics* 20:229–32.

Haegeman, L. (1985) 'The *get*-passive and Burzio's generalization', *Lingua* 66:53–77.

Halitsky, D. (1975) 'Left-branch S's and NP's in English: a bar-notation analysis', *Linguistic Analysis* 1:279–96.

Hasegawa, L. (1968) 'The passive construction in English', *Language* 44–2:230–43.

Hatfield, J. T., Leopold, W., and Zieglschmid, A. J. F. (1930) *Curme Volume of Linguistic Studies*, Baltimore: LSA

Hawkins, J. A. (1978) *Definiteness and Indefiniteness*, London: Croom Helm.

Hill, A. A. (1958) *Introduction to Linguistic Structures*, New York: Harcourt Brace & World.

Hogg, R. (1977) *English Quantifier Systems*, Amsterdam: North-Holland.

Hornstein, N. (1977) 'S and the X-bar convention', *Linguistic Analysis* 3:137–76.

Huddleston, R. (1976) *An Introduction to English Transformational Syntax*, London: Longman.

Huddleston, R. (1978) 'On the constituent structure of VP and AUX', *Linguistic Analysis* 4:31–59.

Jackendoff, R. (1977) *X-bar Syntax*, Cambridge (Mass.): MIT Press.

Jacobsen, B. (1977) *Transformational-Generative Grammar*, Amsterdam: North-Holland.

Jespersen, O. (1909–1949) *A Modern English Grammar on Historical Principles*, London: George Allen & Unwin (Vol. I, 1909; Vol. II, 1914; Vol. III, 1927; Vol. IV, 1931; Vol. V, 1940; Vol. VI, 1942; Vol. VII, 1949, posthumous, N. Haislund (ed.)).

Jespersen, O. (1924) *The Philosophy of Grammar*, London: George Allen & Unwin.

Jespersen, O. (1933) *Essentials of English Grammar*, London: George Allen & Unwin.

Jespersen, O. (1936) *Analytic Syntax*, New York: Holt Rinehart & Winston (reprinted 1969).

Jørgensen, E. (1984) '*Ought*: present or past tense?', *English Studies* 65:550–4.

Juul, A. (1975) *On Concord of Number in Modern English*, Copenhagen: Nova.

Kaplan, R. M. and Bresnan, J. (1982) 'Lexical-functional grammar', in J. Bresnan (ed.) *The Mental Representation of Grammatical Relations*, Cambridge (Mass.): MIT Press, pp. 173–281.

Kayne, R. (1980) 'Extensions of binding and case-marking', *Linguistic Inquiry* 11–1:75–96.

Kayne, R. (1981) 'ECP extensions', *Linguistic Inquiry* 12–1:93–133.

Keyser, S. and Postal, P. (1976) *Beginning English Grammar*, New York: Harper & Row.

Kjellmer, G. (1975) '"The weather was fine if not glorious": on the ambiguity of concessive *if not*', *English Studies* 56:140–6.

Klima, E. (1965) *Studies in Diachronic Transformational Syntax*, Ph. D. dissertation, Harvard University.

Krüger, G. (1897ff.) *Schwierigkeiten des Englischen*, Dresden/Leipzig: C. A. Koch.

Krüger, G. (1914) *Schwierigkeiten des Englischen I* (second edition), Dresden/Leipzig: C. A. Koch.

Krüger, G. (1915) *Schwierigkeiten des Englischen II* (second edition), Dresden/Leipzig: C. A. Koch.

Krüger, G. (1917) *Schwierigkeiten des Englischen III* (second edition), Dresden/Leipzig: C. A. Koch.

Kruisinga, E. (1911) *A Grammar of Present-Day English II-A* (first edition), Utrecht: Kemink.

Kruisinga, E. (1922) *A Handbook of Present-Day English* (third edition), Utrecht: Kemink.

Kruisinga, E. (1925) *A Handbook of Present-Day English* (fourth edition), Utrecht: Kemink.

Kruisinga, E. (1931–1932) *A Handbook of Present-Day English II* (fifth edition), Groningen: Noordhoff (Vol. I, 1931; Vol. II, 1932a; Vol. III, 1932b).

Lakoff, G. and Peters, S. (1969) 'Phrasal conjunction and symmetric predicates', in D. A. Reibel and S. A. Schane (eds) *Modern Studies in English*, Englewood Cliffs: Prentice Hall, pp. 113–42.

Lakoff, R. (1971) 'Passive resistance', in *Papers from the 7th Regional Meeting*, Chicago: Chicago University Press, pp. 149–61.

Langendoen, D. T. (1970) *Essentials of English Grammar*, New York: Holt Rinehart & Winston.

Lees, R. (1957) 'Review of N. Chomsky, *Syntactic Structures*', *Language* 33–3:375–408.

Levin, S. R. (1960) 'Comparing traditional and structural grammar', *College English* 21:260–5. Reprinted in H. B. Allen (ed.) (1964) *Readings in Applied English Linguistics*, New York: Appleton-Century-Crofts, pp. 46–53.

Lyons, J. (1977) *Chomsky*, Hassocks: Harvester Press.

McCawley, J. D. (1973) 'Review of O. Jespersen, *Analytic Syntax*', in J. D. McCawley, *Grammar and Meaning*, Tokyo: Taishukan, pp. 229–36. First published in *Lingua* 46 (1970), 442–9.

McCawley, J. D. (1982) *30 Million Theories of Grammar*, London: Croom Helm.

McKay, J. (1984) *A Guide to Germanic Reference Grammars*, Amsterdam: John Benjamins.

Malone, J. (1978) 'Generative-transformational studies in English interrogatives', in H. Hiz (ed.) (1978) *Questions*, Dordrecht: Reibel, pp. 37–85.

Matthews, P. H. (1981) *Syntax*, Cambridge: Cambridge University Press.

Meijs, W. (1976) 'A Dutch grammarian's English: a reassessment of Poutsma', *Dutch Quarterly Review* 6:139–52.

Meijs, W. (1984) 'Data and theory in computer corpus linguistics', in J. L. Mackenzie and H. Wekker (eds) *English Language Research: The Dutch Contribution 1*, Amsterdam: Free University Press, pp. 85–100.

Miller, G. and Chomsky, N. (1963) 'Finitary models of language users', in R. D. Luce, R. R. Bush, and E. Galanter (eds) *Handbook of Mathematical Psychology*, New York: Wiley, pp. 419–92.

Newmeyer, F. (1969) *English Aspectual Verbs*, Seattle: University of Washington.

Newmeyer, F. (1971) 'Let's eat', *Papers in Linguistics* 4–2:393–4.

Newmeyer, F. (1980) *Linguistic Theory in America*, New York: Academic Press.

Newmeyer, F. (1986) 'Has there been a "Chomskyan revolution" in linguistics?', *Language* 62:1–18.

Nida, E. (1960) *A Synopsis of English Syntax*, Norman (Ok.): SIL.

Nida, E. (1966) *A Synopsis of English Syntax*, The Hague: Mouton.

Nilsen, D. (1973) *The Instrumental Case in English*, The Hague: Mouton.

Ohlander, S. (1980) 'Henry Sweet and Otto Jespersen as transformational grammarians', in J. Allwood and M. Ljung (eds) *ALVAR, a*

Linguistically Varied Assortment of Readings, Stockholm: University of Stockholm, Department of English, pp. 128–69.

Partee, B. H. (1965) *Subject and Object in Modern English*, Ph.D. dissertation, MIT.

Partee, B. H. (1976) 'Some transformational extensions of Montague grammar', in B. H. Partee (ed.) (1976) *Montague Grammar*, New York: Academic Press, pp. 51–76.

Perlmutter, D. (1971) *Deep and Surface Structure Constraints in Syntax*, New York: Holt, Rinehart & Winston.

Postal, P. (1974) *On Raising*, Cambridge (Mass.): MIT Press.

Postal, P. (1976) 'Avoiding reference to subject', *Linguistic Inquiry* 7–1:151–82.

Poutsma, H. (1904–1929) *A Grammar of Late Modern English*, Groningen: Noordhoff (Vol. I–I, 1904, (second edition) 1928; Vol. I–II, 1905, (second edition) 1929; Vol. II–IA, 1914; Vol. II–IB, 1916; Vol. II–II, 1926).

Pullum, G. (1981) 'Evidence against the "AUX" node in Luiseno and English', *Linguistic Inquiry* 12–3:435–63.

Pullum, G. (1983) 'The conduct of *Linguistic Inquiry*', *Natural Language and Linguistic Theory* 1–3:435–40.

Pullum, G. (1985) 'No trips to Stockholm', *Natural Language and Linguistic Theory* 3–2:265–70.

Pullum, G. (1986) 'A guest of the State', *Natural Language and Linguistic Theory* 4–2:283–9.

Pyles, T. and Algeo, J. (1970) *English: an Introduction to Language*, New York: Harcourt, Brace & World.

Quirk, R., Greenbaum, S., Leech, G., and Svartvik, J. (1972) *A Grammar of Contemporary English*, London: Longman.

Quirk, R., Greenbaum, S., Leech, G., and Svartvik, J. (1985) *A Comprehensive Grammar of the English Language*, London: Longman.

Quirk, R. and Greenbaum, S. (1974) *A University Grammar of English*, London: Longman.

Radford, A. (1980) *Transformational Syntax. A Student's Guide to Chomsky's Extended Standard Theory*, Cambridge: Cambridge University Press (reprinted 1982).

Radford, A. (1988) *Transformational Grammar: A First Course*, Cambridge: Cambridge University Press.

Reynolds, A. L. (1969) *On Grammatical Trifles: Otto Jespersen and his Linguistic Milieu*, Ph.D dissertation, Northwestern University.

Reynolds, A. L. (1971) 'What *did* Jespersen say?', in *Papers from the 7th Regional Meeting*, Chicago: Chicago University Press, pp. 519–29.

Rigter, G. and Beukema, F. (1985) *A Government and Binding Approach to English Sentence Structure*, Apeldoorn: Van Walraven.

Roberts, I. (1985) 'Agreement parameters and modal auxiliaries', *Natural Language and Linguistic Theory* 3–1:21–58.

Robinson, I. (1975) *The New Grammarian's Funeral*, Cambridge: Cambridge University Press.

Robinson, J. (1970) 'Dependency structures and transformational rules', *Language* 46:259–85.

Robson, R. A. (1972) *On the Generation of Passive Constructions in English*, Ann Arbor: University Microfilms.

Rosenbaum, P. S. (1967) *The Grammar of English Predicate Complement Constructions*, Cambridge (Mass.): MIT Press.

Ross, J. (1967) *Constraints on Variables in Syntax*, Ph.D. dissertation, MIT.

Sag, I. A., Gazdar, G., Wasow, T., and Weisler, S. (1985) 'Coordination and how to distinguish categories', *Natural Language and Linguistic Theory* 3:117–71.

Sampson, G. (1984) 'Review of Jacobson & Pullum (eds), *The Nature of Syntactic Representations*', *Lingua* 64–4:371–7.

Schachter, P. (1976) 'A nontransformational account of gerundive nominals in English', *Linguistic Inquiry* 7–2:205–41.

Schachter, P. (1980) 'Daughter-dependency grammar', in E. Moravcsik and J. Wirth (eds) *Current Approaches to Syntax*, New York: Academic Press, pp. 267–99.

Schreiber, P. A. (1981) 'Variable surface case in English', *Glossa* 15–2:153–98.

Sebeok, T. A. (ed.) (1966a) *Portraits of Linguists I*, Westpoint: Greenwood Press.

Sebeok, T. A. (ed.) (1966b) *Portraits of Linguists II*, Westpoint: Greenwood Press.

Seppänen, A. (1977) 'The position of *let* in the English auxiliary system', *English Studies* 58:515–29.

Stein, G. (1979) *Studies in the Function of the Passive*, Tübingen: Gunter Narr.

Stockwell, R. P. (1964) 'Transformational grammar in perspective', in G. I. Duthrie (ed.) (1964) *English Studies Today* (3rd series), Edinburgh: University Press, pp. 51–66.

Stockwell, R. P. (1986) 'Grammar as speaker's knowledge versus grammar as linguists' characterization of norms', in D. Kastovsky and A. Szwedek (eds) *Linguistics across Historical and Geographical Boundaries*, Berlin: Mouton De Gruyter, pp. 125–33.

Stockwell, R. P., Schachter, P., and Partee, B. H. (1973) *The Major Syntactic Structures of English*, New York: Holt Rinehart & Winston.

Sturm, A. N. (1986) *Primaire Syntactische Structuren in het Nederlands*, Leiden: Nijhoff.

Stuurman, F. (1985) 'Big a puzzle', in H. Bennis and F. Beukema (eds) (1985) *Linguistics in the Netherlands 1985*, Dordrecht: Foris, pp. 177–86.

Stuurman, F. (1986) 'Alle Nederl*ANS*?', *De Nieuwe Taalgids* 79–6:493–504.

Stuurman, F. (1987) 'Approaching *ought (to)*', in G. H. V. Bunt, E. S. Kooper, J. L. Mackenzie, and D. R. M. Wilkinson (eds) *100 years of English Studies in Dutch Universities*, Amsterdam: Rodopi, pp. 127–38.

Stuurman, F. (1987) 'Review of Emonds, *A Unified Theory of Syntactic Categories*', *Journal of Linguistics* 32–2:469–76.

Stuurman, F. (1988) 'On Poutsma: a context for *A Grammar of Late Modern English*', *Dutch Working Papers in English Language and Linguistics* 4:13–33.

Svartvik, J. and Quirk, R. (1980) *A Corpus of English Conversation*, Lund: C. W. K. Gleerup.

Sweet, H. (1891–1898) *A New English Grammar*, Oxford: Oxford University Press (Vol. I, 1891; Vol. II, 1898).

Sweet, H. (1964) *The Practical Study of Languages* (second edition), London: Oxford University Press.

Tervoort, B. T. (1981) 'Review of De Villiers & De Villiers, *Language Acquisition*', *Lingua* 54:263–7.

Van der Leek, F. (1980) 'Reflexive or non-reflexive', *Dutch Quarterly Review* 10:124–46.

Van Ek, J. A. (1966) *Four Complementary Structures of Predication in Contemporary English*, Groningen: Noordhoff.

Van Essen, A. J. (1983) *E. Kruisinga*, Leiden: Martinus Nijhoff.

Van Riemsdijk, H. and Williams, E. (1986) *Introduction to the Theory of Grammar*, Cambridge (Mass.): MIT Press.

Verkuyl, H. (1981) 'Numerals and quantifiers in X-bar syntax and their semantic interpretation', in J. Groenendijk, T. Janssen, and M. Stokhof (eds) *Formal Methods in the Study of Language II*, Amsterdam: Mathematisch Centrum, pp. 567–99.

Wekker, H. and Haegeman, L. (1985) *A Modern Course in English Syntax*, London: Croom Helm.

Wendt, G. (1914) *Syntax des Heutigen Englisch*, Heidelberg: Carl Winter.

Yim, Y. J. (1984) *Case-tropism: The Nature of Phrasal and Clausal Case*, Ph.D. dissertation, University of Washington.

Zandvoort, R. W. (1937) 'In memoriam Hendrik Poutsma', *English Studies* 19–3:120–2.

Zandvoort, R. W. (1945) *A Handbook of English Grammar*, Groningen: Noordhoff.

Zandvoort, R. W. (1961) '*I found myself walking* (an essay in syntactic substitution)', *English Language Teaching* 16–1:19–24.

Zandvoort, R. W. (1964) *Eindrapport*, Groningen: J. B. Wolters.

Index